Promising Practices for Exceptional Children
Curriculum Implications

Edward L. Meyen
University of Kansas

Glenn A. Vergason
Georgia State University

Richard J. Whelan
University of Kansas

LOVE PUBLISHING COMPANY
Denver • London

Copyright © 1983 Love Publishing Company
Printed in the U.S.A.
ISBN 0-89108-114-3
Library of Congress Catalog Card Number 81-84575
10 9 8 7 6 5 4 3 2 1

Contents

Introduction

Edward L. Meyen
Glenn A. Vergason
Richard J. Whelan

Even though appropriate education for handicapped children has been mandated, much remains to be done to ensure that the education provided is really appropriate. Providing an individualized education program (IEP) with short- and long-term goals and an agreement on placement does not always guarantee that a student's education is appropriate. Yet, many educators in the public schools seem willing to accept the content of an IEP as evidence of appropriateness. In reality, appropriate education occurs when the child's interaction with the instructional process results in maximum learning. Then, *what* curriculum and *how* intervention occurs become the primary considerations in designing and implementing appropriate education. Standards of performance, therefore, emerge as important criteria in judging appropriateness and, in turn, effectiveness of curriculum and instructional interventions.

An examination of our history in special education suggests that although the underlying motivation has been to provide appropriate education, the issues of assessment, labels, and administrative delivery models have tended to receive more focus. As programs grew, however, and the purchasing power of special education increased over the last 15 years, commercial publishers became responsive to the demand for curriculum development in special education.

Not until the late 1960s did the Bureau of Education for the Handicapped (now the Office of Special Education) begin to fund curriculum development research. After that time, several major curriculum projects received support: the science curriculum developed by the Biological Sciences Curriculum Study (BSCS); instructional programs for the moderately handicapped by Project MORE; the social learning curriculum by Goldstein et al.; Project MATH by Cawley et al.; the Pacemaker Primary Curriculum by Ross and Ross; and Project *I Can* in physical education by Wessel et al. These projects were limited primarily to the mentally retarded, and ironically they came into existence during the end of an era in which the special class was the dominant delivery model.

Just when the products of these projects became commercially available, the emphasis in special education was beginning to shift to mainstreaming. The situation was accented by Public Law 94-142, as the regular class became a commonly accepted placement for the mildly handicapped. Though the curriculum projects remain applicable, conditions have changed and further curriculum research and development are warranted.

Some might argue that the primary federal initiative following PL 94-142 should have been a massive infusion of support for curriculum development. This did not occur, though. Instead, the cycle of investing in new concepts of delivery models, assessment instruments, and training models was repeated. Development and modification of curriculum were left largely to teachers. In many cases, this meant that regular class teachers, although lacking time and resources, fell heir to the task of providing appropriate education for the handicapped.

To those who have been in the field for several years, much of what is happening today in special education appears to be history repeating itself. For several years after the first major initiative to establish special classes, state departments of education and large school districts called upon special class teachers to form committees and to produce curriculum guides. The guides did prove useful at the time, but they focused primarily on informational content and did not give sufficient attention to remedial techniques. Teachers were also placed at a disadvantage in that they were asked to be curriculum developers without the benefit of training or resources. Few standards existed by which to judge the merits of the guides, and the general lack of curriculum resources for exceptional children meant that every product identified as being applicable to exceptional children was widely disseminated and used.

Today, teachers are better trained. A reasonable amount of literature on curriculum development has been generated, and demonstrated development models exist. But curriculum development has yet to reach the priority status it deserves. Nondiscriminatory tests are important, as are effective referral procedures and alternative delivery models. Nevertheless, if what the teacher does in the instructional setting does not make a difference, the value of having precision assessment instruments and several alternatives from which to select is lost. Good teachers are resourceful, but faced with teaching children who have serious learning problems, they need and deserve the support of well-designed curricula. To offer them less is to ask the impossible.

An understanding of the promising practices called for by PL 94-142 combines with instructional implications of the IEP to create a set of circumstances favorable to curriculum development. If these promising practices are to be shared, criteria must be designed to differentiate those that are most promising, and professionals must become more sensitive to the significance of special education delivery. The IEP, in theory, represents an instructional decision-making process. At least, it requires assessment data to be considered in the context of instructional needs and options. If these challenges are openly faced, the 1980s may become the decade when special education shifts its emphasis from administrative and psychometric concerns to those of curriculum and instruction. Appropriateness might then be measured by qualitative criteria.

With more exceptional children being served in regular classes through supplemental assistance, new curriculum issues have emerged, including, but not limited to:

- *Parallel adaptation of standard curricula.* Basal series have evolved to a large extent as the curricula for considerable subject matter in regular class programs. Rather than working from curriculum planning in determining what and when students are taught, a series of texts serves as the curriculum for that particular subject. If these texts are inappropriate for an exceptional child integrated into the regular class, the curriculum is inappropriate. Either adaptation of the text(s) or the provision of alternative curriculum materials is then necessary, to allow the student to remain in the regular class while receiving instruction commensurate with his or her needs. If the teacher is required to employ an entirely different curriculum, the advantages of mainstreaming are minimized and the teacher's role is further complicated.

- *Short time frame curriculum materials.* Whereas the self-contained class model allowed the teacher to control the time and length of instruction, instructional time periods in mainstream situations are controlled by other factors. Time segments of 20-30 minutes are the mode. This means that teachers have to introduce an activity and provide instruction through closure in a short time span. Many of the existing curricula for exceptional children are oriented toward group instruction or require extended instructional sessions in order to be effectively employed.

- *Independent learning materials.* Although drill exercises are available for independent use by special students, few resources exist to provide new information or skills that can be acquired with minimum teacher involvement. To avoid having exceptional students spending time in noninstructional tasks, instructional materials must be designed for independent study work. The regular class teacher simply is not able to continuously monitor, let alone constantly interact with, all students. Microcomputers represent an important alternative. The development of software for microcomputers, along with research on how best to use the microcomputer with special students, is beginning to fulfill an important curriculum need.

- *Coping skills.* Work study skills have historically received considerable attention in the upper elementary grades. In curriculum development for exceptional students, this area of instruction has tended to be overlooked or the teaching of work study skills has been unsystematically integrated into other content areas of instruction. Meanwhile, teachers of children with learning disabilities have demonstrated that learning disabled students need a wide range of skills to sufficiently cope with the demands of regular class instruction. These needs undoubtedly generalize to most mildly handicapped students. To a large extent, the teaching of coping skills has been considered a methodology, disseminated through pre- and in-service training. Instructional materials that are applicable to individual instruction and that result in the teaching of coping skills are needed.

- *Bilingual special education instruction.* Considerable emphasis has been placed on assuring that students are assessed in their native language, but similar efforts to consider language preference in offering instruction have not been as serious. To a certain extent, bilingual special education relies more on methodology and appropriately prepared teachers. Curriculum material needs remain. In some cases the need is for translation; in others the language differences are significant and restructuring of materials is required.
- *Minimum competency testing.* Laws within the states that require administration of minimum competency tests vary considerably. Some laws exempt the handicapped; others allow for tests to be modified. From a curriculum perspective, attention should be given to minimum competency testing for the handicapped. This would require establishing standards, or at least goals, that might result in a more systematic approach to curriculum development in special education. At least it would encourage educators concerned with student performance to coordinate their efforts with those of educators responsible for curriculum planning.

These and other issues or areas pointing toward promising practices are addressed by authors of selections in this book. The perspectives of practitioners have been combined with those of researchers and developers. The intent is to provide special educators a resource on curriculum for exceptional children and youth. This resource, we hope, will stimulate more interest and productivity in curriculum planning.

1

The Process of Curriculum Development

Edward L. Meyen

Most educators would agree that the age-appropriate regular class is not the most desirable option for all children. A student may lack the necessary prerequisite skills. Another may be unable to maintain the pace of instruction. The need for specialized instruction can undermine the benefit of curriculum experiences as designed.

For whatever reason, some students have needs outside of the "target band" of the curriculum. This is not necessarily a weakness of a well-developed curriculum. In the graded approach to education, curriculum developers must make assumptions about the target population. The typical approach is to assume that students in the grade(s) for whom the curriculum is intended perform at grade level, or that the learners make some personal adjustment within a rather narrow range to learn from the curriculum, or that teachers modify activities to make the curriculum appropriate to the students.

Even with this adjustment or modification, some students' needs still are not effectively met in age-appropriate settings. One option is to alter the student's placement. For example, if a student is 12 years old and unable to do seventh-grade work, the student could be transferred from the seventh to the fourth grade, or allowances could be made through within-group arrangements. The latter would require the teacher to retain the student in the age-appropriate setting and to modify the curriculum.

If the student's only problem is in learning rate, and if the teacher is willing to simultaneously maintain three or four levels of instruction, the curriculum needs of underachieving students can be accommodated through these types of arrangements. But if students need skills or content different from the curriculum designed for their age-appropriate level, or if their cognitive limitations necessitate functional skills rather than refined academic or occupational skills, merely altering their placement is insufficient.

When shifts in placement no longer result in a good fit between the instructional needs of the learner and the benefits offered by the standard curriculum (as employed through good teaching), curriculum development (or selection of a different curriculum) is indicated. The need for a different or alternative curriculum is apparent in some children as preschoolers. In others it does not become evident until they encounter instruction in basic academic skills during the intermediate grades. Some students may even perform adequately in the regular curriculum until the secondary grades. Whenever the need for a different curriculum becomes apparent, the conditions are set for curriculum development.

Predicting the needs of some groups of children for special curricula can be aided by knowledge of their early developmental patterns. To a large extent, this is what we do in the case of handicapped learners. The more serious the learners' handicaps, the more easily one can hypothesize the uniqueness of their curriculum needs. Being able to ascertain the need for a different curriculum, however, does not tell one how to go about developing curriculum.

TRADITIONAL/HISTORICAL PRACTICES

Historically, in special education, curriculum development has taken the form of modifying the regular curriculum by adapting activities, breaking content down into refined steps or detail, and adding supplemental activities. Often, this has been accomplished through teachers' individual efforts in response to the necessity of accommodating a particular student. Also, state education agencies and local districts have utilized committees to provide curriculum guidance. This has been the pattern, rather than employing systematic approaches to curriculum development. Only in the past 10 to 15 years has much attention been given to achieving an appropriate curriculum through a process of development that approximates the strategies of curriculum design in content subjects for the regular class — and this has been limited to isolated subject matter areas.

Technologies, or at least strategies, of curriculum development do exist and are routinely used to produce curricula. But these practices have not become routine in structuring curricula for handicapped students within the public schools. As pointed out in the introduction to this book, several special education curricula have been produced using the technology of curriculum development. These curricula, however, have in general resulted from heavily funded projects and have tended to be carried out by university-based developers or curriculum development centers. Although local districts and state education agencies have been active in producing curriculum materials, they have tended to undertake less comprehensive development projects and have been more inclined to modify or adapt existing curricula to the needs of the handicapped.

TWO SPECIAL CONSIDERATIONS IN CURRICULUM DEVELOPMENT

Expenditures Versus Benefits

Curriculum development, properly carried out, is expensive. Field testing and production costs alone entail major expenditures. Actual costs, however, must be weighed against ultimate benefits of the curriculum. If rigorous, formative evaluation procedures are employed to maximize effectiveness, expenses are greater. But these procedures also increase the probability that the curriculum will be effective. On the other hand, if one designs a curriculum based on intuition or the collective experiences of informed persons (which is important to development), and implements it without the benefit of field testing, the cost savings can be considerable. At the same time, the probability of producing a curriculum that has omissions or that fails to operate at its potential is greatly increased.

Considering the complexity of designing curricula for handicapped students, a compromise to reduce costs does not seem desirable. Appropriate education will take place only after appropriate curricula are available. This calls for increased investment in curriculum development. Instituting more creative administrative arrangements alone will not likely improve the quality or appropriateness of instruction for the handicapped.

The Teacher's Role

William Mayer, in an article appearing later in this section, implies that a good teacher can make a less-than-adequate curriculum work. This is probably true. Some teachers not only understand learners' characteristics well, but they are also able to extrapolate sufficient guidelines from minimal curriculum directives and bring about student achievement.

The "art of teaching" phenomenon may be what causes administrators not to invest in curriculum development. Knowing that some teachers can translate barely acceptable curriculum guidelines into instructional strategies that result in student achievement may tend to cause administrators to rely on teachers to adapt, modify, supplement, and enrich at the expense of their own efforts. Consequently, curriculum needs that should be addressed through an investment in curriculum development are often ignored. Granted, good teachers abound, but those who are good without the resources of sound curricula appropriate to the needs of students assigned to them are rare. With well designed, appropriate curricula, the effectiveness of most, if not all, teaching is greatly enhanced. At least the conditions then exist for good teaching.

FACTORS AFFECTING CURRICULUM DEVELOPMENT

The standard age-appropriate curriculum is least likely to be appropriate for handicapped students. Further, if students' instructional needs can be met through the regular curriculum without extensive adaptation, by definition they should not be considered handicapped for educational purposes. In practice, special education becomes a matter of providing curriculum couched in the context of appropriate instructional techniques. The exception would be handicapped students who require related therapeutic services to enhance their participation in and benefits from the curriculum. If one accepts this perspective on what constitutes special education, how does one account for the lack of investment in curriculum development that has characterized the history of special education?

Administrative Arrangements

In many ways, accommodating the instructional needs of handicapped students through various administrative arrangements — such as resource rooms, special classes, itinerant teachers, and mainstreaming — represents an attempt to bring about a match between the student's instructional needs and curriculum options (without designing special curricula). This is a form of curriculum response, but not one that involves developing curricula specifically designed to meet the needs of handicapped students. Though alternative administrative arrangements (instructional placements) can result in more appropriate instruction, the results are far less effective than combining placement alternatives with specially designed curricula.

Continuing the search for administrative arrangements that will bring about better matches between instructional needs and available regular curricula ignores the realities of student needs. That logic assumes that the learning problems of handicapped students are merely couched in the context of *rate*. Even if that were true, it would be sufficient grounds to develop special curricula taking into account variances in rate of learning. In periodically altering grade placements as a curriculum strategy, the teacher is still faced with having to independently produce part of the curriculum.

Effects of Mainstreaming

Although skills needed to develop curricula for students with special needs are no more sophisticated than they were 10 or 15 years ago, the conditions under which handicapped students are educated have changed. The focus on placing handicapped students in regular classes has served to broaden the number of persons responsible for educating handicapped students. Although more instructional talent is being applied to maintaining handicapped students in regular classes, most teachers are reporting that the regular curriculum, even with supplemental materials, is not enough. Or they are having to spend inordinate time restructuring materials. Generally, redirection of resources to curriculum is presently placing more emphasis on enabling the students' social acceptance than on what they learn. The former is a concern, of course, but it is certainly a lesser goal than is increasing their overall competence.

IEP Requirements

IEP requirements, as mandated by Public Law 94-142, have raised the consciousness of educators as to the complexity of achieving appropriate education for handicapped students. Merely deciding on short- and long-term objectives based on assessment data can be difficult. This is particularly true if development of an IEP is combined with instructional planning procedures to maintain the handicapped student in a program that is consistently challenging, yet within the student's range of attainment.

Parent Involvement

Increased parental involvement in instructional decisions affecting the education of handicapped students should also help in building an advocacy base for curriculum development. As parents gain awareness of needed instructional resources and question the inappropriateness of available material, they also become sensitive to the need for appropriate curricula. Changing the administrative arrangements by increasing or decreasing the amount of time a student spends in resource rooms, special classes, tutorial sessions, or regular classrooms will have little impact without the proper curriculum resources.

THE FUTURE OF CURRICULUM DEVELOPMENT

Programmatic changes over the past few years, combined with the emerging microprocessor technology, should result in renewed attention to curriculum development. If a broader range of curriculum options is to evolve, a shift in emphasis from administrative arrangements to curriculum must occur.

The above discussion should demonstrate that curriculum options are as important as placement options. Although administrators can alter the roles of personnel and modify time schedules to create administrative options, an expansion of curriculum options will not take place merely through restructuring that which already exists. Investing in the development of new curriculum options is necessary.

Though curriculum development for handicapped students is costly and requires the involvement of personnel with appropriate skills, it is within the realm of local districts. Depending on the scope of the project to be undertaken, alliances with SEAs and universities may be called for. The federal government could obviously play a significant role, but with the prevailing fluctuation in priorities and funding levels, LEAs and SEAs will have to move ahead. Waiting for a federal initiative may place the educational needs of handicapped students at risk.

STEPS IN CURRICULUM DEVELOPMENT AND RELATED QUESTIONS

Needs Assessment

Many special education programs monitor instructional programs and identify curriculum needs through routine monitoring procedures. In some situations, however, specific probes are necessary to ascertain if a curriculum need exists. In the case of major curriculum development projects with national implications, voids in the commercial sector must be identified.

QUESTIONS

- What techniques are routinely employed to monitor strengths and weaknesses of the curricula available to teachers and special students?
- To what extent are data regularly collected on student achievement over time, parental preference for curriculum emphasis, and student preference for instructional formats?
- Is the impact of changes in curricula on student performance checked?
- In examining curriculum options and curricula in use, is an effort made to sort out teacher effects from curriculum effects?
- Is the emphasis on ensuring continuity of the curriculum rather than short-term planning? Is the handicapped student frequently faced with a different curriculum?

Feasibility

When a district has decided to act upon a need for curriculum development, it must determine if the proposed project is feasible or if teaming with another agency is advisable. Before making this decision, the goals and general parameters of the project have to be set.

QUESTIONS

- Is the target population of students clearly definable?
- How is the target population grouped for instruction?
- What expertise is required — and is the needed expertise available?
- What are the financial restraints?
- Who are the primary benefactors of the project (e.g., teachers, students, parents)?

- How does this curriculum project relate to other curriculum needs in the district?
- What external resources are available to aid in developing the curriculum?
- Does the proposed curriculum have applicability outside the district?

Conceptualization of Design

Early in the planning stages the beliefs and principles that will underlie the curriculum must be stated and organized. Development of a model illustrating these beliefs and principles gives credence to the staff's intent and allows others to be informed about the proposed development. This is important in that it allows ideas to be tested and helps ensure that the curriculum to be developed is sound. It also provides the basis for detailing tasks and setting timelines.

QUESTIONS

- What curriculum features are basic to the design?
- How can the design be best illustrated as a model?
- What research or data support the beliefs and principles embedded in the design?
- Can an evaluation procedure(s) be designed to test the model?
- Is the design easily understood by those who will participate in development?

Content Generation

Concern for content, obviously, permeates all steps in a curriculum development process. Content also takes varied forms — some curricula are skill-oriented, others involve the teaching concept or information, still others are concerned with influencing attitudes, and so on. Regardless of the focus, developers must structure systematic procedures for identifying and organizing content.

QUESTIONS

- Will task analysis be applied? If so, what type of analysis?
- What format is most appropriate for organizing the content (e.g., outline, units, objectives)?
- How will an appropriate sequence be determined?
- Is the content developmental?
- What is the best structure for organizing content to enhance the design of activities?
- Who should be involved in the design of instructional activities?

Prototype Design

Early in the development process, but after basic design and content questions have been answered, constructing prototypes of the material to be included in the curriculum can be helpful. These are basically mock-ups and take different forms. After subjecting the prototype to various types of formative evaluation, they are transferred into field-test materials. To the extent possible, the prototype materials should approximate the developers' conceptualization of the final product.

QUESTIONS

- What are the major features of the curriculum, and how are they best accommodated in the design of curriculum materials?
- If mediation appears to be warranted, what are the advantages and the costs?
- What features merit close scrutiny in the evaluation steps?
- Which features will require contractual services from outside the district?
- What are the relative costs of producing a field-test prototype versus evaluating the curriculum in parts and drawing inferences about the effectiveness of the total curriculum?

Evaluation

Evaluation is integral to all steps in development. In addition to employing evaluation procedures in field testing, formative evaluation techniques should be applied to the process of development. This allows greater proficiency in subsequent development projects. Curriculum evaluation is extremely complex because controlling all the variables that will be considered important is not possible. Some good data collection procedures, such as direct observation, are expensive. Therefore, creativity in the design of cost-effective evaluation techniques is necessary. In making decisions on field-test techniques to use, one must keep in mind that the field product depends heavily on the rigor of the field-test procedures.

QUESTIONS

- What evaluation strategies are most appropriate for the nature of your curriculum?
- Which features require particular attention in field testing?
- What resources are available to handle the data reduction and analysis?
- How will the field-test results be translated into revision directives?

- What sampling techniques are essential to the field test?
- What timeline is best given for implementation and dissemination?

Additional steps applicable to curricula developed for national impact include summative evaluation, demonstration, and implementation.

This section of the book presents various discussions concerning curriculum development and adaptation. The introduction has been written with the aim of accenting the importance of and the need for more curriculum options as a prerequisite to appropriate education. Local districts, independently or in cooperation with state education agencies or universities, can pursue curriculum development. The priority, however, should always be on employing systematic development procedures.

Mayer places curriculum development in an historical perspective. The reader is reminded of the importance of curriculum innovation and factors that hinder the implementation of innovative instructional practices. The author draws on his personal experience in presenting the BSCS curriculum development model. He provides a context in which to consider the elements of a systematic approach to curriculum development.

Curriculum Development: A Process and a Legacy

William V. Mayer

People talk about the weather, but no one is able to do anything about it. In educational circles, people talk about the curriculum, but few are even trying to do anything about it. Perhaps the curriculum is no more neglected than other facets of the educational enterprise, but the educational literature, filled with papers on objectives, behaviors, learning theories, discipline, basics, and similar topics, reveals a startling lack of papers dealing with curriculum development. The curriculum is frequently regarded as an unchanging feature around which other educational events revolve. Even the dictionary defines curriculum as "a fixed series of studies." This static nature of the curriculum is accurately satirized in *The Saber-Tooth Curriculum* (Benjamin, 1939).

Curriculum stasis is inexplicable in terms of changes in the world and its human societies. It is explicable only in terms of the interacting components of the educational enterprise. Students training to be teachers are taught how to teach a specific curriculum. Moreover, content and teaching strategies of textbooks either dictate the curriculum or are derived from it. Parents, seeing their children go through the same sequence of study that they themselves experienced, feel that such a curriculum offers a normal and reasonable approach to education. The curriculum prepares students for a sequence of standardized examinations, and the standardized examinations, in turn, reflect the curriculum being taught. Experience, expectation, training, textbooks, and examinations are all linked together to reinforce the status quo and to delay or discourage curriculum change.

A BRIEF HISTORY OF CURRICULUM DEVELOPMENT EFFORTS

Despite the fact that the curriculum has been largely static, still sharing a majority of features with the curriculum of a century ago, concerns about it have been expressed infrequently. These concerns have usually taken the form of reports from prestigious agencies and committees. An heirloom of such reports is the National Education Association's Committee on Secondary School Studies (also known as the Committee of Ten), chaired by Charles W. Elliott, President of Harvard University. This report, issued in 1893, made significant recommendations — followed by no evidence that either teaching practices or curriculum structure was significantly altered as a result of the group's recommendations.

A study by E. G. Dexter in 1906 on the impact of the report of the Committee of Ten noted that little had been achieved by the Committee's recommendations and, indeed, that practice in some instances was running counter to these recommendations. A 1918 report of the Commission on the Reorganization of Secondary Education was designed to orient all courses in the secondary school toward realization of the aims of secondary education stated in the 1893 report. Today's "back-to-basics" advocates would be comforted by knowing that in 1918 one of the cardinal principles of secondary education was to be "command of fundamental processes." The intervening years give evidence that this aim was never achieved in the school curriculum.

In 1927, the report of the Committee on Standards for Use in the Reorganization of the Secondary School Curriculum concerned itself with reorganization of the secondary school curriculum but contained no exciting new developments. By 1932 the Progressive Education Association had renewed a committee examination of the goals of general education in the secondary school and, for the first time, recognized learning theory as a factor in curriculum planning (Commission on Secondary School Curriculum, 1938).

Another shift for the curriculum groups of the 1930s was the acknowledgment of influence by the nature of society and the importance of dealing with student needs and problems. Recommendations that curriculum values for personal and social welfare be considered differed from the emphasis of earlier groups, which had primarily emphasized disciplinary content. The 1945 report of the Harvard Committee concerning general education in a free society noted little progress with these recent ideas of curriculum reform. Nor did the Harvard report result in curriculum reform or improved teaching procedures, any more than did the 1893 study chaired by a member of the same institution.

By 1960 enrollment in high school encompassed 70% of the 14-17 year age group, whereas at the start of the century only 8.4% of that age group was in high school. These 8.5 million students, distributed among 22,000 high schools, presented a range of abilities and interests that the adopted curriculum was simply unable to meet. What had been an academic exercise in curriculum reform over the past 60 years was now a crisis demanding attention. Curriculum recommendations extending back 60 years were reviewed in a new climate in which *action* on behalf of the nation's and society's problems was the prevailing mood.

No one viewed this attention to the curriculum as a panacea. Teacher preparation, physical plant, policy decisions, administration, and a host of other problems faced education but, for the first time, the curriculum was to be singled out for specific attention on a large scale. Attention to learning theory, to the cutting edge of disciplinary content, and to a matrix of modern pedagogy would provide a more effective delivery system than in the past.

Curriculum efforts of the 1960s and subsequent decades were to produce new materials in keeping with the best of precepts. Learning theorists were involved. Professionals in the disciplines concerned presented significant content that reflected the current state of the discipline. Teachers were involved to ascertain whether the curriculum innovations could be handled within constraints of the classroom. For the first time, mixed groups of experts in pedagogy, practical classroom situations, disciplinary content, and educational psychology were brought together to deal with the curriculum in a holistic sense, as well as within the boundaries of a given discipline.

FORMALIZATION OF THE MOVEMENT

Curriculum development began to be formalized, and curriculum development processes started to evolve. A transition from a series of recommendations to an integrated plan of development, production, dissemination, and implementation was initiated. The large-scale curriculum development efforts that were instituted in the late 1950s and carried through the 1960s and 1970s demanded organization, coordination, and planning. The investment of significant sums of money in the process of curriculum development resulted not only in a curriculum but also in a process that could serve as a model for further work.

Individual curricula met different fates. Some did not survive their field tests. Others made a lasting impact. But perhaps more important than the actual curricula developed was the dignifying of curriculum development through the creation of models and processes in a framework of academic respectability and practical feasibility. The legacy of the curriculum development movements may not be so much the materials they produced as their presentation of the curriculum development process in the form of an organized, useful model.

In the classroom, a teacher's ad hoc decisions to use a specific text, to change a certain laboratory, to include a film, to take a field trip or not, or to supplement or complement classroom work by including additional topical information all represent curriculum modification, if not development. On a slightly larger scale, in the bigger schools of the United States, groups of teachers may decide on curriculum changes and the process may be undertaken by an entire school district, a city, or any of the several units into which schools are functionally divided. At the state level, some states issue guidelines, as in California, and others, such as New York, have not only a syllabus but a statewide examination over the syllabus topics. Thus, the picture of curriculum development within the United States is generally disorganized and varied, where it occurs at all.

The first nationally coordinated curriculum exercises were sponsored by the National Science Foundation, which established curriculum studies primarily in the natural and social sciences. This allowed drawing upon a vast reservoir of talent from throughout the country. Geographic boundaries and administrative units could be ignored in selecting personnel, and a combination of Nobel Prize winners, award-winning teachers, and educational researchers could be recognized for their contributions, resulting in a new curriculum synthesis.

Federal Involvement

In terms of the total educational expenditures in the United States, federal monies for curriculum development were limited but powerful in their effect. These were the first monies ever invested to develop innovative curriculum materials on a national basis. The investment not only led to new curricula and new models for curriculum development, but it also awakened the interest of the educational community in the curriculum, at a great variety of levels and from a great variety of individuals and organizations. Hurd (1978) called the period 1960-1975 a "Golden Age" because of the curriculum development movement and the interest and research it generated.

Unfortunately, the curriculum development movement of this period was also hamstrung by administrative timidity and a lack of understanding of what efforts would be required to gain acceptance for truly innovative curricula. The problems of moving a curriculum are similar to those of moving a graveyard — tradition and inertia oppose both, and the energy required to overcome the tradition and inertia is inordinately large.

Although a cadre of teachers gained experience through the field-testing activities of each curriculum study, this group was always limited in numbers. No curriculum development effort funded by the federal government supported its materials sufficiently to ensure that they were established on a sound, competitive basis. The rationale of placing federal monies in curriculum development but withholding federal support for disseminating information and implementing these programs in schools has never been adequately explained.

If the government had feared charges of unfair competition or federal encroachment on local school autonomy, it probably should never have entered the curriculum development field in the first place. Nevertheless, having entered it, and initially withstanding these unfair charges, federal agencies acted like the mother who, having given birth to a child, laid it on a stranger's doorstep, wishing nothing more to do with it. One can only speculate that if sufficient funding had been made available for implementing and disseminating federally-sponsored curriculum developments, the school curriculum might look much different today than it does under the conception and abandonment approach that characterized the federal curriculum efforts.

The MACOS Program

A classic case of federal fear of involvement was that of MACOS — *Man: A Course of Study* — a social science curriculum developed under grants from the National Science Foundation. The MACOS program was prepared, field-tested, revised, and ultimately offered for commercial publication. In the 1,700 or so schools in which it was adopted, it worked well but came under fire from militant school critics, with some aid from the commercial publishing industry. Many of the criticisms of the program, which received wide publicity in the press, were either deliberately or unconsciously misleading. In any case, the hulabaloo raised about MACOS drowned out the rational voices that attempted to explain the program. Not surprisingly, the granting agency was silent in the face of negative publicity, seeming to prefer a mea culpa role to a defense of an innovative, contributory program.

That the MACOS program could be so viciously and unfairly attacked without any consequential defense had a markedly negative effect on the acceptance of federally-funded curriculum programs. First of all, it had a negative effect on curriculum development in general. Second, it created new perturbations within the publishing industry. Individual publishers became increasingly reluctant to sponsor publication of innovative curriculum materials. No publisher wished to be subjected to attacks, no matter how ill-founded, on any of its programs. This concern was larger than the possible negative image of a single program; the publisher's entire product line might become suspect if the publisher were criticized in the public press for programs stigmatized as either immoral or un-American. Thus, commercial publishers who had originally welcomed the products of federally-funded curriculum studies as tested programs, produced under impeccable academic and pedagogic auspices, came to view such products with suspicion.

Implications of the Formalization Movement

Despite the politics of curriculum development as revealed by the MACOS incident, I agree with Paul Hurd that the decades of the 1960s and 1970s were indeed a uniquely active period in education. More ferment and involvement occurred, and more innovative products actually reached the classrooms, than at any other time in the history of the American education. Not only was this a unique phenomenon in the United States, but it was unique throughout the world. As one result, many federally-funded curriculum programs were adapted and translated into other languages. The BSCS programs with which I have been associated, for example, have been adapted for use in more than 60 countries and translated into more than 19 languages. No educational movement has spread so widely or so rapidly. The biological curriculum alone has been changed globally because of the American initiative in curriculum development.

A MODEL FOR THE CURRICULUM DEVELOPMENT PROCESS

The legacy of the curriculum development process itself survives in many models, or as a number of variations on the process developed as each curriculum group strove to formalize its procedures. Some of the models are summarized in *Planning Curriculum Development, with Examples from Projects for the Mentally Retarded* (Mayer, 1975). Others are reported in each curriculum project's development and evaluation reports. Space prohibits recapitulation of the curriculum development patterns of a wide variety of projects, so I will speak only about the one with which I am most familiar. This process has been summarized by Callahan (1976) and delineated further by Mayer (1976).

A curriculum is approached first of all by ascertaining the status of the discipline, its past and its future directions. Second, present and future needs are determined. This needs assessment considers the delivery system in terms of its effectiveness in communicating the content and techniques of a discipline. It considers the teachers' abilities, schools' facilities, students' needs, community desires, parents' expectations, and the social changes with which today's students are likely to be confronted when they operate as tomorrow's citizens. With the knowledge of what is being done and a good idea of what should be done, those conducting the curriculum investigation can begin to plan the curriculum framework.

A systems-design approach enables curriculum developers to identify resources, personnel, processes, and activities associated with specific stages of curriculum development and to evaluate these in a foramtive fashion. The process may be analyzed by the use of a transformation-operation (black box) systems model incorporating a storage unit. The symbols used in one such

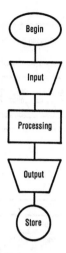

FIGURE 1
General Systems Model

system model are illustrated in Figure 1, where different geometric shapes are used to delineate "Begin," "Input," "Processing," "Output," and "Store." The latter four symbols are used to identify the activity throughout the model.

A typical model used by BSCS to describe and analyze curriculum development consists of 12 stages as presented in Figure 2. This model represents a descending hierarchy of sequential stages related to producing curriculum materials. Note that evaluation is built into the curriculum plan at an early stage rather than being added on at the end, where it can be of no use in the formative design. Two field tests are planned, and revisions are made according to the feedback.

No timeline is indicated, although the process normally requires a year for each field test, feedback, evaluation, and revision. Thus, an extensive curriculum revision minimally takes two years from inception of the plan to delivery of materials to a publisher. The time, however, is a function of the task. Minor revisions can be accomplished in as little as six months. On the other hand, the large-scale, completely innovative initial program of BSCS began with formation of the study in 1958 and was completed in 1963, with the first commercial release of materials.

For illustrative purposes, each of eight stages in Figure 2 has been further delineated in other figures. Only stages 8, 9, 10, and 11 recycle earlier components of the process. These are not separately illustrated. For example, Stage 8 follows a sequence similar to Stage 3, with the addition of the stored information regarding recommendations for curriculum change. Stage 9 is a repeat of Stage 5, with the addition of the changes derived from the first teacher orientation program. Stage 10 repeats Stage 6, and Stage 11 repeats Stage 7.

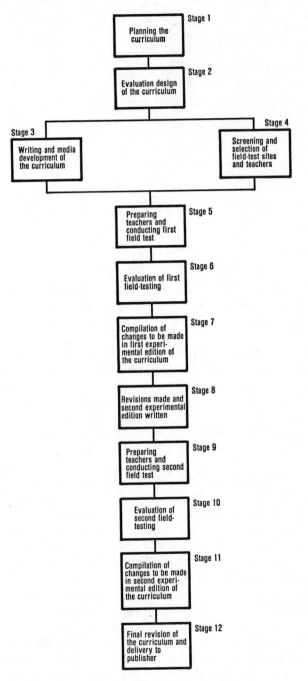

FIGURE 2
Twelve Stages of Curriculum Development

Stage 1, Planning the Curriculum Framework, is elaborated in Figure 3 and shows the curriculum planning process as a collegial one in which the development staff is guided by an advisory board, specialists in the discipline concerned, learning theorists, and the population to whom the curriculum is directed. The general objectives for which the curriculum is to be developed must be clearly delineated and the basic curriculum design established — whether the curriculum is to consists of a textbook, a series of laboratory exercises, a guide for teachers, a resource book, or is to be supported by

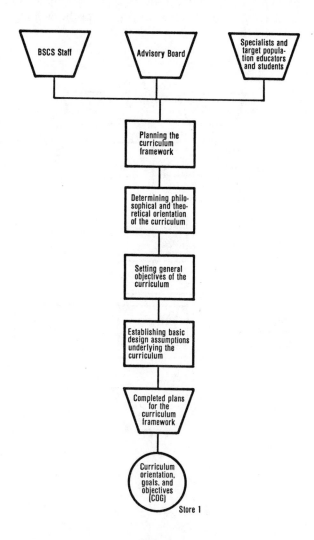

FIGURE 3
Stage 1 — Planning the Curriculum Framework

supplementary materials and demand multimedia approaches. All this must be ascertained early so that the finished curriculum will be an integrated whole. The Stage 1 process results in the curriculum orientation, goals, and objectives that will guide the entire process.

Evaluation, as indicated in Figure 4, must be built into the curriculum from the beginning so that its results can guide the curriculum development. This formative evaluation, if incorporated at the beginning, uncovers weaknesses and gives direction for improving the entire curriculum effort. Ex post facto summative evaluations have little impact on the actual curriculum, appearing as they do several years after the curriculum is in use.

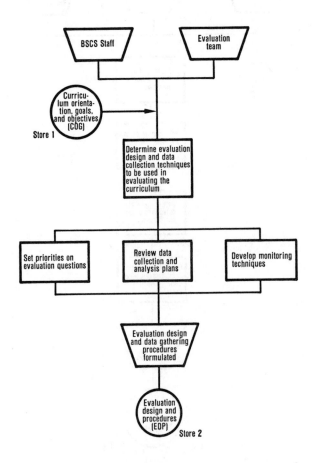

FIGURE 4
Stage 2 — Evaluative Design of the Curriculum

The evaluation team is usually not the same group that is developing the curriculum, for obvious reasons. This team takes the curriculum orientation goals and objectives and develops an evaluation design and data collection technique that will determine whether or not the curriculum meets its own desideratum. The evaluation design and procedures elicited from Stage 2, together with the curriculum orientation goals and objectives, feed into the major effort of formulating and writing the experimental curriculum in Stage 3.

Stage 3, illustrated in Figure 5, is what most people think of as curriculum development. This is usually the biggest, busiest, and most complex stage, and thus tends to overshadow the other efforts — which are equally important. At this stage the content is selected and translated into forms that will constitute the curriculum. If no media accompany the curriculum, the stages of media development are eliminated; the model is altered to meet this situation.

The output of Stage 3 is an experimental curriculum to be placed in the hands of field-test teachers. To do this, field-test teachers and school sites must be screened and selected. Figure 6 delineates that process — Stage 4. Because these schools and teachers will be providing the feedback on the experimental materials, they should represent a cross-section of the target population. The broader the field-test sample, the more representative it can be — and on a national basis geographic representation becomes exceptionally important. Also, urban, suburban, and rural schools stand to benefit, as well as schools with low budgets, schools with high budgets, big schools, little schools, inner-city schools, and specialty schools. Of course, the field-test population should consist of students of the age and grade level to which the curriculum is directed, and should be typical of the target population. This means that academically unsuccessful youngsters along with the gifted and talented should generally be exposed to the experimental curriculum.

We know that outstanding teachers can make anything work, but the population of teachers should be representative. An experimental curriculum intended for use with students of varying abilities will be led astray if tested only by outstanding teachers with high-ability youngsters. Selecting a typical cross-section is not always possible, though, because it depends upon a school administration and a teacher who agree to participate in field-testing for a period that may take several years. The very willingness to become involved in a field-test situation is a self-selecting factor. Field-test teachers, by and large, are risk-takers and have a desire to contribute to innovative programming, thus eliminating teachers who reject change — and who may be the very ones whose concerns could be exceptionally valuable to the developing curriculum. The end product of Stage 4 is the selection of teachers and school sites for the field-testing process.

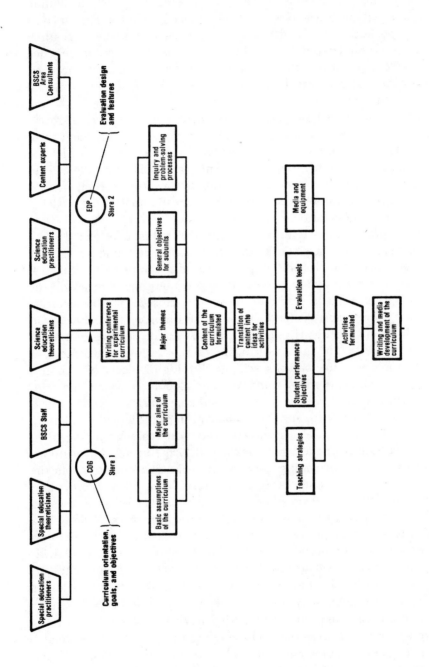

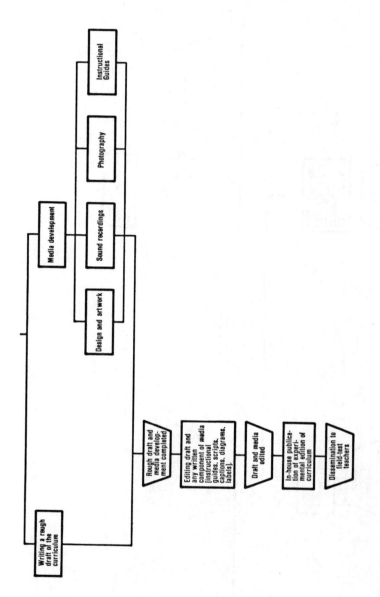

FIGURE 5

Stage 3 — Formulating and Writing the Experimental Curriculum

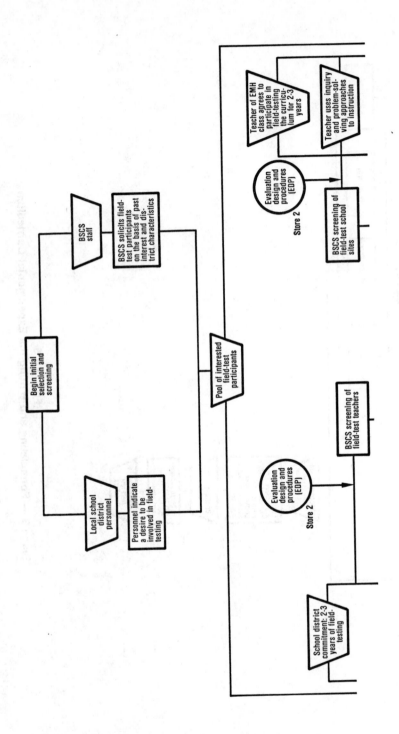

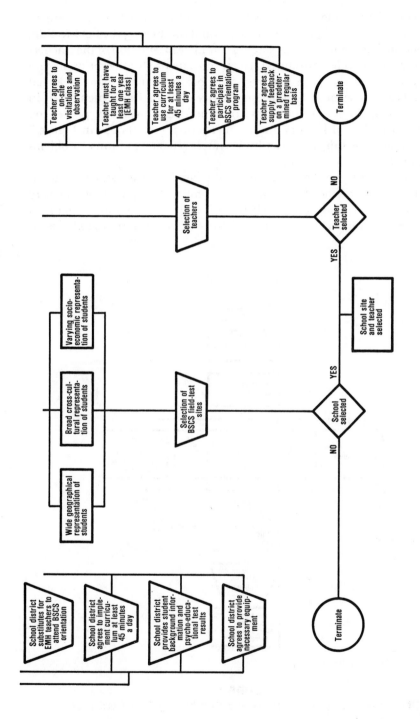

FIGURE 6

Stage 4 — Initial Screening and Selection of Field-Test Teachers and School Sites

After the field-test teachers and sites have been selected, Stage 5 in Figure 7 delineates the stages of preparing teachers and conducting the field-testing. An important component at this stage is complete orientation of the teachers to the curriculum to be introduced. Here, introduction of the rationale and the philosophy of the program may be more important than its actual content. Teachers seem to have less difficulty in changing content than in changing methodology, philosophy, or rationale. Obviously, processing items such as, "Use of inquiry and problem-solving methods" in Figure 7 would change if the subject curriculum is not based on an inquiry, problem-solving mode.

Teachers sometimes have difficulty in using diversified student evaluation techniques or methods of recording student performance that may vary from past practice. Therefore, teachers need help in becoming acquainted with new evaluation techniques and in sifting student responses to focus on

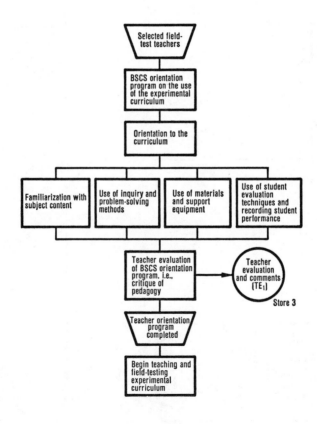

FIGURE 7
Stage 5 — Preparing Teachers and Conducting First Field Test

the more meaningful, contributory ones. After completing the orientation program, the teachers begin teaching and field-testing the experimental curriculum. As a side product, the teachers also provide feedback on the orientation program itself (indicated as Store 3), which is used to further refine future orientation programs for teachers.

The field-testing process is worthless unless it leads to usable results. Figure 8 diagrams the components of Stage 6, dealing with evaluation of field-testing. The various feedback items contribute to evaluation of the field-tested curriculum, each of whose activities is considered individually and whose components are reviewed in terms of teachability. Together with evaluations of student performance, these evaluations — in which the question constantly asked is, "What does the use of this curriculum do to students?" — provide field-test results as Store 4, which lead to Stage 7 in Figure 9.

In Stage 7 the results of field-testing are subject to the scrutiny of curriculum experts, the advisory board, the evaluation committee, and the local staff. This results in recommendations for curriculum revision in Stages 8-11, as noted earlier.

The final revision takes place in Stage 12, as shown in Figure 10, and the end product is a curriculum incorporating the input of as many as thousands of teachers and hundreds of thousands of students, together with the input of specialists such as learning theorists, subject matter experts, and those who have evaluated the curriculum for its teachability. What happens to the final revision depends upon the specific arrangements made. The curriculum developers may arrange various ways for materials to reach the target population, but the assumption of Figure 10 is that the materials will be released through the commercial sector and that the stages followed will vary with the publisher's practices and the developer's desires. If the commercial route is chosen, the production and marketing expertise of a publisher should be involved at an early stage in order for the curriculum to be more of a cooperative enterprise, directed toward successful commercial release.

This systems approach offers a comprehensive view of the elements involved in designing and producing a curriculum. It provides a logical, sequential flow of activities and identifies the components of curriculum development and the various parameters involved in the process. Although the figures illustrate only one model, variations of the process may provide equally viable pathways and products. Most important, the final result offers an alternative to existing curricula for the consideration of educators.

Federal granting agencies now have restricted curriculum development support, as well as the implementation and dissemination activities essential to new curriculum efforts. This vacuum in curriculum development is being partially filled by private foundations along with publishers and distributors of educational materials who have come to recognize that curriculum studies

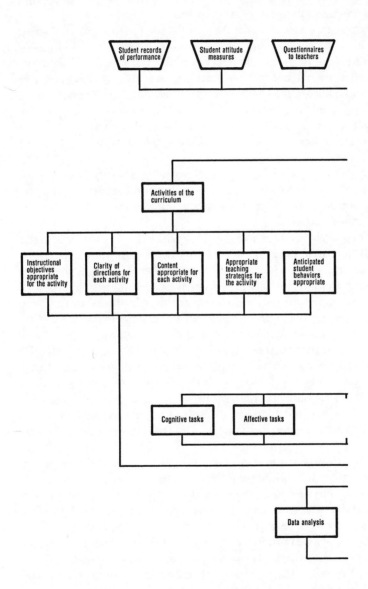

FIGURE 8
Stage 6 — Evaluation of Field Testing

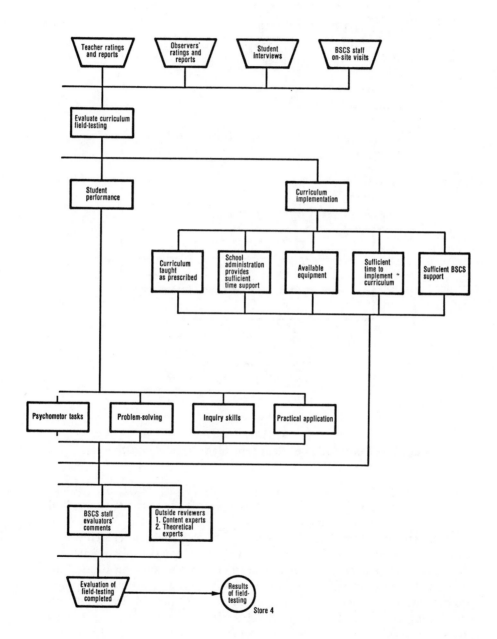

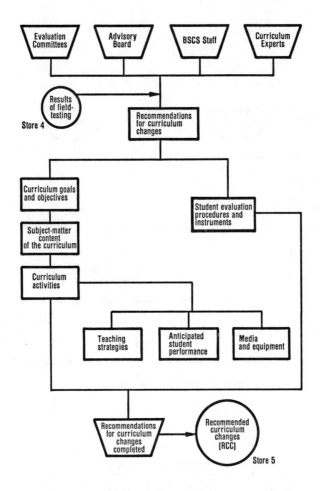

FIGURE 9
Stage 7 — Compilation of Recommended Curriculum Changes

can indeed improve both content and pedagogy. In fact, curriculum studies may now have to look for massive future support to the private sector, both foundations and commercial sources.

Curriculum studies have been a powerful force in American education in the past two decades. They have a fine record of accomplishment. The materials developed have changed the format, content, and emphasis of traditional classroom materials. A formal process of curriculum development has been created as a legacy for curriculum workers of the future. Continued curriculum revision is dictated by our changing knowledge and our societal goals. The process of curriculum development will be easier in the years to

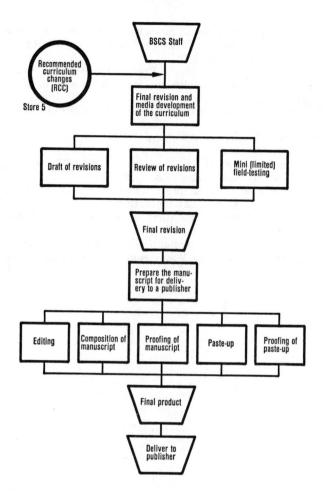

FIGURE 10

Stage 12 — Final Revision and Media Development of the Curriculum

come because of the efforts of those who refined it during the past two decades.

REFERENCES

Benjamin, H. *The saber-tooth curriculum.* New York: McGraw-Hill, 1939, *13*, 139.

Callahan, W. P. Formative evaluation report #5. *Assessing student abilities and performance: Year 3.* Boulder, CO: BSCS, 1976, pp. 22-30.

Commission on Secondary School Curriculum of the Progressive Education Association. *Science in general education* (A report prepared by the Science Committee). New York: Appleton-Century Co., 1938.

Commission on the Reorganization of Secondary Education. *Cardinal principles of secondary education* (Bulletin 1918, No. 35). Washington, DC: Department of Interior, Bureau of Education, 1918.

Committee on Standards for Use in the Reorganization of the Secondary School Curriculum. Report of the committee on standards for use in the reorganization of secondary school curriculum. *North Central Association Quarterly*, 1927, *1*, 510-514.

Dexter, E. G. Ten years influence of the report of the committee of ten. *School Review*, 1906, *14*, 254-269.

Harvard Committee. *General education in a free society*. Cambridge, MA: Harvard University, 1945.

Hurd, P. The golden age of biological education, 1960-1975. In *Biology teachers handbook*. New York: John Wiley, 1978, pp. 28-96.

Mayer, W. V. (Ed.). *Planning curriculum development, with examples from projects for the mentally retarded*. Boulder, CO: BSCS, 1975.

Mayer, W. V. The BSCS process of curriculum development. *BSCS Newsletter #64*. Boulder, CO: BSCS, 1976.

National Education Association. *Report of the committee on secondary school studies —Report of the committee of ten*. Washington, DC: U.S. Bureau of Education, 1893.

Using the IEP as a reference, Poplin introduces the reader to a process of curriculum development, emphasizing the role of the classroom teacher. Particular attention is given to the designed curriculum maps as a strategy for curriculum development. The selection is a classic in the context of curriculum references for special education. And the value of the selection is by no means tied to the IEP. It is one of the few curriculum articles in the literature that places the IEP in a curriculum perspective.

The Science of Curriculum Development Applied to Special Education and the IEP

Mary Poplin

Every year literally thousands of special educators enter their assigned classrooms to face a clean chalkboard, a bare bulletin board, and a list of previously "not so successful" students. Almost every evening throughout the school year, these educators dutifully prepare special materials and aids, spirit masters and individualized programs, in an attempt to stay one step ahead of threatening chaos. Still, each day new questions haunt the special education teacher: "What can I do tomorrow?" "What else is there to math besides the basic facts?" "What makes reading the science text so difficult for the children?" "Exactly what are the social skills that would help these students' integration into the regular classroom environment?"

Often, the only answers to these and countless other questions regarding the education of handicapped youngsters are proposed in the form of objectives inherent in pre-packaged materials, workbooks, and teachers' guides or criterion-referenced skills lists. But rarely are any of these teacher aids or guides adequate to fully answer the questions that concern special education teachers daily.

With the advent of individualized education programs, teachers increasingly have come to look for the answers to their questions in the goals and objectives contained in the student's individual program. While, ideally, IEPs should contain the answers, many times the selected goals and objectives are vague and propose no real continuum for instruction. Often, school psychologists, special education support or administrative staffs, and other non-instructional personnel have composed the educational program with insufficient knowledge of the child. The objectives now mandated and recorded in the student's IEP have, however, served to make us painfully aware of a very real but not so new crisis in special education: *We do not know what we are teaching.*

This author proposes that the single most critical skill a special educator can develop is the ability to define appropriate goals and objectives for the various areas involved in the special education curriculum. A model for achieving this task is presented here, with an emphasis on defining instructional objectives to mastery, and supported by a discussion of purposes, specific procedures, and application of the goals and objectives to development of the IEP.

MAJOR PURPOSES IN SPECIAL EDUCATORS' DEFINING GOALS AND OBJECTIVES

There are two major purposes to be met through active involvement of special educators in defining the goals and objectives encompassing various educational curricular areas: (1) an increase in teacher competence and confidence, and (2) facilitation of appropriate educational programming.

Increased Teacher Competence and Confidence

Every special or regular educator who has been involved in direct instruction of handicapped children has experienced feelings of incompetence at one time or another. These feelings (real or imagined) emanate largely from unanswered questions and doubts concerning the goals and objectives attempted during instruction. Questions and doubts arise in regard to things such as needed prerequisite abilities, appropriate sequence of objectives, the progression of objectives that will reflect true mastery, and the pure knowledge of collective abilities necessary in each of the major educational areas dealt with in special education classrooms. For instance, when Tom cannot count five objects correctly, what prerequisite skills does he need to meet this objective? What is an appropriate sequence of objectives under the goal of mathematical numeration? How would one define mastery of counting five objects? What are *all* of the abilities encompassed under the educational area of mathematics?

Educators in the regular classroom often are plagued by questions similar to those of special educators. In the traditional school program, however, regular classroom teachers have a distinct advantage. For better or worse, traditional school programs are provided with broad-based materials containing a predetermined sequence of curriculum objectives. These materials offer specific guidelines, adding a structure and continuum to classroom experiences that is not characteristic of special education programs. Classroom materials including basal texts in virtually every subject area, teacher manuals, spirit masters, workbooks, and other aids give a sense of security to the classroom environment. Also, basal materials, though certainly not perfect, do approximate what are most often considered appropriate objectives for the normal achieving student. Special education does not, and by its very nature could not, have such standard, reliable guidelines in the preparation of daily objectives.

For many years, special educators have been trained almost exclusively in pedantic features pertaining to the characteristics, etiology, and formal diagnosis of specific handicapping conditions. Regretfully, little of this information is useful when faced with the task of actually teaching handicapped youngsters. For instance, administration and interpretation of formal tests including intelligence tests, electroencephalogram readings, and tests of perceptual and psycholinguistic abilities tell educators little regarding the educational goals and objectives a student needs to develop. Much of this kind of information has been derived from the sciences of medicine and psychology, and it assists educators primarily in determining specific handicapping conditions — largely an administrative function. This determination is, at best, equivocal and rarely guides a teacher in selecting appropriate goals and objectives for handicapped learners. Herein may lie one of the major tasks of the science of education: the definition and study of educational objectives that will lead to mastery of given educational goals.

The science of special education, of which every teacher is a scientist, must involve formal hypotheses and investigations regarding:

(1) delineation of all objectives leading to mastery of an educational goal in the four special education areas of self-help/basic living, pre-academic/academic, career/vocational, and socio-behavioral abilities,

(2) systematic exclusion of objectives not found directly related to given educational goals,

(3) delineation of any possible sequences of objectives that will facilitate goal achievement, and

(4) relationships that exist between specific educational objectives and levels of maturation and cognitive development.

Obviously, before any of these investigations can be started, teachers must have an intuitive grasp of all possible curriculum goals and objectives involved in the instruction of handicapped students. Each teacher must know, in the sense of understanding and application, goals and objectives appropriate for the education of handicapped youngsters.

Teachers can obtain knowledge of curriculum objectives in two primary ways. First and most simply, they can select (or be given) a predetermined scope and sequence or list of objectives to follow. These curriculum aids have become increasingly more available with the advent of individualized education program mandates. Such lists of objectives can be obtained through commercial producers of regular or special education materials, school district curriculum guides, or criterion-referenced test objectives. Special educators who study and use these instruments often find the same sense of security that is afforded their regular education counterparts through basal materials and curriculum guides. Rarely, however, will one find a truly dedicated teacher who remains content and confident with ready-made objectives for long.

Second, educators can become knowledgeable in curriculum by generating their own curriculum goals and objectives. This approach represents more than the mere study and adoption of ready-made curricula. Original construction of curriculum involves an *active process* of careful examination, analysis, synthesis, and evaluation of previously developed curricula that culminates in the re-creation of goals and objectives for the education of handicapped students. Needless to say, creation or re-creation of special education curricula initially requires a great deal more time, study, labor, persistence, and competence on the part of a teacher than does the mere utilization of ready-made objectives. In the long run, though, the advantages of developing original curriculum objectives far outweigh the disadvantages in that the end result for the teacher is less time and labor and an increase in confidence.

The advantages of this approach to a teacher's gaining knowledge in special education curriculum become more apparent upon examination of the goals and uses of such knowledge. One might translate thorough curriculum knowledge into the following special education teacher competencies:

(1) the ability to plan instructional activities for individual students or groups of students that reflect a wide range of goals and objectives needed by handicapped youths — i.e., self-help, vocational, academic, and social goals and objectives,

(2) the ability to solve problems on the spot when students fail to meet certain objectives or once specific objectives are accomplished —i.e., immediate creation or recall of new objectives or the matching of objectives with developmental levels,

(3) the ability to evaluate and select materials available that will assist the teacher in facilitating specific objectives, and

(4) the ability to continuously evaluate student progress and recognize mastery of a given objective.

Each of these abilities requires that the competent teacher have an intuitive understanding of the development and continuum of educational objectives. To solve daily problems, the teacher must be able to immediately recall principles of educational objectives and their sequences. The continuous evaluation of progress can come only from an understanding of how a given objective is or can be objectively defined to represent the principle of mastery. None of the competencies can truly be met by teachers who have not experienced the frustrations and triumphs of actually creating and organizing educational objectives. Well documented studies on the recall, application, and transfer of various scientific principles have established that experience and discovering principles and concepts for oneself produce much better results than merely memorizing or studying given concepts (Bruner, 1963; Piaget, 1970). This holds true for special education curriculum development, in which the intuitive understanding and immediate recall necessary for maximum utilization of educational objectives can come only from teachers who have experienced and discovered the principles of educational objectives for themselves.

An added benefit that can be expected to occur from teacher participation in curriculum development is an increase in teacher confidence. This confidence is derived from the self-knowledge that daily classroom problems can be solved without undue reliance upon administrative and support staffs, and from the rewards inherent in finding solutions to professional problems. This proposition does not necessarily suggest that every special education teacher or group of teachers should always develop a curriculum that is as complete or as well written as that developed by other professionals. Nevertheless, the assumption inherent within this proposal is that teachers can implement a self-designed curriculum better and with more vigor and confidence than they can a curriculum in which they have not been involved.

Additionally, teacher confidence is derived from the accompanying freedom to choose instructional materials according to the objectives they have developed and selected. In many instances, educators operate according to the reverse principle; that is, the material that has been selected or purchased determines the educational objectives presented. This, like undue dependency on support and administrative staffs, gives teachers little leeway in determining which objectives are to be taught. The powerlessness that inevitably results can do little but make teachers the pawns of materials developers and lead to feelings of incompetence.

In contrast, the emergence of more competent and confident special education teachers and their active involvement in special education curriculum development go hand in hand with better educational programming for individual handicapped students. Intuitive knowledge of curriculum along with experience in writing educational objectives simplify the teacher's task of preparing and initiating individualized student programs.

Improved Educational Programming

In addition to an increase in teacher competence and confidence, the special education curriculum development activities proposed here will produce a continuum of educational objectives that will ultimately improve individual educational programming. Delineation of a large number of goals and objectives possible for use in the instruction of handicapped students improves their educational programs by:

(1) providing a sequenced continuum of goals and objectives over the students' school careers,

(2) offering a wide selection of objectives so that the most appropriate ones may be selected for instruction, and

(3) changing the focus in special education programming and services from specific handicapping conditions to educational goals and objectives.

Historically, the special education student's individual program has relied for the most part on the classroom placement for each year. For example, if Don, an educably retarded child, were placed with a teacher who was trained and most comfortable with a unit type of instruction, Don's instruction that year might largely involve units on use of the telephone, time, money, the newspaper, and so forth. The following year, however, Don might be assigned to an academically oriented classroom with an emphasis on reading, writing, spelling, and mathematical skills. Further along in his education, Don could be subjected to arts and crafts oriented programs, therapeutic milieu programs emphasizing social curricula, and pre-vocational programs. Each of these placement changes could alter or repeat educational objectives. After 12 or more years of special education, Don's educational status could very well reveal that the objectives attempted during this instructional period did not represent the continuity necessary for achieving educational goals.

The ideal special education curriculum yields an all encompassing structure of goals and objectives applicable to various special education services and arrangements. Such a structure can improve educational programming for handicapped youngsters by offering a well sequenced continuum of educational objectives across time and classroom settings.

Second, the mere delineation of various objectives believed to be encompassed in academic/pre-academic, self help/basic living, career/vocational, and socio-behavioral education allows for a more comprehensive and simplified selection of appropriate goals and objectives. The very nature of handicapping conditions calls for a rather extensive number of goals and objectives possible for selection in educating individual students. The availability and knowledge of complete curriculum objectives in each of the four areas of special education instruction stated previously allow educators to readily select objectives for individual students, at the same time assuring that important objectives are not overlooked. The annual updates and revisions are also simplified by the provision of continuous objectives leading directly to goal achievement.

This focus on specific objectives that will ultimately lead to goal achievement has the side benefit of downplaying specific handicapping conditions. Regardless of the primary handicap, many students share the same or similar goals or objectives at any given time. The traditional emphasis on placement and programming according to handicapping condition can be resisted only by providing a viable alternative. The creation and study of a special education curriculum as proposed here provides an alternative to grouping by categories of exceptionality. It encourages educators to look beyond the potentially stigmatizing variables and to examine and program the student's education according to appropriate goals and objectives.

Only a few of the many purposes to be accomplished by emphasizing the art and science of special education curriculum development have been discussed thus far, namely:

(1) increasing teacher competence,
(2) improving teacher confidence,
(3) providing a continuum of educational goals and objectives,
(4) simplifying the selection of goals and objectives, and
(5) reducing the emphasis on handicapping condition.

The following section delineates certain procedures that have been used successfully in accomplishing each of the above purposes. Other procedures are possible, of course, but this discussion, at least, will give an indication of the enormous potential in curriculum development activities.

GENERAL PROCEDURES FOR DEVELOPING CURRICULUM

Several procedural strategies must be determined prior to initiating special education curriculum development activities. General procedures involve determining:

(1) who will actually develop the curriculum goals and objectives,
(2) when these goals and objectives will be developed,
(3) in what setting the development will occur, and
(4) in what areas curriculum must be established.

Regarding who will develop the curriculum, the answer is fairly clear when considering one of the major purposes to be accomplished: Special education teachers involved in the direct instruction of handicapped students must be the primary developers of special education curriculum since they are the primary implementors. Ideally, special educators should never be forced to use a set of curriculum objectives that they have not had an active part in developing. Other persons that may contribute to curriculum development include parents, regular classroom teachers, support personnel, and persons from the community at large.

The proper time to develop curriculum goals and objectives necessarily varies from institution to institution. Experience has shown, however, that development of a comprehensive curriculum generally appears best accomplished within highly concentrated blocks of time during which educators' major task can be the examination and creation of curriculum — as opposed to periodic meetings or meetings held at a time when instructional activities in the classroom are occupying most of the teacher's time. For example, the quantity and quality of curriculum material produced sometime during the summer months or in two-week daily workshops has been encouraging. Of course, teachers should be reimbursed in some manner for their time spent in curriculum development of this nature.

The settings reserved for curriculum development can vary widely from pre-service teacher training programs to concentrated in-service programs. Although there are no guidelines to suggest the best setting for special education curriculum development, many school districts have found that participation in this activity as a group is highly appropriate and productive. This format allows development of a satisfying continuum of goals and objectives across school programs within a given district or cooperative entity.

Most special education programs include goals and objectives in four basic areas of education — self-help/basic living, career/vocational, pre-academic/academic, and socio-behavioral education. These are the areas, then, that eventually must be addressed by special educators when developing curriculum. Goals and objectives must be delineated for each of the four areas, to allow for the more thorough selection of objectives for individual pupils. For instance, while some people consider only severely handicapped students as needing objectives that involve self-help/basic living education, many mildly disabled youngsters also have trouble dressing or performing simple consumer skills. Therefore, special educators of all types need some knowledge of and guidelines for developing objectives in each of the four areas.

To take these broad areas of special education and delineate goals and objectives in each, a structure or model is needed around which to arrange these goals and objectives. The more consistent this model is within a local education agency or across agencies, the more readily transferable are the ideas contained in the special education curricula.

A MODEL FOR SPECIAL EDUCATION CURRICULUM

The model to be adopted in developing special education curriculum should be one that can be directly applicable to the individualized education program mandated for all handicapped students. Thus, the model must relate to both annual goals and short-term instructional objectives. Larsen and Poplin (1979) have suggested a curriculum model designed for use in developing individualized education programs for handicapped students. The model consists of three levels of curriculum development: educational goals or constructs, general objectives, and short-term instructional objectives.

The first level or step in curriculum development involves delineating goals or constructs of a given special education area (e.g., academics or self-help). For example, the constructs or goals of the self-help curriculum might include *motor and mobility, hygiene, dressing, feeding,* and *grooming.* The second level of the curriculum represents general objectives — defined as the necessary link between goals and short-term instructional objectives. The primary purpose of this level, as stated by Larsen and Poplin, is to provide content to annual goals and meaning to short-term objectives. For example, general objectives for the construct of feeding might include: drinking from a bottle, eating with a spoon, drinking from a cup, . . . eating in a restaurant. The third level of special education curriculum development involves the breakdown of each general objective into a series of short-term instructional objectives that lead to mastery of a given general objective. Completion of levels one and two (goals and general objectives) results in development of a curricular "map" (discussed next). Completion of level three (described later) results in a specific curriculum guide that can be used directly in the development of IEPs.

Curricular Maps

Curricular maps provide teachers an overview of all major concepts to be covered in a given area of special education. This broad picture of curriculum content lends a sense of continuity to classroom activities and allows for the selection of all goals and general objectives appropriate for a given student's educational program. The structure of a curricular map takes a form similar to that of Figures 1 and 2. This basic structure represents a two-dimensional array of general objectives, organized by construct and by level. Therefore, special educators attempting to develop curriculum maps in each of the areas of special education must first delineate (a) the curriculum maps necessary to adequately cover a given area, (b) the constructs inherent in each curricular map, and (c) the levels along which general objectives will be ordered.

For each area of special education there may be several different curriculum maps. For example, the area of pre-academics/academics might include

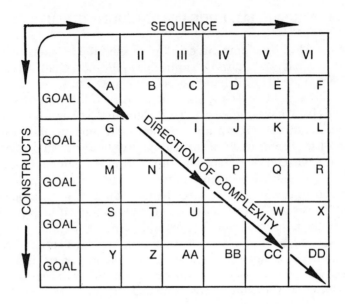

FIGURE 1
Graph of Curricular Map

curriculum in oral language, reading, written expression, and math. Self-help/basic living curriculum may contain maps of motor and mobility objectives, personal skills, and independent living curriculum. Career/vocational maps might include career awareness, career exploration, and occupational maintenance curriculum. Curriculum maps for socio-behavioral education might include the delineation of personal interaction objectives and self awareness objectives, as well as a map of behavior disorders (organized from most to least severe). The above, of course, are examples only; the most appropriate conceptualization of the various curriculum maps for each area of special education is that devised by the group of teachers developing and utilizing the curriculum itself.

The constructs or goals must be specified as the first dimension of the curricular map. These constructs represent the subcomponents or parts of a curriculum map that, when synthesized, reflect the totality of the curriculum itself. For example, the curriculum of written expression would involve the constructs of spelling, penmanship, capitalization, punctuation, vocabulary, grammar, sentence construction, paragraph construction, and theme development. A personal skills curriculum might contain feeding, dressing, grooming, and hygiene constructs. Career awareness constructs might be organized to reflect various occupational clusters. Curriculum maps of self

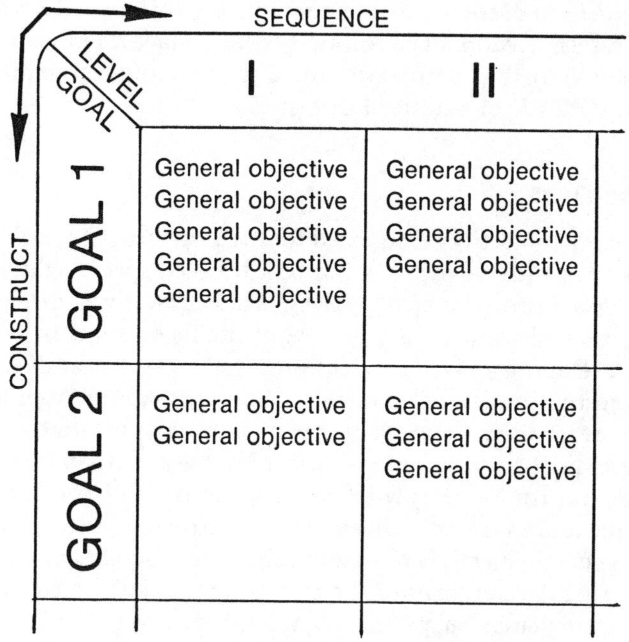

SEQUENCE

Copyright 1979 by Allyn and Bacon. Reprinted by permission.

FIGURE 2
Distribution of General Objectives within the Curricular Map

awareness objectives may be organized around the constructs of body awareness, feelings awareness, response alternatives, and values. The constructs set forth in this first dimension of curricular maps are also appropriate as goals for individual student programs. Thus, the construct dimension not only adds organizational structure to curriculum but is directly applicable to the IEP.

The second dimension of curricular maps also adds to the organizational structure of the special education curriculum. This dimension allows for organization of general objectives along levels of goals or constructs. These levels represent a somewhat subjective organization of general objectives arranged either (a) from simplest to most complex, (b) from high to low priority, or (c) along developmental age levels. Some examples will illustrate these concepts: Mathematical objectives, under the construct of addition, are easily sequenced from simplest to most complex. For example, the objective of "one digit addition" is simpler than, and is often considered a necessary prerequisite to, the objective of "two digit addition without renaming." Language development objectives, under the construct of phonology or articulation, are usually sequenced according to knowledge of the developmental acquisition of speech phonemes in young children. Objectives under the area of career/vocational education generally have no inherent sequence developmentally or by complexity; thus, they are often organized in curriculum on the basis of perceived priorities.

General Objectives

The general objectives delineated for each construct or goal within the curriculum map provide the essential link between special education goals and short-term instructional objectives. These objectives are most adventitiously generated through the process of brainstorming. In this process, educators developing a given curriculum map brainstorm and record all the possible objectives under each construct of the curriculum. After the session, they examine each brainstormed objective and discard duplicate and inappropriate objectives. The remaining general objectives are then (a) written into the proper form conforming with the characteristics of general objectives, and (b) sequenced into levels within each construct.

These general objectives have seven characteristics that one should keep in mind during development of the curriculum map. These characteristics ensure that curricular maps are comprehensive, yet concise enough to provide educators an efficient overview of the curriculum at a glance. The differences between general objectives and goals and short-term instructional objectives become more apparent upon examining the following characteristics delineated by Larsen and Poplin (1979):

1. General objectives can generally be written in three to four words and do not constitute a complete statement.
2. General objectives do not specify a particular behavior that the student is expected to perform.
3. General objectives do not specify conditions under which an objective is to be accomplished.
4. General objectives do not specify criteria necessary to judge success.
5. General objectives are not time specific — that is, mastering one general objective may involve a week or a year's instruction.
6. General objectives do not state desires for improvement.
7. There is a set of general objectives that can be developed and sequenced under each special education goal.

Examination of general objectives delineated and sequenced under several special education constructs serves to illustrate these characteristics.

A curriculum map developed in the academic area of written expression can be used to demonstrate several of the characteristics of general objectives. A curriculum map in written expression, as mentioned earlier, may contain constructs such as penmanship, spelling, capitalization, punctuation, vocabulary, grammar, sentence and paragraph construction. Figure 3 depicts

	I	II	III
Capitalization	The first word of a sentence The child's first and last names The name of the teacher, school, town, street The word "I"	The date First and important words of titles of books the children read Proper names used in children's writings Titles of compositions Names of titles: Mr., Mrs., Miss, Ms.	Proper names, month, day, common holidays First word in a line of verse First and important words in titles of books, stories, poems First word of salutation of informal note, as "Dear" First word of closing of informal note, as "Yours"
Punctuation	Period at the end of a sentence which tells something Period after numbers in any kind of list	Question mark at the close of a question Comma after salutation of a friendly note or letter Comma after closing of a friendly note or letter Comma between the day of the month and the year Comma between name of city and state	Period after an abbreviation Period after an initial Use of an apostrophe in a common contraction such as isn't, aren't Commas in a list

From "Problems in Writing" by D. D. Hammill and M. S. Poplin, in *Teaching Children with Learning and Behavior Problems* (second edition) by D. D. Hammill and N. R. Bartel. Copyright 1978 by Allyn and Bacon, Boston. Reprinted by permission.

FIGURE 3
Partial Curriculum Map of Written Expression

only the constructs of capitalization and punctuation taken from a curriculum map carried across three levels of general objectives. General objectives delineated here, such as "The first word of a sentence" or "Commas in a list" refer to instances in writing in which capitalization or punctuation is needed. The objectives need not be written as complete sentences, and they contain no reference to any behavior that the student is to perform. In looking at this portion of the map of objectives, one receives an overview of the early skills involved in capitalization and punctuation, but with no indication of the instructional activities used in developing these skills. For instance, the objectives do not specify whether students are to locate and correct errors in a given or original selection or incorporate these skills automatically within their original writing. The objectives do not mention any special conditions under which the skills are to be performed, nor do they give the criteria for success. Accomplishing the objective of capitalizing "the first word of a sentence" may require a week or a year or more depending on both the child and the instruction.

Improving the skills listed on the curriculum map is obviously a goal of instruction, but the general objectives themselves do not state a desire to improve or increase these abilities. Although Figure 3 shows only two constructs across three levels, a more comprehensive set of objectives is possible under each of the constructs of written expression.

To further illustrate the characteristics of general objectives, Figure 4 depicts the area of self-help/basic living education on the curriculum map of personal skills. This particular map reflects objectives under the personal skill constructs of feeding, dressing, health and hygiene, and grooming delineated across five levels sequenced from simple to most complex, developmentally, and to some extent by priorities. Again, objectives such as "Use of cup," "Combing hair," "Medical needs," "Make-up" clearly refer to specific skills or information to be acquired, but these objectives make no reference to specific instructional activities, conditions, or criteria for implementation. Timelines and desires for improvement are not indicated within the general objectives shown here. Once again, the curriculum map provides a quick picture of the general content of a given educational area frequently of concern to special educators.

The process of developing and organizing general objectives within the curricular map structure accomplishes several purposes for special educators. In addition to the increased competence and confidence that result from the activity itself, the curriculum map provides an efficient structure for inventorying a large number of objectives often unnecessary for individual student programs. Also, general objectives contained in the curricular map aid educators in making the critical transition between goals and short-term instructional objectives.

Tangential advantages of curricular maps include the possibilities of using these maps and objectives to (a) improve communication with parents regarding selection of appropriate goals and objectives for their handicapped youngsters, (b) simplify the organization of curriculum guides containing short-term instructional objectives, and (c) create informal systems for monitoring individual students' progress. All of these advantages stemming from curricular mapping activities are contingent, of course, upon appropriate use of the curriculum objectives generated.

Two major criticisms of many educational curricula must be considered in order to avoid common pitfalls when developing and utilizing curriculum maps. The first criticism is that often, as in regular education curricula, the objectives themselves determine the students' programs. In other words,

	I	II	III	IV	V
Feeding	Being fed - liquids Being fed - solids Self feeding - bottle Self feeding - hands	Use of cup Use of spoon Use of fork and spoon	Use of knife, fork, spoon Use of bottle drinks Use of can drinks	Table manners Food selection School lunch	Restaurant dining
Dressing	Shoes Socks Coat Shirt	Pants Skirts Gloves Undergarments	Appropriate colors Hose Appropriate sizes Jewelry	Appropriate for season Appropriate for physical characteristics	Appropriate styles Purchasing own wardrobe Accessories
Health and Hygiene	Toilet training Hand washing Face washing	Regular bathing Deodorant Nose care	Medical needs Dental needs Menstruation Other puberty related needs	Medical and dental care - regular Use of over-counter drugs	Regular hygiene Use of prescription drugs Medical and dental emergencies
Grooming	Combing hair Brushing teeth	Washing & drying hair Washing clothes Drying clothes	Shaving Curling hair Ironing Fingernails	Toenails Special skin care Simple repair of clothing	Make-up Styling hair Cologne

FIGURE 4

Example of a Curricular Map of Personal Skills in Self-Help/Basic Living Education

many teachers utilize the general objectives on the curricular map by automatically assigning each objective to every student. In such cases, the idea of individualized programs is fallacious. This criticism of predetermined curriculum is less valid for many special education programs in which variances in handicapped students' abilities are so great as to preclude automatic assignment of identical objectives to every child. Unlike traditional scope and sequence charts that delineate the objectives contained in specific materials, curricular maps should exhibit a much broader perspective. General objectives within curricular maps are designed to represent *all* of the objectives possible in a given special education area. Specific objectives are then selected from that array for individual students. Finally, specific materials are located or designed to assist in instructing the student in the selected objectives.

A second frequent criticism of predetermined curriculum objectives is that they tend to provide only a cursory picture of true abilities in each of the areas of education. For example, a mathematics curriculum usually places much emphasis upon algorithms, calculations, and memorization of number facts, with little attention afforded to development of mathematical concepts. In other words, it is said that the skills oriented educator accepts a "schoolhouse attitude" about educational achievement, often reflected in an overuse of worksheet type activities and objectives that ignores concept learning and thought development. Although this criticism is highly valid, in many instances it can be overcome by giving careful definition of mastery to each general objective on the curriculum map. The concept of mastering curriculum objectives is best applied by perfecting the development of criteria, conditions, and behaviors in the delineation of short-term instructional objectives.

SHORT-TERM INSTRUCTIONAL OBJECTIVES
LEADING TO MASTERY

Two important concepts must be understood and utilized during development of short-term instructional objectives — i.e., the components of these objectives, and the various ways in which mastery can be defined. Once components of instructional objectives and definitions of mastery have been incorporated for each general objective, the results of these activities will produce comprehensive curriculum and instructional guides.

Components of Instructional Objectives

Any short-term instructional objective has three primary components:

(1)   the student activity or observable behavior,
(2)   any special conditions under which the activity will take place, and
(3)   the criteria by which success will be determined.

These components, when spelled out for each general objective, assist special education teachers both in the determination of actual instructional activities for the classroom and in evaluation or assessment strategies for monitoring pupil progress.

Observable Behavior

The student activity denotes a particular student behavior necessary to perform the given instructional objective. For example, will the student be asked to *write* or *say* the answer to a given problem; *drink* from a cup; *correct* an error in capitalization; verbally *name* a common object; or *identify* a cup, sentence, addition sign, or common object? All of these verbs specify an observable behavior that is to occur during instructional and/or evaluative activities. General objectives, on the other hand, do not provide teachers with a student activity that can be observed.

Special Conditions

Any special conditions necessary for performing a given behavior must also be included in short-term instructional objectives. Conditions are sometimes obvious from either the behavior or criteria defined, but in some instances it becomes a most pertinent consideration. For example, if "drinking from a cup" is an objective, transferring this skill from the classroom to home or from one cup to many different cups may be important considerations. The conditions under which a child is expected to function upon returning to a regular classroom may be another consideration. For instance, correctly answering addition problems may be transferable only if the student can record 25 answers in 15 minutes on a single worksheet. Special conditions including rate, quantity, and setting, then, are often important considerations in defining instructional objectives.

Criteria

The third essential component to be delineated in short-term instructional objectives relates to the criteria that must be achieved in order for an instructional objective to be considered mastered. Criteria are generally stated in terms of percentage of accuracy or number of times consecutively performed over a given period of time. Generally, percentage of accuracy or number alone is insufficient to indicate that an instructional objective has been met. For example, achieving "90% to 100% accuracy" on a given list of spelling words rarely assures the successful spelling of those same words tomorrow or next week. Therefore, "90% accuracy measured once every 3-4 weeks" would be a much more appropriate criterion. "Using a spoon during mealtime at home" once would not automatically be considered as an objective achieved; however, if the behavior were to occur over a period of "two weeks," one could be more certain of mastery. Likewise, no one would consider that a student who made one successful bus trip unassisted had mastered the "ability to utilize bus transportation." The delineation of criteria for success, along with the behavior to be performed by the student, and any special conditions, then, are all necessary parts or components of short-term instructional objectives.

Defining Mastery

In developing instructional objectives, initially defining the single short-term instructional objective that will represent mastery of the given general objective is helpful. After that, a series of instructional objectives leading to the mastery objective can be specified. Mastery as a concept is frequently applied to educational or general objectives in three ways: cue reduction, task analysis, and taxonomy of educational objectives (Larsen & Poplin, 1979). These approaches to definition of mastery are most often used in combination rather than as single entities. Each will be discussed below utilizing the lists of short-term instructional objectives contained in Figures 5, 6, 7, and 8 as points of reference.

Cue Reduction

When mastery of an objective depends largely upon the performance of a behavior being accomplished *independently* or *automatically*, it is often best to utilize cue reduction instructional objectives. Cue reduction is merely the specification of instructional objectives whereby teacher assistance is gradually withdrawn from a student activity or behavior. In the several levels of cues that reflect a continuum from most to least teacher assistance:

(1) *priming* represents an activity that is completed with total teacher assistance. An example of a *physical prime* is the formation of letters in handwriting, with the teacher guiding the student's hand through the entire movement. An example of a *verbal prime* would be when a teacher reads aloud each word of a selection with the student.

(2) *prompts* are activities in which the teacher begins or completes some part of the behavior with the child. *Physical prompts* are often used to get children started on manual activities or to assist them at difficult points during the activity. Teachers voice *verbal prompts* to assist students when indicated at varying intervals during a course of instruction (e.g., providing words for students reading aloud when difficulty becomes apparent or is likely).

Self-Help/Basic Living — Personal Skills Map — Feeding

General Objective: Drinking from a cup

Short-Term Instructional Objectives:

Criteria: Ten consecutive trials
Special Conditions: At home and school with three different cups

Behavior	With Physical Prime	With Physical Prompt and Verbal Cue	With Verbal Cue	Independently
1. Reaches for cup				
2. Grasps cup				
3. Brings cup to mouth				
4. Tilts cup				
5. Swallows liquid				
6. Replaces cup				
7. Steps 1-6 sequentially	M.d. 3-79	M.d. 4-79	"drink" M.d. 5-79	*

*Indicates mastery

FIGURE 5

Short-Term Instructional Objectives for "Use of a Cup"

Academics — Math Curriculum — Addition

General Objective: Sums to 18

Short-Term Instructional Objectives: Criteria: 90% accuracy over 3 weeks (6 recordings)

Mechanical Behaviors	5 per page	10 per page	25 per page in 10 min.
1. Records answers to vertically arranged problems, sums to 9, excluding 0's	✓		
2. Records answers to vertically arranged problems, sums to 18, including 0's	✓		
3. Records answers to horizontally arranged problems, sums to 18	✓		*
4. Records answers to vertically and horizontally arranged problems, sums to 18	✓	Md 5-79	
	1 per 5 sec.	1 per 5 sec.	1 per sec.
5. Names answers to vertically arranged problems, sums to 9, excluding 0's	Md 5-79	Md 5-79	Md 5-79
6. Names answers to vertically arranged problems, sums to 18			
7. Names answers to horizontally arranged problems, sums to 18			*

Conceptual Behaviors	With prompt or prime	With cue	Independently
1. Records algorithms vertically when verbally given			Mkl 4-79
2. Arranges concrete objects to denote a given algorithm representing sums to 18	Mkl 5-79		
3. States, records, and solves algorithms when given concrete objects demonstrating sums to 18	Mkl 5-79		
4. Solves own problems involving addition sums to 18	Mkl 5-79		*

*Indicates mastery

FIGURE 6
Short-Term Instructional Objectives for "Sums to 18"

Academics — Written Expression Curriculum — Capitalization

General Objective: Capitalizing first word in a sentence

Short-Term Instructional Objectives:

Criteria: 90% over 6-week period (measured 6 times)

Behavior	With Verbal Cues	Independently
1. Identifies capital letters	AC 10-77	MS 3-78
2. Recognizes first word of sentences	AC 11-77	MS 3-78
3. Identifies errors in capitalizing first word of sentences	AC 12-77	MS 4-78
4. Corrects errors in capitalizing first word of sentences	AC 12-77 / ms. in original comp. 5-78	SC 9-79
5. In original composition, capitalizes first word in sentence	SC 10-79	*

*Indicates mastery

FIGURE 7
Short-Term Instructional Objectives for "Capitalizing First Word in a Sentence"

Pre-Academic — Oral Language Curriculum — One-Word Utterances

General Objectives: Naming common food items

Short-Term Instructional Objectives:

Criteria: 7 consecutive correct responses
Condition: School and home

Behavior	With Prime	With Prompt	With Model or Cue	Automatically
1. Points to object when given the name	MP 1-79 to 5-79	MP 5-79		
2. Points to picture when given the name	MP 1-79 to 5-79			
3. Repeats word				
4. Names when shown object				
5. Names when shown picture of object				
6. Uses noun when requesting or referring to food item				*

*Indicates mastery

FIGURE 8
Short-Term Instructional Objectives for "Naming Common Food Items"

(3) *cues* are merely signals given to students for a certain behavior to occur. *Physical cues* can be hand, facial, or object cues. Modeling is one kind of physical cue. *Verbal cues* include almost any teacher direction — e.g., "An 'o' starts at the top and goes around until it meets again," "Tilt the cup," and "Line up your numbers one under the other."

Most often, verbal or physical cues are begun at the prime and prompt stages so that as these kinds of behaviors are accomplished and withdrawn, the verbal cue remains associated with the activity itself. Verbal mediation skills whereby the child verbally directs him/herself through an activity are predicated upon this assumption.

Examples of cue reduction applied to definition of short-term instructional objectives to mastery are represented in each of Figures 5 through 8. In each instance, cue reduction techniques are listed to reinforce the behaviors to be acquired. For example, in Figure 5 the teacher might physically help children reach for the cup, physically prompt them, or verbally say, "Reach for the cup," or "Cup?" until they independently reach for the cup. Obviously, with some students, application of each of these techniques for every behavior listed would not be necessary. In the event that a student cannot perform a given task independently, however, teachers do have these instructional devices to fall back on in attempting to teach various concepts and/or behaviors. Readers interested in further explanation of cue reduction techniques are referred to Becker, Englemann, and Thomas (1975) and Larsen and Poplin (1979).

Task Analysis

A second means of conceptualizing mastery of general objectives is the process of task analysis. This method is most appropriate for objectives in which mastery requires a series of tasks that must be completed simultaneously or sequentially in order to accomplish the given general objective, such as the steps involved in washing one's hair. Task analysis involves taking a given general objective and dividing it into a series of related sub-tasks. Many self-help/basic living and some vocational tasks are highly appropriate for task analysis activities.

Figure 5 depicts the objective of "Drinking from a cup" broken into sub-tasks like grasping the cup, tilting the cup, and swallowing the liquid. Mastery occurs in Step 7 — the point at which the individual sub-tasks are combined into one activity. To a lesser extent, Figures 6 through 8 represent some task analysis related activities. For instance, in Figure 6, the "Sums to 18" objective is essentially divided into two tasks — "Sums to 9, excluding zeros," and "Sums to 18, including zeros."

In task analysis activities, it is not uncommon to find many students for whom the teaching of each individual sub-task is unnecessary. Instead, the objectives that denote mastery can be instructed directly from the outset. Readers interested in more thorough explanations of this topic are referred to Lovitt (1975a, b) and Larsen and Poplin (1979).

Taxonomies of Educational Objectives

For general objectives in which development of concepts, ideas, or principles is most important, teachers may want to become more familiar with the various taxonomies of educational objectives (Bloom, 1956; Krathwohl, Bloom, & Masia, 1964) and utilize those concepts in developing instructional objectives. The taxonomy of objectives involved in the cognitive domain represents a hierarchy whereby students are required to perform behaviors as simple as rote recall or behaviors that demand application or the complex manipulation of information in order to solve problems and create and evaluate products. The five levels of the cognitive domain, in ascending order, are:

(1) *knowledge objectives*, requiring retention of previously presented information (i.e., memory and recall),
(2) *comprehension objectives*, demanding that the student perform behaviors that indicate his or her understanding of the meaning of acquired information,
(3) *application objectives*, requiring behaviors in which learned material is applied to new situations,
(4) *synthesis objectives*, calling for students to put previously learned information together in new ways to form a new whole, and
(5) *evaluation objectives*, necessitating behaviors whereby materials or information is judged.

Special education teachers are frequently most concerned in helping students reach the level in goals and objectives at which they can apply concepts and facts to their own lives. This view of mastery to application is highly important in special education. For example, knowledge of addition facts offers students only limited assistance until they understand and can apply the concept of addition to their own needs. Nevertheless, preparing students for participation and success within the regular classroom environment commonly requires the achievement of objectives that represent either more or less than that necessary for application. Referring to the general objective of capitalizing the first word in a sentence, this skill is often taught and evaluated on the basis of locating or correcting an error or by rewriting a given unpunctuated sentence. The ability to perform this task falls far short of mastery to application, whereby students automatically capitalize beginning words of their own original sentences. On the other hand, applying addition skills to story problems in which students are given simulated problems to *read* and *solve* requires skills that go beyond the ability to apply addition facts and understanding to their own uses.

When developing short-term instructional objectives, teachers are encouraged to keep both the concepts of mastery to understanding and to application in mind along with mastery as it relates to regular classroom activities. In some instances, when a discrepancy exists between classroom objectives and application, teachers may choose to disregard regular classroom kinds of objectives in favor of more practical application oriented objectives. Application oriented objectives are especially preferred in cases in which the student's abilities in a given special education curriculum area are so deficit as to preclude regular classroom participation for a period of time. Also, in the case of older students, teachers often opt for the more functional objectives, and performance within the regular classroom receives a low priority for the student's education.

In summary, short-term instructional objectives can be defined to mastery by careful use and combination of the concepts of cue reduction, task analysis, and taxonomies of the various educational domains. When defining a series of short-term instructional objectives, it is most efficient to begin by defining the last of the series — i.e., the instructional objective that will represent mastery of the given general objective. Following delineation of the mastery objective, the various techniques outlined here may be incorporated to construct a series of short-term objectives that will hopefully lead to the mastery objective.

Unfortunately, little research information is available to indicate what kinds of instructional activities or objectives actually do contribute to mastery of various educational goals and general objectives. Very likely, differences exist from child to child to the extent that conclusive statements may not be possible to reach. Teachers in situations in which the lack of empirical research on instructional objectives continually manifests itself should be careful to instruct children according to instructional objectives that are as close as possible to the definition of mastery.

After instructional objectives to mastery have been developed for all the general objectives contained in a given curriculum map, the accumulation of listings like those of Figures 6 through 8 will result in a comprehensive, valuable curriculum and instructional guide for instruction. In addition to the new understanding that involved teachers will have gained through these curriculum related activities, well-defined objectives will assist them in appropriate instruction and materials selection.

APPLICATION OF CURRICULUM TO THE IEP

In addition to providing special educators an almost daily guide for instruction (as well as other purposes previously discussed), curricular maps and guides can be used to simplify development of individualized education programs. Application of a well planned, carefully designed curriculum in developing IEPs involves using curriculum maps and guides as:

(1) a source for selecting goals and objectives for individual students, and
(2) a structure for continuous monitoring of pupil progress throughout one or several years of education.

These uses of curriculum maps and guides greatly simplify the development of individual programs and provide students and teachers with a true continuum of educational objectives.

Maps and guides outlining various goals, general objectives, and instructional objectives constitute excellent resources for the special education teacher when selecting goals and objectives for individual programs. A comprehensive curriculum, along with the teacher's knowledge gained in developing the array of goals and objectives, helps ensure that important goals and objectives are not overlooked. A special educator involved in developing numerous educational programs could otherwise have a tendency to repeat the same objectives from program to program and/or to avoid or overlook goals and objectives that are needed but difficult to define. The experience derived from developing a good curriculum does offer an alternative preferable to the likely duplication or omission of goals and objectives.

The concept of individualized education programs does not mean that a new curriculum must be created for each student. It does mean, though, that the range of possibilities for goals and objectives is wide and may be different for each student. During preparation of goals for the student's IEP, teachers are advised to review curriculum maps in the various areas of special education and record the appropriate special education areas, goals, and general objectives directly on the student's IEP form.

Realistically, special education teachers are aware of the virtual impossibility of recording every short-term instructional objective on the IEP form itself. Usually, IEP forms allow approximately one-half page at most for the delineation and evaluation of short-term instructional objectives. Curriculum guides containing short-term instructional objectives offer several alternatives to the tedious recording of instructional objectives on every student's IEP. Following delineation of goals and general objectives, teachers may want to merely refer to the pages and/or numbers in the curriculum guide containing the appropriate instructional objectives or, better yet, to duplicate and attach these pages to the student's individual program. One school district provides the entire guide for each student's program once the appropriate special education curriculum areas have been identified. This guide then follows the student from year to year, program to program, and serves as a continuous monitoring device. The method of delineating short-term instructional objectives as represented in Figures 5 through 8 provides an inherent evaluation form. Progress toward short-term instructional objectives can be marked directly on the form. Criteria, conditions, and behaviors are all contained within the guide.

Referring again to Figures 5 through 8, one sees how these example forms can be used to record progress over time. For example, Figure 5 tells next year's teacher that of the steps, only Step 7 was attempted, and before the end of the school year, the child was drinking from a cup on the verbal cue "drink"; he had not reached mastery, however. The student whose progress was recorded on Figure 6 had not mastered all the mechanical or conceptual skills listed. As another informative aid, teachers had recorded checkmarks during pretesting to indicate skills the student was already able to perform. Figure 7 demonstrates the utility of guides following students through various years of schooling. At a glance, teachers, parents, and administrators can determine past instructional efforts for a given child in the application of capitalization skills. Figure 8 charts the progress of a student having obvious difficulty with one-word utterances. Both initiation and completion dates have been recorded, along with the special education teacher's initials. Progress recorded on Figure 7 for Objective 4 indicates a difference in teaching methods between teachers A.C. and M.S. While A.C. may have given the student ready-made sentences in which to locate and correct errors, M.S. utilized this proofreading objective with the student's own composition. Teaching methods, approaches, and the selection of short-term instructional objectives may differ from teacher to teacher and from child to child, but with a comprehensive monitoring system no essential information goes unrecorded.

The direct application of curriculum goals and objectives to development of individualized education programs prevents useless duplication of efforts and frees teachers for valuable instructional time. Curriculum maps can serve as a source for transferring goals and general objectives directly to the IEP. Curriculum guides containing short-term instructional objectives are most useful as (a) a reference from which teachers can plan instructional activities, (b) a reference that can be duplicated and attached to individual programs, and (c) a continuous monitoring device. Handicapped students' programs then can truly reflect a continuum of goals and objectives that can be easily revised and updated.

REFERENCES

Becker, W. C., Englemann, S., & Thomas, D. R. *Teaching 2: Cognitive learning and instruction.* Chicago: Science Research Associates, 1975.

Bloom, B. S. (Ed.). *Taxonomy of educational objectives: The classification of educational goals. Handbook 1. Cognitive domain.* New York: McKay, 1956.

Bruner, J. S. *The process of education.* New York: Vintage, 1963.

Hammill, D. D., & Poplin, M. S. Written expression. In D. D. Hammill & N. R. Bartel, *Teaching children with learning and behvior problems.* Boston: Allyn & Bacon, 1978.

Krathwohl, D. R., Bloom, B. S., & Masia, B. B. *Taxonomy of educational objectives: The classification of educational goals. Handbook 2. Affective domain.* New York: McKay, 1964.

Larsen, S. C., & Poplin, M. S. *Methods for educating the handicapped.* Boston: Allyn & Bacon, 1979.

Lovitt, T. C. Applied behavior analysis and learning disabilities: Part 1. *Journal of Learning Disabilities,* 1975, *8*(7), 432-443. (a)

Lovitt, T. C. Applied behavior analysis and learning disabilities: Part 2. *Journal of Learning Disabilities,* 1975, *8*(8), 504-518. (b)

Piaget, J. *The science of education and the psychology of the child.* New York: Penguin, 1970.

ADDITIONAL REFERENCES

Bloom, B. S., Hastings, J. T., & Madus, G. F. *Handbook on formative and summative evaluation of student learning.* New York: McGraw-Hill, 1971.

Gronlund, N. E. *Measurement and evaluation in teaching.* New York: Macmillan, 1971.

Teachers are frequently faced with having to make modifications in an existing curriculum. The author provides suggestions that are systematic and directly applicable to the classroom teacher's role. She gives attention to adapting materials, modifying instruction, and altering assignments. The selection is informative, comprehensive, and practical. The content will be of interest to teachers, as well as to individuals with a general interest in the instruction of exceptional children and youth.

A Systematic Approach For Changing Materials, Instruction and Assignments To Meet Individual Needs

Rosemary Anne Lambie

The ultimate purpose of changing existing curricular materials, instructional practices, and assignments is to meet the student's academic, emotional, and physical needs. When the student is not achieving at his or her expected level, three different types of changes can be made: adaptations to the actual commercial product or material; modifications in the manner of delivering instruction; and/or alterations in the nature or scope of the specific assignments. Each of these three variances requires that the teacher change existing practices. They may be combined and do not always have to be planned as singular efforts to meet individual needs.

The value of changing existing practices has been documented by research. Edward (1977) found that changing a curricular approach for fourth-grade students with undesirable conduct resulted in significantly higher percentages correct on examinations. Materials and assignments were changed to meet each student's needs. The changes included audiotapes of the text, learning centers with nonreading tasks, and simplified worksheets to increase probability of successful responding.

A study by Lovitt and Curtiss (1968) investigated the effect of altering an assignment on correct response rate in arithmetic problems. The alteration involved verbalizing prior to making a written response rather than the existing requirement of only writing the response. Results indicated that the subject's error rate decreased and correct answers increased as a result of that alteration.

Harris (1972) investigated the effect on correct spelling responses under two conditions. One group of fifth-grade students received the regular approach. The experimental group received a modified approach that incorporated daily goals and immediate feedback concerning performance. As a result of the modification, the experimental group approximately doubled its correct spelling rate over baseline.

The preceding three studies suggest that changes in existing practices could be justifiable. In addition to research, a national needs assessment was completed through the U.S. Bureau of Education for the Handicapped (Vale, 1980). One finding was that 49% of the teachers sampled thought training in how to adapt media and materials would be of great value. An additional 39% thought it would be of some value. Thus, both the perceived need of teachers and the success found in implementing certain changes support the basic value of the methodology presented here.

Planning for the three types of changes defined in this article should be based upon the specific mismatch of the learner with material, nature of instruction, or assignment. The mismatch is not always unique to the individual. It may be a result of inadequately designed material — in which case the teacher may find many students with the same mismatch. More frequently, though, the teacher finds that students vary individually in their responses to existing materials, method of instruction, or assignments.

The basic premise of the systematic approach presented here is that teachers must determine the type of mismatch that exists, then adapt materials, modify instruction, or alter assignments based upon that determination. Although a listing of "101 changes" may seem desirable to some, the author contends that teachers do not necessarily know when to select which type of the three changes for a specific mismatch. A systematic approach should provide teachers with a framework for facilitating the change process.

REASONS FOR CHANGING EXISTING PRACTICES

As stated initially, the ultimate purpose in changing materials, instruction, and assignments is to meet individual student needs. Other reasons are:

— to avoid having to "reinvent the wheel," and still reach satisfactory solutions. Teachers, sensing inadequacies of materials, often set for themselves the difficult task of constructing what they hope will be the perfect match between learner and material. Not much can be gained in the long run from this laborious and defeating task. Needless to say, teachers have many additional tasks with which they must be concerned. Changes to existing materials and instruction represent an expedient alternative to teacher-made materials. Often simple adaptations will greatly improve upon learner/material match, at the same time freeing the teacher's time for equally important responsibilities.

— to enable students to remain in the least restrictive environment. Pupils are frequently referred for more restrictive placements because they are unable to keep pace within particular environments and settings. Changes based upon identifying specific mismatches may permit the student to remain in the same environment and be able to achieve success — albeit to the beat of a different drum.

— to stretch budget dollars. A limited budget for new instructional materials is a perennial problem for teachers. Sometimes, through a relatively simple change process, the teacher can use already purchased materials to meet students' needs. Adapting, modifying, or altering is far more economical than buying the variety of materials necessary to meet the needs of each student.

EXAMPLES OF THE THREE TYPES OF CHANGES

Most changes in the teaching process fall within the realm of adaptation of materials, modification of instruction, and alteration of assignments. To clarify the differences among these types of change, examples of three different mismatches relating to the same arithmetic assignment are given here. A change procedure is presented for each mismatch. The assignment requires that students complete 30 two-digit addition problems in 20 minutes.

Adaptation of Materials

A behavior disordered student, Chris, found a whole worksheet containing 30 arithmetic problems too threatening. The teacher noticed Chris' avoidant reactions when observing that he was five minutes into the assignment and had not yet completed the first problem of the 30 assigned. The teacher asked Chris if he needed assistance. He replied that there were too many problems to do.

Although a teacher might choose to counsel such a student concerning the perceived threat of solving the 30 problems, he or she might also consider a more expedient strategy involving materials adaptation. The teacher could cut the page in half or in quarters and present only one portion at a time during the 20-minute period. In subsequent drills the teacher could gradually increase the number of problems presented at one time. The student would still complete the same number of problems but in smaller, less threatening blocks. The instructional practice does not change. The nature and scope of the assignment do not change. The only change is in manipulating the commercial product.

Modification of Instruction

A learning disabled student, Pat, failed to learn addition of two-digit numbers when the basal program did not utilize manipulatives. The student was given the 30 arithmetic problems without prior instruction. The five examples provided at the top of the worksheet were assumed ample to allow the student to complete the page. Pat attempted the problems, but the teacher noticed halfway through the worksheet that all the answers were incorrect. When the teacher asked Pat if she needed assistance, the girl said that the examples at the top of the page were not helpful enough when trying to solve the problems.

In this example the teacher could modify the manner of instruction by providing a place value chart and giving direct instruction along with it. A commercial product is involved, but the basic change is with the nature of instruction. The commercial product is not adapted. The assignment is not altered. Rather, the instructional practice is modified.

Alteration of Assignments

An educable mentally retarded student, Tim, worked more slowly than most students in the class and did not complete the 30 arithmetic problems within the stipulated 20 minutes. Observing the student's slow pace, the teacher did notice that Tim was correctly completing each problem. When asked if he needed assistance, the boy informed his teacher that he was just a slow worker.

In that case the change might focus upon altering the assignment of this individual student. The teacher could require the student to complete only 15 of the 30 problems. In doing so, the instruction is not modified and the commercial product is not adapted. The student's assignment, however, is altered to meet an individual need.

These three types of changes that teachers can apply are often combined. Teachers frequently find that materials adaptation has to be combined with modification of instruction or alteration in the assignment. With the arithmetic assignment of the preceding examples, a student might be unable to learn two-digit addition without manipulatives and also could be threatened by too many problems to complete during a 20-minute time period. Then, the teacher might modify instruction by providing a place value chart and adapt the material by cutting the page in half for the 20-minute drill — thus combining two types of changes.

POINTS TO CONSIDER BEFORE MAKING CHANGES

Prior to making a change, the teacher should consider several facets of the total learning process. Possibly, a change involving other than the material, instruction, or assignment is indicated. The following variables should be investigated and eliminated as possible agents of failure before instituting changes of the type advocated.

1. *Sensory acuity.* A student's lack of success in learning may be directly related to visual or hearing problems. In some cases eyeglasses or hearing aids may be all that is needed to turn failure into achievement.

2. *Level of functioning.* If a sixth-grade student is functioning at the fourth-grade level in arithmetic, any changes to sixth-grade materials, instructional procedures, or assignments are inadequate and insufficient. The student must have the necessary prerequisite skills to function successfully at the sixth-grade level. No amount of change at the sixth grade level allows that student's needs to be fully met. Mismatches between a student's level of functioning and the grade level placement must be investigated as possible causative factors before instituting changes like those advocated in this article.

   Related to this concept is that of readability level of instructional materials. The stated readability level of a product is not always the actual readability level. The teacher might apply a readability formula to a material to ensure selection of the appropriate readability level.

3. *Environmental factors.* Factors including lighting, noise level, and proximity of students to any type of distraction must be considered before deciding to institute changes in materials, instruction, or assignments. When environmental factors are found to be causative agents of failure, these elements must be restructured to maximize the learning process. Then the teacher may turn to other adaptations, modifications, and alterations if necessary.

4. *The consequences applied and the contingency or arrangement between the desired response and the consequence.* Adapting materials, modifying instruction, and altering assignments will not work if the cause of failure to learn relates to the contingency or consequence. In the earlier example of the behavior disordered student, assume that there were no mismatch (i.e., the 30 problems were really not too threatening) but that the student knew when he finished the 30 problems he would have to undertake a reading assignment he detested. If, instead of doing reading after the arithmetic, the student would have had the consequence of constructing a model airplane (a highly preferred activity), he would

have been more likely to begin and complete the math problems. The difficulty, under that assumption, was not a mismatch of learner with material presented but was related to the contingency of completing the problems.

In the earlier example of the EMR student, assume that a mismatch did not exist (i.e., 30 problems were not too many). Also assume that the consequence was powerful (e.g., extra recess time) but that the student simply needed more time to complete the assignment. If the student were given 30 minutes instead of 20 to complete the worksheet, a change would have been made in relation to the contingency. This would not require altering the assignment, modifying the instruction, or adapting the material, but simply changing the contingency or time arrangement between the response and the consequence.

Each of the preceding factors must be explored and eliminated as causes of failure to learn before considering any of the changes discussed here. When those four factors have been resolved or ruled out and a student still fails to learn, the teacher should look for the possibility of a mismatch between learner and antecedents (material or instruction provided) or with the response required. Specific mismatches should be identified and followed by systematic changes in existing practices.

GUIDELINES FOR MAKING CHANGES

Some basic guidelines are necessary in actually planning and implementing changes in materials, instruction and assignments Several suggested guidelines are discussed briefly.

- *Use the change process only when a mismatch occurs.* Although implementing change may seem like an interesting process, it should be done only if a mismatch exists between the learner and material, instruction, or assignment. And it should not be undertaken unless all of the prior considerations are eliminated as causative factors in the pupil's lack of learning. This means that the teacher must be certain of no sensory acuity or classroom arrangement problem, that the presentation and requirement are at the student's current level of functioning, and that effective contingencies and consequences are being carried out. Only then should the teacher consider mismatches of materials, instruction, or assignments with the learner.
- *Keep the changes simple.* Elaborate changes may seem pedagogically sound, but teachers should focus on the simplest change process possible that is still effective and efficient. When changes are

too involved, they destroy a major advantage of the change process in that time expenditure becomes magnified.

Figure 1 illustrates, through a student's worksheet, an example of a student/material mismatch. The directions required that students discover a pattern for each horizontal line and fill in the appropriate numbers. For example, the correctly completed top line should read: 2, 4, 6, 8, 10, 12. After looking at the student's worksheet, the teacher diagnosed that the mismatch related to the student's misunderstanding the directions and confusion about directionality. He had tried to form sequential number patterns in all directions, including bottom to top and right to left.

The teacher in that example would have a variety of options to consider in eliminating the mismatch, including: (a) drawing arrows between lines and numbers (adapting material); (b) providing a correctly completed sample (adapting material and modifying instruction); (c) giving oral instruction concerning left to right and top and bottom (modifying instruction); (d) providing a tachistoscopic sheet allowing the student to see only one line at a time (adapting material); or (e) supplying a ruler for the student to move down the page one line at a time (adapting material).

In selecting the change, the teacher should look toward the process that would most expediently eliminate the mismatch and result in student success. Simply giving the student a ruler would be expedient, but he or she probably would not know what to do with it and, thus, would likely continue to do the assignment incorrectly. If, however, the ruler were supplemented with teacher instruction and demonstration, the combined change might result in success. If not, a tachistoscopic window could be introduced in place of the ruler. Each of the above options is potentially workable and simple.

A major advantage of simple changes is that they require little teacher time to plan and implement. The best change is one that is quick and easy and also leads to student success.

2	4	_100_	___	_104_	12
_3_	100	101	___	103	_13_
5	___	_102_	___	25	_14_
95	___	___	98	_26_	100
_96_	10	_19_	20	25	_101_
25	_11_	_41_	40	_26_	50

FIGURE 1
Example of an Incorrectly Completed Worksheet
Showing a Mismatch between Learner and Material

● *Confirm mismatches by evaluating changes made.* The teacher should take data to determine if the change was appropriate. The hypothesis concerning the mismatch and a solution is confirmed when the data show that successful learning has resulted. If the data indicate that the student's need was not met, the teacher should systematically vary the change until achievement is realized.

In the example of Figure 1, assume that the teacher were to introduce use of the ruler along with oral explanation. Figure 2 illustrates 66 percent accuracy on the same worksheet when employing this change. When analyzed using the diagnostic process to determine type of error, the responses on Figure 2 show that the student indeed benefited from the change. But the student did not correctly insert numbers in the 5s sequences unless at least two of the numbers were present initially in the sequence.

In this case the teacher could choose to write those numbers into the sequence (adaptation of material) or instruct the student on how to look at the whole sequence before attempting to write the answers (modification of instruction). By using a diagnostic process and systematically varying the change, the teacher maximizes the probability of meeting individual needs.

● *Minimize teacher time in making changes.* Teachers should not spend too much time on planning or manipulating changes. Change processes that are effective while requiring the least teacher time are desirable. If two or more possible solutions appear to be equally good, selection should hinge upon the change that requires the least teacher time. Teachers should also keep in mind the possible utilization of supporting personnel. For example, cross- or peer-age tutors may be able to help monitor and explain requirements; parents or volunteers might be asked to assist in change processes involving making materials more durable, rewriting information in a different format, and audiotaping lessons.

2	4	6	8	10	12
99	100	101	102	103	104
5	6	7	8	25	26
95	96	97	98	99	100
5	10	15	20	25	30
25	26	27	40	28	50

FIGURE 2
Example of Student Worksheet Showing Improvement
After a Systematic Change Process

- *Keep combinations consistent.* When trying to supplement a program or material that does not allow for enough practice, be sure the supplementary material is compatible with the basic approach. For example, a teacher would not want to use initial/teaching/alphabet materials to supplement the basal reader. In the same manner, a non-inquiry text approach in science should not supplement an inquiry approach. Supplemental materials that differ in basic instructional approach can cause a great deal of confusion in verifying the type of mismatch that exists and the solutions attempted (e.g., supplementary material). On the other hand, a supplementary material that is consonant with the basic approach might be effective.

- *Know the strengths and weaknesses of the instructional material.* If the teacher is aware of the strengths and weaknesses of materials, mismatches with students are easier to identify. For example, if a company tends to publish worksheets with confusing directions, the teacher might guess ahead of time what problems might occur. One product with specific weaknesses presents four different arithmetic operations on one page, gives few examples, and has no illustrations. Knowing this, the teacher can mentally plan for mismatches and can easily make a change if students have difficulty in completing the work satisfactorily.

- *Know the pupil's strengths and weaknesses.* When the teacher is aware of students' strengths and weaknesses, mismatches are easier to identify, as are the types of solutions that might be applied. For example, if the teacher knows that a certain student has difficulty in oral spelling from dictation, a visual written response mode may be indicated.

   One student had considerable difficulty in verbalizing that 167 is greater than 159. She also had difficulty remembering the signs $<$ and $>$. Knowing this, the teacher changed the response mode (alteration of assignment). The student used the same worksheet but was asked to put an X on the larger number in each problem on the worksheet.

   The teacher also benefits from knowing if a student is impulsive or deliberate or has other such characteristics. Sometimes style interferes with learning, and not the material, instruction, or assignment.

QUESTIONS TO ASK IN FACILITATING THE CHANGE PROCESS

Changes in existing practices should be based upon specific mismatches between the learner and material, instruction, or assignment. Systematizing the change process, to maximize the probability that a change will be more effective than existing practices, is accomplished through a questioning or empirical approach. The teacher poses a variety of questions as possible causes of mismatches between learner and materials, instruction, or assignments, then considers tentative solution(s) to the mismatches. Selection of the type of solution (adaptation of material, modification of instruction, or alteration of assignment) is based upon economy of teacher time and probability of eliminating the mismatch. The teacher then systematically varies the change until the mismatch is corrected.

The following questions relate predominantly to antecedents of the instructional process although some relate to the nature or scope of the response required. Each question is followed by hypothetical mismatches and possible solutions to these mismatches.

The key to successful use of the change process is in asking questions that lead to discovery of the type of mismatch that exists. The mismatches and possible solutions presented here are intended to assist teachers in understanding the process by which solutions are planned. They do not represent an exhaustive listing of possible changes but, rather, a sample or cross-section of situations often encountered. The potential solutions are not necessarily the only or best answers, but show some of the options that may be considered.

1. What if there are too many (items, pages, questions, etc.)?

A frequent problem that students face is the "too many" requirement. Two examples are given along with potential solutions.

Too Many Math Problems

The teacher notices that a student does not complete all the assigned math problems in the time allotted. The problems that are solved are correct.

— *Adapting the Material/Altering the Assignment:* The teacher cuts the page in half so the student will not have to complete all the problems. This is a quick and easy alternative but may not represent the most optimum solution. If, as in most practice worksheets, the problems are arranged from easy to difficult, the student may end up with an inaccurate representation of the total assignment. A brief analysis of the material would reveal if this were the case. If not, that solution could be judged worth trying.

— *Adapting the Material/Altering the Assignment:* The teacher selects the problems the student needs for practice, then stars the ones judged most valuable. This is a quick and easy change that takes into account the student's needs and provides a balance from among the total worksheet problems.

— *Altering the Assignment:* The student is asked to do all the odd or even problems. Again, the teacher first has to assess the worksheet to determine what effect this solution will have in relation to worksheet requirements and student needs.

Too Many Pages to Read

A student does not complete all of the silent reading assigned in social studies.

— *Altering the Assignment/Adapting the Material:* The teacher tape records every other page. The student reads one page silently, then listens to the next page. The major change is in the assignment required of the student, as he or she is now required to read only half the amount. It also utilizes another learning modality (auditory).

— *Altering the Assignment:* A similar alteration is to have a peer- or cross-age tutor read every other page to the student. This may be a long and laborious process and requires a more able, patient student to be paired with the slow learner.

2.   What if there is not enough repetition?

This is a major concern when using some developmental materials. Without necessary practice and drill, students with learning problems can easily fail to fix the concepts and skills necessary for retention.

Too Little Problem Solving

After students have been taught a new computation skill, they need enough practice to fix it in their minds before building additional skills. Some texts and materials provide too few practice problems.

— *Altering the Assignment:* The teacher supplements the assignment with materials that cover the same skill and allow extra practice. For example, kits graded and organized for practice according to specific skills can be used to provide the necessary repetition of skills. Although materials are involved in doing this, the real change is in the scope of the assignment. The student is required to do more. This solution is quick and easy. It meets student needs, yet requires little teacher time. A drawback, however, may stem from the budget for materials.

— *Altering the Assignment/Adapting the Material:* The teacher makes worksheets to provide for extra practice. Or the teacher makes transparencies, which are then projected on the blackboard. These solutions are not quick and easy, though. The teacher expends considerable time in constructing the change, even if older students or volunteers assist. Other solutions may be better.

3. What if a lack of feedback results in problems when students use the material independently?

A major consideration in teaching is that of uninterrupted direct instruction of small groups of students. That necessarily requires that some students who are not at the level of the group receiving instruction must work independently at times. As a result, the independent learners may suffer from a lack of immediate feedback.

No Feedback Provided

The student cannot confirm answers and therefore has difficulty in building skills and concepts upon known information.

— *Adapting the Material:* The teacher writes the answers directly in the workbook or text in yellow ink. Before looking at the page, the student places a transparent red plastic sheet, like a theme cover, over it, which neutralizes the answers. The student writes answers on a separate sheet of paper one at a time, after which he or she unmasks the correct answers to see if they match. This is a fairly quick and easy process when only a few students and books are involved.

4. What if the visual presentation is too confusing?

A frequent problem of students — that of focusing on the pertinent elements of visual presentations — sometimes must be facilitated by teachers. Generally, the problem centers on lack of attending to significant detail.

Visually Too Confusing

At times students are given worksheets requiring a variety of responses (e.g., fill in the blank, write a sentence) on one page. This can be confusing for some students.

— *Adapting the Material:* The teacher makes a tachistoscopic window to reveal only a portion of a page at one time. A piece of construction paper is cut such that the right sized window reveals one item at a time. This is a quick and easy adaption of the commercial product if items are all of the same dimensions.

Confusing Transparencies

Sometimes, commercially prepared transparencies are confusing. Students may have trouble focusing on significant details.

— *Adapting the Material/Modifying the Instruction:* The teacher uses carefully cut masks like that described above to focus students' attention on the unmasked stimuli. The teacher also could simply provide a piece of paper that is to be moved downward one line at a time, thereby restricting the detail to which the student is exposed.

5. What if students do not remember or understand the directions?

Many students have difficulty with oral and/or written directions. The teacher should determine if the directions are the sole problem or whether the lesson is too difficult.

Problem with Oral Directions

Teachers frequently give oral directions in class. Some directions require a relatively long attention span as well as good short-term memory. Some students do not recall the sequence or detail of oral directions.

— *Modifying the Instruction:* The teacher tape records directions. These may be expanded, if necessary, with added steps for students who require more detail and smaller increments.

— *Modifying the Instruction:* The teacher appoints a peer tutor to coach students through step-by-step directions. Peers often "speak each others' language" better than the teacher and can more quickly clarify misunderstood directions.

Problem with Written Directions

Written directions may be difficult to understand or follow. The problem may not be with memory in these cases, but with confusion in trying to determine the logical breakdown and sub-steps or increments.

— *Adapting the Material:* When worksheets have paragraphs containing multiple directions, a teacher uses colored dots or numbers to differentiate the separate directions. Each paragraph contains several sentences, and students benefit from knowing where one direction ends and another begins. Thus, they are led to complete one step before starting the next.

— *Adapting the Material:* In a similar circumstance, a teacher uses colored marking pens or pencils, underlining each direction with a different color. This is not as quick and easy as the above adaptation but may be better for younger students.

6. What if the material, lesson, or assignment is not interesting?

Not all things we do in schools or in life have inherent interest. Students should not be deluded into expecting everything to be interesting. At times, though, boredom and sameness reach limits and teachers should turn to forms of motivation.

Oral Lesson Drags

Teachers provide considerable oral instruction in classes. At times the lessons may be boring, yet necessary. For example, teaching parts of speech can be uninteresting to students.

— *Modifying the Instruction:* Teachers use a variety of techniques to make lessons more interesting. Puppets increase interest among younger students. The teacher's personality also makes a big difference. One's voice can elicit a great deal of responsiveness from others. And teachers can point out the relevance of the lesson to students' interests or goals.

Boring Seatwork

Much student seatwork is inherently boring. Teachers tend to drown students in a sea of purple ink that often results in ennui and restlessness. To combat this, teachers can use interest inventories with students as an aid in selecting materials.

— *Modifying the Instruction:* One motivating solution to the boredom dilemma sometimes is found by introducing self-competition. For example, the work is clocked so the student is able to chart progress in correctly completing items within specified times.

— *Modifying the Instruction:* The student is instructed on how to keep data on performance and how to record the results in an interesting way (graphs, charts, using color, and so forth). Self-recording of performance is a relatively quick and easy option. Although it is not effective with all students, it represents a definite possibility in eliciting task behavior of otherwise turned-off students.

7.   What if the product is not durable?

This may be a concern, especially with behavior disordered children. Some pupils tear up instructional materials, rendering them useless. Not all material can be made durable, but it is a factor worth considering. Most important is to make sure that the material used will meet student needs, *then* figure out if it can be made durable. Devising durable material that is unsuitable, of course, is wasted effort.

Paper Product is Destroyed

Some students rip, tear, and otherwise mangle instructional materials. Replacing destroyed materials can be expensive and may result in selection of materials based only on durability factors rather than on pupil material match — an illogical practice.

— *Adapting the Material:* Once a teacher has determined that a certain material meets the needs of a student who tends to be destructive, the teacher investigates the best possible means of making it durable. The most widely applied change is to laminate pages. Another adaptation involves covering pages with clear contact paper. These measures are usually beneficial. Some pupils, however, are so destructive that other measures are necessary. The optimum solution, for small amounts of material, may be to place it on pressed board and spray with acetate. This also allows destructive children to use the adapted material with less supervision than normally would be necessary.

8.   What if the material/lesson moves too rapidly?

Printed and oral instruction is sometimes too rapid for certain students. Slowing down the pace, however, can produce boredom in students for whom the pace is not too rapid. Alternatives must be found and implemented.

Lesson Moves Too Rapidly

Group instruction is not always successful with special education students. One contributing factor is the failure to pace lessons so that students can benefit.

— *Modifying the Instruction:* A peer tutor is assigned to take copious notes. Later, slower students ask questions of the tutor and look at the notes. Also, lessons might be tape recorded for homework.

9.   What if the lesson is too complex?

This situation is frequently encountered in group instruction and when using developmental sources with students having learning problems. When employed strictly as the teacher's manual directs, the lesson can result in failure to meet certain students' needs.

Parts of a Glossary not Understood

Learning to use a glossary or dictionary requires that a variety of skills be called into play. This learning sometimes takes place more readily when it is broken down into separate components.

— *Modifying the Instruction/Adapting the Material:* The teacher makes a base transparency presenting only the words, an overlay adding the diacritical markings, and another overlay with the definitions. This change may be long and laborious, but it might be the only good solution. The transparencies, of course, can be saved and used again and again when similar needs arise.

10. What if the presentation sequence of skills/concepts is too brief and choppy?

Materials often present skills/concepts with little practice provided, then proceed to a new skill/concept. Students with learning problems often need more instruction and practice with one skill/concept at a time.

Teaching Money Handling Too Sporadic

The text presents money handling on five pages every 60 pages. A student has difficulty learning the concepts involved.

— *Adapting the Material/Modifying the Instruction:* The teacher removes all of the pages dealing with money handling. These are placed in a folder or bound for use as a smaller text and presented as a unit. (The change need not be so dramatic. Teachers could assign and cover the pages as a unit by skipping around the book — certainly a quick and easy modification.)

11. What if significant information is not focused upon?

Discerning the most important and useful information is a necessary skill that has to be learned. Without it, students can be mired in irrelevance, unable to bring together features to make realistic conceptualizations.

Significant Written Detail Ignored

Some students have difficulty selecting the important information in reading assignments. The teacher poses comprehension questions that the student answers incorrectly.

— *Adapting the Material:* The teacher uses a color coding system that informs the student of main ideas or significant details. For example, a red mark in the margin could indicate passages dealing with the main idea, and a blue mark could denote significant detail. Undertaking this adaptation would be long and laborious for only one teacher. Therefore, teachers should combine their efforts in marking materials and teacher's editions of texts, and trading them so they can all benefit from the effort. First, they must develop a common coding system that will work for everybody. Then it becomes an ongoing process that could be almost automatic. Assuredly, teachers will encounter students from time to time who need this adaptation, so it does not represent a one-time-only change.

Significant Transparency Detail Ignored

Some students have trouble cueing into significant items of transparencies and chalkboard presentations.

— *Adapting the Material:* The teacher stars the most important points during presentations and underlines other details while raising the voice to connote importance.

Significant Oral Detail Ignored

Students sometimes have difficulty sorting out the most important elements of a lecture or discussion.

— *Modifying the Instruction:* The teacher defines a purpose for listening; for example, "We'll be talking about the sun, with particular attention to how the sun benefits life on our earth." Cueing the student that "this is important" might be enough to elicit specific attention. Also, the teacher could pause at strategic points and say, "You'll want to remember this."

12. What if the language level is too high/different?

Written and oral instruction may be at a level some students do not grasp. The problem may be dialectical, syntactic, or semantic.

Oral Language Misunderstood

A student may not understand implications of an oral lesson. And group situations make it difficult to know whether the student is comprehending the language and conceptualizations.

— *Altering the Assignment:* The teacher devises individualized tasks for the student, using a tape recorder. The feasibility of stopping the tape recording allows the student to replay portions and to use a dictionary if necessary. This alteration is most beneficial when the lesson is no longer than 15 minutes. If required to listen to tapes for long periods, students may become inattentive.

— *Modifying the Instruction:* Students often communicate at a level best understood by peers. Knowing this, the teacher simply requests a "peer translation" when students indicate from time to time that they don't comprehend something in a presentation.

13.   What if purchased commercial products assess recall only?

Although this is a problem with materials rather than students, some students may become dependent upon recall at the expense of comprehension, decision making, and other important facets of learning.

Only Fact Questions Covered

Questions in some teachers' manuals and at the end of reading selections in certain student texts emphasize recall of facts, ignoring the value of inference, drawing conclusions, and total comprehension. This is not a learner/material mismatch but requires attention in changing the material.

— *Adapting the Material:* The teacher supplements existing material with a variety of comprehension questions, written or typed, and duplicated. An answer key could be developed for teacher or student correction. Such changes should be planned for future use and use by other teachers. If several materials require change, other teachers or older, more capable students could take this on as a project. For example, a high school honor society might be willing to do it, or the local chapter of The Student Council for Exceptional Children might adopt it as a project.

14.   What if the material/lesson is biased?

Again, this is a problem with the material, not a student mismatch. But teachers should not condone bias in the products used and should make changes when necessary.

Racial Bias

Minority races are often ignored in material, or portrayed in a discriminatory way.

— *Modifying the Instruction/Adapting the Material:* The teacher discusses discrimination and stereotypes portrayed in print, then asks the students to underline discriminatory statements. Although this does not change the material, it allows students to see it from a different vantage point.

Gender/Career Role Bias

Another form of bias in material is that of sex role stereotyping. For example, physicians and mechanics are generally male, and women are housewives, secretaries, and stewardesses.

— *Modifying the Instruction/Adapting the Assignment:* Before giving an assignment that involves reading, the teacher discusses sex and career role bias and asks the students to look for evidence of that in the reading selection. They could underline or in some other way indicate their findings.

15.   What if verbal response is a problem?

A student may not be able to produce an adequate or correct verbal response.

Inadequate Verbalization

The student may know an answer, yet be unable to verbally respond in an appropriate way because of some handicap. For example, a child may know a cap from a coat but be unable to say, "This is my coat."

— *Altering the Assignment:* If the teacher is working only on receptive vocabulary, it is possible to determine whether the student really knows an answer by changing the response mode required. For example, the student could be instructed to "point to your cap . . . coat." Or a deaf child could sign the answer or underline the correct answer in print.

— *Altering the Assignment:* With other cases of mental or physical handicap, the teacher requires the same response mode, but at a simpler level. For example, the teacher could ask, "Is this your coat?" and require only a yes or no answer or a nod or shake of the head. This may or may not be preparatory to teaching the associated verbalizations.

16.   What if the motor response is too difficult?

Similar to verbal responses, motor responses are too difficult for certain students and may lead the teacher to believe the student does not know something. The student may actually know the correct answer but simply not be able to execute the motor requirement.

Inadequate Motor Response

An example of problems with fine motor skills is shown in illegible handwriting.

— *Adapting the Material:* The student is given a different writing implement, which might be a thinner or thicker pencil; or a rubber gripper is attached to a pencil. Another aid is a wire frame (Zaner Blaser Company) to mold the student's hand in the correct position. Or the teacher wraps tape around the place where the student should hold the pencil.

Written Spelling Words Incorrect

In spelling the student consistently writes the words incorrectly.

— *Altering the Assignment:* The teacher asks the student to respond in a different mode. For example, the student might spell the words orally. Another alteration could be to have the student circle the correctly spelled word of four presented. Or a typewriter could be used by students with fine motor or other physical problems.

CONCLUSIONS

The preceding 16 questions can be helpful to teachers in understanding some of the types of mismatch that exist and possible changes to neutralize them effectively. Focusing on a specific problem allows the teacher to more successfully adapt material, modify instruction, and alter assignments to meet individual needs. The possible solutions to the 16 questions are only representative of the potential answers. Teachers should consider them as merely examples and not bind themselves to using any or all of the solutions given.

The real value of the empirical process recommended in this article is that it liberates the teacher to use a systematic, questioning approach to brainstorm a variety of possible changes. The teacher then can concentrate on selecting a change — preferably as quick and easy as possible — that has a good chance of working to the benefit of students. If the first change is not completely effective, the teacher is free to systematically try other changes. This approach is far superior to the trial-and-error, hit-and-miss or leave-well-enough-alone philosophies that have prevailed in some classrooms for lack of better methodology. It provides a framework and structure for change that can be instituted without undue effort on the part of the teacher — and with results that are demonstrated by student success in learning.

REFERENCES

Edwards, L. L. Curriculum modification as a strategy for helping regular classroom behavior-disordered students. *Focus on Exceptional Children,* 1980, 12(8), 1-11.

Harris, J. H. *The effects of restructuring teaching procedures on the percent of answers correct on the daily spelling assignments of fifth grade inner city students.* Unpublished master's thesis, University of Kansas, 1972.

Lovitt, T. C., & Curtiss, K. A. Effects of manipulating an antecedent event of mathematics response rate. *Journal of Applied Behavior Analysis,* 1968, *1,* 329-333.

Vale, C. *National needs assessment of educational media and materials for the handicapped.* Paper presented at the LINC Special Education Marketing Conference, Philadelphia, 1980.

Edwards compares previous efforts to accommodate the instructional needs of handicapped students in mainstream situations to what she describes as "curriculum interventions." She provides a good analysis of curriculum options to meet the needs of behaviorally disordered students in the regular classroom. This discussion serves as background for presenting the "modified curriculum approach." Edwards reports on a useful approach to curriculum research, which combines an attempt to assess curriculum variables and differing motivational variables.

Curriculum Modification As a Strategy for Helping Regular Classroom Behavior Disordered Students

Linda L. Edwards

The concept of mainstreaming, which in its broadest interpretation refers to the integration of handicapped learners into regular educational programs, has received acceptance from most special educators during the past decade (Keogh & Levitt, 1976). Despite legal, philosophical, and social support for the concept, however, several investigators (Kaufman, Gottlieb, Agard, & Kukic, 1975; Meyen & Moran, 1979) have noted that emphasis to date has been upon administrative arrangements for its facilitation rather than upon instructional or curricular concerns after the initial stage of the process (placement of the handicapped learner within the regular educational environment) has taken place.

In their review of the limitations of mainstreaming, Keogh and Levitt (1976) pointed out that:

> . . . most of the mainstream models provide effective techniques for the placement of the exceptional child in the regular program and identify the

87

kinds of support services needed. Few guarantee, let alone evaluate, what happens to the child once placed . . . Lacking is delineation of possible pupil by program interaction getting at the question of *which* kind of instructional arrangement in the regular program is appropriate for children with *which* kinds of educational characteristics (p. 3).

Several years later, Meyen and Moran (1979) restated this problem from the specific perspective of serving the mildly handicapped mainstreamed pupil. They emphasized that continued effort still has to be given to defining "instructional options that are effective in meeting the needs of students with learning problems" (p. 530). Further, as these options prove to be valid, students in need of them become identified as learning handicapped rather than having identification become the major preoccupation or focus around which program options are later developed.

This article presents a validation of a learning strategy found to be effective in ameliorating some of the educational difficulties of mildly behaviorally disordered students in the regular classroom. The emphasis is on defining an instructional methodology to increase the probability that such learners would be successful — both academically and behaviorally — in this environment.

REVIEW OF PAST STRATEGIES

The literature concerning problems presented by mild and moderate behavior disorders of students in regular classrooms has suggested that these problems traditionally have been approached through a behavior analysis methodology. In general, these studies have been of three types: those focusing upon increasing attention to task as a strategy for improving problematic behavior (or decreasing problematic behavior by improving attention); those examining academic performance in addition to or in relationship to attention to task; and those investigating the manipulation of antecedent events and teaching performance and the resulting effect upon behavior and achievement. Implications of the findings of each of these groups are briefly examined as follows.

Attention to Task

Much of the behavioral literature relative to classroom performance of school age children has been devoted to measuring the effects of reducing problematic behaviors through a direct approach — i.e., "reinforcement for refraining from engaging in disruption" (Ayllon & Roberts, 1974, p. 71). Since it is logical to assume that one must first attend to a task before it can be successfully accomplished, researchers have focused on results of training teachers to modify inappropriate, disruptive behaviors — those that are incompatible with attention to and completion of academic tasks (Hall, Lund, & Jackson, 1968; Thomas, Becker, & Armstrong, 1968).

In other cases, increasing attention to task was the specific focus of the investigation, in the belief that this would produce a concomitant decrease in disruptive behaviors (Walker & Buckley, 1968). Such modification of classroom behavior has been investigated using single subjects (Wasik, Senn, Welch, & Cooper, 1969), entire classrooms (Robertshaw, 1971), and special problem populations (Schmidt & Ulrich, 1969). Strategies for changing disruptive behaviors or increasing attention (use of token economies, group consequences, teacher approval) have also been thoroughly documented (Barrish, Saunders, & Wolf, 1969; Madsen, Becker, & Thomas, 1968).

Results from these numerous studies indicate two clear conclusions. First, teachers can be trained to use behavior modification procedures effectively in their classrooms. Secondly, reduction of disruptive student behaviors results in an increase in attention to task and, conversely, increased attention results in decreased disruptive behaviors.

Attention to Task and Academic Performance

None of the previously mentioned studies was directly concerned with the effects of increasing attention/decreasing disruptiveness upon the academic performance of children. As a result, it was not at all clear whether the reduction of inappropriate behaviors led to improvement in achievement as a function of increased study time (attention to task). In the early 1970s researchers began to challenge the validity of selecting "disruptive behavior" as the major criterion for intervention (Winett & Winkler, 1972). A few studies incorporated a measure of academic performance as a dependent variable and generally concluded that "the relationship between attending behavior and achievement-related behaviors is not clearly understood" (Ferritor, Buckholdt, Hamblin, & Smith, 1972, p. 8).

In 1974, Ayllon and Roberts suggested that instead of relegating the improvement of students' academic skills as secondary to the "all-out effort to maintain orderliness in the classroom," the reversal of these priorities should be investigated; that is, improved achievement possibly could have the effect of decreasing disruptive behavior. In investigating that hypothesis, they found this indeed to be the case. When systematic token reinforcement was applied solely to the reading performance of five fifth-grade disruptive boys, reading improved considerably and rate of disruptions fell as well. Three studies concerned with the relationships between classroom behavior and academic achievement (Ayllon & Roberts, 1974; Ferritor et al., 1972; Robertshaw, 1971) indicated that performance could be increased if appropriately consequated. A precise relationship between attention and performance remained unestablished, however.

Antecedent Events and Teaching Performance

All students whose various behaviors were measured in the previously cited investigations received standard, traditional curricula administered through traditional teaching methods, regardless of possible differing ability levels and interests. No studies could be found that incorporated change in this stimulus dimension along with measurement of its effect upon the possible relationship of achievement and attention to task, despite strong indications that behavior problems increase as age appropriate achievement levels decline (Camp & Zimet, 1975; Graubard, 1971). Several studies, however, have been concerned with alternate ways of presenting curricular tasks or changes in teaching method and the effects of these changes upon the academic performance of behavior problem students in both regular and special classrooms (Gallagher, 1972; Harris, 1972; Lovitt & Curtiss, 1968).

Representative of studies in this latter group is one by Harris (1972), investigating the effects of restructuring teaching procedures for daily spelling lessons of fifth grade pupils who exhibited inappropriate social behaviors in the regular classroom. Subjects were randomly assigned to an experimental or a control group. The experimental subjects were recipients of a teaching procedure that had established daily goals and immediate feedback concerning performance. Students in the control group received a traditional spelling teaching procedure administered to them along with the rest of the class. Correct spelling response rate approximately doubled for the experimental group, while control subjects either maintained constant rates or increased or decreased performance slightly. The effect of the experimental group's dramatic improvement in spelling achievement upon their classroom behavior was not measured.

Each of the cited studies demonstrated that gain in academic achievement through manipulation of the task dimension and/or teaching procedures can be achieved for such children. None investigated the effects of such gains on overt behavior, with the exception of Gallagher (1972), who found that attentional behavior was better in a highly structured, one-to-one (atypical) learning environment.

Since no study examined all of the above elements (relationships between and among attention to task, deviant classroom behaviors, academic achievement, and teaching procedures/task dimensions), and since each factor individually appears to have a bearing upon the successful educational functioning of behavior disordered students, one might profit by attempting to identify the most effective and efficient mix. Some combination of elements possibly could have a synergistic effect. Which factors pertaining to change in the curriculum/teaching procedure dimension and reinforcement of behaviors will lead to optimal academic success and behavioral adjustment for behavior disordered students in the regular class environment? With the perceived and legislated need for establishing individualized education programs for exceptional children of all degrees of handicap (whether these are carried out in a special or regular class environment) comes the research priority of developing and evaluating individualized or specialized approaches.

A STRATEGY FOR INTERVENTION

Recent trends in special education suggest that children who have mild to moderate behavior problems, and who may in addition be underachievers, will be served primarily in the regular classroom, working along with their "normal" peers under the guidance of the regular classroom teacher, rather than being placed in a special classroom. As a cautionary note to this apparent impetus toward mainstreaming practices, some special educators have proposed that past methods which have proved to be effective with handicapped children in special classes *not* be discarded (Adamson & Van Etten, 1972), but also that researchers additionally give attention to which kinds of educational strategies in the regular instructional program are appropriate for which kinds of problems exhibited by mainstreamed exceptional children.

Among the theories about educating behavior disordered children in the special classroom is one postulating that "achievement precedes adjustment" (Phillips, Wiener, & Haring, 1960; Whelan & Haring, 1966). Several studies have investigated this hypothesis, using students from special class populations, with results that have usually been supportive of the intervention emanating from this theory — called the structured approach (Haring & Phillips, 1962; Gallagher, 1972). The strategies employed in this intervention, however, had not been applied or adapted to less severely handicapped children being educated in regular class environments.

The present investigation has as its major purpose to identify and describe an effective learning strategy for use in the regular classroom which would ameliorate some of the educational difficulties of conduct disordered, underachieving, mainstreamed elementary students. If it can be assumed or accepted that achievement precedes adjustment, it is reasonable to hypothesize that increasing the academic success of such children should function to decrease problematic behavior.

Curriculum Intervention

As a strategy for increasing the academic success of conduct disordered, underachieving students, a carefully designed curriculum plan was drawn up. For convenience, it will be called a *modified curricular approach.* "Modified" is used rather than "individualized" since a major objective of the plan's design was to provide a method by which behavior disordered students could proceed through materials and content areas at the same pace as other children in the regular classroom. To assess the effects of the modified curricular approach, a traditional approach was also studied for comparative purposes. Behavior disordered students receiving the traditional approach used the same texts and materials and received the same assignments and teaching procedures as the rest of the students in their classrooms.

Most of the procedures in the modified curricular approach were adapted directly from some of those of the structured approach, drawing heavily upon instructional methods of known effectiveness in the special class education of behavior disordered students. To provide illustrative and comparative examples, these procedures at times will be applied to the framework of a particular unit in some fourth grade social studies curricula, a unit involving comparison of the structures of state and federal governments.

The specific procedures in the modified curricular approach are: formulation of specific instructional objectives drawn from the broader goals; adaptation of content of the unit to meet various instructional reading levels; provisions for immediate corrective feedback; opportunities for visual reinforcement through self-graphing; and modification of existing workbook materials to promote the probability of successful responding.

Formulation of Objectives

As a preliminary strategy, several broad educational objectives were formulated by teachers who had taught the unit's content for several years. These were then translated into specific instructional objectives (Mager, 1975; Popham & Baker, 1970). For example, a broad goal of the curriculum content was for students to be able to identify and differentiate between the two houses of the legislative branch of government. One of the specific instructional objectives of this goal was that students would be able to list, in writing, at least two of the job responsibilities of members of the House of Representatives.

Adaptation of Content

Adaptation procedures are based on three presumptions. The first is that *at least several pupils in a regular classroom will be identified as possibly benefiting from a modified curricular approach.* Research suggests that regular classroom teachers identify approximately 20 percent of their students as exhibiting mild or moderate behavior disorders (Kelly, Bullock & Dykes, 1977). The second assumption is that a common characteristic of behavior disordered students is *underachievement in academic subjects* (Bower, 1969; Graubard, 1971). A study by Camp and Zimet (1975) pointed out that as reading skill levels, in particular, decreased, instances of deviant behavior increased. A third presumption is that *the regular classroom teacher will have the resources necessary to carry out the curriculum adaptations* critical to successful functioning of the mainstreamed behavior disordered students. Regular teachers must receive help in instructing mainstreamed handicapped youngsters. The procedures described, therefore, are designed to be carried out by the regular classroom teacher and a special education consultant teacher (or curriculum consultant with special education expertise) working in cooperation.

After sequential instructional objectives have been delineated, the content of these objectives of a particular unit of material can be adapted to meet individual instructional reading levels. This assumes, of course, that an accurate level is available for each student involved. An additional piece of information that may prove useful at this point is an accurate listening grade level score for students with particularly low instructional reading levels. Once these data have been collected, and the range of abilities ascertained for the pupils involved, adaptation activities can proceed.

A first strategy is to try to determine the existence of other textbooks that might approximate the content of the unit but at a lower reading level. If alternative texts cannot be located, the materials presently being used can be adapted. One possibility to consider is audio cassette taping of the reading content of the unit. Listening comprehension scores for each of the students involved in the modified curricular approach should be known in advance so that appropriate taping strategies can be planned. Two levels of taping of existing materials may be necessary. For students with grade level or above listening level scores, a verbatim reading of the text may be sufficient. (A check of the text's readability level should also be carried out.) Deshler and Graham (1980) have provided some interesting ideas about incorporating text usage and study skills into taped reading assignments.

> While taping a reading assignment, a teacher has an excellent opportunity to demonstrate how to differentiate between main and supportive material within a chapter; how to use illustrations, graphs, charts, etc. to aid comprehension; how to use questions at the end of a section or chapter to determine major points; and how to use chapter titles, section headings, etc., to skim a reading section for main ideas (p. 53).

An additional consideration for students with grade appropriate listening levels is whether or not the student should have the textbook in front of him or her to read along while simultaneously listening to the recorded version. Some research suggests that approximately two-thirds of students with reading difficulties profit from reading and listening concurrently, while the remaining third are confused by the double stimulus (Mosby, 1977). A quick, informal check of which of these two possibilities is most beneficial to a particular student may be necessary before proceeding.

If a student uses the text in conjunction with the tape, teachers might employ a highlighting and/or text marking strategy — a kind of "coding" system. This might involve marking, in various ways, text passages omitted in the recording, indicating others that are paraphrased on the tape, those recorded verbatim, and marking the places at which the student is to stop the tape (Deshler & Graham, 1980). An additional suggestion is to highlight major ideas with a transparent yellow marker, and important names or terms in another color (Mosby, 1977). Alternatively, and depending on the age and capability of the student, the tape might include directions for the student to carry out the highlighting activities.

A different form of taping is necessary when students have listening capabilities significantly below grade level or below the readability level of the textbook. In this circumstance, the taping involves simplifying the language of text passages to be recorded by shortening sentence length and explaining key vocabulary terms at the beginning of the passage. This level of taping might also include repeating major ideas to provide additional emphasis, as well as incorporating use of picture, map, and graph cues provided in the text (Deshler & Graham, 1980).

In planning individual tapes the person responsible for the recording must keep uppermost in mind the specific instructional objectives of the unit and ways of emphasizing these objectives. Additionally, length of recordings should be planned to match the attention spans of pupils who will use the tapes.

If audio cassette taping is a method selected for adaptation of materials, a systematic way of presenting these lessons is essential. One possibility is to provide a listening/learning center where students may listen to the tapes through earphones and where instructional objectives can be reinforced in other ways through non-reading tasks. Although taped materials may require a considerable investment of time initially, once made, students can use them individually as needed, without requiring a great deal of teacher supervision.

Provisions for Immediate Feedback

A further strategy to enhance successful acquisition of material is that of immediate corrective feedback. Knowledge of whether a particular response was right or wrong given in close temporal proximity to the response itself has been demonstrated to be an effective learning procedure (Gallagher, 1972). In the modified curricular approach, immediate feedback was designed to occur after students had responded to a short daily quiz involving a particular instructional objective presented in the day's taped lesson. In addition to allowing quick confirmation of correctness of response, this procedure also allows the teacher to assess student progress toward accomplishment of instructional objectives and to revise the next day's work, if necessary.

Opportunities for Visual Reinforcement through Self-Graphing

Closely related to immediate feedback is the formulation of a way to visually display results of individual work. The daily quizzes mentioned above, for example, provide such an opportunity. Charting daily progress in the form of a bar, line, or other type of graph can be a highly effective extension of immediate feedback. Though students are usually capable of plotting their own graphs, teacher assistance in this activity can serve as a vehicle for praising students' academic accomplishments, thus building in another possible form of positive reinforcement.

Immediate feedback, self-graphing, and teacher praise — while generally effective strategies — may not be individually or collectively reinforcing to some pupils with mild behavior disorders. With those for whom these strategies do not work, alternative reinforcement procedures must be identified and implemented.

Modification of Workbook Materials

As an additional instructional strategy for promoting the successful learning of underachieving behaviorally disordered students, the consumable workbooks that often accompany hard cover texts can often be modified advantageously. Pages pertaining to the unit in question should be carefully examined, looking at the relationship of activities to specific instructional objectives, sequencing, and complexity of activity and response required. Color coding and visual simplification of the pages involved can increase the probability of successful responding in many instances.

An added suggestion is to provide each student with an individual folder in which to keep materials. Graphs, workbook pages, daily quizzes, and perhaps also the cassette tape appropriate for the day's lesson might be included in each child's folder as an organizational aid.

Motivational Intervention

Accompanying curriculum intervention, a second component — motivational intervention — was inserted into the total strategy because of the preponderance of evidence suggesting that increasing task-oriented behavior is a necessary precursor to increasing academic skills (but with a lack of evidence concerning its actual effect upon achievement). Three motivational procedures were initially designed, to determine which would be most effective in combination with modified or traditional curriculum and teaching methods in increasing adaptive behavior and academic achievement of behaviorally disordered mainstreamed students. These procedures, described briefly below, are: (a) reinforcement of attention to task; (b) reinforcement of a specified percent correct on academic tasks, and (c) a non-reinforcement procedure.

Reinforcement of Attention to Task

Among various reinforcement strategies, token economies have been found to be effective and comparatively easy to administer in regular classroom situations. In an attempt to explore and validate the possible effectiveness of this strategy as an intervention for behavior disordered students, points were awarded for a certain percent of attending behavior. To maintain the consistency necessary to evaluate the outcome, one point was given to each student who successfully attended to task for 90% of each 10-minute interval during the social studies period. At the end of each 10-minute interval, points were given (or students were told they had not earned a point), coupled with verbal praise by the teacher. At the end of the day or week, points could be exchanged for a variety of classroom activities or privileges.

Teachers could use a variety of other procedures that would reward attention on a more intermittent basis and thus provide more flexibility and ease of administration. Still, any methodical consequation of attending behavior is a time and attention consuming activity — a major drawback to this motivational procedure in the ongoing regular class.

Reinforcement of Percent Correct

Reinforcement of percent correct — in contrast to reinforcement of attention to task — is a precise and easily administered procedure. By pre-arrangement with the students involved, the teacher can award points on a sliding scale basis. In the case under discussion here, students received one point for 70% correct, two points for 80%, three for 90% and four for 100% correct on daily quizzes or assignments. Again, the teacher accompanied the awarding of points with verbal praise, and points could be exchanged for classroom activities or privileges.

Students could earn a maximum of four points each day under either the procedure of reinforcement of attention to task or the procedure of re-inforcing percent correct.

Non-reinforcement Procedure

In this procedure, students received no systematic reinforcement for any behavior. They operated under the same classroom consequence conditions as their "normal" peers (i.e., no point system was in effect).

EVALUATION OF THE INTERVENTION STRATEGY

A research design was implemented to assess the effects of curriculum variables and differing motivational procedures. Regular classroom teachers identified 23 fourth graders through use of a modified Peterson-Quay Behavior Problem Checklist (Peterson, 1961). (Conduct factor items only were used.) Students scoring in excess of one standard deviation above the mean for all fourth graders rated were considered as possibly behavior disordered. Classroom observation of each student thus identified served to confirm or disconfirm the rating scale selection. This observation revealed that all 23 students were attending to task less than 50% of the time during which they were observed. Upon examining the achievement test scores (Comprehensive Test of Basic Skills) along with the discrepancy scores provided in the achievement testing printouts, each of the 23 students was additionally found to be underachieving in several academic areas. All identified students scored significantly lower in the area of reading comprehension than did other students of the same age, grade, sex, and academic ability.

These 23 children were in four different regular fourth-grade classrooms. The four classrooms were then assigned at random to one of two curricular conditions, modified or traditional, each of which has been described previously. Classrooms rather than students were assigned at random to curricular condition to prevent one classroom from containing students assigned to both curricular conditions. Under the modified curricular approach a social studies unit in the regular curriculum was adapted to meet individual instructional reading levels, along with other modifications including formulation of objectives, provisions for immediate feedback and self-graphing, and adaptation of workbook materials. In the traditional curricular approach students used the same social studies text and received the same assignments and teaching methods as the rest of the students in their classroom. Their teachers were asked to teach as they normally would.

A t-test for differences between two independent means was used to test for differences between the group of students receiving the modified curriculum and the group receiving traditional curriculum on the variables of teacher behavior rating scores, reading comprehension grade level, and IQ scores. Results of these analyses indicated no significant differences between the two groups on any of these measures.

Each student, regardless of traditional or modified curricular condition, was administered each of the three motivational procedures (reinforcement for attention to task, reinforcement for percent correct, and a non-reinforcement procedure) at some point during the evaluation process. Since the non-reinforcement procedure was essentially a baseline condition, all students were subject to this procedure first; the remaining two procedures were administered in random order to help counterbalance an order effect. The unit content was to be covered during a six-week period, so each of the three motivational procedures was in effect approximately two weeks.

The research design employed was a 2 x 3 factorial analysis of variance with repeated measures across one factor (motivational procedure). This method was used to determine significance of results in three areas: academic achievement, attention to task, and number of deviant behaviors. A further achievement measure was evaluated using t-test for the difference between independent means.

Academic Achievement Results

Academic achievement for the group of mild to moderate behaviorally disordered mainstreamed students was measured over a six-week period in two different ways. First, students were given three periodic quizzes, at the end of each two-week interval, coinciding with the conclusion of a given motivational procedure. The quizzes were short (10-question) objective tests covering the social studies content presented during the period in question. Because all four teachers had agreed to cover the unit using the same time and sequence framework, these tests were identical for all students. A second measure was a domain-referenced test reflecting content of the unit developed by the authors of the fourth-grade social studies textbook. This test was administered as a post-test procedure to each identified student along with all other regular class students.

Results of the analysis revealed that the group receiving the modified curricular approach scored significantly higher (at the .05 level) than did the traditional group on both the periodic quizzes and the summative unit test. Unit test scores were a mean of 8.2 percentage points higher for the modified curricular group, which also scored approximately 10 points higher on each of the three periodic quizzes.

Upon first examining the effect of motivational procedure upon academic achievement (within-group differences), the non-reinforcement procedure seemed to produce superior academic gains for both groups over the other two procedures. Although the graphic data in Figure 1 seem to indicate scores for both groups becoming progressively lower, this conclusion is not warranted. As discussed before, the data do not reflect cumulative time spent under reinforcement since two motivational procedures were randomly assigned. Also, the first test, given invariably after the non-reinforcement procedure, pertained to material introductory to the unit in question and thus seemed to be a simpler test than the other two. Therefore, results may possibly be more reflective of item difficulty level of the tests than changes in motivational procedure.

Attention to Task Results

Attention to task was measured using a direct observation technique developed by Madsen, Becker, and Thomas (1968) and modified by Weery and Quay (1968, 1969). This procedure consists of classifying and recording specific overt classroom behaviors of individual children in three major

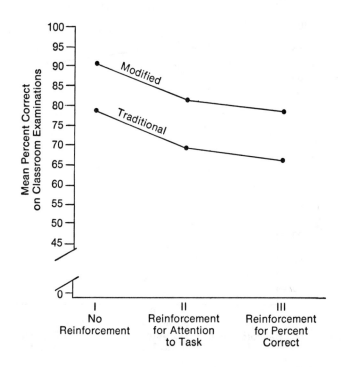

FIGURE 1
Means for Percent Correct on Classroom Examinations for Modified
And Traditional Curricular Groups under Three Motivational Procedures

categories: (a) on-task behavior; (b) deviant behavior; and (c) teacher-pupil interaction. The child is observed for two 20-second intervals per minute and behaviors recorded during the two 10-second rest periods. All behavior disordered students were observed and their behavior recorded daily for at least 15 minutes per student during their social studies period (approximately 40 minutes in length).

Upon analysis, between-group differences on attention to task thus measured were found to favor the modified curricular group. This group had significantly higher percentages of attention to task than did the traditional group (see Figure 2).

All three motivational procedures seemed to produce differential effects upon the two groups. The traditional group attended significantly more when this variable was specifically reinforced than they did under either of the two procedures. For the modified curricular group, however, reinforcement of attention to task produced significantly higher results over the non-reinforcement procedure only. The two procedures of reinforcing attention to task and reinforcing percent correct had an equal effect upon the attention

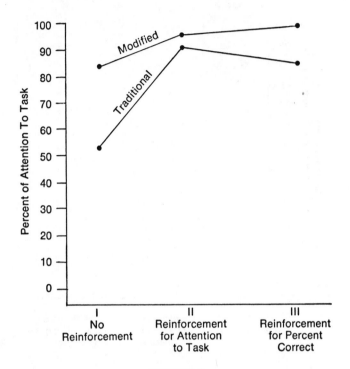

FIGURE 2
Means for Percent of Attention to Task for Modified and Traditional
Curricular Groups under Three Motivational Procedures

behavior of these students. Even for the traditional group, however, reinforcement of percent correct resulted in a significantly higher level of attention than did the non-reinforcement condition. The largest difference between the two groups (approximately 30 percentage points) occurred when no reinforcement was present.

Comparison of Deviant Behaviors

Deviant classroom behaviors of the mainstreamed behaviorally disordered students were measured using the same observation instrument as described under Attention to Task, above. A possible seven different behaviors could be recorded. A simple frequency count of deviant behaviors during social studies was obtained for each child daily. As might be expected, analyses of this factor closely resemble those for percent of attending behaviors.

As can be seen in Figure 3, the modified curricular group exhibited significantly fewer deviant behaviors than did the traditional group. A post

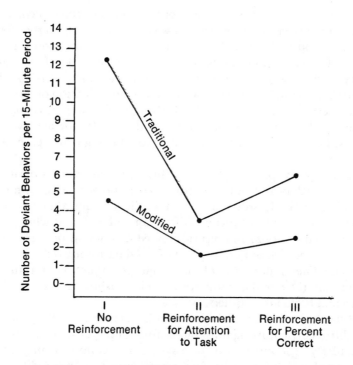

FIGURE 3
Means for Numbers of Deviant Behaviors for Modified and Traditional
Curricular Groups under Three Motivational Procedures

hoc analysis revealed that the traditional group had significantly fewer instances of deviant behaviors when attention to task was being reinforced than they did under either of the other two motivational procedures. However, they also emitted significantly fewer deviant behaviors when academic performance was reinforced than they did when no reinforcement was in operation.

Results of the analysis for the modified curricular group demonstrated that this group had fewer occurrences of deviant behaviors when either attention to task or academic percent correct was reinforced than they did when no reinforcement was given. Again, as in the analysis of percent of attention to task, they performed equally well under both of these two reinforcement procedures. One was not significantly better in decreasing deviant behaviors than the other.

IMPLICATIONS FOR TEACHERS

These data seem to point toward the quantitative superiority of a modified curricular approach over a traditional one when used with behavior disordered students in regular classrooms. Academic achievement as measured by percent correct on examinations was unequivocally higher for students receiving modified curriculum. An interesting implication for teachers is that reinforcement procedures did not seem to have a beneficial effect on the achievement of either group, even when achievement was specifically reinforced. A conclusion to be drawn from this combination of factors could be that a specific and organized change from traditional curricular materials and methods of using them is warranted in order for achievement to be increased for this type of exceptional student being educated in the regular classroom.

The data also provide further verification of the efficacy of strategies and procedures adapted from the structured approach concerning their use within a regular classroom and with a mildly handicapped population. A consultant teacher in cooperation with a regular class teacher possibly can design an educational intervention based on these procedures which will increase the academic performance of conduct disordered, underachieving children. The importance of this concept cannot be minimized when considering the circular nature of the relationship between academic deficiency and behavior disorders.

When attention to task is the factor being measured, the group receiving a modified curriculum again showed superior performances. This effect was particularly pronounced when no systematic reinforcement procedure was being employed. Without reinforcement, students in the modified curricular group attended approximately 85% of the time they were observed, whereas the traditional group had a mean percent of attending of only about 55% under this procedure. When reinforcement of attention to task was specifically reinforced, the traditional group closely approximated the performance of the modified group on this dimension. This increase in attention, however, did not result in a concomitant increase in academic achievement for the group receiving traditional instruction and curriculum. Therefore, the effects of increased attention seem to be directly related to the specific variable being reinforced. Reinforcing academic performance had as beneficial an effect upon the modified curricular group's attention as did reinforcing attention to task itself. Both resulted in significant increases in attention over non-reinforcement, but neither produced significantly better results than the other.

This same effect also operated for decreasing deviant behaviors for the modified group. Implications of this finding for teachers might be that when curriculum and instruction are designed to be appropriate for the needs and abilities of conduct disordered, underachieving students, systematic reinforcement seems to further increase attending and decrease inappropriate behaviors. Importantly, reinforcing percent correct on daily exercises — a procedure that might be more easily managed by the classroom teacher than systematically reinforcing for attending — is equally as effective as reinforcing on-task behavior. Neither of these procedures can be expected to increase achievement, however, whether or not instruction is modified. Modification of materials and instruction in itself resulted in high rates of attending accompanied by significantly higher achievement.

Fewer deviant classroom behaviors were noted for the traditional curricular group when attention to task was reinforced as well as when academic performance was reinforced; and deviant behaviors were significantly fewer than when no reinforcement was operating. Again, though, decreased numbers of inappropriate behaviors did not lead to increased levels of academic performance. Therefore, it seems, without more basic curricular and instructional changes, the effects of systematic reinforcement (i.e., rewarding attention or percent correct) do not lend themselves to academic remediation, but do increase attention and decrease deviancy.

Finally, a major purpose of these explorations was to identify the most effective and efficient combination of factors concerning curriculum variables and reinforcement of behaviors which would lead to optimal academic success and behavioral adjustment for conduct disordered, underachieving students in regular classrooms. Based on the present analysis, this combination seems to be *a modified curricular approach paired with a token reinforcement system in which academic percent correct is rewarded.*

REFERENCES

Adamson, G., & Van Etten, G. Zero reject model revisited: A workable alternative. *Exceptional Children*, 1972, *38*, 735-738.

Ayllon, T., & Roberts, M. D. Eliminating discipline problems by strengthening academic performance. *Journal of Applied Behavior Analysis*, 1974, *7*, 71-76.

Barrish, H., Saunders, M., & Wolf, M. M. Good behavior game: Effects of individual contingencies for group consequences on disruptive behavior in a classroom. *Journal of Applied Behavior Analysis*, 1969, *2*, 119-124.

Bower, E. M. *Early identification of emotionally handicapped children in school.* Springfield, IL: Charles C Thomas, 1969.

Camp, B. W., & Zimet, S. G. Classroom behavior during reading instruction. *Exceptional Children*, 1975, *42*, 109-110.

Deshler, D. D., & Graham, S. Tape recording educational materials for secondary handicapped students. *Teaching Exceptional Children*, 1980, *12*, 52-54.

Ferritor, D. E., Buckholdt, D., Hamblin, R. L., & Smith, L. The non-effects of contingent reinforcement for attending behavior on work accomplished. *Journal of Applied Behavior Analysis*, 1972, *5*, 7-17.

Gallagher, P. A. Structuring academic tasks for emotionally disturbed boys. *Exceptional Children*, 1972, *9*, 711-720.

Graubard, P. S. Relationship between academic achievement and behavior dimensions. *Exceptional Children*, 1971, *37*, 755-756.

Hall, R. V., Lund, D., & Jackson, D. Effects of teacher attention on study behavior. *Journal of Applied Behavioral Analysis*, 1968, *1*, 1-12.

Haring, N. G., & Phillips, E. L. *Educating emotionally disturbed children.* New York: McGraw-Hill, 1962.

Harris, J. H. *The effects of restructuring teaching procedures on the percent of answers correct on the daily spelling assignments of fifth grade inner city students.* Unpublished master's thesis, University of Kansas, 1972.

Kaufman, M. J., Gottlieb, J., Agard, J. A., & Kukic, M. B. Mainstreaming: Toward an explication of the construct. *Focus on Exceptional Children,* 1975, 7(3), 1-12.

Kelly, T. J., Bullock, L. M., & Dykes, M. K. Behavioral disorders: Teachers' perceptions. *Exceptional Children,* 1977, *43,* 316-318.

Keogh, B. K., & Levitt, M. L. Special education in the mainstream: A confrontation of limitations. *Focus on Exceptional Children,* 1976, *8*(1), 329-333.

Lovitt, T. C., & Curtiss, K. A. Effects of manipulating an antecedent event on mathematics response rate. *Journal of Applied Behavior Analysis,* 1968, *1,* 329-333.

Madsen, C., Becker, W., & Thomas, D. Rules, praise and ignoring: Elements of elementary classroom control. *Journal of Applied Behavior Analysis,* 1968, *1,* 139-150.

Mager, R. F. *Preparing instructional objectives* (2nd ed.). Belmont, CA: Fearon Publishers, 1975.

Meyen, E. L., & Moran, M. R. A perspective on the unserved mildly handicapped. *Exceptional Children,* 1979, *45,* 526-540.

Mosby, R. J. *Developmental by-pass techniques.* Union, MO: Franklin County Special Education Cooperative, 1977.

Peterson, D. R. Behavior problems of middle childhood. *Journal of Consulting Psychology,* 1961, *25,* 205-209.

Phillips, E. L., Wiener, D. N., & Haring, N. G. *Discipline, achievement and mental health.* Englewood Cliffs, NJ: Prentice-Hall, 1960.

Popham, W. J., & Baker, E. L. *Establishing instructional goals.* Englewood Cliffs, NJ: Prentice-Hall, 1970.

Robertshaw, C. S. *An investigation of attention to task behavior, arithmetic performance and behavior problems in first grade children.* Unpublished doctoral dissertation, University of Kansas, 1971.

Schmidt, G. W., & Ulrich, R. E. Effects of group contingent events upon classroom noise. *Journal of Applied Behavior Analysis,* 1969, *2,* 171-179.

Thomas, D., Becker, W., & Armstrong, M. Production and elimination of disruptive classroom behavior by systematically varying teachers' behaviors. *Journal of Applied Behavior Analysis,* 1968, *1,* 35-45.

Walker, H. M., & Buckley, N. K. The use of positive reinforcement in conditioning attending behavior. *Journal of Applied Behavior Analysis,* 1968, *1,* 245-250.

Wasik, B. H., Senn, K., Welch, R., & Cooper, B. A. Behavior modification with culturally deprived school children: Two case studies. *Journal of Applied Behavior Analysis,* 1969, *2,* 181-194.

Weery, J. S., & Quay, H. C. A method of observing classroom behavior of emotionally disturbed children. *Exceptional Children,* 1968, *34,* 389.

Weery, J. S., & Quay, H. C. Observing the classroom behavior of elementary school children. *Exceptional Children,* 1969, *35,* 461-470.

Whelan, R. J, & Haring, N. G. Modification and maintenance of behavior through systematic application of consequences. *Exceptional Children,* 1966, *32,* 281-289.

Winett, R. A., & Winkler, R. C. Current behavior modification in the classroom: Be still, be quiet, be docile. *Journal of Applied Behavior Analysis,* 1972, *5,* 499-504.

Guess and Noonan trace the history of curriculum development for the severely handicapped in a comprehensive, analytical review. They examine the present influence of behavioral technology and question its merits as a single approach. The authors emphasize the importance of a holistic approach focusing on the teaching of critical skills that traverse content domains. This article represents essential reading for serious students of curriculum development — particularly those interested in the relatively new field of curriculum development for the severely handicapped.

Curricula and Instructional Procedures for Severely Handicapped Students

Doug Guess and Mary Jo Noonan

Educational instruction among severely handicapped students is an effort barely 15 years old. During this brief history, curriculum development has followed several paths in attempting to identify content and methodology that will meet the needs of a population having severe skill deficits, maladaptive behaviors, and slow rates of achievement. After reviewing and analyzing the major curricula and instructional procedures that have evolved from various theoretical positions, we will give some suggestions for redirections in the field.

THE DEVELOPMENTAL APPROACH

Traditionally, curricula for the severely handicapped have been developmental — designed to replicate the normal sequence of development among handicapped students. Justification for the developmental approach rests on at least three assumptions: 1) normal development constitutes the most *logical* ordering of behaviors in a curriculum; 2) many behaviors within normal development are *prerequisite* behaviors; and 3) behaviors acquired at a particular age by a normal child are *appropriate* objectives for a severely handicapped student at the same level of development (Baldwin, 1976; Haring & Bricker, 1976; Stephens, 1977). On these premises, a multitude of chronologically sequenced behavior scales have been put forth as curricula for the severely handicapped. These curricula describe the "what to teach" and the order in which it should be taught.

Developmental Scales

Normal development serves as the outline of content in the developmental curriculum. Content is sequenced within behavior domains (e.g., gross motor, fine motor, language, social, and self-help) that function as both an assessment and the objectives of the curriculum. Because the assessment and objectives are one and the same, the curricula have been referred to as "assessment-linked" (Bricker, Bricker, Iacino, & Dennison, 1976; Gentry & Adams, 1978).

As developmental curricula were used increasingly with the severely handicapped, two criteria were applied to evaluate a "good" curriculum: 1) fine increments between behaviors; and 2) a broad scope of content. A curriculum with many items would usually be considered superior to one with fewer items for the same levels of development. The more detailed sequence would be more sensitive to behavior change, and an objective targeted through the assessment would be only a small step from behaviors already within the student's repertoire.

Implementation

Use of the developmental curriculum begins with assessment. A student is assessed through a checklist of the normally sequenced behaviors. The first item in each content domain that a student cannot demonstrate is targeted as an instructional objective. Most developmental curricula suggest a behavioral, data-based approach for training objectives. These curricula may include task analyses for objectives or examples of systematic programs for training items. Other curricula include more general training activities that correspond to the behavior in each sequence. Overall, the major utilization of a developmental curriculum is in the assessment and targeting of objectives.

Other Considerations

Proponents of the developmental model have acknowledged that the normal sequence of behaviors may not comprise the complete curriculum for the severely handicapped. In describing the model for preschool severely handicapped, Allen (1978) cautioned against inflexibly adhering to normal sequences, since handicapped children may follow an atypical route of development. An awareness of atypical development as a curricular consideration was expressed by Bricker et al. (1976), who adhere strongly to following the normal sequence but suggest that a "corrective strategy" to decelerate maladaptive and inappropriate behaviors may also be needed.

Modifications of the developmental sequences may at times result in a more appropriate and individualized curriculum. Gentry and Adams (1978), for example, pointed out that in addition to being matched to a student's developmental level, instructional objectives must be immediately useful. Hayden, McGinness, and Dmietriev (1976) described some of these "immediately useful" objectives as "tool skills"— behaviors that are critical for learning more complex skills, such as imitation. An alternative approach for fitting the curriculum to individual needs, discussed by Baldwin (1976), is to modify specific task analyses of objectives by collapsing unnecessary steps or adding steps (branching).

Developmental Curriculum Models

Many developmental curricula for the severely handicapped are presently available. Some are confined to a single content domain, such as a motor curriculum by Folio and Dubose (1974) and a language program by Bricker, Dennison, and Bricker (1976). Developmental curricula that include many content domains and are frequently used with the severely handicapped have been written by Somerton and Turner (1974); Cohen, Gross, and Haring (1976); Fredericks, Riggs, Furey, Grove, Moore, McDonnell, Jordan, Hanson, Baldwin, and Wadlow (1979); Connor, Williamson, and Siepp (1978); and Shearer, 1972.

The *Pennsylvania Training Model* (Somerton & Turner, 1974; Somerton & Meyers, 1976; Meyers, Sinco, & Stalma, 1973) is a good example of a comprehensive developmental curriculum. Its first component is an Assessment Guide, a general assessment that yields an overview of the child's development. The Guide is followed by the major portion of the curriculum, consisting of sequential behavior lists of 14 domains that clearly reflect content areas of importance for the severely handicapped. Individual sequences contain from six items (nasal hygiene) to 80 items (feeding-drinking) organized as checklists. The behaviors are subjectively rated in assessment as (0) 0% correct response, (1) moderate competency, (2) adequate competency, or (3) complete competency. Sample items from the feeding-drinking domain (Somerton & Turner, 1974, pp. 19, 21) illustrate the fine increments among the sequenced behaviors, as well as the comprehensiveness of the curriculum:

_____ 1. Child opens mouth when physically stimulated.
_____ 2. Child closes mouth when physically stimulated.

_____ 3. Child takes fluid from a dropper while in a reclining position.

_____ 4. Child retains liquid in mouth without dribbling.

.

.

.

_____ 78. Child pierces food using fork independently.

_____ 79. Child brings fork with piece of food on it to mouth.

_____ 80. Child returns empty fork to bowl or plate.

Behavior checklists in the *Pennsylvania Training Model* are followed by the third component, a sample of a systematic program and an example of its modification following a period of training. The sample program is written on an individual Prescriptive Planning Sheet that specifies the antecedents, behavior, consequences, and criteria. The fourth component of the curriculum manual consists of two examples of simple data charts to monitor progress. Finally, a flow chart mapping implementation of the total model is presented as a summary of the developmental curriculum process.

The *Pennsylvania Training Model* is fairly representative of developmental curricula for the severely handicapped. Cohen, Gross, and Haring (1976) have presented a more comprehensive compilation of developmentally sequenced behaviors, drawing from 24 previously published scales. Some activity suggestions and explanations for each content domain are included. The curriculum by Shearer (1972) provides, in addition to behavior checklists, many activities for training. A box of activity cards matched to each item (and cross-referenced to related items) complements the checklists.

Fredericks et al. (1976, 1979) and Baldwin (1976) have developed a curriculum that combines task analysis (discussed in the following section) with the developmental model. Skills in the checklists are first broadly task analyzed as "phases," and then broken down into very small "steps" of behavior. It is expected that the curriculum be used only as a guide. Steps that are too detailed should be combined, and additional steps should be added (branching) to individualize the curriculum.

The four curricula that have been reviewed infer or describe skill training *within* content domains. A developmental model by Connor, Williamson, and Siepp (1978), however, outlines and provides examples of strategies for training objectives both within and *across* domains: "(a) a sequential task analysis, (b) a major activity and its possible consequences across developmental areas, (c) integrated activities meeting multiple objectives, and (d) multiple interventions to meet a general behavioral objective" (p. 275). The integration of content domains in strategies (b) and (c) is unique to this curriculum and contributes to its flexibility. Training an activity with consequences in other areas, strategy (b), emphasizes consideration for the impact of goal selection in one content area on other domains of behavior. For example, training reach and grasp may contribute to progress in self-feeding and communication board use, since both skills involve eye, hand, and arm coordination. Strategy (c) involves the training of several target objectives in a single activity, a concept that lends itself to a more natural, meaningful training situation. The Guide recommends, but does not include, normal behavior sequences for the assessment and the selection of objectives, as in other developmental curricula.

Cognitive Models

In addition to the assumptions of the traditional developmental curriculum model (the normal developmental sequence is logical; many behaviors are prerequisites; and objectives at a student's developmental level are appropriate) cognitive developmental models propose three other assumptions that reflect the theoretical orientation of Jean Piaget (Stephens, 1977; Bricker, Siebert, & Casuso, 1980). First, objectives must be slightly beyond the present level of cognitive development to be motivating. In Piagetian terms, the training situations must create psychological "disequilibrium," or conflict, to be resolved by the student. This process of "equilibrium" is deemed critical for developmental progress. A second assumption is that the student must interact with the environment if learning is to occur; the student must be active in the training program. And third, the interrelation of content domains, particularly interrelating the cognitive domain with all other domains, must be considered in selecting appropriate objectives. Cognitive development determines and constrains what can be learned in other content areas. For example, self-feeding with a spoon would not be an appropriate objective for a student who has not demonstrated the simplest levels of means-ends behaviors, because it involves understanding "tool use."

In the cognitive approach, normal sequences of development are used in the same way as previously described for assessment and selecting objectives. But an additional developmental sequence to cover the cognitive domain (as Piaget has described the sequence), such as the *Ordinal Scales of Psychological Development* (Uzgiris & Hunt, 1975), is central and unique to this model.

Training targeted objectives follows behavioral methodology as in other developmental curricula, but special emphasis is placed on the antecedents to the target response (structuring the environment to create disequilibrium). The role of reinforcement is given less emphasis.

Overall, the developmental models (including the cognitive model) are similar to one another and primarily describe the content of instruction. Assessments and objectives for the severely handicapped come directly from normal sequences of skill acquisition. Behavioral methodology is often suggested for training targeted objectives.

Concerns Raised by the Developmental Curriculum Model

The important issue evolving from these approaches is the assumption that behavior must progress developmentally, that certain behaviors must be present in a student's repertoire before other behaviors can be acquired — either through maturation or as a result of direct intervention. This type of developmental logic has been criticized when applied to severely and multiply handicapped children (cf., Guess, Sailor, & Baer, 1978; Switzky, Rotatori, Miller, & Freagon, 1979).

Criticism has been based primarily on: 1) lack of empirical data demonstrating that severely handicapped persons do follow a normal developmental sequence, due, in part, to the presence of severe sensory and motor disabilities; and 2) the fact that many curricula resulting from developmental approaches have included teaching tasks that have been neither age-appropriate nor functional for adapting to environmental realities. For example, the *Pennsylvania Training Model* (Somerton & Turner, 1974) includes the following items:

Child will move object held in his hand to his mouth (p. 17).
Child will fling ball, toy, or paper without direction (p. 17).
Child squeezes and smears pieces of finger food on table (p. 20).
Child plays in bathroom sink by keeping hands under water (p. 27).

These examples, although exaggerated, illustrate a general concern that severely handicapped students are not always being taught the types of skills that will enable them to interact with their present and future environments. As a result, a major effort has been launched to provide more practical instructional programs for severely handicapped students, requiring direct intervention in deficit skill areas. Not coincidentally, this effort has paralleled the emergence of environmental adaptation approaches, including behavioral analysis, as a dominant influence in instructional programming for severely handicapped students.

ENVIRONMENTAL ADAPTATION APPROACHES

Behavioral/Remedial Approach: Developing a Technology for "How to Teach"

Starting in the mid-1960s, applied behavior analysis began to have a major impact on curriculum and, particularly, instructional approaches used with severely handicapped students. Behavioral techniques such as shaping, fading, prompting, and reinforcing were introduced within special education in the attempt to teach severely handicapped students a variety of skills. Skills ranged from self-help to the more complex areas of speech and language. These techniques and procedures were presented primarily by behavior psychologists who were well versed in the operant analysis of behavior. They also combined instructional procedures with a variety of experimental designs (Baer, Wolf, & Risley, 1968; Hersen & Barlow, 1976) aimed at demonstrating the controlling effects of consequences on behavior.

The term *remedial* was soon combined with behavioral to indicate that skills could be taught where none before had existed and that the individual's developmental levels could be minimized when selecting skills targeted for training. Parallel behavior modification techniques were also used among severely handicapped persons to decrease undesirable behaviors. For some cases, professionals perceived a need to eliminate undesirable behavior among severely handicapped persons before attempting to teach new, more adaptive skills. This clinical approach was a derivation of earlier studies in behavior modification that concentrated mainly on the reduction of behavioral deviancies among emotionally disturbed or psychiatric populations (Ullmann & Krasner, 1965). This orientation is still present in many treatment/education programs for severely handicapped persons (cf., Browning, 1980).

The major direction taken in the behavioral approach, however, was to further develop and refine the instructional technology for teaching numerous skills to severely handicapped persons. This was accompanied by an attempt to relate the technology more directly to the field of special education, including classroom instruction and vocational training. One major outcome of this effort was the heavy emphasis on task analysis procedures.

Behaviorists, along with special educators, had become convinced that almost any skill could be taught via operant procedures, if the task could be broken down into sufficiently small (and obtainable) units of behavior. When failures to teach a skill did occur, it was assumed that the task was not broken down sufficiently for the student or that the instructional procedures were not being applied correctly. Some investigators (Gold, 1972; Gold & Pomeranz, 1978) assumed that carefully constructed *task analyses* were sufficient motivation to result in learning.

What followed was a proliferation of task breakdowns for a multitude of skills that might be taught to severely handicapped students. The 1,008-page volume by Anderson, Hodson, and Jones (1974) is an obvious example. Task breakdown was followed by specific information on how to task analyze a skill in preparation for instructional programming (cf., Belmore & Brown, 1978; Cuvo, 1978).

The task analysis approach has been valuable to the extent that it has focused attention on the need to identify behavior in observable units that lend themselves to direct remediation efforts. It has also resulted in identifying many skills that can and should be taught to persons with severe handicapping conditions to enable them to lead more productive, independent lives.

A recent concern, however, is that the systematic, methodical task analysis approach might actually slow down progress for more capable students by taking them through unnecessary training steps (Liberty & Wilcox, 1981a). Another earlier concern was that the task analysis approach was not, by itself, sufficient to teach many skills to severely handicapped students. This concern stimulated the development of even more precise instructional procedures designed to enhance the learning of a skill once it had been broken down into small units of behavior.

These instructional procedures included, for example, the Project MORE model that delineates levels of assistance in teaching a specific response (Lent, 1979; Lent & McLean, 1976) and the delayed prompt procedures that specify increasing time intervals (in seconds) between the presentation of a stimulus and either the self-initiated or, if necessary, the teacher-prompted response to be made by the student (Snell & Gast, 1981). Use of stimulus fading or errorless learning would also fit into this effort to further refine the instructional technology available toward educating severely handicapped students (Touchette, 1971; Schreibman, 1975; Holvoet, 1978).

The more sophisticated procedures have proven to be effective with many severely handicapped students. Skills have been acquired where none have existed before. Instructional procedures have been, in large part, shown to be responsible for learning — at least learning that could be demonstrated in the specific instructional setting, which often required 1:1 training. This latter qualification is important.

A common finding has been that learning occurring under tight instructional control does *not* necessarily generalize to other persons, settings, or materials. This is significant to the education and treatment of severely handicapped students. Newly taught skills will be of little value to the learner if they do not occur in more natural situations and environments. The findings prompted design and development of a new technology to teach generalization in the majority of situations in which it did not occur spontaneously. A frequently cited paper by Stokes and Baer (1977) identified many common and useful procedures for teaching generalization. This additional technology has been viewed as a necessary extension to the education and training of severely handicapped students. Generalization training has attempted to correct original deficiencies in the behavioral approach by adding training requirements to the education process for severely handicapped students.

In retrospect, the behavioral approach has spawned, over the past few years, a sophisticated, how-to-teach technology for severely handicapped students. Continued refinements have increased the complexity. In some respects, the technical nature of many of the procedures has reached a point at which, because of time limitations, teachers will be unable to implement them consistently or effectively in the everyday classroom environment. This situation has been aptly expressed by Liberty and Wilcox (1981a) in their cautions about the overuse of task analysis.

> In the course of their education, most professionals have been trained to perform countless acts of reductionism on a variety of tasks. We are all too familiar with the 76-step task analysis of how to thread a needle, the 42-step analysis of shoe tying, or the 26-step breakout of how to fasten a seat belt. However, once teachers are faced with classrooms of pupils, such detailed task analysis is frequently left behind. (p. 1)

Each new development in the expanding technology leaves less room for additional considerations, because the procedures accruing to the technology are so time consuming that none remains to pursue other approaches. Slavish adherence to a strict behavioral technology, in its narrowness, carries the danger of blocking discovery of other important concepts in teaching severely handicapped students.

A more serious question concerns whether or not the behavioral approach accurately represents a total methodology for changing behavior among severely handicapped persons. Since it probably does not, should the procedures derived from it be used exclusively as the technology of choice? Some indications have already been manifested that strict, exclusive adherence to a behavioral model may have fostered how-to-teach practices that are not conducive to the most effective intervention efforts. Some of these practices and concerns are discussed below.

Splinter Skill Training

In the zeal to demonstrate that many skills can be taught in the absence of developmental prerequisites, behaviorists have tended to teach skills in isolation (teaching content areas separate from one another). Thus, a student might be taught speech at one time, how to dress at another time, and so on. In many cases, the complicated task analyses for specific training programs preclude simultaneous teaching of other skills that require similarly complicated instructions.

As a result of teaching splinter skills in relatively isolated times and settings, generalization to other persons, places, and settings has not always taken place. As already pointed out, this dilemma prompted the design and development of new procedures to *teach* the generalization of skills. A whole new technology was required to overcome a limitation of the original technology. The problem might have been averted if behaviorists had initially recognized interdependence of behavior and skills across and within content domains, as was suggested earlier by some developmental approaches (e.g., Connor et al., 1978).

Nonfunctional Training

Those advocating a behavioral approach have correctly pointed out that many developmentally oriented curricula did not teach functional skills. But behavioral programs have often fallen into the same trap. This is pointed out not so much to direct criticism to the procedures per se as it is to the types of training tasks to which the procedures have led. Behavioral procedures such as response shaping and stimulus fading have been conducted most effectively in massed trial sequences; the same response is emitted over and over again during the session. This format allows the teacher or therapist to build (or shape) the behavior in the desired direction gradually.

On the surface, this format seems logical since learning among severely handicapped students is, at best, slow. But the training outcome, when successful, is often so specific to the training sessions that spontaneous, functional use of the skill is never demonstrated. Indeed, the tasks themselves are often not functional. Teaching a child to raise his or her hand in imitation training, for example, is of dubious value in the real world. We are reminded here of an earlier caution by Wolfensberger (1972) that the means of instruction should be just as normalizing as the ends of the instruction.

One might also add to the discussion here the use of nonfunctional and artificial reinforcers (e.g., foods, liquids, tokens) to maintain an acceptable response rate during mass-trial training. Too frequently, attempts are not made to fade out these reinforcers, or to pair them with more functional and less artificial ones. As a result, the continued use of artificial reinforcers reduces generalization of the training skill to natural environments where these reinforcers are not present. A similar problem exists with the substantial number of severely handicapped students for whom reinforcers are not easily identified (or the reinforcers are so transient that they prove to be nonfunctional for purposes of training). In these cases, the end objective of training is frequently lost to the means — trying to find reinforcers for the student.

Explaining Failures

The literature abounds with published reports that demonstrate the effective use of behavioral procedures in teaching severely handicapped students a variety of useful skills, but probably an equal number of efforts were not successful (and likely not published). Guess, Sailor, and Baer (1978) have reported that approximately 40% of their subjects failed to acquire rudimentary motor and vocal imitation skills in two years of extensive training that used the best behavior modification techniques available.

How can one account for the high number of students who did *not* learn? One explanation is that the technology is far from complete and that better instructional procedures will eventually be designed. Another explanation is that those students did not have the prerequisite skills necessary for learning the type of imitation behavior being taught. This explanation seems more plausible in view of research that has demonstrated certain developmental prerequisites for speech and language skills among severely and profoundly retarded individuals (Kahn, 1975; Leonard, 1978; Lobato, Barrera, and Feldman, 1981).

Thus, the danger exists that some behavioral procedures will be used unsuccessfully when learning is not going to occur unless other skills are also acknowledged as prerequisites, and when other approaches might provide better results. Umbreit (1980), for example, has presented some tentative data suggesting that severely handicapped students acquire skills at a faster rate (fewer number of trials to criterion) when they are developmentally rather than randomly sequenced.

The behavioral approach, in summary, has offered much to the education and training of severely handicapped persons. It has provided many teaching techniques and procedures that should be a part of instructional programming for this population of students, and it has given us a scientific methodology for evaluating and assessing educational intervention efforts. As a comprehensive instructional model, however, it has many limitations. If the training procedures and techniques are viewed as a total and uncompromising explanation of human learning, the potential benefactors of that technology might not have received the best training we are capable of developing. If the behavioral approach is applied judiciously, though, it may reap positive benefits.

Community Adaptation Approach: Selecting Criteria for "What to Teach"

The behavioral approach has not dealt adequately with the issue of "what to teach" or the more fundamental considerations of an integrated, functional curriculum for severely handicapped students. This is likely due in part to the underlying premise that skills can be taught as separate entities if only they are appropriately task analyzed, as well as the reluctance among behaviorists to pursue a more "holistic" approach that fully acknowledges the interdependence among skill domains. The same criticism can be directed at some developmental approaches that both assess and treat behavior deficiencies as isolated units — e.g., teaching motor skills separate from cognitive skills, teaching speech skills separate from cognitive or motor skills.

The behavioral approach did direct attention toward teaching more functional and age-appropriate skills to severely handicapped students. It did not, however, provide any systematic guidelines or rationale for what was to be taught. In the mid 1970s Lou Brown and his colleagues at the University of Wisconsin introduced conceptual systems, or rationale, for designing and organizing curriculum content for severely handicapped students. The impetus for this movement was heavily influenced by a developing philosophy of "normalization"— that severely handicapped persons should be integrated into community life and that they should be prepared, as much as possible, for normal existence in the mainstream of society (Wolfensberger, 1972). Educators, then, had the challenge of initiating curriculum strategies that would enable severely handicapped students to learn a myriad of skills necessary for successfully adapting to the community — as contrasted with teaching skills to prepare them to live in segregated environments and facilities.

In an early publication, Brown, Nietupski, and Hamre-Nietupski (1976) referred to the "criterion of ultimate functioning" as a standard by which classroom curriculum content should be measured for severely handicapped students. This concept "refers to the ever changing, expanding, localized, and personalized cluster of factors that each person must possess in order to function as productively and independently as possible in socially, vocationally, and domestically integrated community environments" (p. 8). They posed six questions for the classroom teacher and other service delivery personnel to consider before initiating education and treatment activities:

1. Why should we engage in this activity?
2. Is this activity necessary to prepare students to ultimately function in complex heterogeneous community settings?
3. Could students function as adults if they did not acquire the skill?
4. Is there a different activity that will allow students to approximate realization of the criterion of ultimate functioning more quickly and more efficiently?
5. Will this activity impede, restrict, or reduce the probability that students will ultimately function in community settings?
6. Are the skills, materials, tasks, and criteria of concern similar to those encountered in adult life? (p. 9)

Given the premise that the curriculum content for severely handicapped students should evolve around teaching skills for eventual community living, the next step taken by the Madison group was to develop strategies to identify skills that should be taught. These strategies were discussed in papers by Brown, Branston, Hamre-Nietupski, Pumpian, Certo, and Gruenewald (1979) and Brown, Branston-McClean, Baumgart, Vincent, Falvey, and Schroeder (1979). The latter publication presented workable guidelines for developing chronological age-appropriate curricular content for severely handicapped adolescents and young adults.

This strategy basically follows an ecological approach to the identification of important skills. These include domestic skills, vocational training, use of leisure and recreational activities, and skills necessary for community living. First, important skills in natural environments (e.g., group homes) and subenvironments within the larger settings (e.g., kitchens within group homes) were to be identified. Next, activities within the subenvironments necessary for community living (e.g., cooking, washing dishes) would be identified, followed by a breakdown of specific responses necessary for engaging in the identified activities. Procedures for delineating the specific skills essentially would follow a task analysis approach, as described by Belmore and Brown (1978). In the final phase, the appropriate skills targeted for remedial training would be taught.

The most significant contribution of the curriculum development strategy summarized by the two Brown et al. studies in 1979 is the emphasis placed on teaching functional, chronological-age-related skills necessary for successful interactions in domestic, community, and vocational settings. These strategies, using an ecological inventory approach, provide specific direction and rationale for selecting and organizing curriculum content for severely handicapped students, especially those of an older age level who are being prepared for "ultimate functioning" in community settings.

Criteria of the Next Educational Environment

The "criterion of ultimate functioning" (Brown et al., 1976) has been difficult to apply to infant and preschool children with severely handicapping conditions because instructional objectives derived from this concept would be so distant (temporally) that they would be irrelevant and essentially nonfunctional. Therefore, the principle was extended downward as the "criteria of the next educational environment" — the public school kindergarten. The logic of this principle implies that the curriculum for young severely handicapped preschool children should be directed toward teaching the skills necessary for successful placement in kindergarten classrooms in public school settings. This approach, described by Vincent, Salisbury, Walter, Brown, Gruenewald, and Powers (1980), is based on their research and observations suggesting that "survival skills" (social and behavioral) are more critical than academic skills in determining the success or failure of children as they are placed in kindergarten settings. Survival skills consist of behaviors such as compliance, attending, social interaction, and following directions.

Vincent and her colleagues (1980) are presently engaged in strategies to identify skills necessary for successful kindergarten placement. When identified, these skills will be used as the instructional objectives comprising the curriculum content to be used with severely handicapped preschool children.

Vincent et al. pointed out that in addition to identifying survival skills as a critical content domain in infant and preschool programs, the criteria of the next educational environment have implications for instructional methodology. They maintain that the precision teaching that characterizes instructional methodology for severely handicapped students does not occur in regular kindergarten classes. Thus, as suggested earlier, instructional technology for the severely handicapped may be moving beyond practical application in contemporary classroom settings and other environments that serve them.

Two ways to modify the instructional environment of special education in consideration of the next environment, as suggested by Vincent et al., are: 1) gradual modification of the special education environment to approximate the kindergarten, and 2) modification of the special education teacher's behavior to approximate the regular kindergarten teacher's behavior.

The positions taken by Brown and his colleagues and Vincent and her colleagues have made a significant contribution to the design and development of curricula for severely handicapped students. Their guidelines and curriculum selection strategies have offered to the field a functional rationale for deciding "what to teach." Accordingly, the "criterion of ultimate functioning" and the "criteria of the next educational environment" provide ecological assessments of what should be taught to severely handicapped students, based on selecting functional and chronologically age-appropriate skills. When the skills to be trained have been identified, the next step is to locate programs designed to teach them. As mentioned in the "how to teach" section, a seemingly endless number of already task-analyzed instructional programs is available from which to choose.

The rationale followed by Brown et al. and Vincent et al. implies that, to a large extent, curriculum development can be separated from instructional methodology for severely handicapped students. This is based on earlier observations in this article that behavioral methodology was a major influence in the development of specific instructional programs, rather than the programs, per se, playing a major role in the design of instructional procedures and techniques. The behavioral technology led to development of splinter skill training programs, most of which served to further isolate content areas. Also, they utilized instructional procedures that eventually led to unacceptable levels of "reductionism."

We believe that the ecological inventory approach advocated by Brown et al. and Vincent et al. provides somewhat more effective means with which to select training objectives. We further believe, however, that it does not lead to the interdependent development of skills across and within content domains.

TEACHING FUNCTIONAL SKILL CLUSTERS: A HOLISTIC APPROACH

We contend that at least two important considerations must be addressed in future curriculum development efforts for severely handicapped students. These include: 1) teaching interdependent skills across and within content domains, and 2) a more integrated relationship between instructional procedures and educational (curriculum) objectives.

Teaching Skill Clusters

Our original concern with many developmental curricula, and with the splinter skill teaching approach evolving from a behavioral technology, was the underlying assumption that behavior consists of isolated responses that can be taught separate and independent from one another. We also were concerned about the disregard for functional interdependence between and among content domains. An earlier reaction to the developmental approach was the frequent omission of teaching functional, age-appropriate skills to severely handicapped students. This resulted in a plethora of carefully designed instructional programs for teaching relevant and ecologically useful skills (e.g., how to ride a bus, make change, go shopping, wash dishes, hold the head up, reach for objects, etc.).

In the rush to teach relevant and useful skills, and to construct procedures for identifying what should be taught, an equally obvious point may have been overlooked: Optimal adaptation to the environment requires the person to emit many behaviors almost simultaneously. Ecologists often refer to the "stream of behavior" as the organism interacts with the environment. Developmental psychologists and others frequently refer to treating the "whole child." As Sailor and Guess (in preparation) have pointed out, "Regardless of one's particular theoretical persuasion, the message is the same; the person must learn to emit many different types of actions either concurrently or in rapid succession if adaptive behavior is to occur."

Present educational efforts with severely handicapped students involve teaching skill areas that have no centrally unifying basis. This forces us into a situation in which we must attempt to teach a likely unobtainable number of discrete skills to achieve even the beginnings of effective adaptive behavior. With these technologies, severely handicapped students simply do not have the time to learn all the skills necessary for adequate functioning in the school, home, or community.

We propose instead that educational programming for the severely handicapped must begin to concentrate on teaching skills that have the widest and most functional applicability across a variety of tasks and content areas. Equally important, the skill clusters taught must cut across traditional content domains. If, for example, a large number of task-analyzed instructional programs were to be lined up side by side, we might be able to identify a number of "critical skills" common across the various programs. Might it not, therefore, be better to teach severely handicapped students a variety of critical skills with specific instructional programs rather than follow the present philosophy and attempt to teach a multitude of isolated instructional programs with the hope that somewhere along the way a more generalized use of the skills will emerge?

Critical skills, as defined here, include behaviors essential to successful performance in numerous tasks, both within and across content domains.

The ability to reach, grasp, and release objects, for example, would be critical skills for many self-help, play, and vocational tasks. The ability to discriminate between objects and events would be equally essential for the above tasks, as well as for the development of academic and communication skills. We are not here advocating the teaching of skills in isolation with the anticipation that these skills will spontaneously emerge within the context of more functional tasks. This approach has failed in the past. We are advocating, rather, the selection of age-appropriate and functional tasks that include common critical skills that will more rapidly generalize to new instructional programs. Current approaches attempt to teach too many tasks consisting of skills that are situation-specific, and yet require excessive amounts of instructional time.

At present, developmental assessment instruments may be needed to help identify critical skill deficiencies. If so, the deficiencies have to be translated into age-appropriate and functional objectives, with instructional programs directed toward development of the identified critical skills. This requires the caution that severely handicapped students might not always exactly follow a developmental sequence, especially severely handicapped students who have accompanying motor and sensory disabilities.

The holistic approach would provide the beginnings of a unified rationale for selecting curriculum content based on a sequence of development. It would provide for the teaching of functional and age-appropriate skills. At the same time, it would avoid the present tendency to attempt to teach skill areas as isolated units with minimal concern for prerequisite skills or the overall amount of instructional time required to attain competency.

If one agrees that critical skills should be taught in place of numerous prepackaged instructional programs, the next concern involves a conceptual framework for teaching these skills. Within this context, we advocate the teaching of skill clusters, defined as a grouping of environmentally appropriate and functional behaviors that cut across typical content domains. This assumes that motor, language, cognitive, and social skills are best taught as interdependent clusters.

A series of articles from the University of Kansas (Mulligan, Guess, Holvoet, & Brown, 1980; Holvoet, Guess, Mulligan, & Brown, 1980) has described a procedure for teaching skill clusters. These articles describe an individualized curriculum sequencing model (ICS) designed to teach skill clusters that combine content areas. A young child might be taught, for example, to look at an object (visual orientation), raise his/her head (gross motor), produce a sound (communication), reach out and grasp the object (fine motor), and then use the object in the appropriate manner (cognitive and motor). This short skill cluster would logically contain skills determined from the child's assessed developmental level, and skills that would enable the child to better interact with his/her environment in an age-appropriate, functional manner. For a young child, the objects in the example might be favorite toys; for an older profoundly retarded student, the objects might be a hair brush, radio, or pencil sharpener.

The ICS model systematically teaches the student to combine skills across content domains and to perceive the relationship between them. In contrast, a more traditional program presents the student with repeated trials for each component of the sequence, separately and independently from one another — and frequently preceded by the verbal directive, "hands in lap."

The analogy can be extended to self-contained instructional programs. One program might teach a student to make change, another to make purchases, and still another to ride a bus to the store. Might it not be better to teach the student all these skills simultaneously? The instructional time may be longer, but in the end the student would have learned a number of interrelated skills germane to the ultimate objective of independent shopping.

This approach of teaching critical skills that traverse content domains will require a basic readjustment of current programming efforts. We must be willing to sacrifice the convenience of prepackaged, task-analyzed instructional programs and start designing and developing programs that effectively interrelate traditional content areas in a more holistic manner. We must be willing to forego the temptations of splinter skill training and undertake the more difficult task of identifying and teaching interdependent critical skills that ultimately will lead to a more naturalized, cohesive instructional program.

Instructional Procedures and Educational Objectives

Within recent years, instructional technology has often been separated from curriculum development in general and from individual education objectives specifically. It has possibly come to the point where the "tail is wagging the dog." A similar observation has recently been made by Liberty and Wilcox (1981b) when they stated:

> The objectives of education, the needs of the individual learner, and even common sense have been supplanted by a superstitious and slavish adherence to certain procedures which have been sanctified in the name of systematic instruction and behavioral technology. The procedures of instruction have become more important than the aim of instruction. (p. 2)

A more holistic approach to the education of severely handicapped students can potentially instill new life in the design and development of instructional procedures for this population. In starting to move away from the overuse of prepackaged instructional programs designed to teach splinter skills, we may begin to see more instructional options to supplement and enhance current behavioral technology. The identification of deficient critical skills among severely handicapped students and the development of training programs that traverse content domains will likely lead us to view the behavior of these students from a more complex and sophisticated level — one that more fully recognizes complicated interactions between cognitive, sensory/motor, and emotional behavior. This realization will, we hope, encourage us to fit the instructional procedures to the identified needs of the student, rather than try to make any one set of instructional procedures or any one approach fit any need. For severely handicapped students, developmental, Piagetian, behavioral, and other approaches may be useful in implementing education and treatment programs.

The important point is that the curriculum objectives must determine, to a large extent, the instructional procedures to be used, rather than vice versa, and that we must become more amenable to using and developing new instructional procedures in the education and treatment of severely handicapped students. This does not imply that we should abandon our current methodology, which requires the systematic collection and analysis of data resulting from intervention efforts. To the contrary — developing and using new instructional procedures and approaches will require an even heavier emphasis on program evaluation for both individual students and groups of students.

SUMMARY

We have described the development of instructional procedures and curricula for severely handicapped students over the past decade. Few would dispute the statement that gains in educating this population have been impressive. The field has come a long way in a relatively short time. Changes are needed, however, if this momentum is to be maintained, and we must seriously reevaluate where our predominant behavioral technology is taking us.

We have argued that the present technology is leading to a not entirely useful level of reductionism, approaching a point at which the technology is neither practical to implement in most classroom settings nor necessarily desirable even if we could do so. We have suggested that future efforts to develop instructional procedures and curricula for severely handicapped students should explore new approaches including, especially, those that teach critical skills across and within content areas, as well as approaches that more fully recognize the inherent complexity of these students' learning needs.

REFERENCES

Allen, K. E. Early intervention for young severely and profoundly handicapped children: The preschool imperative. *AAESPH Review*, 1978, *3*, 30-41.

Anderson, D. R., Hodson, G. D., & Jones, W. G. (Eds.). *Instructional programs for the severely handicapped student.* Springfield, IL: Charles C Thomas, 1974.

Baer, D. M., Wolf, M. M., & Risley, T. R., Some current dimensions of applied behavior analysis. *Journal of Applied Behavior Analysis*, 1968, *1*, 91-97.

Baldwin, V. L. Curriculum concerns. In M. A. Thomas (Ed.), *Hey, don't forget about me!* Reston, VA: Council for Exceptional Children, 1976, pp. 64-73.

Belmore, K. J., & Brown, L. A job skill inventory strategy designed for severely handicapped potential workers. In N. Haring & D. Bricker (Eds.), *Teaching the severely handicapped* (Vol. 2). Seattle: American Association for the Education of the Severely/Profoundly Handicapped, 1978, pp. 223-262.

Bricker, D., Bricker, W., Iacino, R., & Dennison, L. Intervention strategies for the severely and profoundly handicapped child. In N. G. Haring & L. J. Brown (Eds.), *Teaching the severely handicapped* (Vol. 1). New York: Grune & Stratton, 1976.

Bricker, D. D., Dennison, L., & Bricker, W. A. *A language intervention program for developmentally young children.* Mailman Center for Child Development Monograph Series, No. 1. Miami: University of Miami, 1976.

Bricker, D., Seibert, J., & Casuso, V. Early intervention. In J. Hogg & P. Mittler (Eds.), *Advances in mental handicap research.* New York: John Wiley & Sons, 1980.

Brown, F., Holvoet, J., Guess, D., & Mulligan, M. The individualized curriculum sequencing model (III): Small group instruction. *Journal of the Association for the Severely Handicapped*, 1980, *5*, 352-367.

Brown, L., Branston, M. B., Hamre-Nietupski, S., Pumpian, I., Certo, N., & Grunewald, L. A strategy for developing chronological age appropriate and functional curriculum content for severely handicapped adolescents and young adults. *Journal of Special Education*, 1979, *13*, 81-90.

Brown, L., Branston-McClean, M. B., Baumgart, D., Vincent, L., Falvey, M., & Schroeder, J. Using the characteristics of current and subsequent least restrictive environment as factors in the development of curricular content for severely handicapped students. *Journal of the Association for the Severely Handicapped*, 1979, *4*, 407-424.

Brown, L., Nietupski, J., & Hamre-Nietupski, S. Criterion of ultimate functioning. In M. A. Thomas (Ed.), *Hey, don't forget about me!* Reston, VA: Council for Exceptional Children, 1976, pp. 2-15.

Browning, R. M. *Teaching the severely handicapped child: Basic skills for the developmentally disabled.* Boston: Allyn & Bacon, 1980.

Cohen, M., Gross, P., & Haring, N. G. Developmental pinpoints. In N. G. Haring & L. J. Brown (Eds.), *Teaching the severely handicapped* (Vol. 1). New York: Grune & Stratton, 1976.

Connor, F. P., Williamson, G. G., & Siepp, J. M. *Program guide for infants and toddlers with neuromotor and other developmental disabilities.* New York: Teachers College Press, 1978.

Cuvo, A. Validity task analysis of community living skills. *Vocational Evaluation and Work Adjustment Bulletin*, 1978, *11*, 13-21.

Folio, R., & DuBose, R. F. *Peabody developmental motor scales.* Nashville: Institute on Mental Retardation and Intellectual Development, George Peabody College for Teachers, 1974.

Fredericks, H. D., Baldwin, V. L., Grove, D. N., Riggs, C., Furey, V., Moore, W., Jordan, E., Gage, M. A., Levak, L., Alrick, G., & Wadlow, M. *A data-based classroom for moderately and severely handicapped* (3rd ed.). Monmouth, OR: Instructional Development Corp., 1979.

Fredricks, H. D., Riggs, C., Furey, T., Grove, D., Moore, W., McDonnell, J., Jordan, E., Hanson, W., Baldwin, V., & Wadlow, M. *The teaching research curriculum for moderately and severely handicapped.* Springfield, IL: Charles C Thomas, 1976.

Gentry, D., & Adams, G. A curriculum-based direct intervention approach to the education of handicapped infants. In N. G. Haring & D. D. Bricker (Eds.), *Teaching the severely handicapped* (Vol. 3). Seattle: American Association for the Education of the Severely/Profoundly Handicapped, 1978.

Gold, M. W. Stimulus factors in skill training of the retarded on a complex assembly task: Acquisition, transfer, and retention. *American Journal of Mental Deficiency*, 1972, *76*, 517-526.

Gold, M. W., & Pomeranz, D. J. Issues in prevocational training. In M. E. Snell (Ed.), *Systematic instruction of the moderately and severely handicapped*. Columbus, OH: Charles E. Merrill, 1978, pp. 431-440.

Guess, D., Sailor, W., & Baer, D. M. Children with limited language. In R. L. Schiefelbusch (Ed.), *Language intervention strategies*. Baltimore: University Park Press, 1978, pp. 101-144.

Haring, N. G., & Bricker, D. Overview of comprehensive services for the severely/profoundly handicapped. In N. G. Haring & L. J. Brown (Eds.), *Teaching the severely handicapped* (Vol. 1). New York: Grune & Stratton, 1976.

Hayden, A. H., McGinness, G., & Dmietriev, V. Early and continuous intervention strategies for severely handicapped infants and very young children. In N. G. Haring & L. J. Brown (Eds.), *Teaching the severely handicapped* (Vol. 1). New York: Grune & Stratton, 1976.

Hersen, M., & Barlow, D. H. *Single case experimental designs: Strategies for studying behavior change*. New York: Pergamon Press, 1976.

Holvoet, J. *Some general observations about errorless training and some examples of errorless programs used with S M H individuals*. Unpublished paper, University of Kansas, 1978.

Holvoet, J., Guess, D., Mulligan, M., & Brown, F. The individualized curriculum sequencing model (II): A teaching strategy for severely handicapped students. *Journal of the Association for the Severely Handicapped*, 1980, *5*, 337-351.

Kahn, J. Relationship of Piaget's sensorimotor period to language acquisition in profoundly retarded children. *American Journal of Mental Deficiency*, 1975, *79*, 640-643.

Lent, J. R. *Systematic skill training*. Unpublished paper, George Peabody College for Teachers of Vanderbilt University, Project Change, 1979.

Lent, J. R., & McLean, B. M. The trainable retarded: The technology of teaching. In N. G. Haring & R. L. Schiefelbusch (Eds.), *Teaching special education*. New York: McGraw-Hill, 1976.

Leonard, L. Cognitive factors in early linguistic development. In R. Schiefelbusch (Ed.), *Bases of language intervention*. Baltimore: University Park Press, 1978.

Liberty, K., & Wilcox, B. Forum: Slowing down learning. *Association for the Severely Handicapped Newsletter*, 1981, *1* (2), 1-2. (a)

Liberty, K., & Wilcox, B. Forum: Abuse and misuse of systematic instruction and behavior technology: The rabbit test. *Association for the Severely Handicapped Newsletter*, 1981, 7(4), 1-2. (b)

Lobato, D., Barrera, R. D., & Feldman, R. S. Sensorimotor functioning and prelinguistic communication of severely and profoundly mentally retarded individuals. *American Journal of Mental Deficiency*, 1981, *85*, 489-496.

Meyers, D. G., Sinco, M. E., & Stalma, E. S. *The right to education child*. Springfield, IL: Charles C Thomas, 1973.

Mulligan, M., Guess, D., Holvoet, J., & Brown, F. The individualized curriculum sequencing model (I): Implications from research on massed, distributed, or spaced trial training. *Journal of the Association for the Severely Handicapped*, 1980, *5*, 325-336.

Sailor, W., & Guess, D. Curriculum sequencing. In W. Sailor & D. Guess, *Instructional design for the severely handicapped*. Boston: Houghton Mifflin, in preparation.

Schreibman, L. Effects of within-stimulus and extra-stimulus prompting on discrimination learning in autistic children. *Journal of Applied Behavior Analysis*, 1975, *8*, 91-112.

Shearer, D. *The Portage guide to early education.* Portage, WI: Cooperative Educational Agency No. 12, 1972.

Snell, M., & Gast, D. Applying delay procedure to the instruction of the severely handicapped. *Journal of the Association for the Severely Handicapped,* 1981, *6,* 3-14.

Somerton, M. E., & Myers, D. G. Educational programming for the severely and profoundly mentally retarded. In N. G. Haring & L. J. Brown (Eds.), *Teaching the severely handicapped* (Vol. 1). New York: Grune & Stratton, 1976.

Somerton, M. W. & Turner, K. D. *Pennsylvania training model individual assessment guide.* Harrisburg, PA: Pennsylvania Department of Education, 1974.

Stephens, B. A Piagetian approach to curriculum development for the severely, profoundly, and multiply handicapped. In E. Sontag (Ed.), *Educational programming for the severely and profoundly handicapped.* Reston, VA: Council for Exceptional Children, 1977.

Stokes, T. F., & Baer, D. M. An implicit technology of generalization. *Journal of Applied Behavior Analysis,* 1977, *10,* 341-367.

Switzky, H., Rotatori, H. A. F., Miller, T., & Freagon, S. The developmental model and its implications for the severely/profoundly handicapped. *Mental Retardation,* 1979, *17,* 167-170.

Touchette, P. E. Transfer of stimulus control: Measuring the moment of transfer. *Journal of Experimental Analysis of Behavior,* 1971, *15,* 347-354.

Ullmann, L. P., & Krasner, L. (Eds.). *Case studies in behavior modification.* New York: Holt, Rinehart, & Winston, 1965.

Umbreit, J. Effects of developmentally sequenced instruction on the rate of skill acquisition by severely handicapped students. *Journal of the Association for the Severely Handicapped,* 1980, *5,* 121-129.

Uzgiris, I. C., & Hunt, J. *Assessment in infancy: Ordinal scales of psychological development.* Chicago: University of Illinois Press, 1975.

Vincent, L. J., Salisbury, C., Walter, G., Brown, P., Gruenewald, L. J., & Powers, M. Program evaluation and curriculum development in early childhood/special education: Criteria of the next environment. In Sailor, W., Wilcox, B., & Brown, L. *Methods of instruction for severely handicapped students.* Baltimore: Paul H. Brookes, 1980.

Wolfensberger, W. *The principle of normalization in human services.* Toronto, Canada: National Institute of Mental Retardation, 1972.

2
Curriculum Content

Glenn A. Vergason

What is curriculum? How do we decide upon its content? What are the appropriate curriculum experiences? Are certain elements of curricula common to the mildly handicapped, mentally retarded, learning disabled, behavior disordered? How do special educators decide what should be taught? Who controls curriculum content — teachers, administrators, teacher educators? What curriculum changes have resulted from the shift in emphasis from self-contained classes to resource rooms? From resource rooms to the regular class?

Answers to the above questions should be available in any methods or curriculum textbook. But instead of finding answers, one often becomes even more confused. Furthermore, some textbooks are designed to indoctrinate one in a particular teaching approach rather than giving a comprehensive review of curriculum issues. Because issues related to curriculum content for handicapped students are many-faceted, simplistic explanations will not afford teachers an accurate understanding of current concerns in this area.

WHAT IS CURRICULUM?

The Dictionary of Special Education and Rehabilitation (Kelly & Vergason, 1978) defines curriculum as "a systematic grouping of activities, content, and materials of instruction offered under school supervision for the purpose of preparing students to learn and live effectively." This definition is a little different from traditional definitions of curriculum, but it serves special education well because it emphasizes the necessary key elements. It focuses on the systematic or planned sequencing of related materials. It points out that curriculum is the sum total of activities, materials, and methods, as related to future living skills. All these elements seem to be important aspects of curriculum and should be kept in mind as special educators develop curricula.

DETERMINING CURRICULUM CONTENT

Determining curriculum content has posed problems in a variety of areas. The more pervasive ones are listed, and then briefly discussed.

- Special education in the mainstream allows control of only some portion of each school day.
- Much of the special education curricular material currently available was developed when the special class model was the most common practice, and this is no longer true.
- Special education has at times overemphasized methods, materials, or media at the expense of a total curriculum.
- Special education must deal with the increasing discrepancy in ability and achievement as the student gets older.
- In its curricula, special education has to take into account the differences in cultural and ethnic backgrounds of students.
- Special education curricula must accommodate the wide range of intellectual and cognitive differences within the students it serves.
- The various areas of special education have to consider the accompanying differences in curriculum needed.
- Special education has to deal with differences in sequence and scope of materials, because of their effect on curriculum content.
- Educators do not yet know how (or if) curriculum content for the mildly retarded, mildly learning disabled, and mildly behavior disorderd is to be differentiated.

First, special education, for the most part, no longer takes place over the entire school day. Sometimes only a minor portion of the instructional time falls within the realm of special education. Consequently, special education is faced with the task of trying to influence curriculum content within a larger system in which it plays a parallel or only minor role. For that reason, impacting curriculum is becoming a greater challenge than before.

To be effective, the influence of special education and regular education on curriculum must be cooperative. Because mainstreaming has become the standard practice, curriculum content for handicapped and nonhandicapped students is of necessity the same in many situations. Regular education, faced with severe pressures by society to educate large numbers of children having vast intellectual, social, and cultural variances, cannot be expected to be totally responsive to a small subset of the total.

Special education, therefore, has its work clearly cut out to provide leadership in influencing curriculum content in the regular class, providing the proper curriculum content for the resource room, and making sure that all curricula used with children having special needs are appropriate and well coordinated.

Special education can have its greatest influence through the individualized education program, since the IEP may be the most important determiner of curriculum content for a given child. Special educators, together with the parents, are being asked, then, not only to work closely with regular education but to also become skillful catalysts in producing a sequential, rational, effective curricular program for the child.

Second, most special education curricula have been developed for the special class (self-contained) model. Meanwhile, a rapid shift was taking place away from self-contained classes, where the curriculum was 100% special education-generated, to the resource model, in which the time in special education does not exceed 49% and is often far less than that. This change in placement preference stemmed from significant litigation in the early 1970s, including effects of the landmark *Mills* and *PARC* court decisions.

A third challenge relates to special education's emphasis on methods, materials, and media. Special educators tend to overemphasize these three curricular dimensions to the outward exclusion or overshadowing of the total curriculum content. In learning disabilities, at one point the curriculum consisted of training perceptual motor skills. In behavior disorders, behavior modification became the curriculum. In mental retardation, social adjustment became the curriculum. These and other approaches have value as parts of curricula, but they are not sufficient by themselves as a total curriculum.

A fourth concern arises in the discrepancy between a child's potential and the curricular expectations as the child grows older (Wimmer, 1981). Thus, some recent literature emphasizes a differentiated curriculum at the secondary level. One gap in the secondary curriculum that has caused concern has been the absence of or lack of emphasis on appropriate content in social, vocational, and occupational skills. This has led individuals such as Brolin and Kokaska (1979), Clark (1980), and Wimmer (1981) to emphasize a separate career education curriculum.

An even greater differentiation in curricula at the secondary level seems to be a reasonable hypothesis. The schools are realizing that as students' remaining time in school starts to run out, the necessity for acquiring coping skills increases. The ultimate goal for all students is to have some means for earning a living and existing independently in the community.

Curriculum planners also have discovered vast differences in responses to curricula depending upon students' cultural and ethnic backgrounds. This has prompted Almanza and Mosley (1980) to call for curricula that more appropriately respond to the various needs of children with differing backgrounds. They, and others, have emphasized that the overrepresentation of minority students in special education may be a reflection of cultural differences. This point speaks directly to regular education, and all children of non-norm cultural and ethnic backgrounds. The curriculum has to be relevant for culturally diverse students, their occupational expectations, and their way of approaching learning materials.

Another concern relates to the wide differences in the intellectual and mental capacities of students within and among schools. A child in the mildly retarded range may be successfully mainstreamed and able to deal effectively with the curriculum in a school where the backgrounds and intellectual levels are not too far above this child. But a child with similar ability attending a socioeconomically favored school in which the average IQ is above 120 may be unable to cope with the curriculum adopted to accommodate the prevailing population of that school.

The seventh problem area relates to differences in curriculum advancement in various areas of special education. The field of mental retardation, for example, has over 50 years of experience in curriculum development. Though much of this curriculum was developed for the special class, it does provide a framework and strategies for instruction. In contrast, the fields of learning disabilities and behavior disorders have had relatively few years of experience in developing curricula. In fact, so little emphasis has been placed on curricula for use by teachers trained in behavior disorders that learning disability resource teachers are often incorporated into IEP conferences when behavior disordered children are being staffed. Since much of the curriculum in mental retardation has already been applied to other areas of education, content in areas other than mental retardation possibly can be applied across additional areas as well.

The eighth consideration discussed here concerns materials. Regular classroom materials, and those for special education, usually follow a sequence and scope, which many times are out of step with the needs of handicapped children. Sometimes teachers, including special education resource personnel, follow these materials without questioning the appropriateness of the sequence or the scope. Teachers may tend to think that if a textbook publisher put it there, it must be right.

Teachers should be encouraged to develop confidence in their own judgment. They should try to acquire the flexibility, creativity, and competence to program the materials to meet the needs of their students. Teachers are in a better position to make decisions about the best sequencing of skills and scope of curriculum content for individual students in their classes than are textbook authors who have not experienced those unique situations.

The final point of discussion here relates to differentiating curriculum content for the mildly retarded, mildly learning disabled, and mildly behavior disordered. Because these are the most prevalent groups of handicapped students in the schools (other than the speech/language impaired, for whom programs seem to be generally well-defined), and because space imposes limitations, the following pages focus primarily on the former groups. Again, since the longest tradition of curriculum development is in the field of mental retardation, research and material are more abundant in that area and for that reason receive emphasis in the ensuing discussion.

CURRICULUM APPROACHES

Heiss and Mischio (1971) suggested three directions that curriculum, particularly for the retarded, could take: (1) the unit approach; (2) task analysis; and (3) social learning approaches. The first two approaches bear directly upon the issue of how the curriculum is organized. The third bears directly upon curriculum content.

The Unit Approach

Based on the work of Ingram (1935), the unit approach entails developing specific integrated learning segments based on life experiences. For example, a unit might be developed around buying groceries and might include a visit to a grocery store; development of a grocery within the special class; and use of that grocery to teach selection of foods, the value of money, and computational, writing, and spelling skills. This type of curriculum is concrete, practical, and experienced-based. A unit is not always sequenced and sometimes neglects prerequisite skills. But the unit approach has provided direction and a basis for curricular products such as the *Illinois Curriculum Guide* (Goldstein & Seigle, 1958). Heiss and Mischio (1971) believed, however, that materials used in the unit approach were not systematic enough and were not properly sequenced.

The Task Analysis Approach

The basic concept underlying the task analysis approach to curriculum is that the teacher selects an activity or content a student is to learn and then breaks it into the various tasks involved in mastering the material. In the classic example of tying shoes, one can come up with a list of 17-35 motor steps needed to learn that skill.

The task analysis approach was facilitated by curriculum banks or inventories, as exemplified by the Brigance Inventory (1977); Meyen's Objective Cluster Bank (IBAS) (1976), the Desired Learner Outcomes (DLRs) (Cawley, 1974), and career education materials such as Brolin and Kokaska's (1979). This type of package is clearly a boon to teachers who are attempting to introduce flexibility and individualization into their teaching strategies, but task analysis is an approach toward the presentation and sequencing of materials only.

The Social Learning Curriculum

One major approach that tries to integrate curriculum with guiding theoretical construct is the social learning curriculum. Goldstein (1969) proposed that social competence is the goal of curriculum and that social competence has two characteristics: the ability to think critically and the ability to act independently. The social learning curriculum sets forth a model for integrating the social, psychological, and physical aspects of life's need areas.

Theoretical issues related to the social learning curriculum appear to be difficult for the average special education teacher to conceptualize. The theory is, however, carefully researched and conceptualized. A teacher does not have to be able to understand all the theoretical constructs of this curriculum to use it. Excellent curricular materials drawn from this model are on the market and available to teachers. The emphasis on socio-occupational areas and social competency seems quite in line with the predictions and emphasis suggested by Safer, Burnette, and Hobbs (1979) in their article, "Exploration 1993." Those authors projected that the special education curriculum will have much more socio-occupational emphasis in the future.

CATEGORIZING CURRICULUM CONTENT

Content material may be grouped into the following three categories: (1) use of the regular curriculum; (2) adaptation or modification of the regular curriculum; or (3) development of a specialized or different curriculum.

Regular Curriculum

Some programs for the handicapped advocate close adherence to the regular curriculum, insofar as possible. One example of a program successfully used to teach regular class material to special education students is based on English and biology materials researched by Breuning and Regan (1978). Mean IQs of the subject students ranged from 78 to 84. Breuning and Regan reported that the material ordinarily taught to regular class children was mastered by the 125 mildly retarded students who participated in the study. The main instructional differences in the above study involved teaching English for two hours broken into four 30-minute segments, and the same for biology. The program utilized small-group instruction and incentives such as release time to accomplish the instructional objectives.

Another option is the Directive Teaching Instructional Management System (DTIMS). This system, described by Hartman (1979), involves direct teaching of the behaviors the students need and for which they have demonstrated prerequisites. The system is based on a structured assessment of specific skills emphasizing systematic, well spelled-out objectives. Part of the system's strength is in its management or monitoring emphasis, through which teachers carefully evaluate each student's performance. The focus is on instruction in the basic skill areas of reading, spelling, math, and the like. Special education students do not follow a different curriculum;

rather, they are helped to progress as far as possible on academic skills and concepts contained in the regular curriculum.

Modified or Alternative Curriculum

An alternative curriculum called the Parallel Alternate Curriculum (PAC) has been developed by Hartwell, Wiseman and Van Reusen (1979) for mildly handicapped high school students. It translates required courses into a nonreading format including taped books, videotaped materials, movies, slides, lectures, and the like. This approach is said to be of value to children with learning and behavior disorders, especially those with reading difficulties. McDowell and Brown (1978) advocated for the behavior disordered high school student an adaptation of the traditional curriculum for some of the students and a different curriculum for others. Edwards (1980) proposed that the regular curriculum be modified for behavior disordered children in several ways. First, a different but parallel text would be written at a lower reading level. Second, poor readers would use tape recordings of regular curriculum materials. She also suggested the use of incentives such as self-graphing and reinforcement for percent correct responses.

Another example of a modified curriculum approach is that advocated by Meisgeier (1981), called the Social/Behavioral Curriculum (SBC), or synergistic approach. Meisgeier conjectured that in the mainstreaming process students are rejected by their peers because they often lack social skills, and this works against learning. The SBC program, advanced primarily for the learning disabled but applicable to others, stresses learning of social and behavior skills with primary goals to help students:

(a) communicate and interact effectively and appropriately with peers and adults;
(b) accept responsibility for personal behavior and decisions through autonomous inner-directed behavior;
(c) cope appropriately with frustration and stress;
(d) be appropriately assertive without being aggressive or passive-aggressive; and
(e) develop rational problem-solving behavior.

A similar program by Silverman, Zigmond, and Sansone (1981) advocates teaching learning strategies to help learning disabled secondary students cope with the regular curriculum and life. The skill areas to which the learning strategies apply are reading, writing, mathematics, thinking, social interaction, speaking, and listening. Listening skills, among several other areas, has only recently received the attention it deserves. The article by Robinson and Smith (1981) in this section provides many practical suggestions for a listening skills approach.

Alley and Deshler (1979) envisioned their learning strategies approach, intended primarily for the learning disabled, as being used with secondary students with reading skills above third-grade level, who can deal with symbolic as well as concrete reasoning, and whose IQs are above 85. Thus, their alternative curriculum approach is applicable to a broader range of students than just those classified as learning disabled. Within their stated parameters, some of the mildly retarded and others could benefit from it.

Special Curricula

Before the onset of the resource room movement, special curricula abounded. The unit or experience approach for mental retardation has already been discussed. Others, such as the engineered classroom (Hewett & Taylor, 1980) and the structured-stimulus approach (Cruickshank, Bentzen, Ratzeburg, & Tannhauser, 1961), were also utilized. Some professionals would argue that these programs are really teaching approaches rather than curriculum. Granted, the engineered classroom does emphasize behavior modification and token economy, but the overall approach also specifies what much of the curricular content will be. The various instructional centers (order, mastery, etc.) set up the expected content on a hierarchical basis.

In the years following mainstreaming, educators have come to realize that some special education students still need special curricula. The Social Learning Curriculum, discussed earlier, is one specific example (Goldstein, 1969). It is unique in scope and represents a major change from traditional regular class curricula.

McDowell and Brown (1978) espoused a different curriculum for behavior disordered students, organized around five functional life skill areas: (1) social curriculum; (2) academic curriculum; (3) vocational curriculum; (4) vocational training; and (5) work-study experiences. Interestingly, this curriculum bears close resemblance to many previous curricula programs for the retarded that, too, advocate use of the social-learning curriculum. McDowell and Brown's program includes some ecological elements — a highly structured environment, acquisition of specific competencies, control of time.

Clark (1980) and Brolin and Kokaska (1979) focused on a career education curriculum. They pointed out that beyond ordinary academics, the regular curriculum does little to equip the mildly handicapped for life. Clark grouped instruction around four developmental areas: (1) values, attitudes and habits; (2) human relationships; (3) occupational information; (4) job acquisition and daily living skills. Brolin and Kokaska's three major areas are similar to those of Clark. Wimmer (1981) recommended a special career education curriculum developed by the Department of Defense Dependents Schools (DODDS). It does not differ drastically from those mentioned above but does center more on small, group-directed community and vocational experiences.

DIFFERENTIATING CURRICULUM CONTENT

Children near the normal in intelligence and general functioning may be able to master much of the traditional curriculum. On the other hand, special classes and special curricula still appear best for children with lower functioning and in the moderate range of retardation.

Before 1971 special educators tended to believe that curricula for the retarded, learning disabled, and behavior disordered had to be differentiated. In actuality, much of what is appropriate for one group has also worked with others. Although behavior disordered children were viewed as having a basically affective problem, this was often accompanied by significant academic retardation. Glavin and Annesley (1971), in a study of 130 behavior disordered children, found that 81% of them were underachieving in reading and 73% were underachieving in math. More commonalities than differences may exist among the mildly handicapped.

Dangel (1981a) has differentiated curricular approaches to content in a slightly different way. He applied the terms *functional, maintenance* and *remedial.* The functional is exemplified by the Social Learning Curriculum (Goldstein, 1969) or any curriculum that differs drastically from the regular curriculum and emphasizes basic skills needed to live and cope with life's demands. The Hartwell, Wiseman and Van Reusen (1979) approach is a good example of a maintenance program. The teacher teaches or tutors skills that will allow the child to stay within the regular curriculum, by adjusting the material down to the student's level of functioning. Remedial programs, in contrast, focus on the student's developing the skills necessary to meet academic and social demands of mainstream classes. An example is the Directive Teaching Approach (Hartman, 1979), through which students are taught academic subjects to a mastery level. Figure 1 presents these three classifications, along with the most significant features of each.

In the area of academic content, one is always faced with the questions of how much, what type, how to teach it, and so on. These questions are not easy to answer. Most of the traditional areas of curriculum do appear in special education curricula or modifications of the regular curriculum. The readings that follow are directed at language, reading, spelling, written composition, math, and science curricula. Additional areas that many readers may not have thought of in connection with curriculum, such as coping strategies and listening skills, are addressed. Other unique areas, including motor development, outdoor education, and career education, are also covered. Additional areas that could have been included would be teaching good citizenship, legal rights, sex education (see Meyen, 1970, for example), and more. These topics are equally applicable to all children and represent content areas in which mainstreaming can be practiced to the optimum.

	Functional	Maintenance	Remedial
Goals	Prepare student to meet life-related demands as an alternative to mainstream program.	Support and tutor student in mainstream program, with graduation as a goal.	Remedy learning and behavior problems so the student can master mainstream material.
Procedures	Provide career and vocational programs, functional curriculum, with nonacademic emphasis.	Tutor student in mainstream to enable sufficient attainment to qualify for diploma.	Ensure basic skills (reading, written language, organizing work, etc.) needed for success in regular class.
Advantages	• Tends to be motivating. • Relevant to later life. • Student sees payoff.	• Meets school requirements. • Enhances cooperation with mainstream teachers. • Student sees payoff.	• Deals directly with the problem. • Relevant to long-term success. • Programming dictated by student's needs.
Disadvantages	• Removed from mainstream. • May require extensive support system. • May not deal with handicap.	• Doesn't deal with handicap. • May lack relevance. • Programming dictated by content rather than student's needs.	• Student may not see immediate relevance. • Payoff is long-term, not immediate. • Lacks good incentive for regular class teacher.

(from Dangel, 1981a)

FIGURE 1

Curricular and Programmatic Approaches in Special Education

A MODEL FOR CURRICULUM CONCEPTUALIZATION

Models serve a worthwhile purpose in helping to analyze and understand curriculum. One of these, developed by Heiss and Mischio (1971), is directed at the educable mentally retarded and has as its basis the Social Learning Curriculum. The model is cubical and has the three major dimensions of: curriculum (focusing on social learning, communication arts, quantitative thinking, and other), social-behavioral contexts (emphasizing a gradient from self to community), and psychoeducational processes based on those projected by Johnson and Myklebust (1967) for the learning disabled. While this model is helpful, a broader representation may be beneficial in understanding approaches, content, and skill areas. It is shown as Figure 2.

In this figure, Dimension A represents academic areas that are part of most courses of study within elementary and comprehensive high schools. Dimension B covers a large number of techniques and programs used to help students learn. Numerous other techniques/programs could be listed, but these, particularly, illustrate the relationships among academic areas, programs, and curriculum. Many techniques and programs are incorporated within the articles in this section. Dimension C represents social, psychological, and other skills necessary for students to progress effectively in school. Dimension C is not always hierarchical, but students are usually expected to develop skills from left to right on the figure. This dimension helps the teacher identify possible prerequisite skill areas that require programming and areas in which to extend existing skills. Curriculum thus involves the systematic interplay of the Dimension B techniques and programs with the Dimension C skill areas to accomplish the desired curricular outcomes under Dimension A.

WHAT FACTORS COME INTO PLAY
IN DECIDING ON A CURRICULUM?

Teachers and administrators are often faced with making curricular decisions without much to guide them. They ask how one decides if a child should go into a particular program or how one can determine if a child will succeed. Dangel (1981b) has developed the Curriculum Inventory for Decision Makers (CIDM) as an attempt to help answer many of these questions. It is represented in Figure 3.

In the CIDM, curricula are categorized by the three groupings of: functional skills (an emphasis on non-regular class or alternative experiences), maintenance (support and tutoring the student in the mainstream), and remedial (instruction viewed as necessary for the student to master the regular curriculum — e.g., teaching reading so students can learn academic subjects).

In looking at a student's records at an IEP or staffing conference, the student factors will have an effect on placement. According to this Inventory,

DIMENSION A: ACADEMIC CONTENT

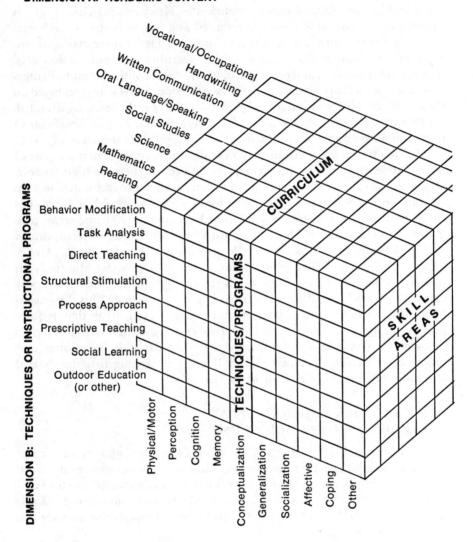

FIGURE 2
A Model for Conceptualizing Curricular Approaches, Content, and Skill Areas

	FUNCTIONAL SKILLS	MAINTENANCE	REMEDIATION
STUDENT FACTORS			
Intelligence	----------average and below----------		
		----------average and above----------	
Motivation	--------------turned off-----------------		
		----------average and above----------	
Grade Placement	--running out of time--		
		-----have some time remaining------	
Achievement Level	----< 1/3 of GP------	------------->1/3 of GP---------	
			--->1/2 of GP--
Responsibility	-----limited self-responsibility-----		
		------adequate self-responsibility--	
Expectation	--average and below--	------average and above---------	
PARENT FACTORS			
Expectations	------------low------------	------average and above------	
Support	----------------------low--------------------		
		--------------average or above--------	
MAINSTREAM ENVIRONMENT			
Level of Other Students	-----high achievers-----	---------below average---------	
		-----none----------	
Curricular Alternatives	----------none--------	----several options available----	
Teacher Acceptance	--------limited--------	-------------good-----------------	
		-----limited-----	
Teaching Style	------rigid-----------	---------------flexible----------------	
		-------rigid-------	
Administrative Support	-------limited-----------	---------------average------------	
		--excellent--	

(continued)

FIGURE 3
Curriculum Inventory for Decision Makers (CIDM)

	FUNCTIONAL SKILLS	MAINTENANCE	REMEDIATION
MAINSTREAM ENVIRONMENT (continued)			
Vocational Education Options	-------good-------	----------------none----------------	
			---limited---
Scheduling Flexibility		------none------	
	--------------------------------good--------------------------		
Credits	--given to SPE-- courses	--none for SPE-- courses	--given for SPE-- courses
SPECIAL EDUCATION ENVIRONMENT			
Caseload	----------average or above----------		
	--average or below--		--average or below--
Materials	-average or above--	--limited--	-average or above--
Teacher Training	---------------average---------------		--average or above--
	---limited---		
Teacher Motivation	---------------average---------------		--average or above--
	---limited---		
Grouping Options	-----large groups----	------------small groups------------	
Other SPE Support	------------another teacher----------------		
	---------------no other support----------		

FIGURE 3
Curriculum Inventory for Decision Makers (CIDM) (continued)

children in the lower ranges of intelligence, for example, are more likely to need a functional curriculum and less likely to benefit from maintenance or remediation programs and curricula, while those in the higher ranges may benefit most from maintenance or remediation programs and least from functional curricula. The CIDM also ascribes a substantial role to motivation and suggests that the functional curriculum is more likely to be appropriate for students who are "turned off" or doubt their ability to compete; the chances for success in maintenance and remedial programs are better if the motivation is greater.

Those involved in making curriculum content decisions for a child should also consider grade placement and achievement level. If the student has low academic skills and is in the upper teens, a specialized occupa-tional/life skills program may be appropriate. With further reference to the CIDM, responsibility and expectations are two learning contingency factors that are often overlooked but that bear upon the optimum curriculum content. Most teachers can name students whose IQ, achievement, and other factors would not suggest that they would reach an independent level, and yet these students have surpassed even the highest expectations. The teachers will tell you that those students had great drive and wanted to succeed.

The CIDM also implies a relationship between the school environment and students' success in learning. Students in high achieving schools may be less successful than they would be in schools with average or below average grade level achievement. Further, teacher acceptance and teaching style have an effect on the learning environment, though these factors are difficult to evaluate. The CIDM indicates that maintenance and remedial programs under these two areas can be either a positive or a negative force. Finally, the CIDM focuses on learning contingency factors within the special education environment.

Most teachers and administrators have at one time or another taken all these factors into consideration in curricular placement and content deci-sions, but this has usually not been done systematically. The CIDM offers a systematic look at the total learning factors. Although the factors are not intended to carry equal weight and will vary from student to student, they offer, in total, a framework within which one should be better able to reach conclusions about curriculum.

This discourse has not answered some of the questions it posed initially, but it has provided discussion and another perspective for the reader. The total curriculum is far from being negotiated at the IEP meeting, and increased understanding of the many dimensions of curriculum will help special educators to better evaluate what curriculum content for each student should be.

REFERENCES

Alley, G., & Deshler, D. *Teaching the learning disabled adolescent: Strategies and methods.* Denver: Love Publishing Co., 1979.

Almanza, H., & Mosley, W. Curriculum adaptations and modifications for culturally diverse handicapped children. *Exceptional Children,* 1980, 46, 608-614.

Breuning, S., & Regan, J. Teaching regular class material to special education students. *Exceptional Children,* 1978, *44,* 180-187.

Brigance, A. *Diagnostic inventory of basic skills.* North Billerica, MA: Curriculum Associates, 1977.

Brolin, D. K., & Kokaska, C. J. *Career education for handicapped children and youth.* Columbus, OH: Merrill Publishing, 1979.

Cawley, J. *Behavior resource guide.* Wallingford, CT: Educational Sciences, Inc., 1974.

Clark, G. H.   Career education: A concept — A challenge. In D. E. Schwartz (Ed.), *Institute on career education for the handicapped.* University, AL: Project Retool, 1980.

Cruickshank, W., Bentzen, F., Ratzeburg, F., & Tannhauser, J.   *A teaching method for brain-injured and hyperactive children.* Syracuse, NY: Syracuse University Press, 1961.

Dangel, H.   *Curricular and programmatic approaches in special education.* Unpublished material, Georgia State University, 1981. (a)

Dangel, H.   *Curriculum inventory for decision makers.* Unpublished material, Georgia State University, 1981. (b)

Edwards, L.   Curriculum modification as a strategy for helping regular classroom behavior disordered students. *Focus on Exceptional Children,* 1980, *12*(8), 1-11.

Glavin, J. P., & Annesley, F. R.   Reading and arithmetic correlates of conduct-problem and withrawn children. *Journal of Special Education,* 1971, *5*, 213-219.

Goldstein, H.   Construction of a social learning curriculum. *Focus on Exceptional Children,* 1969, *1*(2), 1-10.

Goldstein, H., & Seigle, D.   *A curriculum guide for teachers of the educable mentally handicapped.* Springfield, IL: Dept. of Public Instruction, 1958.

Hartman, C.   The directive teaching instructional management system: How it can help teachers. *Directive Teacher,* 1979, *1*, 3-5.

Hartwell, K., Wiseman, D., & Van Reusen, A.   Modifying course content for mildly handicapped students at the secondary level. *Teaching Exceptional Children,* 1979, *12*, 28-32.

Heiss, W. E., & Mischio, G.   Designing curriculum for the educable mentally retarded. *Focus on Exceptional Children,* 1971, *3*(2), 1-10.

Hewett, F. M., & Taylor, F. D.   *The emotionally disturbed child in the classroom: The orchestration of success.* Boston: Allyn & Bacon, 1980.

Ingram, C.   *The slow-learning child.* New York: Ronald Press, 1935.

Johnson, D., & Myklebust, H.   *Learning disabilities.* New York: Grune & Stratton, 1967.

Kelly, L. J., & Vergason, G. A.   *Dictionary of special education and rehabilitation.* Denver: Love Publishing Co., 1978.

McDowell, R., & Brown, G.   The emotionally disturbed adolescent: Development of program alternatives in secondary education. *Focus on Exceptional Children,* 1978, *10*(4), 1-14.

Meisgeier, C.   A social/behavioral program for the adolescent student with serious learning problems. *Focus on Exceptional Children,* 1981, *13*(9), 1-15.

Meyen, E. L.   Sex education for the mentally retarded. *Focus on Exceptional Children,* 1970, *1*(8), 1-8.

Meyen, E. L.   *Objective Cluster Bank Index (IBAS).* Bellevue, WA: Edmark Associates, 1976.

Robinson, S., & Smith, D.   Listening skills: Teaching learning disabled students to be better listeners. *Focus on Exceptional Children,* 1981, *13*(8), 1-14.

Safer, N., Burnette, J., & Hobbs, B.   Exploration 1993: The effects of future trends on services to the handicapped. *Focus on Exceptional Children,* 1979, *11*(3), 1-24.

Silverman, R., Zigmond, N., & Sansone, J.   Teaching coping skills to adolescents with learning problems. *Focus on Exceptional Children,* 1981, *13*(6), 1-20.

Wimmer, D.   Functional learning curricula in the secondary schools. *Exceptional Children,* 1981, *47*, 610-616.

Listening is a skill that can be improved with training, according to research findings. It is also a skill that may be deficient in children with learning disabilities. Significantly, this skill is required during about 45% of our waking hours. Listening exceeds talking, writing, and reading in hours of the day, and other learning and communication depend upon it.

The authors emphasize the place of listening skills in the instruction of children with learning disabilities. They propose a model to define and sequence the behaviors contained in listening, including observational guidelines to pinpoint where instruction should begin. Listening skills turn out to be complex in terms of their full scope. The authors examine the subject from the standpoint of input considerations, cognitive skills in listening, and output considerations. For each of these areas, they offer strategies for remediation and information on some of the available programs.

Listening Skills: Teaching Learning Disabled Students to be Better Listeners

Suzanne Robinson and Deborah D. Smith

A person's ability to listen with understanding is essential to good communication. Its importance in all life settings — school, job, and social interaction — cannot be denied. In the 1980s the primary forms of information dissemination require one to listen; these include TV, radio, telephone, teachers, supervisors, and friends. Research verifies that people spend the majority of each day engaged in communication, and most of that time is in listening. Rankin's (1930) thorough and often cited study of verbal communication found that 70% of an average adult's waking time was spent in either reading, writing, listening, or speaking. Further analysis of the data showed that subjects spent 30% of their waking hours each day speaking, 16%

reading, 9% writing, and 45% listening. Wilt (1949) found that children in elementary school spent 54% of their time listening. As children progress from elementary to middle to high school, listening is required for increasingly more of the school day.

Yet, the teaching of listening is often ignored or, at best, inconsistently addressed as an integral part of any school curriculum. Many teachers assume that listening skills develop automatically with other communication skills. In these areas that "develop automatically," however, the exceptional child often has great difficulty. In fact, the little research that has been conducted concerning exceptional students and listening has revealed that the learning disabled do not exhibit "normal" developmental levels of listening comprehension (Bauer, 1977; Kotsonis & Patterson, 1980). In the studies, learning disabled students as compared with "normal" peers remembered less and did not monitor whether they understood what they heard.

This difficulty with listening is observed so frequently (if not validated empirically) that the *Federal Register's* definition of learning disabilities cites disorders in listening as an identifying characteristic of the learning disabled child. Despite this, teachers often expect their learning disabled students to supplement or compensate for poor reading and writing skills with listening via tapes, films, filmstrips, or lecture. Therefore, teachers might be doing their exceptional students a disservice if they do not instruct them in how to be better listeners.

Substantial research documents that better listening can be taught. Devine (1978) reviewed this body of literature and found that direct instruction can improve listening skills. In another study Cosgrove and Patterson (1978) found that not only could listening be taught, but when given a task approach strategy (or plan on how to listen effectively) to use with one set of stimuli, the training generalized to different stimuli. In this case the task approach strategy consisted of instructions to stop the speakers and ask questions to help clarify what was heard. Often, a gain in other communication skills, such as speaking, was noted as well (Sonnenstein & Whitehurst, 1980).

Since listening skills can be taught and learning disabled children have difficulty with listening, this area of instruction should be included in curricula for these children. We are suggesting a viable approach to teaching better listening skills, in this article. We are proposing a model to define and sequence the behaviors contained in listening and observational guidelines to pinpoint where instruction should begin. These are followed by exploration of instruction using approach or cognitive strategies as a way to facilitate better listening. A review of materials currently available concludes the article.

DEFINITIONS FOR LISTENING

There is no widely accepted definition of listening. Agreement exists, however, on a few points. First, listening is more than hearing; it is more than attending to sounds. Barker (1971), after reviewing numerous definitions, defined listening as "the selective process of attending to, hearing, understanding and remembering aural symbols" (p. 17). Alley and Deshler (1979) supplemented this definition by including attention to and comprehension of nonverbal messages along with verbal messages. The nonverbal component incorporates *paralinguistic* communication, or tone of voice, loudness, speed, and pauses that convey meaning by emphasis or lack of it; and *visual* communication, which includes the visual impression the speaker creates by dress and hair style. The third element of the nonverbal component is *kinesic* communication or body movement, which consists of posture, facial expressions, and use of body parts (e.g., pointing, hand waving).

Listening also is defined qualitatively. Barbara (1957) differentiated between active and passive listening by stating:

> In the former, the individual listens with more or less his total self — including his special senses, attitudes, beliefs, feelings and intuitions. In the latter, the listener becomes mainly an organ for the passive reception of sound, with little self-perception, personal involvement, gestalt discrimination, or alive curiosity. (p. 12)

These three definitions combined describe the act of listening. More emphasis, however, should be placed on the interactional nature of listening, and any operational definition must consider the possible variations in each component.

A MODEL TO DEFINE LISTENING

Although the definitions describe the act of listening, they lack criteria that would enable the teacher to know when the listener has indeed "listened well." They do not help the teacher decide where to begin when instructing youngsters in listening skills, and they do not clearly delineate components that could be modified to improve listener performance.

Listening may indeed elude a simple behavioral definition. Yet, research has shown that identifying specific components of a task is the initial step to efficient instruction (Mager & Beach, 1967; Smith, 1981). Direct observation and measurement of a student's performance are known to be effective, when paired with instruction, in knowingly causing child change (Smith, 1981). Because listening is a complex task, this is difficult to do. Nevertheless, a model is suggested here to facilitate discussion of possible teaching strategies to increase good listening (see Figure 1).

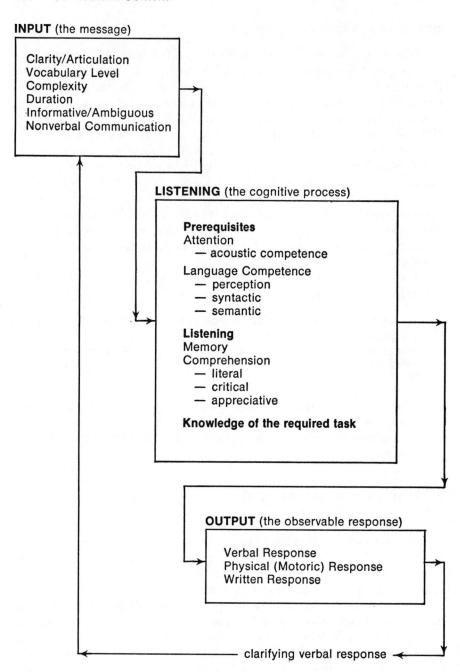

INPUT (the message)

Clarity/Articulation
Vocabulary Level
Complexity
Duration
Informative/Ambiguous
Nonverbal Communication

LISTENING (the cognitive process)

Prerequisites
Attention
— acoustic competence

Language Competence
— perception
— syntactic
— semantic

Listening
Memory
Comprehension
— literal
— critical
— appreciative

Knowledge of the required task

OUTPUT (the observable response)

Verbal Response
Physical (Motoric) Response
Written Response

clarifying verbal response

FIGURE 1
A Model to Define Listening

Listening skills are divided into three major parts: input (or the message), listening, and output (or observable response). An awareness of all three is essential for appropriate instruction. Each part of the listening sequence has several components. A description of each follows.

Input — the Message

Input, or the message, consists of the words, sounds, and nonverbal message the "speaker" conveys to the "listener." The way in which these components interact has an effect on listening (Alley & Deshler, 1979; Barker, 1971; Ironsmith & Whitehurst, 1978; Sonnenschein & Whitehurst, 1980). A short description of each characteristic of the message follows.

Clarity/Articulation

Clarity of articulation refers to the mechanics of creating sounds. If someone's speech is poorly articulated, or if there is a difference in dialect, the message is more difficult for the listener to perceive. If competing sounds or noises are present in the environment, this also interferes with the clarity of the message.

Vocabulary Level

The speaker's level or range of vocabulary influences the listener's ability to respond appropriately. If the vocabulary in the message is too difficult, the listener is not likely to understand the message.

Complexity

Complexity refers to the type of message the speaker wants to convey. The conceptual level expressed, though possibly framed in simple vocabulary, may be more sophisticated than the listener has encountered in past experience.

Duration

The length of the message can affect the listener. Too much material or repetitions of the same information can be confusing.

Informative/Ambiguous

Research has shown that children have difficulty detecting the difference between ambiguous and informative messages, although this ability improves at a consistent rate through the beginning of adolescence (Asher, 1976;

Ironsmith & Whitehurst, 1978). Therefore, quality of the message plays a part in the listener's ability to respond appropriately.

Nonverbal Messages

Much has been written about the messages people convey nonverbally (Gordon, 1970; Shelton, 1974). In addition to auditory clues, the listener must comprehend visual clues that signify certain emphases. For example, mood, emotional importance of the message to the speaker, or important points can be conveyed nonverbally.

Obviously, the message can become complex, and the possible variations are infinite. The listener must exhibit great flexibility in listening, to receive and then act upon many different messages.

Listening — The Cognitive Process

What is necessary for the listener to take a message and transform it into an appropriate response? At this point in the listening process, the exceptional child often has difficulty. Yet, little research has been done to examine the learning disabled child's listening behavior. Some possible components necessary for good listening behavior, however, have been identified.

Prerequisite Skills

Attention. First, there are some prerequisite skills to listening. One of these is attention. The listener must attend to the speaker.

Acoustic competence. The next prerequisite skill is acoustic competence. The listener must be able to hear correctly that which was said. A person's acoustic competence, or acuity, must be sufficient for accurate reception of the messages.

Language competence. The third prerequisite skill is language competence. One must be able to *perceive* and discriminate the various sounds and combinations of sounds used to create words. One must have the *syntactic* and *semantic* skills to allow understanding of what the speaker is saying. Within the child's repertoire must be the vocabulary to allow for decoding and understanding the message. The level of language competence, therefore, either facilitates or interferes with good listening.

Listening

Comprehension. What a person does to "understand" or "comprehend" is not clearly understood. One can tell, however, when comprehension occurs because of the response the listener gives. For example, a person may give a complex set of directions over the phone to meet a friend somewhere. That person does or does not arrive at the destination depending on whether the message was understood. Or a child, after hearing a story, might later restate it to someone else, indicating that the child "understood" what was heard.

Memory. Memory appears to be important and intrinsic to comprehension. If the information is not encoded or remembered, the cognitive processes to interpret the information cannot occur (Humphreys, Hall, & Wilson, 1980). Comprehension activities, which incorporate memory, range from simple to complex. Alley and Deshler (1979), in their review of listening taxonomies, compiled a detailed sequence (please refer to Table 1) that can be used to further define the many levels of comprehension.

TABLE 1
Listening Sequence to Define Comprehension

1. Understanding words and concepts, and building a listening vocabulary

2. Understanding sentences and other linguistic elements of language

3. Auditory memory

4. Listening Comprehension (literal)

   a. Understanding the relationship of details to main ideas
   b. Following directions
   c. Following the sequence of the message
   d. Listening for details
   e. Listening to a question with an intent to answer
   f. Repeating what has been heard

5. Critical Listening (evaluative/inference)

   a. Recognizing absurdities
   b. Recognizing propaganda
   c. Correct me
   d. Finishing stories
   e. Distinguishing between fact and opinion
   f. Detecting bias and prejudice
   g. Distinguishing between emotive and report language
   h. Evaluating speaker's argument
   i. Drawing inferences and making judgments
   j. Understanding sales pressure
   k. Recognizing repetition of the same idea in different words

6. Appreciative Listening

   a. Listening to visualize
   b. Listening for rhythms of speech
   c. Recognizing tone and mood
   d. Appreciating speaker's style
   e. Interpreting character from dialogue
   f. Understanding effect on listeners of speaker's vocal quality
   g. Understanding effect of audience on listener's reactions.

From *Teaching the Learning Disabled Adolescent: Strategies and Methods,* by G. Alley and D. Deshler (Denver: Love Publishing Co., 1979), p. 282.

Output — The Observable Response

The third major component of the listening model is output, or the listener's response. This component is necessary for teachers to have verification that acceptable listening has taken place. Instructional success, therefore, must be measured by evaluating the listener's response. Three outputs or responses are possible: a *motoric* response (body movement), a *verbal* response, and a *written* response. A verbal response that clarifies the input and starts the sequence again is in fact a strategy to increase comprehension and is discussed in greater depth later.

IMPLICATIONS FOR INSTRUCTION

Pinpointing Areas of Difficulty

Direct observation and measurement of a child's performance represent an effective way to target the learner's entry level in any instructional situation. Difficulties in using this procedure to measure listening performance stem from the lack of consensus regarding the essential components of listening and difficulty in controlling the environment (or the message) sufficiently to measure listening adequacy consistently. Still, if one adopts a sequence of listening behaviors, observational data about various listening tasks and the child's listener characteristics can be collected.

The first step for efficient instruction is to identify the listening skills the learner possesses or lacks. The second step is to analyze the speaker's message or communication skills. Finally, one must be aware of the interaction and environmental climate in which the listener and speaker are involved.

Attention

Referring back to the listening model (see Figure 1), it is evident that learning disabled children often have difficulty in many or all of the skills involved in the cognitive process of listening. Research on attentional deficits in learning disabled students is substantial (Tarver & Hallahan, 1974). The learning disabled child often has difficulty filtering out extraneous stimuli and attending selectively to the focal task. The absence of this prerequisite skill may inhibit good listening behavior; thus, attempts should be made to identify it at the learner's entry level.

Language Competence

Language competence is another prerequisite skill. The possible language problems a learning disabled child may have are well documented

(Wiig & Semel, 1980). If a child's semantic and syntactic language skills are not as sophisticated as those contained in the message, the child could have trouble responding properly.

Memory

In recent years learning disabled children have been characterized as "inactive learners" (Torgesen, 1977). Inactive learners do not approach tasks efficiently, and they are not aware of the responsibility in utilizing information to complete learning tasks independently. Active participation requires learners to be aware of their own cognitive processes, strengths and weaknesses, and demands of the task. Active learners use this awareness to apply cognitive strategies to ensure goal completion. Children who actively organize and structure the information they receive do better on memory tasks than children who do not.

From research on the development of memory, the concept of active participation in learning appears intrinsic to normal development. Researchers have demonstrated the importance of active rehearsal strategies in memory tasks (Flavell, 1971; Hagen, 1967; Keeny, Cannizzo & Flavell, 1967). Others (Bauer, 1977; Hallahan & Kneedler, 1979; Lloyd, 1980) have shown that the lack of such strategies (such as rehearsal or organization) in memorization attempts by both learning disabled and normal children results in poorer performance than was exhibited by those who used such memory strategies. Therefore, a child deficient in memorization strategies could experience difficulty in responding accurately after listening to a message.

Comprehension

If a child does not comprehend the information given, that child will have difficulty responding appropriately to the message. Research has shown that a child's monitoring comprehension (that is, the ability to evaluate one's level of understanding of incoming messages) progresses developmentally throughout the elementary years. Younger children do not discriminate as easily as do older children whether information given is adequate for understanding (Ironsmith & Whitehurst, 1978; Markman, 1977).

Little research has compared the development of comprehension monitoring in normal children to that of learning disabled children. In one study, Kotsonis and Patterson (1980) found that learning disabled youngsters of varying ages consistently felt they had enough information to do the task when in fact they did not. Their skills in comprehension monitoring were significantly less than those of their normal peers. This lack in evaluation of message quality could cause difficulty in successfully completing a listening task.

Knowledge of the Task Required

Finally, the teacher must make sure the child can in fact do the requested task. For example, if the child is asked to respond to a message by writing, the child must know how to write. The child must also be able to write the words required in the response. Assessment by the teacher of the appropriateness of the performance mode is essential to planning an instructional sequence.

INTERVENTION STRATEGIES

Modifying Speaker Input

Listening skills can be taught in a variety of ways. An underlying structure or sequence is desirable to increase the flow of skill acquisition. Using the model suggested here, intervention strategies either modify and control the input, modify the listening behavior, or modify both at the same time. First, intervention can take place with the speaker (see Table 2). The message can be modified to increase attention, accommodate listener language competence, or facilitate the listener's memory and comprehension skills. This controlled message can be varied, depending on listener competence, at each level of the comprehension sequence (i.e., literal comprehension, critical listening, appreciative listening, and their respective subskills).

Controlling input to accommodate the learner's level of task proficiency is an instructional strategy often used in teaching exceptional children. To control the content of the message, the speaker must first be aware of factors influencing listener comprehension: clarity, vocabulary level, complexity of ideas presented, duration, informative quality, and nonverbal components. Specific modifications of the input, depending on listener characteristics, can then take place.

Attention

The speaker can facilitate listener attention in a variety of ways. Telling the child to listen or indicating that what will be said next is important can focus the child's attention on the task. Some researchers have found reinforcement or teacher attention to be an effective strategy to increase attending (Hallahan & Kauffman, 1975; Kazdin, 1973). Controlling the environment by reducing extraneous noise or increasing proximity of the speaker to the listener are other useful techniques to promote attention. The speaker can also use a visual aid to focus the listener on important points.

TABLE 2
Strategies to Modify Input (The Message)

INPUT	INTERVENTIONS
Attention—Focusing the listener's attention on the speaker	1. Give direct instruction (Example: "Listen to what I'm going to say").
	2. Shorten input.
	3. Use visual aid.
	4. Reduce extraneous stimuli.
	5. Increase proximity of speaker to listener.
Language	1. Simplify vocabulary.
	2. Restate message.
	3. Simplify syntax.
Memory—The speaker's facilitating listener recall	1. Use high frequency words.
	2. Disseminate group information in easily associated categories.
	3. Use groupings categorized by semantic membership (what they are) rather than where or when.
	4. Control message length.
	5. Control linguistic (or surface) structure.
	6. Control restatements — should be exact or will confuse.
	7. Control serial position of information — information given last is remembered best, information given in the middle is forgotten most easily.
	8. Use careful phrasing — can group words or elements for listener.
	9. Increase relevance of material to listener — increases recall.
Comprehension	Provide practice at all levels of literal, critical, and appreciative comprehension.

Language Competence

The speaker must be aware of the listener's functional levels in areas of syntax and vocabulary. Input can then be simplified, shortened, or restated to facilitate task completion by the listener. When adequate listening performance is hampered by the student's lack of language proficiency, in-depth language development intervention could be necessary.

Memory

Enhancement of listener recall can be consistently and systematically addressed if the speaker is knowledgeable of the organizational strategies used in memorization. Wiig and Semel (1980) have discussed in depth various elements that can be controlled in intervention. These variables are word frequency, associative strength, logical relationships, linguistic structure, length, serial position, information, and salience or immediate relevance.

Words commonly used in everyday speech are considered high frequency words. High frequency words tend to be recalled more easily than low frequency words (Wiig & Semel, 1980). Therefore, this variable should be controlled in planned interventions. Numerous resources that list high frequency words are available (Dolch, 1936; Thorndike & Lorge, 1944).

Associative strength refers to the connection that can be made between important words in a message. Words that have a strong association, such as "knife, fork, spoon," are easier to recall by chunking together than is a series like "dog, car, apple." This logical grouping can be analyzed further. The type of association between important words is hierarchical in ease of recall. Words that can be grouped by semantic class membership (*what:* fruits — apples, oranges, peaches) are easier to remember than those grouped spatially (*where:* in the refrigerator — milk, catsup, meat) or by temporal relationships (*when:* at night — moon, dark, sleep) (Wiig & Semel, 1980).

Other variables that can be controlled to facilitate recall are: linguistic structure, length, and serial position. Wiig and Semel (1980) stated that interchanging words with similar meaning (as in restating a message) go unnoticed when they occur within 25 to 30 seconds. Changes are noticed (and can thus confuse), however, if the delay between repetitions of similar statements is longer than 30 seconds. Conversely, restatements that change the meaning of the sentence are recognized if the delay between repetitions is no more than 45 seconds. Therefore, restating a message must be done carefully because, if done poorly, it can confuse the listener and impair recall.

Simplifying sentence structure is another modification that can improve listener recall. At times, simplification of sentence structure entails shortening the sentence or decreasing the number of clauses or transformations. But not all long statements are difficult to remember. Related clauses can be chunked together and more easily remembered than an equal number of critical, unrelated words contained in one short sentence.

The position of critical words or ideas in a sentence can facilitate recall. Final words are easier to remember than initial words, and ideas or words in middle positions are most difficult to recall. These effects are called *primacy* (initial word) recall in contrast to *frequency* (last word) recall. Many learning disabled and developmentally delayed youngsters remember the last words or ideas presented and forget those given first (Bauer, 1977; Hallahan & Kneedler, 1979). The sequence of ideas or elements in the message can be controlled so that essential information is presented last.

Finally, intonational features and relevance of the message can influence recall. Phrasing, which chunks groups of words together, can facilitate listener recall. Also, relevance of the words or message to the listener can affect desire and ability to remember. The speaker must be aware of what is important or relevant to the listener and formulate messages with that in mind. This can be done by asking the listener about interests, hobbies, and preferences, and then incorporating that information in framing the message.

Comprehension

When planning interventions that modify the speaker's role, all these elements that facilitate adequate listener performance must be considered. Then, message types accommodating the different levels of comprehension skills must be formed and the child's competence at each level noted

Modifying Listening Behavior

Whenever possible, controlling input can ease the burden of children who have difficulty listening well, and it can facilitate their learning the lesson or message. To control all input (considering the variables listed), however, is a formidable, if not impossible, task for even the most conscientious of teachers. Also, one must question whether this would be in the youngster's best interests. Since so much time is spent listening to a wide variety of messages in differing contexts for varied purposes, students should learn strategies that enable them to distill meaning from uncontrolled messages.

Interventions, therefore, should be directed at changing listening behavior. Cognitive and task approach strategies seem appropriate for a number of reasons. First, these intervention techniques appear to promote generalization of strategies learned to other similar situations (Cosgrove & Patterson, 1978; Douglas, Parry, Marton, & Garson, 1976; Keogh & Barkett, 1979). Uncontrolled messages require situation-specific task performance by the listener. Strategy training that generalizes across classes of problems, therefore, appears to be a logical instructional tactic. Second, the focus of these techniques is on creating change in the child's cognitions (the way he or she thinks). Considering how complex and variable listening tasks are, training cognitive skills rather than changing situation-specific behaviors seems more practical.

Cognitive strategies have been defined by Meichenbaum (1980) as strategies that focus on the learner's self-control, self-awareness, and conscious participation in organizing learning. Cognitive strategies typically require students to act as their own trainers or teachers. Verbalization of the instructional sequence or strategy by the learner is typically included. The teacher models the tactic, and then the child practices it and is encouraged to delay responding, to evaluate different alternative approaches. For example, the child might verbalize, "It's time to listen. What's my plan? Am I following my plan?" Cognitive strategies are more general in nature than are task approach strategies. Task approach strategies (or attack strategies) are more specific to a particular problem and require learning a small set of rote subskills or rules to apply to a specific class of problems (e.g., learning specific strategies that aid memorization) (Lloyd, 1980).

The combination of both intervention techniques seems appropriate to teaching general listening strategies. Maker (1981), in reviewing some of the literature on listening and the learning disabled, found many researchers to be in agreement: *Students deficient in listening skills can perform as well as normal children after training consisting of verbal rehearsal, strategies of associative clustering, general organizational strategies, or mnemonics.* Specific intervention tactics that focus on changing the listener's approach without controlling the input are listed here (and in Table 3) for each level of the listening sequence.

Attention

A number of recent studies exploring attentional deficits of the learning disabled found that modeling, self-instruction, and reinforcement, in combination increased attention in the learner (Camp, Blom, Herbert, & vanDoorninck, 1977; Douglas et al., 1976; Meichenbaum & Goodman, 1971). As an example of such an instructional strategy, the teacher might first provide a verbal model: "Okay, I'm getting ready to listen. I have to remember to listen for important points . . ." After listening to a message, the teacher then models: "Now what was said?" (restates the message) "What are the important points? What am I supposed to do next?" The child practices the self-instructional techniques and then does the task. Feedback on completion of the task, along with reinforcement, completes the instructional sequence. Finally, the child fades out verbalized self-instruction and then uses internalized speech to direct task performance.

TABLE 3
Strategies to Modify Listening Behavior

LISTENING BEHAVIOR	INTERVENTIONS
Attention	1. Peer modeling.
	2. Teacher modeling.
	3. Verbal rehearsal.
	4. Reinforcement.
	5. Physical guidance.
Language	1. Increase in vocabulary.
	2. Increase in knowledge of multiple word meanings.
	3. Increase in syntactic skills.
Memory	1. Rehearsal during listening.
	2. Clustering or chunking information.
	3. Coding information (POP for people, organizations, populations; etc.).
	4. Visualization.
	5. Question asking.
	6. Identifying organizational cues (First . . ., second . . ., etc.).
	7. Rehearsal after listening.
	8. Summarizing message after listening.
	9. Comparing information received to develop categories.
Comprehension	1. Practice at all levels of literal, critical, and appreciative comprehension.
	2. Practice identifying nonverbal messages.

Abikoff (1979) evaluated 13 studies that used cognitive training to decrease impulsivity and hyperactivity and increase attending, and found the success of such strategies equivocal. The major difficulty appeared to lie not with the strategy itself but in the assumption that all impulsive or attentional behaviors belong to one response class (e.g., assuming impulsive task approach is similar to impulsive, inappropriate class behavior). No evidence suggests that such is the case. Therefore, although cognitive strategies are effective in improving attention when measured within the context of one response class (listening as contrasted with classroom play or written assignments), careful assessment of task requirements should take place before instruction. If the task requirements are similar, generalization or transfer of attentional skills for listening should occur.

Language Competence

If a student appears to be having difficulty in completing listening tasks because of deficiencies in language development, instruction in specific areas of language development is most appropriate. Interventions aimed at increasing *vocabulary*, knowledge of word meanings, and syntax might all be necessary. Language instruction, however, is not the focus of this article. Readers interested in specific language strategies should consult Wiig and Semel (1980) or any of the excellent language development programs commonly in use.

Memory

General memory and organizational strategies given here are a compilation from a number of sources (Alley & Deshler, 1979; Barker, 1971; Lundsteen, 1971; Maker, 1981). Instruction in such strategies is aimed at facilitating recall of messages containing any type or amount of information. Again, the intervention is planned to change listening behavior.

Strategies Used During the Task

Rehearsal has been shown to be an effective strategy in increasing recall. The listener should repeat and review what was said during the listening situation. The difference between thought speed and speech speed makes this possible. People can process information twice as fast as they can speak. Rehearsal strategies encourage active participation by the listener — a noted deficiency in many learning disabled youngsters.

Clustering or chunking information is another memory strategy. The student is taught to group ideas under an identifying characteristic. This strategy is facilitated by verbal rehearsal.

Coding is another mnemonic device. Here, the student needs to remember the first letter of each word in a series. The letters cue the appropriate response. Arranging such cues in a more easily recalled sequence (e.g., forming a word with the letters) is a variation of this tactic.

Students also can be encouraged to visualize the information contained in the message. The effectiveness of this technique depends on the type of information given. Concrete information is more easily visualized in an appropriate environment.

Asking questions of the speaker appears to activate participation in listening and recall besides clarifying unfamiliar vocabulary or concepts (Cosgrove & Patterson, 1978; Patterson & Massad, 1980). Many learning disabled children, however, have difficulty monitoring their comprehension, and thus may be unable to formulate information-enhancing questions.

Sonnenschein and Whitehurst (1980) found that children improve their communication (speaking and monitoring comprehension) by watching poor communication between peers, but they did not improve when watching an adult engaged in poor message giving. A possible instructional strategy derived from this study is to have children model a communication situation with a speaker and listener and then have other children analyze good as contrasted with poor question asking. As a result, listeners might learn to modify the message and message giver to meet their comprehension needs.

Another memory strategy is to look for organizational cues. The student learns phrases that speakers use to organize and emphasize important information. Phrases like, "the next three steps," "the main point I want to make," "first, second . . . finally," and so on should be used to focus attention. Comparing information is another organizational tool. The listener is to note similarities and differences, and then categorize the information accordingly. Identifying main ideas and supporting details and separating them from irrelevant information is another skill that organizes input and aids recall. Taking notes is an extension of this skill and can aid memorization for older students.

Strategies Used After Listening

Some memory strategies can be applied after the listening task. Students can verbally review what they heard. They might be asked to identify the organizational strategies they are using to remember the information. Reviewing notes is a similar strategy to increase retention of material. Requiring the student to summarize the message can also enable synthesizing or active participation with the input and can enhance comprehension.

Comprehension

Comprehension and memory strategies are interconnected. The content of the message provides a vehicle for practicing the aforementioned strategies. Learning to apply general or specific learning strategies at one level of comprehension does not inevitably generalize to a different level of comprehension, but research does indicate that general or specific attack strategies enhance generalization across classes (Keogh & Glover, 1980; Lloyd, Saltzman

& Kauffman, 1980). Therefore, learners must have practice in each area of comprehension. For example, messages in literal, critical, and appreciative listening must be provided, along with training in how to interpret nonverbal messages, to measure listening proficiency. Video tapes or modeling of nonverbal message giving could be used to elicit evaluation of possible meanings.

Cognitive strategies appear to be viable aids in the measurement of listener success. By requiring verbalization before and after listening, the teacher can evaluate the student's level of success with specific or general comprehension strategies. Depending upon evaluation of the verbal, written, or motoric responses required of the listener, the teacher can plan more practice, a different intervention, or conclude current instruction depending upon the degree of behavior change exhibited.

MATERIALS REVIEW

Many commercial materials are available to aid the teacher in listening instruction. The complexity of listening skills, however, means that no one material meets the needs of all exceptional students. Variables such as language level, attention span, reading level, response format of the material, and *always* an assessment of the specific listening skills in which each student needs instruction must be considered before matching materials to instructional plans. A short review of a few commercial materials available is included here, to illustrate the range of skills addressed in various programs.

Listening to the World, by R. Goldman & M. E. Lynch. Circle Pines, MN: America Guidance Service, 1980.

This program has been designed to teach five listening skills: (1) auditory discrimination (environmental as well as speech sounds), (2) selective auditory attention (listening for important sounds and ignoring distracting sounds), (3) auditory vigilance (listening for particular words or sounds), (4) hypothesis testing (identifying words obscured or absent from sentences and then filling in by context clues), and (5) auditory memory skills (including visualization, rehearsal, grouping, and linking). The program provides for practice at varying levels of difficulty as well as lessons that combine the various skills.

The materials are intended for children in kindergarten and early primary grades, and the content reflects the interests of that age level. The 90 lessons can be presented in a variety of ways, including oral presentation by the teacher, tapes and records, songs to be played on the piano, and use of rhythm instruments. Lessons run 15 to 25 minutes each, and the children respond orally, motorically, or by using a gameboard. Reading is not required by the student.

This program is adaptable to use with exceptional students and includes suggested behavioral objectives for individualized education plans. Extra activities are not provided for students requiring more practice, though there are suggested activities to be done at home with the family. Teacher participation and instruction is intrinsic to the program, the student could not use this material independently.

Auditory Perception Training II: Listening Skills, by R. Willette, B. Galofaro, & I. Peckins. Niles, IL: Developmental Learning Materials, 1980.

This new program is modeled after and is a continuation of the well-known *DLM Auditory Perception Training Program.* It has been developed for middle school or junior high students with identified listening skills deficits. It has been designed to train listening skills in the areas of: figure ground (attending to instructions while ignoring background noise), memory (including practice in remembering sequence and fact recall), imagery (forming a visual image from verbal information), and motor responding (following verbal directions with various motoric responses). The content reflects interests and activities common to middle and junior high students.

Reading proficiency at approximately third grade level is needed to complete lessons in the memory component. Proficiency in simple addition, subtraction, writing of three place numbers, and knowledge of money concepts, as well as reading are required to complete some lessons in the figure ground component. Little or no reading is required in the motor and imagery sections of the program.

Lessons are 10 to 15 minutes in duration, and students respond on worksheets while listening to the tapes. This program's format allows for the students' independent use. The 20 lessons are divided into two levels for each component. A short list of activities is suggested, in the teacher manual for each component, for students requiring more practice.

Auditory Perceptual Enhancement Program, Volumes 1-4. Tulsa, OK: Modern Education Corporation, 1978.

Four separate components make up this listening skills program. Volume I consists of nine tapes, two lessons per tape, called "Auditory Memory Chunking Techniques." This component contains lessons in the memory organizational skills of chunking by association and categorization. Volume II contains 11 lessons in discrimination of words in isolation and in sentences. Volume III's 18 lessons provide instruction in following directions. Volume IV is titled "Improving Listening Skills: Critical Listening and Speed Listening." This component's objectives are to increase alertness, to evaluate orally presented information, and to retain factual information.

The program is designated by the publishers as appropriate for elementary students through gifted and junior/senior high school students. This suggests a substantial range in material difficulty within each program, with little practice at any desired level. Previewing the tapes may be a more appropriate way to assess difficulty of materials. Lesson length varies from 7 to 20 minutes. The student listens to a taped lesson and responds on a worksheet or paper. This format allows for individual pacing and independent use of the material.

Scholastic Listening Skills. Unit I: Easy Ears. Unit II: Ear-power (H. Benham, Ed.). New York: NY: Scholastic Book Services, 1977.

Many educators consider listening comprehension and reading comprehension as complimentary skills, and this program combines listening skills with reading. Unit I consists of 40 lessons that cover: following directions, sequence, main idea, predicting outcome, understanding character, drawing conclusions, discrimination of selected sounds, and rhyming. Targeted age ranges are first through third grades, and the worksheets require reading at the first to second grade level. Unit II also contains listening comprehension instruction and specifically addresses listening for significant details, sequencing, finding proof, main ideas, identifying supporting details, predicting outcomes, inferences, drawing conclusions, discriminating between fact and opinion, problem solving, and finding word meaning through context.

This unit is intended for upper elementary age children, and worksheets require reading at approximately the third to fourth grade reading level, though some sheets demand more reading than others. Youngsters can work independently at their own pace because of the tape format, which includes instruction, though independent student usage is not recommended by its authors.

These programs are only examples of the variety of materials available to teachers. The range of listening skills covered by the different programs is evident, and the need for teacher discretion in material selection is essential. Assessment of students' entry levels and instructional needs in relation to the listening skills sequence is necessary for appropriate instruction to take place.

IMPLICATIONS

Evidence that instruction in listening should be incorporated in comprehensive curricula for exceptional children cannot be refuted. Demands often are placed on these children to listen more in lieu of inefficient or dysfunctional reading and writing skills. Therefore, it seems somewhat

shortsighted that the issues in developing systematic instructional procedures have been skirted by many special educators. We believe that by
developing an operational definition to frame an intervention sequence and
then systematically applying those interventions, measurable improvement
in listening behavior can occur. Cognitive and task attack strategies seem a
logical approach to intervention. Teaching youngsters strategies that generalize across response classes is practical and efficient considering the
variability of messages.

Research substantiates these assumptions, but the need for considerably
more research centering on the listening behavior of exceptional children is
evident. Research should be directed toward identification of listener characteristics in exceptional children and verification of intervention effectiveness. Until a broader research base is developed, the paradigm for listening
instruction developed here is a viable and reasonable approach to instruction.

REFERENCES

Abikoff, H. Cognitive training interventions in children: Review of a new approach. *Journal of Learning Disabilities*, 1979, *12*, 129-135.

Alley, G., & Deshler, D. *Teaching the learning disabled adolescent: Strategies and methods.* Denver: Love Publishing Co., 1979.

Asher, S. R. Children's ability to appraise their own and another person's communication performance. *Developmental Psychology*, 1976, *12*, 24-32.

Auditory Perceptual Enhancement Problems, Vols. 1-4, Tulsa, OK: Modern Education Corp., 1978.

Barbara, D. *The art of listening.* Springfield, IL: Charles C Thomas, 1957.

Barker, L. L. *Listening behavior.* Englewood Cliffs, NJ: Prentice-Hall, 1971.

Bauer, R. H. Memory processes in children with learning disabilities: Evidence for deficient rehearsal. *Journal of Experimental Child Psychology*, 1977, *24*, 415-430.

Benham, H. (Ed.). *Scholastic listening skills.* New York, NY: Scholastic Book Services, 1977.

Camp, B. W., Blom, G. E., Herbert, F., & van Doorninck, W. J. Think aloud: A program for developing self-control in young aggressive boys. *Journal of Abnormal Child Psychology*, 1977, *5*, 157-169.

Cosgrove, J. M., & Patterson, C. J. Generalization of training for children's listener skills. *Child Development*, 1978, *49*, 513-516.

Devine, T. G. Listening: What do we know after 50 years of research and theorizing? *Journal of Reading*, Jan. 1978, pp. 296-304.

Dolch, E. W. A basic sight vocabulary. *Elementary School Journal*, 1936, *36*, 456-460.

Douglas, V. I., Parry, P., Marton, P., & Garson, C. Assessment of a cognitive training program for hyperactive children. *Journal of Abnormal Child Psychology*, 1976, *4*, 389-410.

Flavell, J. H. What is memory development the development of? *Human Development*, 1971, *14*, 272-278.

Goldman, R., & Lynch, M. E. *Listening to the world.* Circle Pines, MN: American Guidance Service, 1980.

Gordon, T. *Parent effectiveness training.* New York: Peter H. Wyden, 1970.

Hagen, J. W. Some thoughts on how children learn to remember. *Human Development*, 1967, *14*, 262-271.

Hallahan, D. P., & Kauffman, J. M.   Research on the education of distractible and hyperactive children. In W. M. Cruickshank & D. P. Hallahan (Eds.), *Perceptual and learning disabilities in children: Research and theory* (Vol. 2). Syracuse, NY: Syracuse University Press, 1975.

Hallahan, D. P., & Kneedler, R. D. *Strategy deficits in the information processing of learning disabled youngsters* (Technical Report #6). Charlottesville, VA: University of Virginia Learning Disabilities Research Institute, 1979.

Humphreys, M. S., Hall, J. W., & Wilson, K. P. *Incomplete encoding and susceptibility to interference among children with school achievement problems* (US HEW OE 300770493). Chicago: University of Illinois Institute for Learning Disabilities, 1980. (Research paper)

Ironsmith, M., & Whitehurst, G. J. The development of listener abilities in communication: How children deal with ambiguous information. *Child Development,* 1978, *49,* 348-352.

Kazdin, A. E. The effect of vicarious reinforcement on attentive behavior in the classroom. *Journal of Applied Behavior Analysis,* 1973, *6,* 71-78.

Keeny, T. J., Cannizzo, S. R., & Flavell, H. H. Spontaneous and induced verbal rehearsal in a recall task. *Child Development,* 1967, *38,* 953-966.

Keogh, B. K., & Barkett, C. J.   An educational analysis of hyperactive children's achievement problems. In C. Whalen & B. Henker (Eds.), *Hyperactive children: The social ecology of identification and treatment.* New York: Academic Press, 1979.

Keogh, B. K., & Glover, A. T. The generality and durability of cognitive training effects. *Exceptional Education Quarterly,* 1980, *1,* 75-82.

Kotsonis, M., & Patterson, C. J.   *Comprehension monitoring in learning disabled youngsters* (Technical Report #19). Charlottesville, VA: University of Virginia Learning Disabilities Research Institute, 1980.

Lloyd, J. Academic instruction and cognitive techniques: The need for attack strategy training. *Exceptional Education Quarterly,* 1980, *1,* 53-63.

Lloyd, J., Saltzman, N. J., & Kauffman, J. M. *Predictable generalization in academic learning by preskills and strategy training* (Technical Report #23). Charlottesville, VA: University of Virginia Learning Disabilities Research Institute, 1980. (BEH/OE 300770495)

Lundsteen, S. W. *Listening: Its impact on reading and the other language arts.* Urbana, IL: National Council of Teachers of English, Educational Resources Information Center, Clearing House on the Teaching of English, 1971.

Mager, R. F., & Beach, K. M., Jr. *Developing vocational instruction.* Belmont, CA: Lear Siegler, Inc./Fearon Publishers, 1967.

Maker, C. J.   Problem solving. In D. D. Smith, *Teaching the learning disabled.* Englewood Cliffs, NJ: Prentice-Hall, 1981.

Markman, E. Realizing that you don't understand: A preliminary investigation. *Child Development,* 1977, *48,* 953-956.

Meichenbaum, D. Cognitive behavior modification with exceptional children: A promise yet unfilled. *Exceptional Education Quarterly,* 1980, *1,* 83-88.

Meichenbaum, D., & Goodman, J. Training impulsive children to talk to themselves: A means of developing self-control. *Journal of Abnormal Psychology,* 1971, *77,* 115-126.

Patterson, C. J., & Massad, C. M. Facilitating referential communication among children: The listener as teacher. *Journal of Experimental Child Psychology,* 1980, *29,* 357-370.

Rankin, P. T. Listening ability: Its importance, measurement and development. *Chicago Schools Journal,* 1930, *12,* 177-179.

Shelton, M. N. Body language in the classroom. *New Mexico School Review,* 1974, *50*(4), 24-25.

Smith, D. D. *Teaching the learning disabled.* Englewood Cliffs, NJ: Prentice-Hall, 1981.

Sonnenschein, S., & Whitehurst, G. J. The development of communication: When a bad model makes a good teacher. *Journal of Experimental Child Psychology,* 1980, *3,* 371-390.

Tarver, S. G., & Hallahan, D. P. Attention deficits in children with learning disabilities: A review. *Journal of Learning Disabilities,* 1974, *7,* 560-569.

Thorndike, E. L., & Lorge, T. *The teacher's workbook of 30,000 words.* New York: Teacher's College, Columbia University, 1944.

Torgesen, J. K. The role of nonspecific factors in the task performance of learning disabled children: A theoretical assessment. *Journal of Learning Disabilities,* 1977, *10,* 27-34.

Wiig, E. H., & Semel, E. M. *Language assessment and intervention for the learning disabled.* Columbus, OH: Charles E. Merrill, 1980.

Willette, R., Galofaro, B., & Peckins, I. *Auditory perception training II: Listening skills.* Niles, IL: Developmental Learning Materials, 1980.

Wilt, M. A. *Study of teacher awareness of listening as a factor in elementary education.* Unpublished doctoral dissertation, Pennsylvania State University, 1949.

Adolescents have a great need to be perceived as normal and to be able to deal with the curriculum and social situations. Unfortunately, learning disabled students have great difficulty in these areas and often drop out of school without specific programs to assist them.

The authors offer a number of suggestions. Of special interest is the School Survival Skills Curriculum (SSSC). The three strands in it are: (1) behavioral control, (2) teacher-pleasing behaviors, and (3) study skills. These terms are fairly indicative of the content. Each strand has a number of components, and the authors expand upon their use. The article advocates this program in addition to the regular curriculum as a survival approach.

Teaching Coping Skills To Adolescents With Learning Problems

Rita Silverman, Naomi Zigmond, and Jan Sansone

All adolescents, whether learning handicapped or not, are in a confused and confusing state as they enter high school. They are struggling to achieve some independence from their families. They are attempting to develop an identity and set of personal values. They are adjusting to the physiological changes that accompany the teenage years and trying to understand and control the emerging, sometimes frightening, feelings of sexuality. They are working to establish and maintain relationships with same sex and opposite sex peers, and to be accepted into a peer group. And they are beginning to consider what they will do after high school and for the rest of their lives (Conger, 1977).

For students with learning problems, adolescence may be an especially difficult time. Many of these students have serious problems with peer acceptance. Because they may be developing physically, cognitively, and socially at a slower pace, they are often out of synchrony with their age peers. Adolescents seem to have an overwhelming need to perceive themselves as "normal" (Erickson & Friedman, 1978). This need for sameness is demonstrated in the fads and cliques so common among teenagers. Subtle differences in the rate of physical and intellectual development, or subtle delays in the emergence of sexual characteristics (beards, deep voices and body hair in boys; breasts, pubic hair, and menstruation in girls) may contribute to the rejection of educationally handicapped students by their peers (Erickson & Friedman, 1978).

Handicapped adolescents may also be grievously lacking in experience. Their parents may have considered them too vulnerable or too gullible to be permitted many independent, unsupervised forays into the outside world. They may have been educated in self-contained, segregated elementary school programs, thereby limiting their access to nonhandicapped students and to models of appropriate social behaviors. Furthermore, if they lacked the coordination or social aptitude required for the sports teams or other neighborhood activities in which nonhandicapped children took part, they were probably excluded from those experiences as well.

Even adolescents who have had opportunities for peer interactions and modeling as children may have failed to learn social skills. Many learning handicapped youngsters have as much difficulty learning social skills as they have with reading, writing, and arithmetic. They reach adolescence with inadequate social tools to choose the right clothes to wear, the right things to say, the right things to do. They often do not seem to develop a broad enough repertoire of social behaviors to react differently to different situations. As a result, their behavior is often inappropriate. They also seem to lack social judgment. They are continually getting themselves and their peers into trouble, both in school and in the community (Zigmond, 1978).

Thus, learning handicapped adolescents often enter high school lacking experience in independent, responsible decision making. They are on the periphery of peer groups that could provide support and models of appropriate teenage behavior. They may be deficient in the development of verbal and nonverbal social behaviors that could help them interact appropriately with peers and adults.

Difficulties of the educationally handicapped adolescent are exacerbated by the very structure of a secondary school. Students are expected to move from class to class independently and promptly, to adjust their behaviors to a wide variety of teachers' styles and requirements, to navigate large complex buildings and grounds, to develop work habits so they can cope with increased academic pressures and expectations. The majority of educationally handicapped students cannot be expected to "make it" through high school unless their school experience provides them some form of support.

Many communities have addressed this problem by offering students alternative high school programs. Some of these emphasize vocational or prevocational training. Some offer a self-contained, lower track, less demanding curriculum. Some provide tutorial assistance from special education teachers to help students in regular mainstream courses. These alternatives may help a student complete the requirements for high school graduation, but they do not address a critical issue: Most learning handicapped adolescents need explicit instruction in social skills or they will leave high school unprepared to function independently and responsibly.

Recognition of this need has led us to develop a School Survival Skills Curriculum, which we believe should be an integral part of any comprehensive program to serve secondary school-age students with learning and behavior problems. Its purpose is to prepare students to deal effectively with demands of the secondary school environment and the world beyond school.

SCHOOL SURVIVAL SKILLS CURRICULUM

The School Survival Skills Curriculum is divided into three strands of activities, each strand focusing on a set of skills that seems to be lacking in high school students with learning problems. The Behavior Control strand of the curriculum is designed for students who are always getting into trouble, who consistently do the wrong things, and who are often suspended or punished. These students do not seem to understand the role they play in influencing the consequences that accrue to them. In the Behavior Control strand the goal is to help students alter their locus of control and regain control over their environment. Students learn that they can change the consequences because they can control their own antecedent behaviors.

The second strand of the curriculum, Teacher-Pleasing Behaviors, is for students who have difficulty coping with the demands of the regular classroom. This strand helps students acquire behavior patterns that usually lead teachers to consider students more positively. Most students learn, in an incidental fashion, that certain behaviors ingratiate them with teachers. They learn to make eye contact, to look interested, to respond, to look busy. Many students with learning problems do not learn these behavior patterns. They need to be taught explicitly that their classroom behaviors have an impact on how the teacher responds to them and that, depending on the behaviors they display, the teacher's response will be positive or negative.

The third strand in the curriculum deals with Study Skills. Most special education students do not have adequate reading and writing skills. But the problems they face in mainstream classes are a function of more than just limited academic skills. These students do not know how to organize their time, how to approach a textbook, how to take notes, how to organize information, how to study for tests, how to take tests. The goals of the Study Skills strand are to teach students some "tricks" or shortcuts to gathering and retaining information. Students learn systematic methods for approaching classroom tasks and strategies for compensating for deficiencies in basic skills.

These strands in the School Survival Skills Curriculum will be examined in detail after we have described the format for delivering the SSS Curriculum to high school students and an approach to assessing competence in School Survival Skills that should be used before beginning any instructional sequence.

Format for Instruction in School Survival Skills: The Group Meeting

A weekly small-group meeting provides the format for implementing the School Survival Skills Curriculum. In a resource room program in which students receive basic skill instruction for one or two periods daily, one period a week is reserved for group instruction in school survival skills. During that period individually prescribed activities in reading, math, or written language, or tutorials in content area subjects, are set aside and students engage in a group activity designed specifically to teach some aspect of the School Survival Skills Curriculum.

Because adolescents are particularly responsive to their peers, this small-group format provides an effective context for exploring, developing, and practicing new coping skills. Peers are usually more credible than teachers as models of behavior and as sources of feedback. They provide authentic sources of social information. Peers interacting together, supporting one another, learning from one another are the backbone of the school survival skills lessons. Therefore, the School Survival Skills Curriculum is implemented in a group setting. We recommend that the curriculum be included as part of the students' schedules, and that the group meet on a regularly scheduled basis, not in a random fashion.

Ideally, the special education teacher would decide on the composition for each group by scheduling students with common skill needs or compatible personalities for given periods. But the exigencies of secondary school schedules usually preclude this. Therefore, the group composition may be quite diverse and not lend itself automatically to interactions that facilitate teaching the School Survival Skills. To overcome this constraint, the teacher must plan initial activities that will foster group cohesion and allow students to feel comfortable in a structured group environment. Teachers usually begin by helping establish the rules for what will be acceptable and unacceptable behavior in the group meeting. Generally, the teacher does not set up the rules but instead leads a discussion in which the students design the rules themselves. Although the teacher may have to enforce the rules at first, with time the group itself is encouraged to monitor individual behavior problems.

A discussion of the purpose of the group meeting should be the next step. Students require reassurance that the class will relate only to school goals and will not explore personal lives. A chart outlining general goals and sample activities to reach those goals could be introduced. Audio-visual equipment such as a Polaroid camera, tape recorder, or videotape machine might also be introduced, and students could explore how multi-media equipment might be used to help them understand their present behaviors and to help them learn new behaviors.

After rules have been established and students understand the purpose of the group meeting, the teacher begins a series of activities designed to develop group cohesion. The activities are based on the concept of cooperation and sharing information among group members as a requisite to reach a goal or solve a problem. In accordance with this, one application is to create a problem which, when solved, leads to a reward for the students. Clues — of which each student is given one — must be "pieced together" to find the solution. "Red herrings" can also be included. The "problem" can be putting together a puzzle, solving a "crime," or following a recipe.

Following are some additional activities that can be used to facilitate group interaction:

- The students are paired randomly, and each interviews his or her partner to find out something about the student no one else knows. Each student then "introduces" the partner to the rest of the group and includes the new piece of information in the introduction.
- Each student writes down something about himself or herself that he or she thinks the group does not know. The teacher reads each statement and the group tries to match the statement to the appropriate person. (If the teacher also takes part in this activity, barriers between students and teacher may begin to break down.)
- Students (and the teacher) in turn describe themselves to the group by naming their favorite food, TV program, sport, or similar items.
- Everyone anonymously finishes the statement, "If I could be anyone, I would like to be . . ." The written responses are transferred to the chalkboard, and the group tries to match the responses to the correct persons.

Many variations of these activities can be designed and tailor-made to fit the group's composition. Initially, students may be most comfortable with short, written responses or paired interviews because these activities structure the group interactions and are less threatening than speaking in front of the entire group. Eventually, students will feel comfortable enough to share their ideas with the whole group. The more willing the teacher is to participate in the interactions, not just by leading the group but by taking part in the activities, the more willing the students will be to participate.

The teacher has the responsibility to keep the group moving, to involve all the students, to plan activities that are appropriate for the students' interests and experiences, and to determine when the group is ready to move from this initial phase to working on the actual School Survival Skills

Curriculum. Although developing group cohesion is essential to meeting the goals of the curriculum, it is only an enabling activity and the curriculum itself should be introduced as soon as possible.

Assessment of Student Needs in School Survival Skills

Because the program of instruction in School Survival Skills must be tailored to the needs and characteristics of the adolescents who comprise each instructional group, the teacher cannot begin to teach School Survival Skills until these needs have been assessed. And because the curriculum is taught to a group, the assessment procedures do not end with a determination of individual needs. The teacher must summarize several sets of information to ascertain common needs in each instructional group. Skills needed by all or most of the group members become the priority and focus for instruction. The teacher identifies which of the curriculum strands will be taught to each group and which objectives from within each strand will define the curriculum based on the group needs.

Sources of Information

We have found no useful tests or formal assessment tools to assess student competence in school survival skills. Instead, teachers may rely on three methods of data collection: reviewing school records, observations, and interviews.

Records. Over the student's years of attending school, various facets of behavior and school experience are permanently recorded, and these are often accessible and useful in understanding how well the student has managed to cope. School records give an overall picture of student grades from year to year, subject by subject. They also reveal student attendance patterns. This information helps the teacher place the student's current performance into a context. In addition to past records, current information is available in the records kept by the student's present teachers. By assembling the information on a student's past and present grades, attendance, behavior, and rate of progress, the special education teacher can get a clearer picture of how well the student is functioning in school.

Observations. A revealing way to assess how well a student can cope is to observe the student in a mainstreamed class. This firsthand observation gives the special educator an opportunity to note the teacher's expectations for the students, the classroom organization and management patterns to which students must adapt, and the extent to which the target student is using teacher-pleasing behaviors and study skills in the classroom. To contrast observation data on students in classes in which they are succeeding and in classes in which they are failing may be particularly revealing.

Figure 1 is an example of a form that entails observation by the teacher. This particular one is generated by the resource room teacher. The same

---

In addition to remediating reading, math, and written language, the Resource Room helps students develop the behavior and study skills necessary for success in their mainstream classes. So that we may concentrate on the specific skills required in your class, please check off areas below in which this student needs to develop further.

Student_____ Date_____

Subject_____

Teacher_____ Period, Days_____

Study Skills

_____ using the text
　　_____ table of contents
　　_____ index
　　_____ glossary
　　_____ finding specific information
　　　　　　in chapters

_____ taking notes or copying
　　_____ from lecture
　　_____ from the board
　　_____ from the text
　　_____ from transparencies, filmstrips

_____ doing homework

_____ taking tests

_____ keeping a notebook

_____ listening for important facts
　　_____ from lecture
　　_____ from A-V

_____ bringing necessary supplies to class
　　_____ text
　　_____ pencil
　　_____ paper
　　_____ homework

_____ following directions
　　_____ oral
　　_____ written

Academic

_____ reading skills

_____ math skills

_____ writing skills

_____ other
　　　　(please specify)

Behavior

_____ on time

_____ in seat

_____ paying attention

_____ raising hand

_____ peer interaction
　　_____ individual
　　_____ small group
　　_____ whole group

Other (please specify)

FIGURE 1
Information From Teacher: Behavior and Study Skills

basic form, minus academic areas, could be given to the student to check off areas in which he or she sees a need for help.

Observation of student behavior outside the classroom can provide additional information. By observing students interacting with peers and teachers in the halls, in the lunchroom, or in the gym, the teacher can obtain a more complete picture of behavior patterns, social skills, and ability to understand and use appropriate behavior. Observations provide information on student weaknesses and also on strengths. A student who demonstrates poor social skills and poor behavior control may need specific instruction; a student who has good social skills may serve as a leader in the instructional group and as a peer model in role playing activities.

Whenever possible, students should be observed more than once in each setting. Although the observations may be unstructured and informal, the special education teacher should keep written records of each observation by noting any evidence of deficiencies or strengths in School Survival Skills. An additional effect of observational data is that the special education teacher is able to validate information obtained from students and teachers in conversation and interviews.

Interviews. Interviews represent another way of gathering assessment information. They can help teachers determine expectations for students in mainstream classes and special education students' performance patterns in the areas of academic achievement, behavior control, teacher-pleasing behaviors, and study skills. To obtain the necessary information for planning the School Survival Skills Curriculum, regular education teachers and special education teachers must maintain mutual, ongoing dialogue. This dialogue can take place only after the special educator has established some rapport with the school faculty and has become an integral part of the school environment. Then, through both formal, prearranged meetings and informal conversations while sharing a duty period or a lunch break, special educators and regular educators have opportunities to share information about specific students' progress and needs.

Interviewing students also provides valuable assessment information. Many students are eager to share their perspective on the mainstream — the expectations of their various teachers and their own strengths and weaknesses. Interviews give students an opportunity to help shape their curriculum by defining the skills they need to learn to become more successful in school. Through the interview the teacher may also uncover areas of special interest to the students, and this information may be useful in developing motivational schemes or more stimulating lessons.

These three methods of data collection are used to compile information on critical aspects of each student's school experiences. By focusing on grades, attendance and suspension patterns, tardiness, interactions with peers and teachers, and noteworthy experiences outside of school, the special education teacher can begin to identify the needs of individual students.

Information to Collect

Student Grades. Unsatisfactory grades are common among high school students who have learning problems. Many teachers interpret this to mean that the students lack the required academic skills to handle mainstream content area classes. In our experience, this is an incomplete interpretation. Although unsatisfactory grades *may* indicate deficient skills, they may also reveal that the student lacks the teacher-pleasing behavior and study skills that might permit him or her to "get by" despite relatively poor academic skills. The special educator must probe for evidence of problems other than academic deficits that contribute to these grades. Indications of inappropriate behavior patterns or poor study skills may clarify which aspects of the School Survival Skills Curriculum should be taught.

Consider, for example, the case of Bill, a poor reader who may fail social studies because the assignments require high level reading skills. If Bill could talk to the teacher and present himself as an interested, industrious student, a more positive outcome might result. He might draw the teacher's attention to another of his skills, such as his drawing ability. He could learn to negotiate with the teacher for alternative or supplementary assignments or projects that require less reading. He could learn to analyze the classroom rules and be sure that he is following them. He could learn to compensate for poor reading skills by learning how to follow directions on worksheets, how to find key words and headings in the social studies text, and how to keep a notebook.

Attendance. A major problem in today's schools is poor attendance. Many students simply do not attend classes. Students with learning problems are no exception, but these students are often systematic in their attendance patterns. They attend classes in which they are interested and successful and do not attend classes they find difficult, frustrating, or boring. In these latter classes they often receive unsatisfactory grades. Information about students' attendance patterns is frequently useful in planning the School Survival Skills Curriculum.

Many students who have erratic attendance patterns do not understand that this has a negative impact on the teacher and that it eventually results in negative attitudes toward the student, and poor grades. Some students have to be taught that neither their grades and skills nor their teachers' attitudes are likely to change unless they attend school regularly.

Suspension Rates. In examining student records, teachers should not be surprised to find that students who have poor grades and poor attendance patterns are frequently suspended from school. Students are suspended for such things as continual absence, tardiness, failure to hand in required work, or sleeping in class. These students may need instruction within the Teacher-Pleasing Behavior strand of the School Survival Skills Curriculum. Other students are suspended either because of infractions of school rules or because of negative interactions with teachers or peers. These students should be taught the objectives within the Behavior Control strand of the School Survival Skills Curriculum. Interviews with them often reveal that they need to accept greater responsibility for their behaviors and the consequences.

Interactions with Teachers and Peers. Students with learning problems often have a "reputation" by the time they reach high school. A student's name may conjure up a specific negative image in both peers and teachers. This reputation may be more damaging to the student's interactions with peers and teachers than his or her actual behavior.

As special educators gather information about each student, they should consider the student's reputation and the kinds of interactions students actually have with peers and teachers. Does the reputation match the behavior? Has it become a self-fulfilling prophecy? Are negative interactions situation-specific (e.g., the student is unruly in classes in which the teacher requires a great deal of reading) or generalizable across situations (the student is unruly in every class)?

Consistent negative interactions in school may lead to suspension, detention, loss of privileges, or exemption from extracurricular activities. These punishments establish or confirm the student's reputation as a troublemaker, and the likelihood of "making it" becomes even more remote.

Of course, not all students with learning difficulties have consistently negative interactions. Students with positive peer and teacher interaction patterns should not be exempt from the School Survival Skills meeting but should serve as leaders for group activities in those areas.

Experiences Outside of School. Adolescents are complex people whose lives and identities are only partly defined by school. Many other experiences contribute to the person we classify as "student." Some factors in students' lives outside of school reinforce the special educators' efforts in teaching school survival skills. Others do not. Information about the student's life outside of school completes the teacher's picture of the student and leads to selection of more realistic teaching objectives in the School Survival Skills Curriculum.

No one can know everything about all students. And one should take care not to pry into sensitive areas. Yet, certain information is critical. For example, if a student is working on study skills, the teacher would benefit from knowing if the family can support this effort at home. The student may need quiet and privacy for 30 minutes of homework. Is this possible? Can someone at home help the student practice math facts or study for a test? Will the student receive praise or acknowledgment for improved grades or for staying out of trouble for some time? If reinforcement from outside of school is not forthcoming, the teacher and student must plan accordingly. The student will have to accept more responsibility for changing his or her behavior, and the teacher will have to find a different way to reinforce new behaviors outside of school.

Other information about the student's life circumstances may help explain some behaviors. For example, a student who is chronically tardy may be irresponsible — or may have overwhelming responsibilities at home that contribute to tardiness to the first period class. The correct interpretation may help define what should be taught to this student.

Knowing something about how a student spends time outside of school is also useful. Information about a student's job or interests can help the teacher select activities and materials that are motivational.

Individual Assessment Summary

Figure 2 summarizes assessment information collected on Sidney, a ninth grade boy. Systematic use of such information leads the teacher to curricular decision making.

The teacher, Mrs. Miller, has collected and recorded information in each assessment area. She has noted that Sidney got a D in his science class. Science is his first period class, and Sidney has reported that he hates to get up in the morning and also that he doesn't like science class. Through informal observations and interviews with his other teachers, she became aware that Sidney's attendance record at other classes is fine and that his interactions with teachers and peers are usually good (although he sometimes gets into fights in the halls).

The next step is to interpret the information to see how the student's individual behaviors and experiences interrelate, and the implications for instruction. The teacher in this example linked Sidney's tardiness and detention record to his science class. She concluded that Sidney needs to become aware of the relationship between his attitude and behavior and his grades. He needs structure and direction for his interactions with his science teacher.

A profile emerges. The teacher begins to identify appropriate strands from the School Survival Skills Curriculum. In the example the teacher concluded that Sidney needs instruction in Behavior Control and Teacher-Pleasing Behaviors, and she checked these areas on the Assessment Summary Form. She did not have any reason to suspect that Study Skills were poor.

Finally, the teacher selects a priority for instruction. A rating scale like that of Figure 2 is suggested. Sidney's teacher indicated that the greatest need seemed to be for instruction in Behavior Control.

Assessment of Group Needs

After collecting information on all individual students, the teacher must organize the data to identify overlaps in student needs. Figure 3 illustrates how this can be done, to create a profile of group needs. The skills representing the collective needs of the group of students become the initial focus of instruction.

Student: Sidney   Date: September, 1980

ASSESSMENT AREAS	ASSESSMENT INFORMATION	INTERPRETATION	STUDENT NEEDS		
			BC[1]	TPC[2]	SS[3]
Grades	D in science; C's in others.		X	X	?
Attendance	Frequently marked tardy for 1st period science class — attendance otherwise OK	Impact of tardiness on teacher attitude —			
Tardiness		tardiness and grades related		X	
Suspension			X		
Detention	Frequent detention for tardiness	Link detention to tardiness			
Interactions — with teachers — with peers	OK — sometimes gets in fights in halls			X	
Experiences Outside of School	Works part-time at McDonald's Takes care of younger siblings at home in a.m.	Discuss with counselor parental response to his oversleeping	X		
			2	1	?

Rating Scale: 0 = no problem
                1 = moderate problem
                2 = severe problem
                ? = no data

[1]BC   = Behavior Control
[2]TPC = Teacher-Pleasing Behaviors
[3]SS   = Study Skills

FIGURE 2
Assessment Summary — Individual Student

Day_____ Period_____	Date		
NAMES OF STUDENTS	BEHAVIOR CONTROL	TEACHER-PLEASING BEHAVIORS	STUDY SKILLS
Sidney	2	2	?
Mary Kay	2	1	?
Tom	2	1	1
Vicky	1	.1	2
Robert	2	?	1
TOTAL:	10	7	6

Notes: Begin Behavior Awareness; link to impact on teachers

Code:
0 = no problem
1 = moderate problem
2 = severe problem
? = no data

FIGURE 3
Group Skill Summary

The group of students presented in Figure 3 (including Sidney, whose profile is given in Figure 2) need instruction in all three curriculum strands, but the need for instruction in Behavior Control seems most acute. This is where the teacher might choose to begin the School Survival Skills Curriculum. After the initial assessment of student competence in School Survival Skills, the teacher continues to monitor student performance in the mainstream and to note evidence of progress or new problems. Through continued conversations with students, teachers, and parents, and repeated observations of student behavior, the special educator obtains new information that helps to clarify individual and group needs and to define further objectives of the School Survival Skills Curriculum.

Principles of Instruction

Students who need to be taught SSS do not learn easily. If they did, they would probably have picked up these coping skills early in their school careers, by observing and modeling others, interpreting teachers' facial expressions and body language, intuiting appropriate and acceptable behaviors, and generalizing across social settings. Instruction in SSS must therefore be planned carefully and systematically if it is to be effective. New skills should be taught in three phases: presentation, practice, and mastery.

In the presentation phase the skill is introduced. The student is given a reason to learn the skill and a structure for learning it. The presentation phase is teacher-directed. The teacher enables the students to be sufficiently organized to learn the skill, makes learning the new skill relevant to the students' lives, explains what is expected from the students, and offers them appropriate strategies for learning the skill. Many students need more than one lesson when a new skill is introduced. The presentation phase should be continued, using a variety of activities, materials, and teaching techniques, until the students are prepared to begin independent practice.

The goal of the practice phase is for students to gradually increase their competence. The teacher manipulates instructional variables so the students are engaged in activities that systematically stretch their capacities to perform. These variables include, but are not limited to: the amount of teacher direction, the immediacy of corrective feedback required, the number and type of cues, the concreteness and relevance of materials, the level of memory required in the activity, and the size of the task. Practice activities continue until the student can perform when less teacher direction is required, when feedback is delayed, when cues are no longer provided, when materials are abstract, when the level of memory required has moved from recognition to recall, and when tasks are longer and more complex.

Then the student may be said to have mastered the skill, but the mastery phase branches out in two dimensions — mastery in isolation and mastery in application. When students first demonstrate mastery, they perform the skill in a familiar environment, for an encouraging teacher, with materials that are appropriate, interesting, and consistent with those used in practice. This is mastery in isolation. While it is an essential step in the learning process, full mastery has not occurred until the student can demonstrate the ability to apply the skill in varied settings, without the teacher present, and using different materials. This is mastery in application, which completes the sequence.

The stages in a teaching sequence and the directions in which the variables of instruction change are illustrated in Figure 4. When teaching the School Survival Skills Curriculum, each skill should be taught through all four phases to increase the probability that new skills will be applied in the mainstream setting.

Teaching the Curriculum

For each of the three strands of the SSS Curriculum, we have identified a set of teaching components and a terminal behavioral objective for each component. These terminal objectives should be considered hierarchical; that is, earlier skills should be taught before later ones and considered prerequisite to later ones. Figure 5, 6, and 7 give the components and terminal objectives for Behavior Control, Teacher-Pleasing Behaviors, and

VARIABLE	PRESENTATION STAGE		PRACTICE STAGE		MASTERY STAGE — ISOLATION		MASTERY STAGE — APPLICATION
Teacher Direction	Total	→	Less	→	Independent	↑	
Feedback	Immediate	→	Less Immediate	→	Delayed	↑	
Cues	Total	→	Fading	→	Internalized	↑	
Materials	Concrete	→	Similar	→	Similar	↑	Different and More Abstract
Level of Memory	Matching	→	Recognition	→	Recall	↑	
Size of Task	Few items	→	More	→	More	↑	Many items

FIGURE 4
Stages in a Teaching Sequence

Components of Strand	Terminal Objectives of Instructional Module for Component
1) Behavior awareness	1) Students will be able to identify the behaviors they exhibit in typical school situations.
2) Impact of behavior	2) Students will be able to say how their behavior in specific situations affects others.
3) Behavior consequences	3) Students will understand that the consequences they experience are the result of behaviors they exhibit.
4) Behavior options	4) Students will be able to identify options to their present behaviors in typical school situations.
5) Behavior change	5) Students will be able to identify and substitute another option to a habituated behavior which results in negative consequences (in a contrived setting).
6) Practicing change	6) Students will practice substituting a behavior option in a specific school situation when negative consequences usually occur.
7) Exerting control	7) Students will generalize their awareness and knowledge of options to any situation (school, home, job, etc.) by selecting and exhibiting behaviors that lead to positive consequences.

FIGURE 5
School Survival Skills Curriculum Strand: Behavior Control

Study Skills. The following sections describe sample activities for each component and terminal objective. These samples suggest the types of lessons teachers might design and provide the barest outline of the curriculum. In implementing the SSS Curriculum, teachers are to expand, adapt, and modify these to provide appropriate, interesting, and motivating presentation, practice, and mastery activities for students in each unique instructional group.

Teaching Behavior Control

Component 1: Behavior Awareness. Often, students who would benefit from the SSS Curriculum are not sensitive to their own or others' behaviors. To begin the process of sensitizing students, the teacher creates a story of a typical school situation. It could center on a fight in the halls, an altercation between a teacher and a student, or a student caught with a cigarette by a security guard. The teacher reads the story and asks the students to identify how the actors in the story behaved (after having explained that the purpose

Components of Strand	Terminal Objectives of Instructional Module for Component
1) Rules	1) Students will be able to identify the overt and covert rules in each of their classrooms.
2) Classroom requirements	2) Students will be aware of the requirements of one classroom and be able to identify the behaviors they exhibit which match the requirements and those which do not.
3) Appropriate behaviors	3) Students will be able to identify appropriate behaviors in a variety of classroom settings.
4) Behavior change	4) Students will be able to substitute more appropriate behaviors for identified inappropriate classroom behaviors in contrived settings.
5) Using Teacher-Pleasing Behaviors	5) Students will select a mainstream teacher and an inappropriate behavior, and contract to substitute a Teacher-Pleasing Behavior in the mainstream setting.
6) Improving Teacher-Pleasing Behaviors	6) Students will generalize Teacher-Pleasing Behaviors to more settings and/or more teachers.

FIGURE 6
School Survival Skills Curriculum Strand: Teacher-Pleasing Behaviors

of the activity is to have students focus on and describe student actions and reactions).

In a follow-up practice activity, the teacher presents a school situation in a story without an ending. Each student responds by discussing how he or she would act in that situation. The next activity might involve the students' identifying how they think other students in the group typically respond to a given situation.

A final activity in learning to identify behaviors uses a real-life situation. The teacher or the student(s) recreates a recent school event that turned out badly for the student(s) involved. Students are expected to identify the behaviors they exhibited in the situation.

Figure 8 shows how these four activities for the first component of the Behavior Control strand are examples of systematic teaching. Note that the presentation and practice activities involve contrived (teacher-created) situations, and the application activity is a real-life situation. Our experience has shown that students are better able, initially, to meet the demands of the task if they are not too personally involved and if the task is not too threatening. But they must be able to demonstrate, by applying the new skill in a real-life situation, that the objective has been mastered.

Component 2: Impact of Behavior. Role playing in conjunction with audio and video taping is a useful tool in helping students recognize that

Components of Strand	Terminal Objectives of Instructional Module for Component
1) Organizing assignments and study time	1) Students will be able to organize assignments for more efficient use of study time.
2) Following directions —written —oral	2) Students will be able to follow oral and written directions in the regular classroom setting.
3) Listening for information from lecture	3) Students will be able to listen to a lecture and identify the central theme, and facts to support that theme.
4) Locating information in a text	4) Students will be able to use the table of contents, index, and glossary to find specific information from a text.
5) Taking notes from a text	5) Students will be able to identify and record pertinent information from a textbook using an organized procedure.
6) Preparing for tests	6) Students will be able to use notes from lecture and reading to study for different types of tests.
7) Taking tests	7) Students will be able to apply strategies for taking different types of tests.

FIGURE 7
School Survival Skills Curriculum Strand: Study Skills

Objective	Presentation Activities	Practice Activities	Application Activities
Students will be able to identify the behaviors they exhibit in typical school situations.	Teacher-created story; students identify behaviors.	Teacher-created story without ending. Students identify how they would typically respond. Teacher-created story without ending. Students identify how they think other students would typically respond.	Teacher or students describe recent incident. Students identify their own behaviors.

FIGURE 8
Curriculum Strand: Behavior Control Component: Behavior Awareness

their behaviors have an effect on other pupils with whom they interact. The teacher creates scenarios, and the students assume various roles. A typical scenario might be a confrontation between a teacher and a group of students in the lunchroom, or a meeting between the principal and two students. The scene is taped, and the students listen to or watch the interactions.

Students are directed to recognize that others respond to their own behaviors. They learn to identify the impact that a certain tone of voice or facial expression has had on the person with whom they were interacting. They are taught to notice body language, eye contact, gestures, and voice intonations while watching the tapes.

In application activities students are asked to articulate how a certain set of their behaviors has had an impact on another person. These application activities are neither teacher-created nor contrived; they grow naturally out of the group interactions. Competency is demonstrated when students can answer a question like, "Norm, what was Jim's reaction when you put him down?"

Component 3: Behavior Consequences. This set of activities follows naturally from students' new awareness of the impact of their behaviors. In fact, some teachers may choose to combine Components 2 and 3. We have separated them to emphasize the significance of each as part of the Behavior Control strand.

In this component students become aware that both the positive and negative consequences they experience result from their own behaviors and, therefore, are within their control. To introduce this concept the teacher describes to the group a series of events with a variety of endings (or consequences). Students are asked to choose the appropriate ending based on the behaviors of the students in each vignette. The teacher then leads a group discussion. Students are helped to recognize that consequences occur because of earlier behaviors: If Student A hits Student B in the presence of a teacher, the negative consequence that ensues to Student A (being suspended) is a result of Student A's behavior (hitting Student B). Students are encouraged to understand that consequences (in this case, suspension) do not occur randomly and do not occur simply because the teacher does not like the student. Rather, consequences are the result of behaviors the student exhibits.

In application activities students identify the behavior(s) they exhibited in a recent interaction that ended negatively. When students change their response to the question, "Why are you being punished?" from "I dunno" to "I did . . . ," they have mastered this component.

Components 4 and 5: Behavior Options/Behavior Change. As students begin to deal with the knowledge that their behaviors may lead to negative consequences, they need to understand that their behavior patterns are not fixed, even though many of their responses are quite automatic. They have to come to realize that alternative ways of behaving are possible. One activity involves introducing a typical school situation and listing several ways in which students might behave. Students are asked to identify potential consequences for each of the options presented. In a second activity the teacher describes another typical school situation, and the students are asked to think of all the possible responses they can for that situation. The students then break into smaller groups and each group puts the alternative behaviors in order from least likely to produce negative consequences to most likely.

Another activity involves a teacher-made game. Using a simple game board with spaces and dice, students roll the dice and land on either blank spaces or situation spaces. If a player lands on a blank space, the next student takes a turn. Any player who lands on a situation space draws a situation card. The card descibes a school situation, a behavior option, and a consequence. If the behavior has led to a positive consequence, the student takes another turn. He or she loses a turn if the consequence is negative. The first student to reach the "finish" space wins the game.

Another useful activity involves role playing. The teacher creates a variety of situations for the students to act out. The students take turns playing the main character, who role plays three behaviors: one that will lead to a positive sequence, one to a neutral consequence, and one to a negative consequence. Students demonstrate mastery of this component when they can consistently identify the behavior options that lead to positive consequences.

Component 5: Behavior Change. At this point students begin to apply the earlier competencies they have learned. They identify one of their current behaviors that leads to negative consequences and work on substituting a more appropriate behavior *in a contrived setting* — for example, during group meetings in the resource room. This affords the student an opportunity to become more comfortable with a new behavior in a supportive environment. It also allows students to have responses from their peers as to how the new behavior appears. Is it sincere? Is it appropriate? Is it consistent?

Component 6: Practicing Change. The next step is for the student to practice the behavior *in a specific school situation.* If, for example, the new behavior is to make eye contact when talking with someone, the student may decide to practice it in a social studies class. Students are taught to monitor and record how often they practice the new behavior and what responses they receive. The student might carry a simple form on an index card to record this data, under the headings: Behavior, Date, Time, Who, and Response.

We recommend that several different behaviors be included in components 5 and 6 (Behavior Change and Practicing Change) until the students' day-to-day interactions or school records reflect that they are exerting control and changing previously negative consequences.

Component 7: Exerting Control. Students must apply all the skills learned in the Behavior Control strand. They must demonstrate that they

have accomplished all the objectives by exhibiting more appropriate behaviors in a variety of settings in and outside of school. Changes in student
behavior can be verified both by student self-reports and by talking with
school personnel and parents. Further verification should come from school
records indicating a decline in the number of suspensions, detentions,
demerits, or similar factors. Even when students seem to be controlling
behavior at this high level, teachers should return to activities in the
Behavior Control strand regularly to review skills with students — just as
they review arithmetic algorithms or punctuation rules.

Teaching Teacher-Pleasing Behaviors

Component 1: Rules. Secondary school teachers generally have definite
expectations for student behaviors, but they are seldom explicit about these
classroom rules. Furthermore, the rules are not always the same from teacher
to teacher or class to class. Students need to be able to identify both the overt
and covert rules in all their classes. Before they can do that, they must
understand that rules are necessary, that rules may be fair or unfair, but that
failure to follow teachers' rules has consequences. They must also understand
the difference between overt and covert rules. To begin, the teacher engages
the student in a familiar game, then suddenly announces that no rules will
be in effect during the next five minutes. A follow-up group discussion
centers on what happened when no rules were in force.

In a second activity, the teacher asks the students to give examples of
circumstances in which rules are necessary and when they are not. To
reinforce the idea that some rules are necessary, the students read a teacher-
created, open-ended story of an episode in which rules are suspended.
Students discuss how the story would end if rules would be reinstated and if
they would not.

Next, students list the rules they must follow in the world outside of
school, and the group discusses which of the rules seem legitimate and
which do not. The teacher might use traffic signals as an example: Are traffic
lights as necessary in the middle of the night as during the middle of the day?
Should one have to wait for red light to turn green at 1:00 a.m.? What are the
possible consequences of not waiting for the light to change? This same task
could be repeated, but focusing on school rules. Students identify the school
rules and discuss which they feel are needed and which seem unfair.
A discussion of the consequences of not following school rules follows
naturally. At this time the teacher should introduce the concept of overt and
covert rules. Students list the types of classroom behaviors that lead to
negative consequences. For each behavior listed, they supply the consequence
and the rule that was broken. The teacher then asks them how they knew a
rule existed. Figure 9 is an example of one final product from this activity.

Behavior	Consequence	Rule Broken	How did you know?
Didn't do home-work	Failing	Must hand in homework	Teacher said so
Swore at teacher	Sent to office	Can't swear in class	Everyone knows that
Late to class	Detention	Be on time to class	Posted on board
Punched Tony	Suspension	No fighting	Posted on board
Talked to friend	Teacher yelled	Can't talk in class	Teacher said so
Didn't answer teacher's question	Teacher got mad	Answer when called on	I just know
Took money	Suspension	No stealing	School rule
Cut class	Detention	Must attend	Posted on board
Misbehaved for substitute	Lowered grade	Behave for substitutes	Teacher told us later

FIGURE 9
Example of Student Responses to Activity Involving Overt and Covert Rules

The various answers to "How did you know it was a rule?" demonstrate the difference between overt rules (those posted) and covert rules.

In the application activity students are to list the rules for each class they attend. Then they are to indicate which rules are overt and which are covert.

Component 2: Classroom Requirements. Students with learning problems often feel inadequate in academic classes and take the position that they cannot succeed. To help them begin to recognize that they might be successful in those environments, a first activity could be to have the students list all the behaviors on which teachers base grades. A typical list generated from this activity is shown in Figure 10.

Turning in homework	Having the textbook
Coming to class on time	Grades on tests
Not cutting	Answering questions
Staying in your seat	Working quietly
Not talking to your friends	Not going to the bathroom
Not swearing	Raising your hand to talk
Having a pencil and notebook	

FIGURE 10
An Example of Students' Listing of "What Teachers Base Grades On"

After the students have completed the list, the teacher asks the students which of the items on the list require reading or writing skills. As a result, the students will become aware that grades are based in large part on behaviors that even academically deficient students can exhibit.

Each student chooses one class in which he or she is having problems and generates a list of behaviors on which the teacher of that class bases grades. The students identify which of the classroom requirements they are meeting. They then compare their own behaviors over a one-week period with those of another student who is more successful. Students might use notecards similar to the one shown in Figure 11.

Component 3: Appropriate Behaviors. The last activity in Component 2 leads naturally into this area. The teacher directs a discussion on the observable, non-academic behaviors exhibited by a "good student." Students generally characterize a "good student" as one who: attends class regularly, comes on time, is prepared (with pencil, books, etc.), and follows the overt rules for "good" behavior. Many students, however, fail to notice additional verbal and nonverbal behaviors that contribute to the impression of a "good student": tone of voice, eye contact, posture, displays of effort. The teacher elicits these from the group by using some of the role playing or audio-video taping activities described in the Behavior Control strand. If these activities have already been introduced, the teacher may only have to remind students of them and help them bridge the gap from general behavior awareness to awareness of specific classroom behaviors. If these activities have not been used, this would be an appropriate time to introduce them.

An application activity for this component might be for each student to identify appropriate behaviors for various classes. The ability to do the activity would indicate mastery of the component.

Component 4: Behavior Change. Now that students have identified classroom requirements and "good" behaviors, they are ready to attempt to choose appropriate behaviors and practice them during group meetings or at other times in the special education class. The behaviors to be changed are

Classroom Requirements	Me	Jimmy
Contributed in class	/	╫╫ ///
Raised hand	//	╫╫
Brought pencil and notebook	//	╫╫
Handed in homework	O	///
Came on time	///	╫╫

FIGURE 11
Behavior Comparison Chart

ones students have identified as those that get them into trouble with mainstream teachers and ones that they have chosen to change. The risk that students will return to former, more automatic behavior patterns is reduced when they are able to articulate that a behavior is inappropriate and that they will attempt to change it.

The teacher's role is to help the student find a way to remember to try the new, more positive behavior and to reward the student when he or she consistently substitutes the appropriate behavior for the inappropriate one. The nature of the reward and the schedule for delivering the reward should be negotiated between student and teacher. For example, if a consistently tardy student is going to try to come to class on time, the student and teacher may decide that the student will earn 20 minutes to listen to a record album if he or she exhibits this on-time behavior 90 percent of the time over a two-week period. At this point, students are asked only to demonstrate mastery of this component in isolation. Once the student has changed an inappropriate behavior in the special education setting, he or she is ready to generalize the behaviors.

Components 5 and 6: Using and Improving Teacher-Pleasing Behaviors. These components represent the mastery in application phase of the teacher-pleasing behavior skills. Students begin to substitute more appropriate behaviors in several of their mainstream classes and perhaps even demonstrate that they can generalize these behaviors and exhibit "boss-pleasing behaviors," "parent pleasing behaviors," and so forth.

A useful technique is to have students enlist their classroom teachers as they practice new behaviors. They explain to the teachers that they are going to try to come to class on time, turn in homework, be prepared, and so on. Each day they present the teacher a simple chart like that of Figure 12. The teacher is asked to initial the items the student has fulfilled that day. This chart is a constant reminder to the student of the behaviors he or she is working on, and it also alerts the teacher to the efforts the student is making in class.

Behavior	Mon.	Tues.	Wed.	Thurs.	Fri.
Be on time Have book Have pencil Turn in homework					

FIGURE 12
Suggested Chart for Teacher-Pleasing Behaviors

Students who learn to use teacher-pleasing behaviors report that their grades improve and their interactions with teachers are generally more positive. The TPB strand appears to be most helpful to students who seem to have given up. They do not come to class on time or do not attend at all; they do not carry books and pencils; they do not hand in homework; their body language and attitudes indicate disinterest; they no longer believe that they can be successful in school. Instructing these students in the components of the Teacher-Pleasing Behaviors strand is a concrete way to change their defeatist, failure-ridden attitudes. In our experience, it is a much more successful approach than the hackneyed refrain, "If you would only try harder."

Teaching Study Skills

An appropriate time to begin a unit on study skills is shortly before the first report cards are issued. During the group meeting students are given a sheet of paper with each of their class subjects listed vertically down the left side, and two columns headed across the top by "Grade I Think I'll Get" and "Grade I Got." They record the grades they think they will receive. After students receive their report cards, they compare their actual grades with their predictions. Invariably there will be some discrepancies. The teacher should discuss with the students why the grades they received were different from those they had anticipated. The students then are to sort their grades into two categories: "OK" grades and "not OK" grades. They analyze reasons for the "not OK" grades and try to identify the differences in academic and social behaviors between the classes in which they received "OK" and "not OK" grades. Analyses of this kind encourage the students to take responsibility for their grades and for their behaviors. Finally, each student selects one "not OK" class in which to focus by applying new study skills, as described in the following paragraphs.

Component 1: Getting Organized. This component covers three areas of organization: notebook, time, and assignments.

Organizing a notebook: Students are required to keep and use a notebook in many of their classes. The notebook is supposed to help students collect relevant class information in an organized way. It provides a format for students to keep track of their assignments. Teachers check to see if the student's work is current. Often, students are graded on the quality of their notebooks.

Activities involving organizing a notebook first ask students to identify which teachers require a notebook, how the teacher wants it used, and the purpose of the notebook in that class. Then the group is exposed to two sample notebooks. Each is a three-ring binder containing folders with pockets, color-tabbed dividers, and several sheets of paper, including vocabulary lists, worksheets, study guides, two quizzes, and an assignment sheet.

Some of the papers are wrinkled; others are torn. The students are divided into two groups. Each group gets one of the notebooks and "grades" it according to neatness and organization. Then the students modify the notebook so it will receive an improved grade. The two groups compare their evaluations of the notebooks and their improvements. The teacher records their findings, and the entire group creates some basic guidelines for organizing notebooks.

Next, students bring their own notebooks to the group and spend time analyzing and improving them. The students can use group time to redo their notebooks, with the guidelines developed during previous group meetings as reference points.

As students learn to create acceptable notebooks, they can begin to use them in their mainstream classes. Responses from mainstream teachers and students' own reports on the effectiveness of the notebooks reinforce the students for taking part in this set of activities.

Organizing time: To make students more aware of how they spend their time, they could be asked to keep a schedule for one week, recording what kinds of activities occupy their time from school dismissal until bedtime. The activities are recorded in half-hour segments. A sample activity log is given in Figure 13.

In analyzing their logs after one week, most students will recognize that several slots each day *could* be used for studying. The students are to compare their logs, discuss what they do during after-school hours, and allot study time. They continue to record their after-school activities for one more week to see if their study time increases. Logs are compared again after that week, and students who have increased their study time are given some type of reward or bonus.

Organizing assignments: Students frequently say they have no homework, no tests to study for, and no project due, when in reality they cannot remember what their assignments are. To help them keep track of assignments, the students could talk about and then create some possible assignment sheets. Figure 14 is an example of a student-created assignment sheet. The teacher makes copies of the various assignment sheets for everyone, and group members practice using them.

In an accompanying activity the students might be asked to create a series of assignments that approximate those typically delivered by classroom teachers. They write each assignment on a separate card and place the cards in the middle of a table. The students take turns role playing a teacher, by taking a card, standing before the group, and "giving the assignment." The other students use the newly designed assignment sheets to record the assignments. This activity affords the students immediate feedback on the effectiveness of the various assignment sheets. It also provides practice in listening for important information and recording it in an organized way. During the activity students role play "student" as well as teacher. They

	Mon.	Tues.	Wed.	Thurs.	Fri.
3:30–4:00 p.m.					
4:00–4:30 p.m.					
4:30–5:00 p.m.					
5:00–5:30 p.m.					
5:30–6:00 p.m.					
6:00–6:30 p.m.					
6:30–7:00 p.m.					
7:00–7:30 p.m.					
7:30–8:00 p.m.					
8:00–8:30 p.m.					
8:30–9:00 p.m.					
9:00–9:30 p.m.					
9:30–10:00 p.m.					
10:00–10:30 p.m.					
10:30–11:00 p.m.					

Name _____   _____ Week

POSSIBLE CATEGORIES

TV	Eating	Family	Friends	Outdoors	Nothing
	Telephone	Talking	Messing Around	Work/Chores	

FIGURE 13
Sample Form for Organizing Study Time

NAME: *Leo*

Week of: *March 16*

Day	Class	Assignment	Date Due
Monday	*English* *Science*	*Read pages 117- 128* *do questions* *term paper*	*Wednesday* *March 26*
Tuesday			
Wednesday			
Thursday			
Friday			
Notes:			

FIGURE 14
Sample Assignment Sheet

practice raising their hands and asking for information to be repeated or to be written on the board.

Component 2: Following Written Directions. Students should be made more aware of the impact of written directions on their everyday lives. Through discussion and demonstration, group members can generate evidence to this effect. Job applications, instruction manuals, bus schedules, telephone directories, and labels on products verify the importance of being able to interpret and follow written directions. To reinforce this concept, the teacher might use a cooking activity in which each student must follow the directions for one of the steps. This activity has the additional benefit of an edible reward for following directions and for working cooperatively with other group members to achieve a goal.

A number of activities may be required to reinforce the importance of attending to written directions and to help students develop their skills in this area. Some of these activities might involve group discussions on the many contexts within the school where following written directions is essential — the school handbook, bulletin board announcements, hall posters, worksheets, tests, and textbooks, to name just a few.

Component 3: Listening. Typically, adolescents have highly refined, if selective, listening skills. When asked to recite lyrics from a "hit" song, they do so with ease. With a cue to a TV commercial, they readily fill in the rest. But they need to generalize these listening skills to school situations in attending to oral directions, key facts, and central ideas in the classroom.

One suggested listening activity entails either the teacher or one of the students reading aloud an interesting set of paragraphs, such as a write-up of Saturday's football game, a description of a rock concert, or a portion of a horror story. Then the students try to paraphrase what they heard and assess who could most accurately restate the content. The "reader" could also create five or six questions based on the content and see which listeners can answer them most accurately. The school's TV or radio could be utilized for this type of "listener's quiz," with new or other broadcasts as a basis.

As another activity, the teacher might tape the same material three or four times, but omit increasing amounts of information with each recording. The listeners would then "fill in the blanks" as practice in attending to relevant information.

Materials to enhance listening may have to be highly motivating to the students at first. But material from actual classes should be introduced as soon as possible so they can begin to apply their listening skills to the prevailing oral language, style, and content of their regular classes. For example, students might obtain permission from a classroom teacher to tape part of an oral presentation, and this tape could be used for listening tasks. Or students may select one class as a target and be responsible for bringing back to the next group meeting a specified number of "facts" from an oral presentation in that class. Several students from the same class might compare the information they remember.

Activities that afford the students practice in following oral directions are appropriately introduced at this point. One such activity involves preparing Language Master® cards, each with an instruction such as, "Find a social studies book and turn to page 80," or "Go to the board and write your name backwards." The Language Master is connected to a listening post, and each student has a set of headphones with which to listen to the directions on the cards. The activity itself can develop in a number of ways. For instance, students might take turns selecting a card, putting it through the Language Master, and following the directions. Or they could each create their own directions cards, pool them, and practice following each other's directions.

To increase the interest level, the initial items could be silly or humorous, but eventually the students should create a set of cards with oral directions typical of those used by their regular classroom teachers. In developing an appropriate set of directions, students could be asked to pay attention to all oral directions in their classes for one week and come to the group meeting with a collection of these directions.

Variations of the above activities include using a tape recorder in lieu of a Language Master; or writing out the oral directions on index cards or strips of paper, taking turns being the teacher, and reading the directions aloud while other group members take turns following them.

Component 4: Locating Information.   Before engaging in actual activities, the students should be given a multiple-choice pre-test to determine their knowledge of textbook components and their ability to use an index, a table of contents, and so forth to locate information. This should be followed by a discussion that emphasizes the need for understanding how textbooks are organized.

Then, one activity involves placing several texts, each from a different content area, in various locations of the room. The students sit at a table, in the center of which is a pile of colored index cards. The color of the card has been coded to one of the texts (e.g., social studies - blue, math - red, etc.). Each student picks a card, goes to the area of the room where the text is, and uses it to follow the directions on the card. Each card contains three (or other number of) items such as, "What is the title of Chapter 3 in the history text?" "Use the index in the science text to find the page with information about gorillas." "The glossary of the math text has a definition for *fraction*. What is the definition, and on what page did you find it?"

The students record their findings on an answer sheet that has been placed next to the text. When they finish, they return with their texts to the central table. After all group members have completed their tasks and are at the table, each student in turn reads his or her items and demonstrates how he or she used the textbook to find the answers. This way students have an opportunity for immediate corrective feedback on their answers. Moreover, they have an opportunity to learn by watching other group members use textbooks to find specific information. If desirable, the activity could be turned into a competitive game, with points awarded for finishing first and for each correct use of the text.

In the follow-up activity, students come to the group meeting a week later with a textbook they are using in a mainstream class, along with an assignment. The students exchange books and make up questions for each other that require use of the index, glossary, or table of contents. Next, students look at their class assignments and determine how to use the textbooks to find the information.

Variations of these activities can be devised to give students practice in using reference books like a dictionary, an encyclopedia, an atlas, or the *Reader's Guide*. The format for the series of activities can remain basically the same. First the teacher determines that the students lack the ability to locate information efficiently in reference books. The students then are directed to consult the sources and review their organizational components. The teacher should consider the motivational factor when selecting topics for students to "research" as practice in locating information in various reference books.

Component 5: Developing Notetaking Skills. For students to become competent in taking notes, activities should stress how to listen to and look at information systematically. Students may have to be taught that information is usually presented in a structured way and that they must look for cues and use them to record relevant information.

For example, in teaching that chapters within a text follow a consistent pattern, each student in the group might be asked to bring one of his or her texts from the regular classroom. First the teacher points out that key words and ideas are highlighted in the book (italicized or listed at the beginning of each chapter or set in bold type, etc.). Then students practice finding and copying headings and sub-headings within chapters and locating information summaries and chapter check-ups. Also, they learn to look at pictures, charts, graphs, photographs, maps, time lines, number lines, and any accompanying captions as sources of information.

Component 6: Preparing for Tests. Studying can be described as the process of assimilating key information and remembering it. It is systematic preparation for a demonstration of knowledge.

To help students learn how to study for tests, they must first learn to look at their sources (e.g., notebooks, notes, word lists, study guides) and organize the information available. The next step is to commit this information to memory. Students may benefit from working in pairs or small groups to study and master the content. They could make tapes for themselves or for each other and study from these. They also may have to communicate with their teachers about their problems in taking tests and the possibilities of arranging alternative ways of demonstrating competence. Finally, systems for organizing and remembering information, such as SQ3R, are introduced and the students practice learning an appropriate system.

Component 7: Taking Tests. The steps involved in taking tests include reading directions, asking questions for clarification if necessary, going through the test item-by-item answering the items that are known and skipping those that are not known, and coming back to answer unknown items as time permits. Teachers should outline these steps to the students and as a subsequent practice activity, teach them how to create cue cards for themselves.

Later, using actual tests as vehicles for teaching how to take tests will help students recognize that tests represent an obstacle they can overcome. These tests should be adaptations of what the students face regularly. Thus, if content teachers typically include true-false, multiple choice, or matching sections on their tests, several practice tests should be created for each type of test item.

CONCLUSION

The School Survival Skills Curriculum we have proposed purposely links special education content to mainstream requirements. This curriculum is considered to be mastered only after the students have demonstrated the competencies in their content area classes. We believe that installing such a curriculum for secondary students with learning handicaps is one way to facilitate integration of these students into mainstream education.

Students who have had this curriculum generally report better interactions with peers and adults, more passing grades, and fewer altercations with authority figures. Teachers report that the students seem to be better prepared, more involved in their classes, and less abrasive in social situations.

Of course, the curriculum has not worked for all the students who have been exposed to it. Some have continued to be suspended and receive failing grades. Others have dropped out of school. We acknowledge that the School Survival Skills Curriculum will not solve all the problems of adolescents with learning problems. No single curriculum could do that. Nevertheless, our experience suggests that a curriculum like that described here can be a crucial component of a comprehensive model of services.

REFERENCES

Conger, J. J. *Adolescence and youth: Psychological development in a changing world.* New York: Harper & Row, 1977.

Erickson, C. F., & Friedman, S. B. Understanding and evaluating adolescent behavior problems. *Journal of School Health,* 1978, *48*(5), 293-297.

Zigmond, N. A prototype of comprehensive service for secondary students with learning disabilities: A preliminary report. *Learning Disability Quarterly,* 1978, *1,* 39-49.

Cratty examines the history of movement activities as a part of special education. He poses a number of questions such as: Who should receive motor development services? What are the benefits? How many types of services should be offered? He sets out to answer these questions and then outlines the essentials of a motor development program.

Motor Development For Special Populations: Issues, Problems, and Operations

Bryant J. Cratty

Historically, the use of movement activities for various special groups of people has paralleled the interest of individuals and societies in exceptional populations. Centuries before the birth of Christ, physicians in the Orient, Greece, and India were caring for the needs of physically handicapped people with exercises, which in modified forms are a part of contemporary therapy programs (Licht, 1965). Still later, at the end of the 1700s, sensory-motor activities began to be applied to those with sensory handicaps, and the retarded as exemplified by the work of Sequin and the legendary book, *The Wild Boy of Aveyron* (Itard, 1932). Marie Montessori used movements of both the larger and smaller muscle groups in formulating her program for the culturally deprived in the slums of Rome around the turn of this century. After World War II, the learning disabled segment was exposed to various movement tasks (Getman, 1952; Ayres, 1972).

The programs of still other exceptional groups might be enriched with movement activities designed especially for them. These populations include the gifted and the developmentally disabled young adult. And the special movement needs and capacities of the deaf and hard-of-hearing still have received only cursory attention by both researchers and practitioners (Cratty, 1980).

The historical antecedents just cited, along with firsthand observation, prompted the insertion of various types of movement imperatives in Public Law 94-142, exemplified in statements of objectives and in descriptions of program content for handicapped groups. Thus, one is now able to find a variety of delivery systems in both general and special education incorporating efforts to enhance the movement attributes of various atypical populations (Gearheart & Weishahn, 1976).

For the most part these attempts at enriching movement experiences are useful, and the practitioners involved are often capable, energetic, knowledgeable, and well motivated. But sometimes school districts have employed part-time help with sketchy backgrounds, merely to throw balls at special children and youth 15-20 minutes a day for one or two sessions each week. Efforts in this latter case may be meeting the letter of the law but not the intent of PL 94-142.

At times, when time and experience permit, the adapted physical education teacher, physical or occupational therapist, or another whose responsibility involves incorporating movement experiences into special programs formulates credible, achievable goals when writing the individualized education program. Other times, when both experience and time are lacking, the IEP meeting is superficial and the written goals involving motor development tasks are unachievable, less than meaningful, or developmentally unsound.

To provide meaningful services for the physical needs of youngsters and adults with special problems, certain issues must be confronted and problems solved. Such confrontation should result in reasonable and sound operations, which in turn are likely to produce real change in the movement capacities of those served.

One can easily pontificate about what should be done, but one must also realize that school districts are being confronted with the most difficult kinds of decisions. On one hand, taxpayers, by their support of PL 94-142 and other legislation at the state level, are demanding increased services. But these same taxpayers meanwhile are pleading to cut the "meat" out of the often sparse budgets required to supply these essential kinds of educational enrichment. With these conflicts in mind, I will outline what I perceive as some of the most important issues within the context of motor development services for exceptional students, and then outline certain operational procedures that may be useful to consider.

ISSUES AND PROBLEMS

1. *Who should receive motor development services and in what form?*

Simply mainstreaming a handicapped youngster within a regular school's academic program may not go far enough when the child is faced with the school's physical education program. Even recess may prove trying. To illustrate the kind of problem that might arise — I received a phone call recently from a mother of a young girl with spina bifida. The mother reported that her daughter was doing fine in the academic program and had a heightened feeling of self-worth upon realizing that she was equal or superior to many of her "normal" classmates. In informal play and during physical education, however, the girl was experiencing anguish. The difference between her own physical capacities and those she observed in the other children seemed "overwhelming", the distraught mother told me. While my response was perhaps more tranquilizing than truly helpful, the realization remained that the girl was being served well in one sense — in that the concept of "least restrictive environment" *was* being met within the classroom — but the environment in which the child had to play and function physically was proving to be more restrictive both physically and emotionally than that of the school for the handicapped that she had attended previously.

Physical activities for special children and youth range from impera-tives needed by the obviously physically handicapped (Cratty & Breen, 1972) and the profoundly and severely retarded (Edgar, 1970), through helpful modifications required by the moderately and mildly retarded, sensory handicapped, emotionally disturbed, and learning disabled, to what might be termed "helpful and creatively different tasks" for the gifted. Schools should take care to provide a reasonably exact "fit" in physical development services for the handicapped. Permitting a child in a wheelchair to merely keep score or administering physical activities for typical children without regard for a handicapped student in their midst is not serving his or her needs. Likewise, allowing an emotionally disturbed child to remain on the fringes is not being sensitive to his or her needs.

Rather, many special children and youth may be exposed to a helpful mix of both special and regular educational services throughout a school day. The prevailing policy should be one that provides for optimum integration of given attributes, including physical capacities, of special and regular services within the school program — not one that mindlessly places atypical youngsters with typical ones in all phases of the school curriculum, to sink or to swim as best they can.

Among the variety of delivery forms of enrichment in motor develop-ment are the following possibilities:

(a) the help of a "student guide" in a regular physical education class;
(b) special physical education classes catering to certain motorically deficient children and youth in regular school settings;
(c) traveling physical development teachers who would work on a 2:1 or 3:1 ratio with physically impaired children in regular school settings;

(d)   special physical or occupational therapy services to which handicapped children might travel or which may be provided by an
itinerant physical therapist (PT) or occupational therapist (OT)
during visits to regular schools twice a week or so.

2.   *How many types of services should be offered within a physical
development program?*

The content of a physical development program may vary greatly
depending upon the available time and resources, the expertise and background of specialists assigned to the job, the philosophy of the school
district, and specific needs of individual children needing services. The more
expansive programs provide a broad range of movement experiences including rhythmics, sports skills, fitness activities, and the like, along with
manual dexterity tasks, self-care skill development, relaxation training
intended to reduce hyperactivity, practice in printing and writing, and
activities designed to reduce manneristic behaviors.

More and more people are earning graduate degrees focused on the
physical needs of special children and youth, and so are becoming better
equipped to provide the breadth of services described. At the same time, the
roles of the PT and OT are becoming defined more broadly than was true
during the 1960s and early 1970s.

Thus, I think that in the decade ahead the physical development
specialist will more and more provide special children, youths, and adults
with a broader range of services including those listed above. These
specialists may improve the physical capacities and skills of youngsters in
direct ways as well as by serving as helpful consultants to classroom teachers.

3.   *What are reasonable goals to expect from the application of a physical development program to special populations?*

Hopefully, the presence of better educated motor development specialists
within school systems will:

(a)   bring about an increased ability to provide the breadth of services
discussed under issue 2, above;
(b)   enable interpretation of research findings; which in turn will
(c)   subject expansive claims made for motor development activities to
rational and scientific scrutiny (Freeman, 1967; Hammill, 1972;
Glass, 1967; Hammill & Wiederholt, 1972).

For the most part, research indicates that the folksy axiom heard in
many contexts applies when attempting to formulate reasonable goals for a
motor development program for special populations: "You get out of
something what you put into it!" Stated in another way, one had better

include in a motor development program content that corresponds rather closely with stated goals or one may be disappointed with outcomes (Cratty, 1972; Seefeldt, 1974).

The research indicates that, within limits, movement capacities may be improved if children and youth are exposed to properly sequenced, reasonable movement tasks (Cratty, Ikeda, Martin, Jennett, & Morris, 1970). This improvement is more likely if the children are younger and the movement problems are moderate rather than severe.

Many of the surveys by numerous writers over the past 15 years stating expansive claims for outcomes of movement programs are less than realistic (Myers & Hammill, 1976). One must focus rather directly upon the specific type of movement capacity one is hoping to change. Rolling on the floor or otherwise subjecting a child to a variety of activities using the larger muscle groups is not likely to help him or her print better or exhibit better self-care skills, which require use of the smaller muscle groups.

Crawling on the floor, patterning, scooter board work, and balance activities, if applied intelligently, may aid certain movement capacities. But assertions that these and similar sensory-motor experiences will somehow influence higher thought processes, auditory and visual perceptual skills, reading, and other academic activities are not supported by the available research.

Motor development specialists of a variety of titles, somehow seduced by the "movement magicians" whose ideas have found their way into print, may initially recruit enthusiastic volunteers, easily collect monies, and gain support to institute what appear to be viable programs. Later, however, evaluation of the outcomes of such programs by more sophisticated specialists within the district may bring embarrassment to many well meaning but misguided zealots.

To provide a sound program of motor development, a rather close correspondence should exist between three components:

(a) the list of objectives put forth;
(b) the nature of the content of evaluation devices employed before and after the program takes place; and
(c) the activities offered to participants on a daily basis.

4. *What skills focusing on atypical populations should motor development specialists possess?*

More and more useful legislation at the state level is specifying the critical skills needed by those who impose motor tasks upon handicapped children and youth. Now, these individuals may be required to have, in addition to regular teaching credentials, physical education, special education, and, often, advanced graduate work in their specialty. As a result, these people are more likely to bring to the job a useful balance between practical and applied skills gained via internship programs and a theoretical sophistication enabling them to determine *why* they may be exposing a given child or youth to a given task or tasks.

This enlarged background is also spawning people with finely honed assessment skills that should enable them to:

(a) evaluate the technical integrity of a given test or test battery including assessment of its reliabilty and validity, as well as a careful look at the population upon which it has been normed;

(b) formulate developmentally sound, sensible, situation-specific check-lists for use by various handicapped groups. Such lists may be useful, for example, in attempting to determine improvements that may be made within a given school's environment and classroom situation by children confined to wheelchairs (Cratty, 1980);

(c) construct useful test batteries by selecting from among those available either entire testing instruments or selected parts of more than one instrument which, when applied, will yield useful information before, during, and after application of a motor development program.

Finally, motor development specialists should possess patience and warmth. These qualities may be ascertained in advance by taking a look, before making a permanent job offer, at the way in which they relate to special populations while they serve as part-time aides or volunteers.

5. *How can people from more than one discipline be aided in working together to optimize the motor development of a given child or a group of atypical children, youths, or adults?*

A lack of supervision or integration of physical services may cause less than optimum outcomes and even regression in an individual's physical capacities. For example, a physical therapist may be training a child with spastic cerebral palsy to walk by reducing the tendency for a scissor-like gait. During another part of the day, a well meaning but maladroit swimming instructor may be teaching the elementary backstroke — and thereby strengthening the muscles that *cause* scissoring. At still another point in the school day, the traveling "perceptual-motor lady" may take an apparatus from the back of her station wagon and proceed to decrease the capacity for a wide, stable gait pattern by placing the child on a narrow balance beam.

To cite yet another example, a robust physical educator, assuming that the "drainage" theory of physical activity is valid, may attempt to calm hyperactive children by exposing them to vigorous exercise. In truth, however, he or she is probably raising their activation levels too high for any kind of meaningful academic work that is to follow the physical activity.

I once observed an army of specialists working with a number of profoundly and severely retarded individuals in a large, expensive facility. These specialists, in their own sessions, were requiring what in sum were virtually identical tasks. The speech therapists, occupational and physical therapists, physical educators, and dance specialists were, unknown to each other, eliciting the same responses despite what each "specialist" considered his or her special type of effort.

Integration of services is not difficult. It primarily requires frequent, continual communication between and among movement specialists and others concerned for the clients' welfare. The legislation requiring IEPs is serving in some ways to reduce the types of problems mentioned above.

Many other issues could be mentioned, most of which are interrelated and are modifications of those already presented here. Four of these are briefly suggested below, and the following discussion of various operations alludes to the same and other issues.

— Formulating reasonable administrative and supervisorial structures and policies to promote motor development program components is important. At present, budgetary situations tend to restrict the number of adequate supervisory personnel. And those who do function in that capacity often do not have the appropriate academic background and techniques to supervise therapists, adapted physical education teachers, and others interested in motor development. Or their supervisory duties are so fragmented that enhancing motor development occupies only a small part of their time and mission. Legislation at the state level, to provide for supervisors with graduate level degrees in motor development as overseers of adapted physical educators and others, seems advisable.

— Adequate provision for meaningful parent participation in motor development programs is usually lacking within the school system. The following section speaks to the issue of operationalizing this kind of interaction.

— Policies are needed to provide adequate guidelines for evaluation, and at times to impose restrictions upon the kinds of things motor development specialists are permitted to evaluate. At this writing, one of the larger school districts in the country, with the help of a university teacher-educator in physical education, has provided its adapted physical education teachers with an evaluative instrument containing numerous items that purportedly evaluate visual-perceptual functions. The real danger in an unqualified person using such an instrument is the perhaps spurious assumption by parents that if school personnel involved in the evaluation find no visual problem, none exists; thus, parents will be less inclined to seek further help for their children from professionals trained to detect atypical vision and ocular function.

— Policies are needed to spell out exactly how much time should be allotted for direct contact between a motor development specialist and a child each week. With mainstreaming this direct contact has often been drastically reduced because the time spent traveling from school to school is interpolated into the specialist's working day. Any real change in a child's motor competencies, however, will not take place without a minimum of two to three contacts per week between specialist and client, with each session lasting 20-45 minutes.

OPERATIONS/PROCEDURES

The operations and procedures discussed here bear upon the quality of service rendered to pupils. The guidelines are based upon optimizing contact time between motor development specialist and child or youth, yet are reasonable in relation to the budgetary circumstances confronting most school districts.

1. *Providing for facilities and equipment.*

Maximum use of facilities and equipment may be encouraged by considering the following ideas:

- Equipment, balls, and the like need not all be "store bought." The mark-up for relatively simple equipment and apparatus is great. As an alternative, many pieces of equipment may be made by the children themselves. Often, the special ownership and feelings about equipment like beanbags are enhanced if the children themselves have made them (Corbin, 1972).
- Special children could be accorded playground and gym use, with proper supervision of specialists, at times when the other children are not using these facilities. Self-conscious children with motor problems do not usually enjoy having their more competent peers judge their progress toward achieving adequate play skills, and hyperactive children can become more focused if they are not subjected to the confusion of the usual playground situation.
- Cubicles, or carrels, may be helpful to distractible children who are involved in crafts projects.
- Studies have shown that the modifiability of play materials enhances both physical and mental participation by youngsters of all ages (Cratty & Breen, 1972). Thus, for example, giving children large sheets of thin plastic often prompts a variety of construction behaviors, and a water source further enhances the activity (a system of "lakes?"). Large IBM printout sheets similarly prove stimulating to groups of children in a play situation. I once observed a young

group of atypical youngsters beginning to construct "buildings" of IBM sheets early in the day. Later, artistic paper-tearing activities evolved, and by the end of the day the paper had been reduced to "snow," which was sprinkled on the heads of all participants!

● Equipment normally purchased for the gymnasium — large, foam-filled mats, for example — may be constructed with the contribution of scraps from a foam-furniture shop, which are bundled within a large, old volleyball net. This type of mat may be constructed in various shapes and used as a downhill or uphill surface, or as a level, soft, therapy-like mattress.

2. *Proceeding developmentally.*

No practitioner of the "motor development arts" can be too well-versed in the sequences and subsequences permeating the motor development patterns of normal children (Cratty, 1979). The adapted physical educator and others should be aware, for example, of the subsequences involved in crawling (i.e., a hand-knee support, then reaching out, then a random-pattern crawl, and finally a cross-extension crawl).

Similar knowledge of the subsequences of scribbling, to cite another example, represents a tool in what may be termed "parallel-scribble play" alongside a motorically deficient youngster (Keogh & Smith, 1967). As a result of this strategy, the youngster is encouraged indirectly, through the teacher's efforts, to be gradually stimulated by increasingly sophisticated types of scribbling — efforts that promote the control needed to form primitive geometric figures and, later, letters. An excellent text by Rhoda Kellogg (1969) provides guidelines for this type of early enrichment.

As the child attempts to print, the motor development specialist should be familiar with developmental sequences of figures that may be drawn (i.e., first a + then a O, then a square, triangles, and so on. During this stage templates may be constructed to aid the child in partially making figures and letters and then, after removing the template, completing the figures. Examples of both inside (easiest to manage) and outside templates are shown in Figure 1.

Motor development specialists should also be familiar with the order in which lines are drawn in various directions relative to the body and the order of difficulty of various block printed letters, rather than starting by asking the child to print his or her name. Right angle letters are easiest (e.g., H I T), then circular letters (C O), then combinations (B P), and then slanted lines (X V K W A) and those combining curves and slants (R). The compound curved S is the most difficult.

My test in adapted physical education (Cratty, 1980) contains numerous sequences and subsequences underlying the important act of walking. These

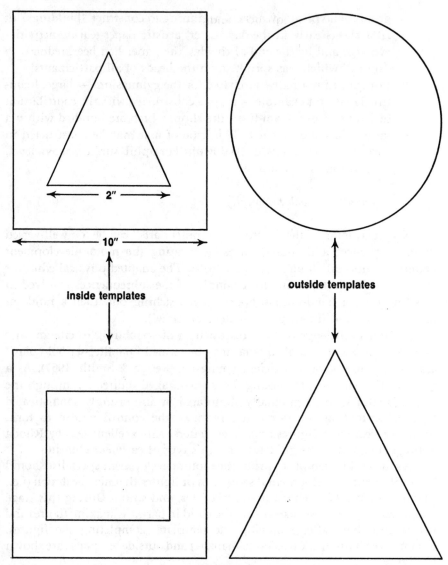

FIGURE 1
Examples of Inside and Outside Templates

sequences should be kept in mind, particularly when more than one motor specialist converges on a given youngster each day or week. The specialists should consult each other about meaningful substages, where the child is at the present time, and the best way in which to move the child upward and forward.

Among the other sequences and subsequences of which the motor development specialist should be aware are the following:

- Intercepting a thrown or bounced ball is not a first step for motorically handicapped children. If a child cannot manage this, balls of various shapes, sizes, and weights should simply be passed from hand to hand, and held. Also, balls should be rolled, and trapped, first in a seated position and later standing. These things should be accomplished before asking a motorically deficient child to catch a ball of any size. A first step for many handicapped children may be to merely watch a moving ball.
- The use of beanbags may not aid ball catching because the hands have to "give" as a ball is contacted and this is not necessary in catching a beanbag. Beanbags, frisbees, and other missiles, however, should be experienced by all children, including the handicapped.
- The stages in throwing a ball are first to give it impetus with the hands or feet, then to propel it without any weight shift (usually two-handed at first), then to make a weight shift, stepping with the foot on the same side as the throwing arm. Finally, the mature throw requires a simultaneous weight shift, using the leg opposite to the throwing arm. By having the child on a small tilting platform when releasing the ball, the weight shift may be heard and exaggerated.
- Developmentally sound ways to proceed with various rhythmic movements are based, for example, on the fact that vertical and horizontal movements are easier than lateral and spiral movements. Failure of a child to participate successfully in the best intended rhythmic program may result if a teacher ignores these sequences.

This main purpose of possessing a detailed knowledge of developmentally sound sequences relates to the formulation of valid, useful program content. Many subpopulations of atypical children and youth, including the retarded, emotionally disturbed, and motorically deficient, evidence marked insecurities when confronted with physical tasks. Their background of failure has led to a disinclination to exert effort in motor skills, and this in turn leads to a further reduction of capacities.

To reverse this failure syndrome, the sensitive instructor should first introduce tasks that are slightly below the students' skill levels — tasks that permit a build-up of success. As success is realized, more difficult tasks slightly ahead of the individual's level of function should be introduced gradually in order to promote positive change and elicit progress.

In determining what tasks are likely to produce success and those that are likely to be slightly difficult, one must be aware of the performance level of a given individual and group and, thus, which tasks are likely to be achieved, and which tasks are likely to elicit change through the promotion of slight stress. To make these important judgments, one must be aware of the nature of several motor task sequences normally seen in the maturing child and youth.

3. *Helping in therapy.*

One of the most frequently seen mistakes when observing uninitiated or inexperienced people work with atypical children in motor activities involves overenthusiastic help. A therapist may literally carry the child through some tasks (e.g., walking a balance beam). On the other hand, the experienced therapist affords a child minimal help in motor tasks. The exercise should be done by the child, not the therapist! Thus, the good therapist molds the child's actions with minimum help at critical times. If a child seems to seek or require too much help, the experienced therapist reduces the difficulty of the task (e.g., by taking the child off a balance beam and instead having the child work on walking lines painted on the ground) or perhaps gives the youngster some relaxation activity so he or she will be able to approach the task less fearfully.

Overassistance not only may fail to produce any real change in the motor capacities of the client but, if the assistance is too vigorous, may actually prove counterproductive. A child's struggling movements imposed on the nervous system can produce patterns that are antagonistic to those required in various tasks.

4. *Using physical activities to enhance intellectual growth.*

Several publications over the past decade have suggested helpful ways to aid learning through movement activities. Such learning games, using action, can promote the acquisition of important academic, intellectual, and social-psychological abilities (Cratty, 1975, 1981; Mosston, 1972; Gilbert, 1977). If applied well, they prove motivating to those exposed to them and at the same time provide obvious evidence to the observing teacher of the nature and rate of learning taking place.

In essence, these games are based on the premise that movement can improve intellectual and academic abilities to the extent to which these abilities are combined with movement tasks in *direct* and *obvious* ways. The question that motor development specialists should ask, however, is whether both motor development and academic progress are possible, given the time constraints and other areas of learning required. At times, promoting both is possible. At other times, academic/movement games are best left to the classroom teacher of younger or developmentally handicapped individuals. In our studies we have found that moderate physical improvement *was* elicited at the same time children were using movement activities to expand their prereading, reading, and spelling skills. We also found that the most improvement in *physical* skills accrues from programs designed to enhance physical rather than mental attributes (Cratty et al., 1970).

5. *Involving the parents.*

School district personnel, particularly those involved in improving movement capacities of children, often pay lip service to parent involvement. These same individuals, however, often confidentially relate their difficulties in achieving the cooperation of parents in devising physical development programs for atypical youngsters.

Parents of nonhandicapped children often have a hard time gaining the cooperation of their children in the development of new skills. The frequency with which parents reward and punish their offspring tends to blunt their efforts at motivating their progeny to attempt and improve in new skills. Not surprisingly, then, parents of atypical youngsters, where relationships with their children may be more strained, similarly have difficulty initiating home practice sessions that would aid and enhance their child's motor development.

At the same time, little technical support is offered to parents in this regard. Workshops in which "experts" pontificate are sometimes sponsored by school districts for participation by teacher-professionals and parents alike. But parents' vital questions may remain unanswered because of the reluctance of many parents to speak out in front of professionals whom they may perceive as more knowledgeable than are they.

The following operations may be helpful toward gaining parent participation in motor development programs for atypical children, youths and young adults.

- Workshops could be designed specifically for parents, with the basic purpose of meeting their needs for information. These workshops should be as practical as possible, and conducted either by "experts" or by knowledgeable members of the school district staff. Parents should be encouraged to listen, to ask questions, and to participate in the movement activities themselves, so they will be able to better understand the potential benefits. A parent who is unenthusiastic and who places little value on physical activity is unlikely to "sell" its advantages to either normal or atypical youngsters.
- The use of balance activities, as well as locomotor activities, should be explained to parents at information sessions.
- Parents should be invited to be real partners in motor therapy of their children. For example, a detailed schedule might be drawn up denoting times for the parent to engage in fine-motor activities with the child on Tuesday, Thursday, and Saturday, while the school is scheduled to provide sessions in large muscle activity on Monday, Wednesday, and Friday.

- Fathers should be involved in a larger sense than the usual tendency to play catch with the child in the backyard.
- The advantages of relatively brief but regular practice sessions should be explained to parents. Parents often either ignore a home program or compensate in the other direction, believing that the more one does of something the better. In the latter instance they may schedule long, physically oppressive programs containing arduous content which, when applied, is likely to have a negative rather than a positive effect upon their child's progress.
- Parents may be trained as classroom aides. During this training, they should be exposed to motor training facilities, equipment, and techniques. As a result of exposure, they not only will "pick up" technical skills but should perceive that other children have problems similar to their child's and that remediation may indeed take place if reasonable motor tasks are patiently applied. Parents are advised, however, to not work in a school context with their own children.

6. *Rewarding and motivating.*

Lack of motivation is a frequent problem encountered in working with atypical youngsters through physical activities. Their background of failure may be extensive and, therefore, accepting new and often difficult tasks may provoke various kinds of withdrawal reactions. Sometimes the withdrawal is obvious; the child may simply run away. At other times the negativism is more subtle; the child may seem to "space out," evidence distractibility, or otherwise detach himself or herself from the immediate surroundings.

Progress can be elicited by offering tangible rewards. Behavioral modification does work. Indeed, in all life situations obvious intrinsic or more subtle intrinsic social rewards are present and mold performance either negatively or positively. To bestow rewards effectively, however, several points must be kept in mind:

- No reward should be extended unless a real change is perceived by *both* the child and the helper. Constantly rewarding the same behavior will cease to produce the desired changes and progress.
- The kind of reward being extended by parent or teacher may not be perceived by the youth as rewarding. Thus, before setting up a reward system, one must gain firm knowledge of what is truly rewarding, and also keep in mind that the nature of the reward may have to be changed from day to day or even from moment to moment because of the child's shifting feelings.

A graduate student recently completed a case study in which coding games (see Cratty, 1981) were applied in an attempt to teach a retarded 9-year-old boy to read action verbs. At first extrinsic rewards seemed to work as he became able to jump when shown the letter *J*, and then to hop when shown an *H*. Later, as the letters were "stretched" into complete words, however, learning seemed to become more difficult. The highly perceptive boy had come to realize that his learning was important to the graduate student and that when he made an error, he could incite sometimes obvious but usually subtle signs of tension and negativism in her. Thus, *her* reactions to his failures became more powerful rewards than the pretzels she had been extending. The rewards extended — her tensions — began to mold his behavior in a direction opposite to that desired.

- Both the pupil and the teacher or parent extending the rewards must know when some change in behavior has taken place. One of the reasons why behavioral modification techniques do not always work with the severely retarded, for example, is because they cannot connect their behavior to the reward extended or they are not cognizant of any real changes that may be taking place.

Atypical individuals often have a narrow range of acceptance regarding the difficulty of tasks presented to them. When normal children are presented with difficult tasks, they tend to try harder, insofar as they have had a background suggesting that "trying hard pays off." These same normal youngsters may passively participate in easy, even boring tasks, having also learned that conformity pays off. The atypical youngster, on the other hand, is often threatened by difficult tasks and is easily insulted by tasks that are too easy. Thus, motivating these children through the intrinsic nature of motor tasks is not easy. The difficulty of the task must be compatible with the narrow band of acceptance in children and youth who have experienced derision and failure. Well trained adults must become sensitive as to why an individual withdraws, asking themselves if it is because the task was perceived as too easy (insulting) or too difficult (threatening). Then difficulty level should be adjusted accordingly for maximum motivated participation.

7. *The gifted?*

Although the title of this article contains the word *special*, most of this discourse has focused on *handicapped* students. Children and youths who are labeled *gifted* comprise a special group, too, whose needs have rarely been accorded specific consideration by those offering them physical activity. Studies of the gifted (Terman & Oden, 1951) demonstrated that the stereotype of gifted children as being physically inferior may be in error, that the gifted population contains as many physically vigorous youngsters as are found within average populations. I suspect also — without the support of any available data — that the academically gifted population contains about as many motorically handicapped youngsters as are found within groups of academically average individuals. In a program I have administered during the past 18 years for the needs of awkward children, a number of intellectually superior youngsters have been served whose movement attributes were far less than average.

Thus, for the most part, cognitively gifted youngsters are likely to be as physically able or unable as intellectually average youngsters. To enhance their gifts while incorporating physical development, the following provisions might be made when working with academically gifted students.

- Gifted youngsters should be given an important role in the formation of their own activity programs. This participation could be preceded by learning about the nature of human body functions, including the cardiovascular and neuromuscular systems.
- Gifted students may at times be given a chance to make up new games using "different" equipment (e.g., a broken box) and rules formulated especially for the game. And they could be invited to modify game rules from traditional games to create other games. They could be challenged with "absolute novelty" in inventing games unlike any of the traditional games to which they have been exposed.
- Gifted pupils could be asked to integrate specific academic learning into physical development classes by devising their own exercise programs to suit their individual needs.
- Game selection can be aided by historical reviews of presently available game forms. Surveys of games played around the world, both in past and contemporary times, could spark interest on the part of gifted youngsters to devise their own versions of these games, using authentic equipment, rules, and facilities.

AN OVERVIEW

As a result of current national and state legislation, administrators of special education programs must give more than lip service to providing services intended to improve the physical functioning of their charges. The degree to which youngsters are served in this area of the curriculum depends in part upon the background of the adapted physical educator and others offering these services, including the dance specialist, occupational therapist, physical therapist, and recreational therapist.

Understanding the nature of normal motor development is important in serving special needs individuals. Atypical youngsters, the axiom goes, develop as do typical ones but at a different rate, exhibiting the same qualities but at a different time of their lives. Thus, motor development specialists should be well versed on the sequences and subsequences of this development.

The integration of personnel — lay, parent, and professional — provides the best basis for improving movement capacities of special populations — all of which can benefit to varying degrees from such programming. With a sound underlying structure and well trained people to carry out the programs, the issues and problems of today can be steadily resolved.

REFERENCES

Ayres, J. *Sensory integration and learning disorders.* Los Angeles: Western Psychological Services, 1972.

Corbin, C. *Inexpensive equipment for games.* Dubuque, IA: W. C. Brown, 1972.

Cratty, B. J. *Physical expressions of intelligence.* Englewood Cliffs, NJ: Prentice-Hall, 1972.

Cratty, B. J. *Teaching about human behavior through active games.* Englewood Cliffs, NJ: Prentice-Hall, 1975.

Cratty, B. J. *Perceptual and motor development of infants and children* (2d ed.). Englewood Cliffs, NJ: Prentice-Hall, 1979.

Cratty, B. J. *Coding games: Active ways to enhance reading and thinking.* Denver, CO: Love Publishing Co., 1981.

Cratty, B. J., & Breen, J. E. *Educational games for the physically handicapped,* Denver, CO: Love Publishing Co., 1972.

Cratty, B. J., Ikeda, N., Martin, M., Jennett, C., & Morris, M. *Movement activities, motor ability, and the education of children.* Springfield, IL: Charles C Thomas, 1970.

Edgar, C. L. The adaptation of perceptual-motor training techniques to the profoundly retarded. In *Some educational implications of movement.* Seattle, WA: Special Child Publications, 1970.

Freeman, R. D. Controversy over "patterning" as a treatment for brain damage in children. *Journal of the American Medical Association,* 1967, *202,* 385-388.

Gearheart, B. R., & Weishahn, M. W. *The handicapped child in the regular classroom.* St. Louis, MO: C. V. Mosby Co., 1976.

Getman, G. N. *How to develop your child's intelligence — A research publication,* Luverne, MN: G. N. Getman, 1952.

Gilbert, A. G. *Teaching the three R's through movement experiences.* Minneapolis, MN: Burgess Publishing Co., 1977.

Glass, B. B. *A critique of experiments on the role of neurological organization in reading performance.* Champaign, IL: Center for Instructional Research and Curriculum Evaluation, University of Illinois, 1967.

Hammill, D. D. Training visual perceptual processes. *Journal of Learning Disabilities,* 1972, *5,* 552-559.

Hammill, D. D., & Wiederholt, J. L. Review of the Frostig visual perception test and the related training program. In L. Mann & D. Sabatino (Eds.), *The first review of special education.* Philadelphia: Grune & Stratton, 1972.

Itard, J-M G. *The wild boy of Aveyron.* (G. & M. Humphrey, trans.). New York: Appleton-Century-Crofts, 1932.

Kellogg, R. *Analyzing children's art.* Palo Alto, CA: National Press Books, 1969.

Keogh, B., & Smith, C. E. Changes in copying ability of young children. *Perceptual & Motor Skills,* 1967, *26,* 773-774.

Licht, S. History. Chapter 13 in S. Licht (Ed.), *Therapeutic exercise* (2d ed). Baltimore, MD: Waring Press, 1965, pp. 426-471.

Mosston, M. *Teaching: From command to discovery.* Belmont, CA: Wadsworth Publishing Co., 1972.

Myers, P. L., & Hammill, D. D. The perceptual motor systems. Chapter 9 in *Methods of learning disorders* (2d ed.). New York: John Wiley & Sons, 1976.

Seefeldt, V. Perceptual-motor programs. In J. Wilmore (Ed.), *Exercise and sport sciences reviews* (Vol. 2). New York: Academic Press, 1974, pp. 265-288.

Terman, L. W., & Oden, M. The Stanford studies of the gifted. In P. Witty (Ed.), *The gifted child.* Boston: Heath, 1951, pp. 23-24.

ADDITIONAL REFERENCES

Cratty, B. J. *Adaptive physical education for handicapped children and youth.* Denver, CO: Love Publishing Co., 1980.

Goodman, L., & Hammill, D. D. The effectiveness of the Kephart-Getman activities in developing perceptual-motor and cognitive skills. *Focus on Exceptional Children,* 1973, *4*(9), 1-9.

Hammill, D. D., Goodman, L., & Wiederholt, J. L. Visual-motor processes: Can we train them? *Reading Teacher,* 1974, *27*, 469-486.

Humphrey, J. H., & Sullivan, D. D. *Teaching slow learners through active games.* Springfield, IL: Charles C Thomas, 1970.

Johnson, D. L., Brekke, B., & Harlow, S. D. Appropriateness of the motor-free visual perception test when used with the mentally retarded. *Education & Training of the Retarded,* 1977, *21*, 312-315.

Mann, L. Perceptual training, misdirections and redirections. *American Journal of Orthopsychiatry,* 1970, *40*, 18-23.

Robbins, M. P., & Glass, G. V. The Doman-Delacato rationale: A critical analysis. In J. Hellmuth (Ed.), *Educational therapy* (Vol. 2). Seattle: Special Child Publications, 1968.

Whitsell, L. J. Delacato's "neurological organization," a medical appraisal. *California School Health,* 1970, *3*, 1-13.

Wiederholt, J. L., & Hammill, D. D. Use of the Frostig-Horne visual perceptual program with kindergarten and first grade economically disadvantaged children. *Psychology in the Schools,* 1971, *8*, 268-274.

Zigler, E., & Seitz, V. An experimental evaluation of sensorimotor patterning, a critique. *American Journal of Mental Deficiency,* 1975, *79*, 483-492.

Handwriting is an important yet greatly neglected area of the curriculum Graham and Miller indicate that teachers and student teachers alike list handwriting as last in their perceived areas of preparation to teach. Considerable research relating to handwriting is reviewed, including the relationship of handwriting to reading, fluency, legibility, and manuscript versus cursive.

The authors suggest that most instruction is not based on research but should be. They review the research basis for teaching handwriting, including which letters to introduce when. They offer a model for handwriting and also discuss the assessment of handwriting skills, reviewing the various scales available to teachers. Finally, they offer many practical suggestions on subjects such as posture, methods of instruction for left-handed students, and remedial approaches.

Handwriting Research and Practice: A Unified Approach

Steve Graham and Lamoine Miller

A man walked into a New England bank and shoved a piece of paper under one of the teller's windows. The teller carefully examined the note, then kicked the alarm button. Within minutes police officers converged on the scene and arrested the man. They later discovered that the suspect was a respected businessman suffering from laryngitis and illegible handwriting. The note was a poorly written request for a new checkbook (O'Brien, 1959).

The aftereffects of malformed print are usually not so bizarre. Nonetheless, within today's schools poor handwriting has aptly been dubbed an instructional time thief (Enstrom, 1967). Students with handwriting difficulties often lose considerable time completing assignments, and teachers forfeit precious time attempting to grade papers marred by illegible letters and words. Poor penmanship is a barrier to both expressive writing and spelling achievement (Strickling, 1973). Further, regardless of content, teachers assign higher scores to papers with handwriting of good quality (Briggs, 1970; Chase, 1968; Markham, 1976; Rondinella, 1963; Soloff, 1973).

Poor penmanship has at least two possible causes. First, a learner may bring to the task certain predilections that impede effective instruction. For example, a spastic paraplegic with poor motor coordination may not respond well to standard techniques of teaching handwriting (Bachmann & Law, 1961). This is not the case for most students, though. Legible handwriting has not been found to relate significantly to either eye-hand coordination, race, intelligence, or anatomical age (Harris, 1960). Handwriting problems also do not seem to be particularly associated with mental retardation (Kvaraceus, 1954; Love, 1965).

The second explanation — that most handwriting difficulties are the result of inadequate instruction — seems more viable. Enstrom (1966) has suggested that handwriting is the most poorly taught element of the elementary school curriculum. Only one of every 10 schools requires its teachers to have some kind of handwriting training (King, 1961). There is little instructional individualization, and some schools have no formal program for handwriting (Addy & Wylie, 1973; King, 1961; Wolfson, 1962). Additionally, handwriting is an unpopular subject with teachers (Greenblatt, 1962). And student teachers rank handwriting last among subjects they feel prepared to teach (Groff, 1962). Failure to adequately teach handwriting is analogous to "the woodcutter who is so busy with his chopping that he hasn't time to sharpen his axe" (Enstrom, 1965, p. 185).

The teaching of penmanship appears to be based primarily on public opinion rather than on research (Groff, 1960). Even though most of the published literature is of a nontechnical and descriptive nature (Andersen, 1965), the twentieth century has witnessed considerable scientific interest in handwriting. While empirical evidence is available, it has not been applied, for the most part.

If handicapped and normal students are to receive adequate handwriting instruction, they must have relevant experiences and considerable practice in developing specific skills. Handwriting instruction should be teacher directed, should contain a variety of relevant instructional options, and should be based on a foundation of research evidence. In this article, we present a model of handwriting instruction based on research and experiential knowledge. The model is designed primarily for mainstreamed handicapped students but could be adapted for use with most school-age children.

DEVELOPMENT OF HANDWRITING SKILLS

Children become interested in writing at an early age. By the age of two, they are usually fascinated with scribbling. At approximately age three, many children begin to realize that people make marks on paper purposefully. Somewhere between the ages of four and five, most children attempt to formulate both letters and numbers.

Formal instruction in handwriting begins in first grade. Initially, the student's quality of penmanship is poor, gradually improving with practice (Andersen, 1969; Covert, 1953; Groff, 1964). Similarly, speed in writing increases from about 36 letters per minute in grade two to 50-72 letters per minute in grade six (Freeman, 1915a; Groff, 1961). Both speed and quality tend to vary together (Wills, 1938).

Although most children are eager to learn how to write, some students develop an aversion to penmanship (Quint, 1958). Boys are more likely than girls to dislike handwriting. Moreover, girls are often better handwriters than are boys (Andersen, 1969; Gates & LaSalle, 1924; Groff, 1964; Horton, 1969; Lewis, 1964; Love, 1965; Trankell, 1956).

Although the errors are comparable, adults' handwriting is frequently less legible than that of upper elementary and junior high school students (Newland, 1932). This is, in part, related to experience and increased fluency. As students write more and acquire speed, they have a tendency to become careless and take shortcuts in forming letters. This eventually results in the individual's developing a personal style of handwriting (Eagleson, 1937; Harris & Rarick, 1959; Quint, 1958; Seifert, 1959).

Writers also commonly exhibit different standards of penmanship depending upon the exercise. To illustrate, students customarily write better on a copying task than on a written composition (Lewis, 1964; Wills, 1938). In general, good handwriters evidence more intrapersonal variability than do poor handwriters (Covert, 1953).

THE HANDWRITING CURRICULUM

Handwriting is essentially a tool for expressing, communicating, and recording ideas. Among the basic skills it is unique because it results in a tangible product. Handwriting is considered primarily as a means to an end, not an end unto itself, and should therefore be produced with maximum efficiency and minimum effort.

The handwriting product should be easy to learn, read, and write. Nevertheless, there is no accepted standard alphabet form used in instruction (Herrick & Otto, 1961). Although there are similarities, each letter of the alphabet has many variant forms. Considerable variation is found in the speed, stability, and legibility of different forms of the same letter (Boraas, 1936). Thus, a teaching alphabet should be simple, and selected on the basis of readability and speed of production.

In planning a handwriting curriculum, then, which letter forms should be taught, and which skills should receive primary consideration? With respect to the former concern, controversy endures over the merits of manuscript versus cursive writing. With regard to the latter, students should develop handwriting that is both legible and fluent.

Manuscript Versus Cursive

Humankind has always used at least two styles of writing (Enstrom, 1968, 1969). One, a formal script, has been used for special documents and books. The other is a rapidly produced, informal cursive style.

Traditionally, writing by hand was an adult skill passed from parent to child. When the formal education of children began, the adult skill of cursive writing was emphasized. But cursive handwriting was difficult for many young children to learn. Consequently, in 1913, Edward Johnston proposed that a simplified script would be easier for children. Teachers soon discovered that primary students could learn the new style of writing. This simplified print later was termed *manuscript*.

Manuscript writing was first introduced in the United States in the early 1920s. Its acceptance gradually spread during the next 20 to 30 years. Today, both manuscript and cursive writing are taught in the majority of American schools (Addy & Wylie, 1973; Herrick & Okada, 1961; Owen, 1954; Soltis, 1963; Wolfson, 1962). Manuscript is commonly introduced in grades one and two, and instruction in cursive writing usually begins in grade three.

Despite the widespread practice of teaching both forms, some experts espouse the use of only one style. These advocates suggest that mastering two styles is more difficult than perfecting one. They further point out that there is no natural transition from manuscript to cursive.

Authors and educators who have championed manuscript writing for developmental and remedial penmanship include Hildreth (1963), Myklebust and Johnson (1967), Mecham, Berko, and Palmer (1966), and Templin (1964). Proponents of manuscript writing indicate that it: (a) is more legible than cursive handwriting; (b) closely resembles book print and therefore is an aid to both reading and spelling instruction; (c) consists of simple movements and hence is easier to learn than is cursive writing; (d) can be written as fast as the cursive style; (e) is required on documents including employment applications; (f) may be the preferred style for children with poor vision or motor difficulties; (g) requires fewer reciprocal movements and changes of letter forms than does cursive writing; and (h) promotes the independence of letters within and between words.

Authorities who have promoted cursive writing for developmental and remedial penmanship include Cruickshank, Bentzen, Ratzeburg, and Tannhauser (1961), Early (1973), Fernald (1943), Kaufman and Biren (1979), McGinnis, Kleffner, and Goldstein (1963), and Strauss and Lehtinen (1947). Proponents indicate that the cursive style: (a) is faster than manuscript handwriting; (b) is continuous and connected and therefore is perceived as whole units; (c) may be the preferred style for orthopedically handicapped children; (d) results in less directional confusion than manuscript and therefore fewer reversals; (e) is preferred by parents, students, and teachers; (f) is more rhythmical and less cramping than the manuscript form; (g) is a prerequiite to reading cursive script; and (h) is easier to write.

Not all the claims advanced by supporters of either style of handwriting have been substantiated by empirical evidence (see Figure 1). For instances, research examining the comparative speed of the two styles and the effects of manuscript writing on spelling achievement has been inconclusive. The ability to write cursive letters also does not appear to be a necessary prerequisite to reading cursive script. There is considerable evidence, however, that manuscript is more legible than cursive writing, leads to greater gains in reading achievement, can be written as fast, and is easier to learn. The bulk of the evidence, then, tends to support the claims of manuscript style proponents. Nonetheless, the evidence is not conclusive and the relative effectiveness of the two styles has not yet been adequately demonstrated. To illustrate, the two-minute speed test used in many handwriting studies may yield misleading results (Enstrom, 1964). On a longer time sample, cursive script may be faster, more durable, and result in less fatigue.

Which letter forms should be taught? We recommend that manuscript print be maintained throughout the instructional program. Once a student acquires legible and fluent manuscript writing, the instructor should, when appropriate, teach cursive script as a separate but related skill. For many students, acquiring and maintaining two styles of handwriting does not present any overwhelming problems. Most students are eager to learn cursive script, and research suggests that the initial procurement of manuscript does not have a detrimental effect on the subsequent attainment of cursive. writing. Still, cursive script should not be viewed as a replacement for manuscript. If both styles are taught, they should be learned and used throughout life.

For a small number of students, the cursive style may be a necessary alternate to manuscript. This practice is recommended for students who are unable to master manuscript or repeatedly refuse to use this form because it looks "babyish."

Legibility

Conventionally, the quality of handwriting had been rated on the basis of legibility. Legibility refers to the ease with which writing can be read. It is not a unitary characteristic but a composite of simpler elements. Research by Andersen (1969), Craig (1965), Jackson (1970), and Quant (1946) has indicated that readability of print is affected by: letter form, uniformity of slant, size of letters, compactness of space within and between words, alignment, and line quality. For the most part, these elements are interrelated. A change in one element frequently results in a change in another. Thus, no single

Relationship to Reading and Spelling

- The initial use of manuscript writing facilitates learning to read and leads to greater gains in reading than does cursive script (Cutright, 1936; Houston, 1938; Long & Mayer, 1931; Voorhis, 1931).
- The initial use of manuscript writing does not lead to greater gains in spelling in comparison to cursive script (Byers, 1963; McOmber, 1970; Varty, 1938).
- The initial use of manuscript writing leads to greater gains in spelling in comparison to cursive script (Cutright, 1936; Lindahl, 1938).
- The initial use of cursive script does not adversely affect spelling or reading achievement (Early, Nelson, Kleber, Treegob, Huffman, & Cass, 1976).

Reading Cursive Print

- Manuscript writers have little difficulty reading cursive script (Hendricks, 1955; Plattor & Woestehoff, 1967).

Transition

- The initial learning of manuscript has no detrimental effect on the later learning of cursive script (Crider, 1932; Gates & Brown, 1929; Goetsch, 1934; Heese, 1946).
- The acquisition of manuscript writing can improve a person's cursive script, and vice versa (Conrad & Offerman, 1930; Goetsch, 1934).
- Many students favor learning both manuscript and cursive writing (Gates & Brown, 1929).

Ease of Learning

- For young children, manuscript is both quicker and easier to learn than is cursive writing (Gates & Brown, 1929; Hildreth, 1936; Townsend, 1951).

Legibility

- Regardless of the mode of instruction or age of the writer, manuscript tends to be more legible than cursive handwriting (Boraas, 1936; Foster, 1957; Freeman, 1936; Gates & Brown, 1929; Jackson, 1970; Templin, 1958; Turner, 1930).

Fluency

- If instructional emphasis and practice are equivalent, students and adults write manuscript as fast as cursive script (Hendricks, 1955; Hildreth, 1945; Jackson, 1970; Turner, 1930; Washburne & Morphett, 1937).
- Students and adults write cursive script *faster* than they do manuscript (Foster, 1957; Gates & Brown, 1929; Gray, 1930).
- The speed of manuscript writing can be significantly increased through direct instruction (Conrad & Offerman, 1930; Gates & Brown, 1929).
- With substantial increases in speed, the quality of manuscript writing deteriorates less rapidly than cursive (Hendricks, 1955).

Parents

- Parents generally object to their children using manuscript writing beyond the primary grades (Renaud & Groff, 1966).

FIGURE 1
Synopsis of Research on Manuscript and Cursive Writing

factor distinguishes between samples of good and poor handwriting (Herrick, 1960).

Legible handwriting is generally neat and uniformly arranged. Letters are well-proportioned and properly formed. Words are evenly aligned, and the spaces within and between words are not extreme. The slant of each letter is regular, left to right, and not too acute (Brogden, 1933; Quant, 1946). Line quality is characterized by a light to medium gray line (i.e., if using a pencil). Conversely, handwriting of poor quality may differ on one or a combination of these traits.

Fluency

If handwriting is to be functional and done with ease, it must be fluent. Fluency, or speed in writing, is an essential skill for taking notes, capturing one's thoughts, completing timed exercises, and so on. Speed of writing is a highly individual and relative matter (Harris & Rarick, 1957). Students who are forced to write faster than their normal rate may produce less legible handwriting.

Freeman (1954) indicated that an adult may easily reach a speed of 130 letters per minute. Earlier he had proposed the following norms (Freeman, 1915a): (a) grade two -36; (b) grade three - 48; (c) grade four - 56; (d) grade five - 65; (e) grade six - 72; (f) grade seven - 80; and (g) grade eight - 90. Groff (1961) suggested that these norms may be too high and recommended the following: (a) grade four - 35; (b) grade five - 41; and (c) grade six - 50.

Scope and Sequence

Figure 2 presents a handwriting scope and sequence divided into eight levels. Each level represents approximately one school year. Depending upon the student's characteristics and the severity of the handicapping condition, the rate of progression through the curriculum may be either decelerated or accelerated. In any case, the fundamental sequence of skills should remain intact.

Within the program, letters are introduced in groups that share common formational characteristics. Lower case and capital letters are presented separately. The formation of each letter is first overlearned, then practiced in context. For manuscript letters, we recommend an alphabet with oval shape letters rather than the more difficult circle and slant letters.

	Level 1	Level 2	Level 3	Level 4	Level 5	Level 6-8
PRE-WRITING SKILLS						
MANUSCRIPT Lower Case:						
(l,i,t), (o,c,a,e)						
(r,m,n,u,s)		----- Review ------→				
(d,f,h,b)						
(v,w,k,x,z)						
(g,y,p,j,q)						
Capitals:						
(L,I,T,E,F,H)						
(O,C,G,Q)		----- Review ------→				
(R,V,S,D,B,P,J)						
(A,K,N,M,V,W,X,Y,Z)						
Numerals: (0-9)		----- Review ------→				
Contextual Practice						
Speed						
Pre-Cursive Skills						
CURSIVE Lower Case:					------ Review ------→	

(i, u, w, t, r, s)
(n, m, v, x)
(e, l, b, h, k, f)
(c, a, g, d, q)
(o, p, j), (y, z)

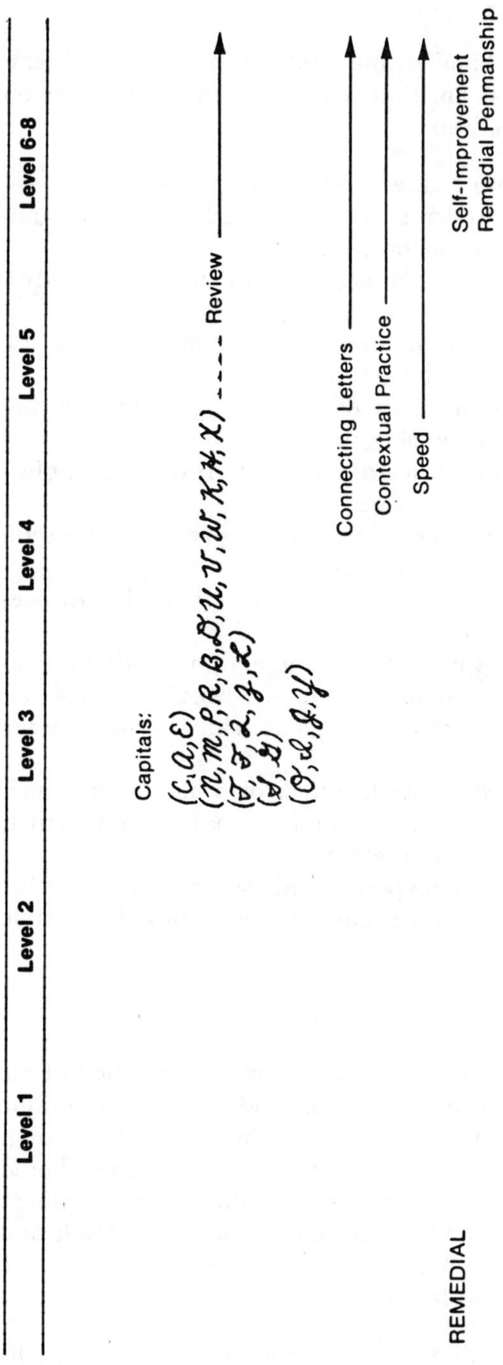

FIGURE 2
Handwriting Scope and Sequence

THE HANDWRITING MODEL

The major objective of the handwriting model is to develop efficient, legible writers. To meet this goal, an effective program should be based on the following principles and conditions:

1. Handwriting instruction is direct and not incidental.
2. Because handicapped students exhibit a diverse range of handwriting achievement, instruction is individualized.
3. The handwriting program is planned, monitored, and modified on the basis of assessment information.
4. Successful teaching and remediation depend upon the flexible use of a wide variety of techniques and methods.
5. Handwriting is taught in short daily learning periods during which desirable habits are established.
6. Skills in handwriting are overlearned in isolation and then applied in meaningful context assignments.
7. Teachers stress the importance of handwriting and do not accept, condone, or encourage slovenly work.
8. Effective handwriting instruction is dependent upon the attitudes of both student and teacher.
9. The instructional atmosphere is pleasant, and motivation is promoted through incentives, reinforcement, success, and enthusiasm.
10. Teachers practice lessons prior to presentation and are able to write a "model" hand.
11. Students are encouraged to evaluate their own handwriting and, when appropriate, actively participate in initiating, conducting, and evaluating the remedial program.
12. Although students do develop personal idiosyncrasies, the teacher helps them maintain a consistent, legible handwriting style throughout the grades.

Assessment

Assessment is integral to handwriting instruction. Examination of the student's present level of performance, strengths and weaknesses, unique learning needs, and progress is necessary for formulating, implementing, and evaluating an effective program. Evaluation of student progress should be made individually, and a suitable analysis should at least consider: (a) readiness for formal instruction; (b) general handwriting level; and (c) immediate causes of poor performance.

A few general principles are as follows:

1. A variety of both standardized and informal procedures should be used.

2. Fluency and legibility should be measured on both copying and free writing exercises.
3. For assessment purposes, students should be told to write as well and as rapidly as they can.
4. The formation of letters should be assessed both in isolation and in written context.
5. Results of various assessments should not be considered as discrete, separate entities but should be analyzed for possible relationships.

Readiness

As in other content areas, all children are not equally prepared to begin handwriting instruction. Students who have not attained sufficient mental maturity, motor control, or perceptual development are scarcely ready to participate in a formal program. How is handwriting readiness assessed? Generally, a student should demonstrate: (a) a mental age of 4-0 to 5-0 (Simon, 1957); (b) an interest and desire to write; (c) adequate muscular coordination; (d) the ability to make visual discriminations; (e) an understanding of the concept of left-to-right progression; (f) a writing hand preference (left or right); and (g) the ability to draw a circle, diagonal line, and horizontal line. Specific readiness activities have been described by Page (1964), Peterson (1975), Towle (1978), and Wright and Allen (1975)

Handwriting Scales

Various standardized scales are available for measuring a student's general handwriting legibility and fluency. Figure 3 lists the most useful of these. In addition, the *California Achievement Tests* (Tiegs & Clark, 1970) and the *Test of Written Language* (Hammill & Larsen, 1978) each include a handwriting subtest.

Even though the use of an appropriate handwriting scale usually results in more reliable measurement than does informal teacher evaluation (Andersen, 1965), relatively few schools utilize scales to assess children's writing (Herrick & Okada, 1963; Wolfson, 1962). At least four factors are responsible. First, most handwriting programs have been designed to instruct children but not to measure the growth of that instruction. Second, handwriting scales are fairly crude instruments and, thus, not very useful for instructional purposes. Third, many teachers are insufficiently aware of the criteria for grading handwriting samples and ultimately rely on their own opinions (Rondinella, 1963). Fourth, what one teacher thinks is good or poor handwriting will most likely not agree with the judgment of another teacher (Feldt, 1962; Manuel, 1915; Watts, 1971). These four determinants, however, should not be considered as proof that handwriting scales serve no useful

Scale	Style	General Description
• Bezzi Scale (1962)	Manuscript	A series of five-step scales for rating manuscript writing at the first, second, and third grade levels. Measures both quality and speed. Normed on a sample of 7,212 specimens.
• Thorndike Scale (1910)	Cursive	A 15-step scale for rating cursive writing in grades 1-12. Measures the general merit of a student's handwriting. Normed on a sample of 1,000 specimens.
• Ayres Scale (1912)	Cursive	An eight-step scale for rating cursive writing in grades 2-8. Measures the general legibility of a student's writing. Normed on a sample of 1,578 specimens, which were read by 10 judges.
• Freeman Scale (1915b)	Manuscript and Cursive	A series of five-step scales for rating manuscript (grades 1-2) and cursive (grades 2-8). Developed by collecting samples from throughout the United States. Legibility measured by examining letter form, uniformity of slant, uniformity of letter alignment, quality of line, and spacing between letters and words.
• West Scale (1926)	Cursive	A series of seven-step scales for rating cursive writing at each grade level. Measures both legibility and speed.
• Herrick & Erlebacher Scale (1963)	Cursive	A master continuum of rated samples for analyzing a wide variety of elements in handwriting. From the master scale, any number of subscales with predetermined elements can be used to evaluate cursive writing of intermediate grade students.

FIGURE 3
Handwriting Scales

purpose. The reliability of a teacher's evaluations can be heightened by providing additional training and averaging student scores from several independent sessions (Feldt, 1962). Further, Otto, Askov, and Cooper (1967) found that teachers experienced in using handwriting scales can make reliable judgments regarding legibility of a student's handwriting.

Informal Procedures

Because using handwriting scales on a day-to-day basis is impractical, most handwriting evaluation is done informally (Addy & Wylie, 1973).

Unfortunately, examining a student's themes or other written work provides only a limited amount of information. Obtaining samples of a student's handwriting under reasonably controlled conditions is more beneficial (Otto, McMenemy, & Smith, 1973).

Two simple ways of obtaining a measure of a student's fluency and legibility are copying and free writing exercises (Brueckner & Bond, 1955). On a copying exercise a student is typically given a sample sentence to reproduce. The sentence should contain all the lower case alphabet letters and be simple enough so the student knows the phrase thoroughly and how to spell each word. A sentence that meets this criteria is: "The quick brown fox jumps over the lazy dog."

On a free writing exercise, the student is asked to write from memory a sentence or simple selection, like a short, well known poem. For both copying and free writing exercises, fluency is determined by the number of letters the student can copy per minute over a short time. To judge legibility, the teacher concentrates on letter formation, uniformity and degree of slant, alignment, line quality, spacing between letters and words, letter size, general neatness, beginning and ending strokes and, where appropriate, the joining of letters.

In securing either a copying or free writing exercise from students, a teacher's directions often affect their performance. Otto, McMenemy, and Smith (1973) therefore have recommended that the teacher obtain a sample of each of the student's usual, best, and fastest writing. Specifically, the student first becomes familiar with the test sentence. Then the teacher instructs the student to write the sentence X number of times, "at your usual rate." (At least a two- or three-minute sample should be obtained.) Next, after a period of relaxation, the student is told to write the test sentence, "as well and as neatly as you can." Finally, after another relaxation period, the student is instructed to write the test sentence, "as rapidly as you can in three minutes." These procedures allow the teacher to identify students who are unable to meet minimum standards of fluency and legibility and whose quality of handwriting deteriorates markedly under the requirement of speed.

In addition to copying and free writing exercises, the teacher should examine the student's knowledge of how to write letter forms and numerals. This can be done by asking the student to: (a) write the numbers 0-9 and the letters of the alphabet; (b) write letters and numbers as they are pronounced; and/or (c) copy specific letters and numbers. Further, written assignments can be examined periodically for possible causes of illegibility (see Brueckner & Bond, 1955, p. 390).

Self-Evaluation

Since self appraisal is basic to all learning, it seems reasonable that students should assist in the evaluation process. Harris and Herrick (1963), however, reported that few children could judge the quality of a handwriting sample and use this as a basis to improve their own performance. Kaplan (1957) found that poor handwriters were less successful at rating the legibility of their writing than were good handwriters. These findings indicate that students should not be given the primary responsibility for evaluating their own handwriting, but the teacher should assist them in noting their progress over time. Also, teachers can train some students to evaluate letter formation through use of a letter template designed to slide under a semitransparent worksheet (Stowitschek & Stowitschek, 1979).

Handwriting Posture, Grip, and Position

Early studies by Judd (1911) and Freeman (1918) revealed that children and adults use a combination of finger, hand, and arm movements during sustained writing. From this pioneering work a certain grip-movement pattern has come to be accepted as a standard. Essentially, the pen or pencil is seen as an extension of the forearm, and the writing movement combines vertical and side strokes to produce moderately slanted print. The hand is turned so that it rests on the third and fourth fingers and can move smoothly across the writing surface as the fingers form each letter (see Figure 4).[1] The writing instrument is held lightly between the thumb and the first two fingers, about an inch above the point. The first finger rests on the top of the instrument, while the end of the bent thumb holds it high in the hand, near the large knuckle, and pointed in the direction of the shoulder.

The student is seated comfortably so that the hips touch the back of the chair and both feet rest on the floor. The body leans slightly forward in a straight line, with both forearms resting on the desk and the elbows extended slightly. For vertical or manuscript print the student places the paper perpendicular squarely in front of him or her with the left side at about the center of the body. The student's left hand holds the paper in place and moves it along as needed. For slanted or cursive writing the paper is placed counterclockwise on the desk, as shown in the figure.

Not all good handwriters hold their writing instruments the same way (Little, 1943). For example, Callewaert (1963) suggested an alterative grip designed to relieve pressure and prevent fatigue. The writing instrument is placed between the middle and index fingers rather than between the thumb and index finger as in the traditional grip. And the wrist and hand are turned more sharply to the side. Otto, Rarick, Armstrong, & Koepke (1966) reported that this modified grip results in acceptable levels of speed and legibility.

Appropriate handwriting movements should be established as soon as possible and sustained throughout school. Probably the most common procedure for teaching posture, grip, and position is to model the correct

---

[1] Adjustments for left-handers are illustrated in Figure 6.

Posture

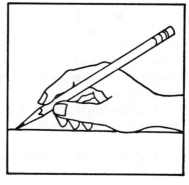

Pencil Grip

Paper Position for Vertical Print

Paper Position for Slanted Print

Illustration by Susan Crouder

FIGURE 4
Posture, Grip, and Paper Positions for Right-handed Writers

response, physically prompt the student, and provide corrective feedback and reinforcement. Some teachers draw stick figures on the chalkboard to demonstrate these skills. Tape or a rubber band can also be placed on the writing instrument to remind students where to place their fingers (Foerster, 1975; Mendoza, Holt & Jackson, 1978).

Letter Formation

Developmental and remedial procedures for teaching letter formation are the same for both manuscript and cursive writing. Letters are first overlearned in isolation through concentrated drill and practice, then applied within a written context. The initial formation of letters depends upon external prompts (e.g., copying, tracing) until eventually becoming internalized.

A combination of various instructional and motivational procedures is used to teach letter formation. These procedures include:

Modeling. The teacher writes the letter and names it. The student observes the number, order, and direction of the strokes.

Noting critical attributes. The teacher compares and contrasts the stimulus letter with letters that share common formational characteristics.

Physical prompts and cues. The teacher physically directs the student's hand in forming the letter. Additionally, the direction and order of strokes can be guided through use of arrows or colored dots outlining the letter shapes.

Tracing. The student forms the letter by tracing dot-to-dot patterns, dashed letters, a faded model, raised letters, or an outline.

Copying. The student copies the letter on a piece of paper or in wet sand (calling upon the tactile sense).

Self-verbalization. The student verbalizes the steps as the letter is written (using the auditory mode).

Writing from memory. The student writes the letter without the aid of cues.

Repetition. The student practices forming the letter, through concentrated multisensory drills.

Self-correction and feedback. The student corrects malformed letters with the assistance of a visual aid (e.g., desk or wall alphabet charts) or under the teacher's direction.

Reinforcement. The teacher praises the student and gives primary reinforcers for correct letter formation.

Even though all these procedures are not supported by empirical evidence, research does indicate that letter formation is enhanced through: (a) dramatiztion of progress (Johns, 1976); (b) copying and tracing (Hirsch & Niedermeyer, 1973); (c) verbalizing self-guiding instructions (Furner, 1969a; Kosiewicz, Hallahan, Lloyd, & Graves, 1979; Robin, Armel, & O'Leary, 1975); and (d) reinforcement and corrective feedback (Fauke, Burnett, Powers, & Sulzer-Azaroff, 1973; Hasazi & Hasazi, 1972; Lahey, Busemeyer, O'Hara, & Beggs, 1977; Nichols, 1970; Smith & Lovitt, 1973; Stromer, 1975). Moreover, Askov and Greff (1975), Gates and Taylor (1923), and Hirsch and Niedermeyer (1973) found that copying is a more effective technique than tracing. And a combination of several procedures appears to be superior to a single technique (Fauke et al., 1973; Kosiewicz et al., 1979; Robin et al., 1975).

Specific instructional strategies for teaching letter formation are given in Figure 5. With a few simple modifications these procedures can be used to teach number formation as well. Letter qualities like size, slant, alignment, and spacing can be improved by using lined or graph paper, slant guides, corrective feedback, reinforcement, and self-evaluation.

Fluency

Remedial procedures to improve speed are relatively straightforward. After the mechanics of handwriting have become automatic or habitual, speed is gradually increased by having the student apply and practice the skills on meaningful, written assignments. For some students, though, it may be necessary to provide self competition on timed exercises plus motivation through reinforcement. Fluency can also be improved by increasing on-task behavior (Hallahan, Lloyd, Kosiewicz, Kauffman, & Graves, 1979).

Cursive Writing

The acquisition of cursive as a second style of writing is usually made sometime between first and fourth grades. This is primarily a matter of tradition since little evidence exists to support any of the widely used transition periods (McOmber, 1970; Otto & Rarick, 1969). A student's readiness to acquire a second style of writing should be determined on an individual basis rather than arbitrarily.

When should students begin formal cursive instruction? First, they should be proficient at writing and reading manuscript. Second, they should express an interest in learning the cursive style. Enstrom (1968) further indicates that it is helpful if the student's manuscript writing is slanted.

Fauke Approach (Fauke et al., 1973)

1. The teacher writes the letter, and the student and teacher discuss the formational act.
2. The student names the letter.
3. The student traces the letter with a finger, pencil, and magic marker.
4. The student's finger traces a letter form made of yarn.
5. The student copies the letter.
6. The student writes the letter from memory.
7. The teacher rewards the student for correctly writing the letter.

Progressive Approximation Approach (Hofmeister, 1973)

1. The student copies the letter using a pencil.
2. The teacher examines the letter and, if necessary, corrects by overmarking with a highlighter.
3. The student erases incorrect portions of the letter and traces over the teacher's highlighter marking.
4. The student repeats steps 1-3 until the letter is written correctly.

Furner Approach (Furner, 1969a, 1969b, 1970)

1. Student and teacher establish a purpose for the lesson.
2. The teacher provides the student with many guided exposures to the letter.
3. The student describes the process while writing the letter and tries to write or visualize the letter as another child describes it.
4. The teacher uses multisensory stimulation to teach the letter form.
5. The student compares his or her written response to a model.

VAKT Approach

1. The teacher writes the letter with crayon while the student observes the process.
2. The teacher and student both say the name of the letter.
3. The student traces the letter with the index finger, simultaneously saying the name of the letter. This is done successfully five times.
4. The student copies and names the letter successfully three times.
5. Without a visual aid, the student writes and names the letter correctly three times.

Niedermeyer Approach (Niedermeyer, 1973)

1. The student traces a dotted representation of the letter 12 times.
2. The student copies the letter 12 times.
3. The student writes the letter as the teacher pronounces it.

Handwriting with Write and See (Skinner & Krakower, 1968)

The student traces a letter within a tolerance model on specially prepared paper. If the student forms the letter correctly, the pen writes gray; if it is incorrect, the pen writes yellow.

FIGURE 5
Letter Formation Strategies

Once instruction begins, the cursive style can be learned in as little as six months (Crider, 1932; Gates & Brown, 1929). Initially, students practice drawing ovals and curved lines (O , $\smile$, $)$). They should also be told that all lower case letters are connected,[2] that they start at the baseline, and that cursive script is to be slanted. Cursive letters are usually connected by overcurves ($\frown$) and undercurves ($\smile$). Therefore, teaching each letter and its connecting curve together ($\frown$ + d = d ; $\smile$ + c = c) is advisable.

The Left-handed Writer

A student's hand preference is probably the most obvious difference between individual writers. Approximately one of 10 children is left-handed, with boys slightly outnumbering girls (Enstrom, 1957). Without intervention, many of these children develop an awkward, hooked writing position. Left-handed students should therefore receive special assistance as soon as formal instruction begins.

A common belief is that left-handed writers are less fluent and their writing less legible than their right-handed counterparts. Research by Guilford (1936), Horton (1969), and Lewis (1964) tends to support this supposition. Investigations by Clark (1957), Groff (1964), Smith and Reed, 1959), and Trankell (1956), however, found no significant differences between the two groups. This conflicting evidence may result from differences in instructional procedures rather than actual differences between left-handed (sinistral) and right-handed (dextral) students.

What special provisions should the teacher make for the left-handed student? First, before beginning instruction the student's hand preference should be determined. Second, left-handers in a class might be grouped in the front right corner of the room facing the chalkboard. Third, the desk of a left-handed student should be slightly lower than that of a right-handed child of the same height. Fourth, the left-handed child should be provided a left-handed person as a model. Fifth, to help the student establish left-to-right direction, practicing on rightward sliding exercises is beneficial. Sixth, the student should be encouraged to do a lot of writing on the left side of the chalkboard. Finally, the left-handed student should always keep his or her writing paper turned somewhat clockwise and hold the pencil slightly farther back than right-handers do. Figure 6 presents four relatively effective approaches to writing with the left hand (Enstrom, 1957). Adjustments one through three are recommended unless a student has used hook writing for a long time or is unable to conform to any of those adjustments. Then, adjustment four might be effective.

---

[2] Not all capitals are joined to lower case letters.

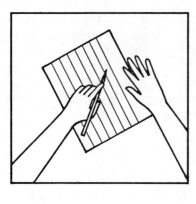

Adjustment Number 1

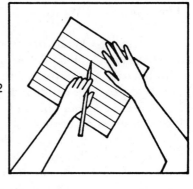

Adjustment Number 2

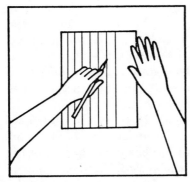

Adjustment Number 3

Adjustment Number 4

Illustration by Susan Crouder

FIGURE 6
Approaches to Writing With the Left Hand

Diagnostic and Remedial Instruction

After the basic letter forms have been mastered, the bulk of the instructional program should be geared to helping students remedy specific difficulties. For the most part, this process is straightforward and uncomplicated. Examination of children's and adults' handwriting indicates that a few errors account for a large percentage of the illegibilities in writing (Horton, 1969; Kvaraceus, 1954; Lewis, 1964; Newland, 1932; Pressey & Pressey, 1927; Rollstin, 1949). For example, only four symbols — a, e, r, t —account for about 50 percent of all the malformed letters at any grade level. By focusing remedial and diagnostic instruction on the most common types of errors (see Otto, McMenemy, & Smith, 1973), the remedial teacher can improve both the student's quality and speed of handwriting.

Even though elimination of common errors can decrease illegibilities by more than one-half (Lewis, 1964), a student's specific difficulties still must be identified. Individualizing instruction so that students' practice is confined to the problem areas is an effective instructional strategy for improving handwriting skills (Bradley, 1933; Cole, 1935-36, 1939; Scruggs, 1931; Tagatz, Otto, Klausmeier, Goodwin & Cook, 1968). Teachers can pinpoint specific handwriting strengths and weaknesses by using one of the various diagnostic charts available in many commercial programs or the *Criterion Test of Cursive Penmanship* (Starkel, 1975).

A type of error that deserves special consideration is the written reversal. Although reversal errors are generally rare after seven or eight years of age (Chapman, Lewis, & Wedell, 1970; Schonell, 1942), a few older students continue to reverse letters and numbers.

In many instances, reversals disappear without direct intervention. For instance, Sidman and Kirk (1974) found that written reversals dissipate simply as a result of continued testing. Some students, however, do require direct instruction. The following are examples of direct intervention strategies:

1. The student simultaneously traces and names the problem letter.
2. The student writes the reversed letter to the right of the midline of the paper. If the symbol is written correctly, the student makes a row of letters moving toward and recrossing the midline so the end of the row falls into the proper writing place (Zaslow, 1966).
3. The teacher presents the student with a visual model of the problem letter and reinforces the correct written response (Cooper, 1970).
4. When initially teaching a commonly reversed letter, the teacher uses heavy black lines, color cues, or drawings to indicate directionality. The cues are then slowly and systematically withdrawn.
5. The student associates the problem letter with another letter that is not commonly reversed (e.g., c and d).
6. The teacher gives the student a verbal cue for correctly writing the letter (e.g., "B — right!").

ADDITIONAL CONSIDERATIONS

In designing an appropriate handwriting program, the proposed methods, materials, reinforcers, and daily activities should be realistic with respect to the instructional time available. Our recommendation is to allot 50 to 100 minutes per week to handwriting instruction. The allocated time can be maximized by advantageous use of tutors and by assigning specific teaching responsibilities to the student's special and regular classroom teachers.

Beginning writers commonly are given comparatively large writing tools, but no objective evidence supports use of the beginner's pencil (Tawney, 1967; Wiles, 1943). The current practice of having students learn to write using large tools and later changing to smaller instruments may not be necessary in most cases. Neither does evidence support use of paper with widely spaced lines.

Finally, the effectiveness of an instructional program depends greatly upon the student's interest and motivation. Teachers can help students develop a "handwriting consciousness" by showing examples that reveal the importance of legible handwriting and by encouraging pride in their written products. And teachers should practice their own recommendations, serving as role-models for their students.

REFERENCES

Addy, P., & Wylie, R. The "right" way to write. *Childhood Education*, 1973, *49*, 253-254.

Andersen, D. Handwriting research: Movement and quality. *Elementary English*, 1965, *42*, 45-53.

Andersen, D. What makes writing legible? *Elementary School Journal*, 1969, *69*, 365-368.

Askov, E., & Greff, K. Handwriting: Copying versus tracing as the most effective type of practice. *Journal of Educational Research*, 1975, *69*, 96-98.

Ayres, L. *A scale for measuring the quality of handwriting of school children.* New York: Russell Sage Foundation, 1912.

Bachmann, W., & Law, K. Manuscript writing with the cerebral palsied child. *Exceptional Children*, 1961, *27*, 239-244.

Bezzi, R. A standardized manuscript scale for grades 1, 2, and 3. *Journal of Educational Research*, 1962, *55*, 339-340.

Boraas, H. An experimental study of the relative merits of certain written letter forms with respect to legibility, with speed and stability as related factors. *Journal of Experimental Education*, 1936, *5*, 65-70.

Bradley, L. *A diagnostic and remedial study of handwriting difficulties.* Unpublished master's thesis, University of Chicago, 1933.

Briggs, D. Influence of handwriting on assessment. *Educational Research*, 1970, *13*, 50-55.

Brogden, W. *The trigonometric relationship of precision and angle linear pursuit movement as a function of the amount of practice.* Unpublished master's thesis, Columbia College, 1933.

Brueckner, L., & Bond, G. *Diagnosis and treatment of learning difficulties.* New York: Appleton-Century-Crofts, 1955.

Byers, L. Relationship of manuscript and cursive handwriting to accuracy in spelling. *Journal of Educational Research*, 1963, *57*, 87-89.

Callewaert, H. For easy and legible handwriting. In Herrick, V. (Ed.), *New horizons for research in handwriting*. Madison: University of Wisconsin Press, 1963.

Chapman, L., Lewis, A., & Wedell, K. A note on reversals in the writing of eight-year-old children. *Remedial Education*, 1970, *5*, 91-94.

Chase, C. The impact of some obvious variables on essay test scores. *Journal of Educational Measurement*, 1968, *5*, 315-318.

Clark, M. *Left-handedness*. London: University of London Press, 1957.

Cole, L. A successful experiment in the teaching of handwriting by analytic methods. *Journal of Psychology*, 1935-1936, *1*, 209-222.

Cole, L. Instruction in penmanship for the left-handed child. *Elementary School Journal*, 1939, *39*, 436-438.

Conrad, E., & Offerman, E. A test of speed and quality in manuscript writing as learned by adults. *Teachers College Records*, 1930, *31*, 449-467.

Cooper, J. *Eliminating letter and number reversal errors with modeling and reinforcement procedures.* Unpublished doctoral dissertation, University of Kansas, 1970.

Covert, S. *An evaluation of handwriting in certain Iowa schools.* Unpublished doctoral dissertation, University of Iowa, 1953.

Craig, M. *An analysis of the relationship between the ease of reading sixth grade handwritten papers by peers and teacher evaluation of the handwritten papers with selected handwriting factors.* Unpublished doctoral dissertation, Ball State University, 1965.

Crider, B. The adaptability of pupils to manuscript writing. *Elementary School Journal*, 1932, *32*, 617-622.

Cruickshank, W., Bentzen, F., Ratzeburg, F., & Tannhauser, M. *A teaching method for brain-injured and hyperactive children.* Syracuse, NY: Syracuse University Press, 1961.

Cutright, P. Script-print and beginning reading and spelling. *Elementary English*, 1936, *13*, 139-141.

Eagleson, O. The success of sixty subjects in attempting to recognize their handwriting. *Journal of Applied Psychology*, 1937, *21*, 546-549.

Early, G. The case for cursive writing. *Academic Therapy*, 1973, *9*, 105-108.

Early, G., Nelson, D., Kleber, D., Treegob, M., Huffman, E., & Cass, C. Cursive handwriting, reading, and spelling achievement. *Academic Therapy*, 1976, *12*, 67-74.

Enstrom, A. *The extent of the use of the left hand in handwriting and the determination of the relative efficiency of the various hand-wrist-arm-paper adjustments.* Unpublished doctoral dissertation, University of Pittsburgh, 1957.

Enstrom, A. Research in handwriting. *Elementary English*, 1964, *41*, 873-876.

Enstrom, A. Hen-tracks in high school. *Journal of Secondary Education*, 1965, *40*, 184-186.

Enstrom, A. Handwriting: The neglect of a needed skill. *Clearing House*, 1966, *40*, 308-310.

Enstrom, A. Improving handwriting. *Improving College and University Teaching*, 1967, *15*, 168-169.

Enstrom, A. But how soon can we really write? *Elementary English*, 1968, *45*, 360-363, 382.

Enstrom, A. Those questions on handwriting. *Elementary School Journal*, 1969, *69*, 327-333.

Fauke, J., Burnett, J., Powers, M., & Sulzer-Azaroff, B. Improvement of handwriting and letter recognition skills: A behavior modification procedure. *Journal of Learning Disabilities*, 1973, *6*, 25-29.

Feldt, L. The reliability of measures of handwriting quality. *Journal of Educational Psychology*, 1962, *53*, 288-292.

Fernald, G. *Remedial techniques in basic school subjects.* New York: McGraw-Hill, 1943.

Foerster, L. Sinistral power! Help for left-handed children. *Elementary English*, 1975, *52*, 213-215.

Foster, E. *A comparison of intermediate grade manuscript and cursive handwriting in two typical elementary school programs.* Unpublished doctoral dissertation, University of Iowa, 1957.

Freeman, F. Handwriting. *Fourteenth Yearbook*, National Society of the Study of Education, Part 1. *Public Schools*, 1915. (a)

Freeman, F. An analytical scale for judging handwriting. *Elementary School Journal*, 1915, *15*, 432-441. (b)

Freeman, F. *The handwriting movement.* Chicago: University of Chicago Press, 1918.

Freeman, F. An evaluation of manuscript writing. *Elementary School Journal*, 1936, *36*, 446-455.

Freeman, F. Teaching handwriting. *What Research Says to Teachers*, 1954, *4*, 1-33.

Furner, B. The perceptual-motor nature of learning in handwriting. *Elementary English*, 1969, *46*, 886-894. (a)

Furner, B. Recommended instructional procedures in a method emphasizing the perceptual-motor nature of learning in handwriting. *Elementary English*, 1969, *46*, 1021-2030. (b)

Furner, B. An analysis of the effectiveness of a program of instruction emphasizing the perceptual-motor nature of learning in handwriting. *Elementary English*, 1970, *47*, 61-69.

Gates, A., & Brown, H. Experimental comparisons of print-script and cursive writing. *Journal of Educational Research*, 1929, *20*, 1-14.

Gates, A., & LaSalle, J. Study of writing ability and its relation to other abilities based on repeated tests during a period of 20 months. *Journal of Educational Psychology*, 1924, *15*, 205-216.

Gates, A., & Taylor, G. Acquisition of motor control in writing by pre-school children. *Teachers College Record*, 1923, *24*, 459-468.

Goetsch, W. *The effect of early training in handwriting on later writing and on composition.* Unpublished master's thesis, University of Chicago, 1934.

Gray, W. An experimental comparison of the movements in manuscript writing and cursive writing. *Journal of Educational Psychology*, 1930, *21*, 259-272.

Greenblatt, E. An analysis of school subject preferences of elementary school children of middle grades. *Journal of Educational Research*, 1962, *55*, 554-560.

Groff, P. From manuscript to cursive — Why? *Elementary School Journal*, 1960, *61*, 97-101.

Groff, P. New speeds in handwriting. *Elementary English*, 1961, *38*, 564-565.

Groff, P. Self-estimates of teaching ability in elementary school subjects. *Journal of Teacher Education*, 1962, *13*, 417-421.

Groff, P. Who are the better writers — The left-handed or the right-handed? *Elementary School Journal*, 1964, *65*, 92-96.

Guilford, W. *Left-handedness: Its effects upon the quality and speed of writing of pupils in the fifth and sixth grades.* Unpublished master's thesis, College of Puget Sound, 1936.

Hallahan, D., Lloyd, J., Kosiewicz, M., Kauffman, J., & Graves, A. Self-monitoring of attention as a treatment for a learning disabled boy's off-task behavior. *Learning Disability Quarterly*, 1979, *2*, 24-32.

Halpin, G., & Halpin, G. Special paper for beginning handwriting: An unjustified practice? *Journal of Educational Research*, 1976, *69*, 267-269.

Hammill, D., & Larsen, S. *Test of written language*, Austin, TX: Pro-Ed, 1978.

Harris, T. Handwriting. *Encyclopedia of educational research,* New York: Macmillan, 1960.

Harris, T., & Herrick, V. Children's perception of the handwriting task. In Herrick, V. (Ed.), *New horizons for research in handwriting,* Madison: University of Wisconsin Press, 1963.

Harris, T., & Rarick, L. The problem of pressure in handwriting. *Journal of Experimental Education,* 1957, *26,* 151-177.

Harris, T., & Rarick, L. The relationship between handwriting pressure and legibility of handwriting in children and adolescents. *Journal of Experimental Education,* 1959, *28,* 65-84.

Hasazi, J., & Hasazi, S. Effects of teacher attention on digit-reversal behavior in an elementary school child. *Journal of Applied Behavior Analysis,* 1972, *5,* 157-162.

Heese, D. The use of manuscript writing in South African schools. *Journal of Educational Research,* 1946, *40,* 161-177.

Hendricks, A. Manuscript and cursive handwriting in Brookline. *Elementary School Journal,* 1955, *55,* 447-452.

Herrick, V. Handwriting and children's writing. *Elementary English,* 1960, *37,* 248-256.

Herrick, V., & Erlebacher, A. The evaluation of legibility in handwriting. In Herrick, V. (Ed.), *New horizons for research in handwriting.* Madison: University of Wisconsin Press, 1963.

Herrick, V., & Okada, N. The present scene: Practices in the teaching of handwriting in the U.S.-1960. In Herrick, V. (Ed.), *New horizons for research in handwriting.* Madison: University of Wisconsin Press, 1963.

Herrick, V., & Otto, W. *Letter from models advocated by commercial handwriting systems.* Madison: University of Wisconsin Press, 1961.

Hildreth, G. Copying manuscript and cursive writing. *Childhood Education,* 1936, *13,* 127-128.

Hildreth, G. Comparative speed of joined and unjoined writing strokes. *Journal of Educational Psychology,* 1945, *36,* 91-102.

Hildreth, G. Simplified handwriting for today. *Journal of Educational Research,* 1963, *56,* 330-333.

Hirsch, E., & Niedermeyer, F. The effects of tracing prompts and discrimination training on kindergarten handwriting performance. *Journal of Educational Research,* 1973, *67,* 81-86.

Hofmeister, A. Let's get it write. *Teaching Exceptional Children.* 1973, *6,* 30-33.

Horton, L. *An analysis of illegibilities in the cursive handwriting of 1,000 selected sixth-grade students.* Unpublished doctoral dissertation, Ohio State University, 1969.

Houston, H. Manuscript writing and progress in reading. *Elementary School Journal,* 1938, *39,* 116-118.

Jackson, A. *A comparison of speed and legibility of manuscript and cursive handwriting of intermediate grade pupils.* Unpublished doctoral dissertation, University of Arizona, 1970.

Johns, J. *The effect of training, self-recording, public charting, and group contingencies on manuscript handwriting legibility.* Unpublished doctoral dissertation, Ohio State University, 1976.

Judd, C. *Genetic psychology for teachers.* New York: Appleton Press, 1911.

Kaplan, H. *A study of relationships between handwriting legibility and perception adjustment and personality factors.* Unpublished doctoral dissertation, University of Wisconsin, 1957.

Kaufman, H., & Biren, P. Cursive writing: An aid to reading and spelling. *Academic Therapy,* 1979, *15,* 209-219.

King, F. Handwriting practices in our schools today. *Elementary English,* 1961, *38,* 483-486.

Kosiewicz, M., Hallahan, D., Lloyd, J., & Graves, A. *The effects of self-instruction and self-correction procedures on handwriting performance.* (Technical Report No. 5). Charlottesville, VA: University of Virginia Learning Disabilities Research Institute, 1979.

Kvaraceus, W. Handwriting needs of mentally retarded children and of children in regular grades. *Elementary School Journal*, 1954, *55*, 42-44.

Lahey, B., Busemeyer, M., O'Hara, C., & Beggs, V. Treatment of severe perceptual-motor disorders in children diagnosed as learning disabled. *Behavior Modification*, 1977, *1*, 123-140.

Lewis, E. *An analysis of children's manuscript handwriting.* Unpublished doctoral dissertation, University of California, Berkeley, 1964.

Lindahl, H. The effect of manuscript writing on learning to spell. *Childhood Education*, 1938, *14*, 277-278.

Little, M. Current opinions, experimentation, and study on handwriting problems. *Elementary School Journal*, 1943, *43*, 607-610.

Long, H., & Mayer, W. Printing versus cursive writing in beginning reading instruction. *Journal of Educational Research*, 1931, *24*, 350-355.

Love, H. Comparison of quality, speed, and use of handwriting among special and regular classroom children. *Journal of Educational Research*, 1965, *58*, 475-477.

Manuel, H. Use of an objective scale for grading handwriting. *Elementary School Journal*, 1915, *15*, 269-278.

Markham, L. Influence of handwriting quality on teacher evaluation of written work. *American Educational Research Journal*, 1976, *13*, 277-283.

Mecham, M., Berko, F., & Palmer, M. *Communication training in childhood brain damage.* New York: Charles C Thomas, 1966.

Mendoza, M., Holt, W., & Jackson, D. Circles and tapes: An easy teacher-implemented way to teach fundamental writing skills. *Teaching Exceptional Children*, 1978, *10*, 48-50.

Myklebust, H., & Johnson, D. *Learning disabilities: Educational principles and practices.* New York: Grune & Stratton, 1967.

McGinnis, H., Kleffner, R., & Goldstein, R. *Teaching aphasic children.* Washington, DC: The Volta Bureau, 1963.

McOmber, J. *A study of the relationship between handwriting form and spelling performance of intermediate grade pupils using manuscript and cursive handwriting.* Unpublished doctoral dissertation, Utah State University, 1970.

Newland, E. An analytic study of the development of illegibilities in handwriting from the lower grades to adulthood. *Journal of Educational Research*, 1932, *26*, 249-258.

Nichols, S. Pupil motivation: A rewarding experience. *Modern English Journal*, 1970, *8*, 36-41.

Niedermeyer, F. Kindergarteners learn to write. *Elementary School Journal*, 1973, *74*, 130-135.

O'Brien, R. Can you read what you write? *Reader's Digest*, 1959, *75*, 222-226.

Otto, W., Askov, E., & Cooper, C. Legibility rating for handwriting samples: A pragmatic approach, *Perceptual & Motor Skills*, 1967, *25*, 638.

Otto, W., McMenemy, R., & Smith, R. *Corrective and remedial teaching.* Atlanta: Houghton-Mifflin Co., 1973.

Otto, W., & Rarick, L. Effect of time of transition from manuscript to cursive writing upon subsequent performance in handwriting, spelling, and reading. *Journal of Educational Research*, 1969, *62*, 211-216.

Otto, W., Rarick, L., Armstrong, J., & Koepke, M. Evaluation of a modified grip in handwriting. *Perceptual & Motor Skills*, 1966, *22*, 210.

Owen, M. Just where do we stand in handwriting? *Instructor*, 1954, *63*, 57.

Page, S. What's involved in getting ready to write? *Instructor*, 1964, *74*, 44, 74.

Peterson, G. An approach to writing for kindergarteners. *Elementary English*, 1975, *52*, 89-91.

Plattor, E., & Woestehoff, E. The relationship between reading manuscript and cursive writing. *Elementary English*, 1967, *44*, 50-52.

Pressey, S., & Pressey, L. Analysis of 3,000 illegibilities in the handwriting of children and adults. *Educational Research Bulletin*, 1927, *6*, 270-273, 275.

Quant, L. Factors effecting the legibility of handwriting. *Journal of Experimental Education*, 1946, *14*, 297-316.

Quint, G. *Aversions to handwriting.* Unpublished doctoral dissertation, Boston University, 1958.

Renaud, A., & Groff, P. Parents' opinions about handwriting styles. *Elementary English*, 1966, *43*, 873-876.

Robin, A., Armel, S., & O'Leary, K. The effects of self-instruction on writing deficiencies. *Behavior Therapy*, 1975,, *6*, 178-187.

Rollstin, D. *A study of the handwriting of college freshman.* Unpublished master's thesis, University of Iowa, 1949.

Rondinella, O. An evaluation of subjectivity of elementary school teachers in grading handwriting. *Elementary English*, 1963, *40*, 531-532.

Schonell, F. *Backwardness in basic subjects.* London: Oliver & Boyd, 1942.

Scruggs, S. Remedial teaching for improvement in handwriting. *Journal of Educational Research*, 1931, *23*, 288-295.

Seifert, E. *Personal styles of handwriting in grades six, seven, eight, and nine.* Unpublished doctoral dissertation, Boston University, 1959.

Sidman, M., & Kirk, B. Letter reversals in naming, writing, and matching to sample. *Child Development*, 1974, *45*, 616-625.

Simon, J. French research in the teaching of reading and writing. *Journal of Educational Research*, 1957, *50*, 443-458.

Skinner, B., & Krakower, S. *Handwriting with write and see.* Chicago: Lyons & Carnahan, 1968.

Smith, A., & Reed, F. An experimental investigation of the relative speeds of left- and right-handed writers. *Journal of Genetic Psychology*, 1959, *94*, 67-76.

Smith, D., & Lovitt, T. The educational diagnosis of written b and d reversal problems: A case study. *Journal of Learning Disabilities*, 1973, *6*, 20-27.

Soloff, S. Effect of non-content factors on the grading of essays. *Graduate Research in Education and Related Disciplines*, 1973, *6*, 44-54.

Soltis, R. Handwriting: The middle "R." *Elementary English*, 1963, *40*, 605-607.

Starkel, J. *Demonstration of reliability and validity of the criterion test of cursive penmanship.* Unpublished master's thesis, University of Kansas, 1975.

Stowitschek, C., & Stowitschek, J. Evaluating handwriting performance: The student helps the teacher. *Journal of Learning Disabilities*, 1979, *12*, 70-73.

Strauss, A., & Lehtinen, L. *Psychopathology and education of the brain-injured child.* New York: Grune & Stratton, 1947.

Strickling, C. *The effect of handwriting and related skills upon the spelling score of above average and below average readers in the fifth grade.* Unpublished doctoral dissertation, University of Maryland, 1973.

Stromer, R. Modifying the number and letter reversals in elementary school children. *Journal of Applied Behavior Analysis*, 1975, *8*, 211.

Tagatz, G., Otto, W., Klausmeier, H., Goodwin, W., & Cook, D. Effect of three methods of instruction upon the handwriting performance of third and fourth graders. *American Educational Research Journal*, 1968, *5*, 81-90.

Tawney, S. An analysis of the ball point pen versus the pencil as a beginning handwriting instrument. *Elementary English*, 1967, *44*, 59-61.

Templin, M. *A comparative study of the legibility of handwriting of 454 adults trained in three handwriting styles: all manuscript, all cursive, or manuscript-cursive.* Unpublished doctoral dissertation, New York University, 1958.

Templin, E. Manuscript and cursive writing. *NEA Journal,* 1964, *53,* 26-28.

Thorndike, E. Handwriting. *Teachers College Record,* 1910, *11,* 83-175.

Tiegs, E., & Clark, W. *California achievement tests.* Monterey: McGraw-Hill,.1970.

Towle, M. Assessment and remediation of handwriting deficits for children with learning disabilities. *Journal of Learning Disabilities,* 1978, *11,* 43-50.

Townsend, E. A study of copying abilities in children. *Genetic Psychology Monographs,* 1951, *43,* 3-51.

Trankell, A. The influence of the choice of writing hand on the handwriting. *British Journal of Educational Psychology,* 1956, *26,* 94-103.

Turner, O. The comparative legibility and speed of manuscript and cursive handwriting. *Elementary School Journal,* 1930, *30,* 780-786.

Varty, J. *Manuscript writing and spelling achievement.* New York: Teachers College, Columbia, University, 1938.

Voorhis, T. *The relative merits of cursive and manuscript writing.* New York: Bureau of Publications, Teachers College, Columbia, University, 1931.

Washburne, C., & Morphett, M. Manuscript writing: Some recent investigations. *Elementary School Journal,* 1937, *37,* 517-529.

Watts, I. *Reliability of a rating system of handwriting improvement.* Unpublished master's thesis, Utah State University, 1971.

West, P. *Chart for diagnosing elements in handwriting.* Bloomington: Public School Publishing Co., 1926.

Wiles, M. The effect of different sizes of tools upon the handwriting of beginners. *Elementary School Journal,* 1943, *43,* 412-414.

Wills, I. An investigation of the relationship between rate and quality of handwriting in the primary school. *British Journal of Educational Psychology,* 1938, *8,* 229-235.

Wolfson, B. The teaching of handwriting. *Elementary English,* 1962, *39,* 55-59.

Wright, J., & Allen, E. Ready to write! *Elementary School Journal,* 1975, *75,* 430-435.

Zaslow, R. Reversals in children as a function of midline body orientation. *Journal of Educational Psychology,* 1966, *57,* 133-139.

Research and practices in the teaching of spelling are reviewed first. The authors point out that teachers and spelling basal series base their instruction more on practice than on research findings. The article presents a number of research findings, including the fact that instruction in 2,000 carefully selected words can handle 95% of students' spelling needs. A model for spelling instruction is presented, along with suggestions on assessment and methodological practices. Readers will find this to be a highly useful research review.

Spelling Research and Practice: A Unified Approach

Steve Graham and Lamoine Miller

Although spelling is neither the most important nor the least important aspect in writing, it is a crucial ingredient. Good spellers are able to express their thoughts on paper without unnecessary interruptions. Poor spellers are hampered in their ability to communicate freely through the written word. For a grocery list or personal reminders, accurate spelling is not essential, but material to be read by others should be free from the distraction of misspelled words.

Spelling is a traditional element of the elementary school curriculum, where considerable amount of time and energy are devoted to its mastery. Moreover, the general public often associates correct spelling with educational attainment, accuracy, neatness and cultivation, while the inabilty to spell is frequently linked with illiteracy (Personkee & Yee, 1971). Because the public and the educational community emphasize the importance of spelling achievement, the inability to spell may adversely affect an individual's educational and occupational status.

Unfortunately, many school-age children have difficulty learning to spell. The majority of students who are presently labeled handicapped exhibit spelling problems. Learning disabilities, mental retardation, emotional disturbance, and crippling and other health impairments may unfavorably affect spelling performance (Kyte, 1949; Miller & Graham, 1979). These realizations are compounded by an ever present and growing concern that our schools' overall spelling achievement is lower than it was 30 or 40 years ago (E. Horn, 1960).

Unsatisfactory spelling progress may be attributed, in part, to inadequate contemporary classroom instruction, poorly designed commercial materials, and the absence of spelling programs based on research findings. Further, contemporary classroom instruction rarely accounts for individual student differences. On Monday each student usually is introduced to the same list of spelling words. On Tuesday the teacher administers a pretest, and on Wednesday each student uses the spelling words in sentences. Thursday's activities are designed to teach phonic skills and/or words missed on Tuesday's pretest. A final posttest is administered on Friday. This pattern or one that is strikingly similar is common in most American classrooms (Rowell, 1972). Although some students may profit from such large-group oriented instruction, many others do not. Children do not learn at the same rate, nor do they encounter the same difficulties in learning to spell.

The actual spelling procedures used in many classrooms are influenced heavily by commercial materials that form the foundation of most spelling programs. Spelling texts ordinarily offer a set pattern of instruction with little variety (Dieterich, 1973); and a recent survey revealed that direct teacher involvement is limited in most spelling books (Jobes, 1975).

"Teacher proof" materials with little diversity might be acceptable if the content were appropriate. Regretably, this is not the case. For instance, in a study evaluating current commercial materials, Cohen (1969) identified five major categories of activities or exercises common in sixth grade spellers, and their aggregate percentage of emphasis by text, as follows: phonics (33.6%), affixes and inflectional endings (23.7%), language arts skills (20.2%), word meaning (14.6%), and syllabication (7.9%). Cohen found that some of the exercises actually deterred learning while others were merely ineffectual. As late as 1976, spelling books still contained a large proportion of inappropriate activities (Graves, 1976). Results of the Cohen and Graves studies point to the need for reevaluation of spelling texts and their contents.

As disturbing as it may seem, evidence reveals that instructional practices in spelling are influenced more by habit than by research results. In a study involving 1,289 second through sixth grade elementary teachers, Fitzsimmons and Loomer (1977) found that teachers seldom use research-supported practices in their classroom. The insignificant role of research in spelling *instruction* is paradoxical, since spelling is one of the most thoroughly researched areas in the language arts. Many earlier findings are substantiated by more recent research (Allred, 1977). Even so, improvement in spelling programs is not commensurate with research efforts. While existing evidence will continue to be refined and expanded, it is basically useless if it is not applied.

If handicapped and nonhandicapped students are to receive adequate spelling instruction, teachers need viable alternatives to current spelling texts and instructional practices. The building materials for such options are presently available — A solid research foundation already exists, and the Elementary and Secondary Education Act created a landslide of spelling techniques, approaches, and materials (Fitzsimmons & Loomer, 1977). In designing appropriate alternatives, the present day educator runs the risk of choosing ineffectual activities and/or neglecting the current research foundation. Therefore, spelling instruction should be teacher directed, should contain a variety of relevant instructional options, and should be based on a foundation of research evidence.

THE DEFINITION AND PROCESS OF SPELLING

Unless one first knows the nature of what one is trying to teach, a discussion of methodology and organization seems pointless. Yet, much of the literature evidences this characteristic, mainly because most definitions do not capture the full essence of the spelling process. For example, Hanna, Hodges, and Hanna (1971) define spelling as the "process of encoding, or of rendering spoken words into written symbols" (p. 264). Similarly, Brueckner and Bond (1955) define spelling as the "ability to produce in written or oral form the correct letter arrangement of words" (p. 346). Neither of these definitions is complete. Spelling is not based upon a single act but requires a variety of skills euphemistically called "spelling." *For the purpose of this article, spelling is defined as the ability to recognize, recall, reproduce, or obtain orally or in written form the correct sequence of letters in words.*

Spelling begins with a felt need to spell a word (see Figure 1). This need may be in response to a written assignment, a request for aid, a spelling text, and so forth. Ordinarily, students are able to immediately write or recall spellings of words appropriate to their level of learning with little or no conscious effort. Occasionally, students are able to spell words correctly but first need to use intrinsic or extrinsic strategies to determine if a word is (a) a homonym (semantic information), (b) capitalized (syntactic information), and/or (c) hyphenated (human or written aid). Once they have this information, they immediately recall the word from memory.

If the correct spelling of a word is uncertain or unknown to a student, there are two main resources upon which to draw. One, a person could use *intrinsic strategies* to determine a "possible" correct sequence of sound-symbol associations. These strategies include direct phonemic spelling, the generate-and-test process, and morphemic information (Simon & Simon, 1973). In direct phonemic spelling, students apply their knowledge of

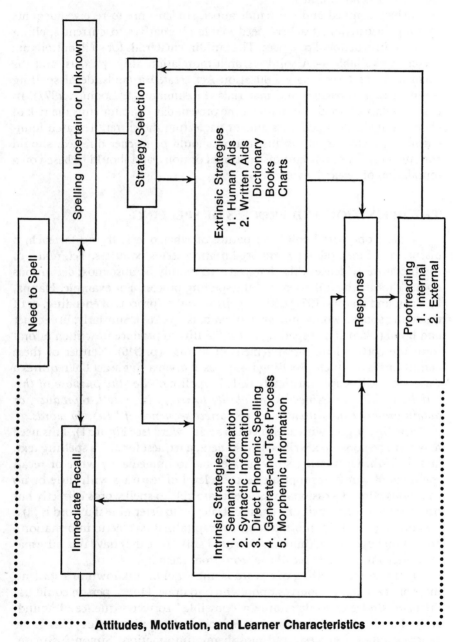

FIGURE 1
The Spelling Process

phoneme-letter associations and phonemic rules to produce a phonetic spelling of the word. This strategy is successful for only about one of every two words (Hanna, Hanna, Hodges, & Rudorf, 1966). The generate-and-test process is a trial-and-error procedure in which the student produces alternative possible spellings and tries to recognize the correct written response. Although this procedure is superior to direct phonemic spelling (Simon & Simon, 1973), it, too, is prone to error. Each of these two strategies may be supplemented by the use of morphemic information. Auditory recognition of a morphemic element (e.g., *and*) provides spelling information that may be used to derive the correct spelling of words containing that component.

If intrinsic strategies prove inadequate for a particular situation, a student may refer to *extrinsic resources* such as aid from a teacher or friend, the dictionary, spelling books, and so forth. Sometimes, intrinsic and extrinsic strategies are used concurrently; e.g., a student may generate a possible spelling and then use a dictionary to check that response.

A student does not need to be able to recall the full spelling of a word in order to recognize whether or not it is spelled correctly. The process involved in this phenomenon is commonly referred to as "proofreading." Once a response is generated either through immediate recall or a spelling strategy, the student may scan the word in an effort to see if it is spelled accurately. Although this procedure is not exact, it often uncovers incorrect spellings. After a suspected error is detected, the student might use extrinsic or intrinsic resources to determine whether or not the response is correct.

In defining the spelling process, a distinction must be made between the mature speller and the beginning speller. A mature speller can immediately spell nearly all of the words encountered on usual writing tasks and can appropriately select intrinsic or extrinsic strategies to correctly spell words that are unknown. The beginning speller, in contrast, has a limited spelling vocabulary and does not have access to a wide variety of spelling skills. Research suggests that students in the primary grades progress through several stages in the development of spelling strategies (Beers, 1974; Beers & Henderson, 1977; Gentry, 1977). First, students tend to omit essential sound features of the word (e.g., vowels). At the next level, spelling is primarily phonetic. During the third stage, attributes of the English orthographic system begin to appear. At the fourth stage, students recognize and recall the correct lexical representation of the word.

THE SPELLING CURRICULUM

The preceding discussion points out that spelling is multifaceted and requires mastery of a variety of skills. Learning to spell is not an easy task. The speller faces many difficulties including, but not limited to, foreign spellings, 26 letters representing 44 sounds, silent letters, variant and invariant sounds, and 300 different letter combinations for 17 vowel sounds

(Allred, 1977). To illustrate, the word "circumference" can be spelled over *396,000,000* different ways phonetically (Peters, 1970). In addition to orthographic barriers, the English language contains the largest vocabulary in the world, with approximately 490,000 words plus another 300,000 technical terms.

In planning a spelling curriculum, then, what should be taught and which skills should receive primary consideration? With respect to the latter concern, an enduring controversy regards the regularity of the English language. There are two major theories (and consequent curricular applications) based on divergent views regarding the consistency of English orthography.

Synthetic Alphabet/Whole Word Approach

One theory holds that English orthography is irrational and consequently difficult to master. This view is responsible for the two distinct methodological interpretations that (a) instruction should be based on a special synthetic alphabet (e.g., Initial Teaching Alphabet); and (b) whole words should form the core of the spelling curriculum.

At present, however, special synthetic alphabets are not a viable or pragmatic approach to spelling instruction because they require an additional step in the learning process — transition from the synthetic alphabet to English orthography. Upon cursory examination, the whole word approach also appears to be impractical. The average person uses perhaps 10,000 words freely and can recognize another 30,000 to 40,000 (Monson, 1975). Mentally handicapped students are not likely to be able to memorize this many spelling words.

Fortunately, to be an effective speller, a student does not have to be able to correctly spell all the words in his or her listening, reading, and writing vocabulary. Studies by E. Horn (1926), Fitzgerald (1951a), T. Horn and Otto (1954), and Rinsland (1945) indicate that a basic spelling vocabulary of 2,800 to 3,000 well-selected words should form the core of the spelling program. To illustrate, 8 words account for 18% of all the words children use in their writing, 100 words for 50%, 1,000 words for 89%, 2,000 words for 95%, 3,000 words for 97%, and 4,000 words for 99% (Hillerich, 1977; E. Horn, 1926); Otto & McMenemy, 1966; Rinsland, 1945. After several hundred words have been learned, the law of diminishing returns begins to operate (Allred, 1977). To require a student to master a spelling vocabulary significantly larger than 3,000 words is out of harmony with research.

Phonemic Approach

The second theory views English orthography as a patterned but incomplete system. Supporters of this theory suggest that the systematic properties of orthography should be used in spelling instruction. This view stresses the application of phonics and spelling rules as a means of developing spelling abilities.

There are several notable challenges to the application of phonemic skills. Those objecting to phonics instruction point out that: (a) most sounds are spelled many ways; (b) most letters spell many sounds; (c) more than one-third of the words in the dictionary have more than one accepted pronunciation, more than half contain silent letters, and about a sixth contain double letters; (d) unstressed syllables are difficult to spell; and (e) children do not understand word-attack principles (E. Horn, 1960). In addition, detractors indicate that most misspelled words are phonemically correct (Hahn, 1960; Tovey, 1978) and that intensive phonics instruction is not superior to non-phonics methods (Bedell & Nelson, 1954; Grottenthaler, 170; Hahn, 1964; Ibeling, 1961; Personkee & Yee, 1971; Warren, 1970).

Those who favor phonics instruction indicate some fairly consistent characteristics of English spelling (Horn, 1960). For example, Hanna et al. (1966) reported that 49 percent of 17,000 words could be spelled correctly using phoneme-grapheme correspondences and another 37 percent could be spelled with only one error. Furthermore, a large body of research supports the contention that intensive phonics instruction creates greater gains in spelling than non-phonics approaches (Baker, 1977; Block, 1972; Dunwell, 1972; Gold, 1976; K. Russell, 1954; Thompson, 1977). Some evidence shows that children learn the more essential phonic principles whether or not formal instruction in phonics is offered (Schwartz & Doehring, 1977; Templin, 1954). In summary, both theory and evidence suggest that phonics instruction may be of some benefit in learning to spell.

Spelling Rules

The issue surrounding use of spelling rules is more clear-cut: Only those rules, with few exceptions, that apply to a large number of words should be taught; and teaching generalizations without regard to utility of the spelling rule is wasteful. For instance, Clymer (1963) found that only 18 of 45 generalizations are useful. Other researchers have suggested that even fewer spelling rules should be taught (Cook, 1912; E. Horn, 1954a; King, 1932). Supporting the statement that spelling rules should be unambiguous, Archer (1930) and Personkee and Yee (1971) indicated that the use of spelling rules may lead to errors because students often misapply generalizations they do not clearly understand. Spelling rules, as a whole, are deemed not very useful in improving overall spelling achievement (Davis, 1969; King, 1932; Turner, 1912; Warren, 1969).

Returning this question of what should be taught and which skills should receive primary consideration, we suggest that a basic vocabulary of 2,000 to 3,000 words should be supplemented by direct phonics instruction accompanied by limited use of spelling rules. In addition, the student should be able to detect spelling errors (i.e., proofread)[1] and be able to effectively use a dictionary.

Figure 2 presents a spelling scope and sequence divided into eight levels. Each level represents approximately one school year. Depending upon the student's characteristics and the severity of the handicapping condition, the rate of progression through the curriculum may be either decelerated or accelerated. In any case, the fundamental sequence of skills should remain intact.

Within the program, the spelling vocabulary is arranged from the most frequently used words to those used least often. Because of the significant overlap between children's and adult's writing vocabularies (Fitzgerald, 1951b; E. Horn, 1954b), the curriculum is comprised of the words most common to both — attending to the student's future as well as present spelling needs.

Initially, any of a number of lists of "most common words" (e.g., Dolch, Fry, etc.) can be taught. For example, Fitzgerald (1951b) identified a permanently useful core of 449 words for beginners and the retarded, which account for more than 76 percent of the words used in children's and adults' writing. Once the vocabulary in the selected list of "most common words" is learned, additional words are taken from one of the following sources: Fitzgerald (1951b), Hillerich (1976), E. Horn (1926), or Rinsland (1945). Before teaching any word from these sources, the teacher should make sure that the word is already part of the student's listening and reading vocabulary.

Since correct spelling in place of phonetic misspelling is a major goal in spelling instruction, only essential phonic skills and spelling rules are incorporated into the curriculum. The nucleus of the phonics program includes base words, prefixes, suffixes, and consonant, consonant blend, digraph, and vowel sound-symbol associations. Spelling rules are limited to the following:

— Proper nouns and most adjectives formed from proper nouns begin with capital letters.
— Rules for adding suffixes (changing *y* to *i*, dropping final silent *e*, doubling the final consonant).
— The use of periods in writing abbreviations.
— The use of the apostrophe to show possession.
— The letter *q* is followed by a *u* in common English words.
— English words do not end in *v*.

---

[1] Research indicates that proofreading skills can be improved and that proofreading programs lead to gains in spelling achievement (Frasch, 1965; McElwee, 1974; Oswalt, 1961; Personkee & Knight, 1967; Valmont, 1972).

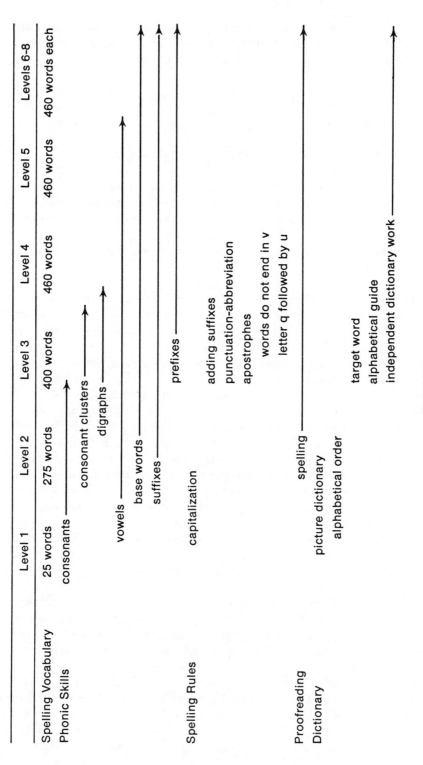

FIGURE 2
Spelling Scope and Sequence

Dictionary work includes picture dictionaries, alphabetizing skills, word location skills, independent dictionary skills, and pronunciation skills. Proofreading involves detecting and correcting errors.

THE SPELLING MODEL

The major objectives of the spelling model as presented here are to:

1. Help students become proficient at standard spelling.
2. Maintain and promote spelling growth.
3. Teach students how to spell words they use in writing.
4. Help students develop effective methods of studying new words.
5. Promote students' use of the dictionary in learning to spell unknown words.
6. Develop in students a spelling conscience — a desire to spell words correctly.

To meet these goals, an effective remedial spelling program must be based on a number of well-defined principles. First, spelling instruction must be direct and not incidental. Studies by Allen and Ager (1965) and Knoell and Harris (1952) found that spelling is an independent skill and that transfer effects from other areas of the curriculum should not be expected. Although students learn many words outside of specific spelling instruction, this incidental learning is applied primarily by the good spellers (Gilbert & Gilbert, 1944; Tyler, 1939). Thus, for poor spellers, basing remedial spelling procedures on reading or other language arts activities may not be justified.

A second assumption inherent in the model presented here is that spelling instruction must be individualized. A wide range of spelling ability and achievement is apparent at every grade level (Ayer, 1951; E. Horn, 1960). The skills and needs of each student are different. Teachers who fail to account for individual differences often rely on hodge-podge procedures that produce hodge-podge results (Schell, 1975). For example, Guiler and Lease (1942) found that pupils at all levels of spelling ability benefited from a program based on individual needs and made substantially greater gains than students receiving instruction formulated on a conventional group basis.

Third, effective remedial spelling instruction depends upon continuous evaluation. Assessment data are used to determine if progress is adequate or if alterations in the instructional plan are necessary. Teachers who do not monitor a student's spelling program carefully cannot adapt instruction to meet individual needs.

Fourth, successful remediation is based upon flexible use of a wide variety of techniques and methods. Regrettably, no one best method or technique has emerged for teaching spelling (Blair, 1975). Likewise, what works with one student may not work with another. Because handicapped students exhibit a diverse range of problems, teachers require access to an extensive assortment of methodological techniques.

Fifth, the effectiveness of spelling instruction is heavily dependent upon the attitudes of both student and teacher. Students must be shown that spelling is personally important to them. Desirable attitudes in students can be encouraged by teachers who (a) provide students with efficient learning techniques, (b) present words of high social utility, (c) emphasize student progress, (d) use a variety of interesting activities and games, (e) structure tasks so that the student can succeed, and (f) limit instruction to relevant and critical skills. Spelling, however, is one of the subjects teachers most dislike to teach (E. Horn, 1960). This is unfortunate, because teachers may be the key variable in students' learning to spell (Blair, 1975).

Assessment

Public Law 94-142 requires that an Individualized Education Program (IEP) must be developed for each student receiving special services. The IEP is a management tool designed to facilitate the process of instructional delivery. While the scope of this article does not allow an in-depth discussion of the IEP, it is necessary to discuss procedures for establishing the present level of performance and evaluating student progress. Readers interested in a systematic planning model for development of the IEP are referred to Hudson and Graham (1978).

The procedure through which the present level of performance is established has to vary from one student to another. Nonetheless, a suitable analysis should consider the student's (a) readiness for formal instruction, (b) general spelling level, (c) spelling errors, and (d) proofreading, phonic, and dictionary skills. This information is used to plan the student's educational program (i.e., annual goals and short-term objectives).

Before describing specific assessment techniques, a few general principles should be noted:

1. A variety of both standardized and informal procedures should be used.
2. Since writing is the most common response mode in spelling, written tests are preferable to oral tests.
3. Spelling behavior should be assessed in both isolation and written context.
4. Recall tests are more difficult than recognition tests.
5. Results of various assessments should not be considered as discrete, separate entites but should be analyzed for possible relationships.

Readiness

Before direct spelling instruction is planned, the student must be intellectually able and emotionally willing to learn. Students who have not attained sufficient mental maturity and linguistic experiences are scarcely ready to participate in a formal spelling program. How is spelling readiness assessed? Read, Allred, and Baird (1972) recommend that students should be able to: (a) name and write all the letters of the alphabet, (b) copy words correctly, (c) write their names from memory, (d) enunciate words clearly, (e) recognize common letter-sound combinations, (f) write a few words from memory, and (g) demonstrate an interest in spelling. If students do not meet these criteria, they should take part in activities (see Hildreth, 1962) aimed at developing spelling readiness.

Overall Achievement

Various standardized tests are available for measuring a student's general spelling level. Among these instruments are the *Iowa Spelling Scale* (Ashbaugh, 1921), the *Phonovisual Diagnostic Test* (Schoolfield & Timberlake, 1949), the *Ayer Standard Spelling Test* (Ayer, 1950), the *Seven-Plus Assessment* (Lambert, 1964), and the *Kelvin Measurement of Spelling Ability* (Fleming, 1933). Each of these tests examines recall processes and requires that students write words that have been presented orally, used in a sentence, and presented orally again.

Several informal methods are also available for measuring spelling ability at the survey level. Word lists developed by Kottmeyer (1959) and a coefficient of misspelling both yield a general estimate of spelling achievement. Using the latter, the teacher obtains from the student a written specimen containing approximately 200 words. The total number of misspelled words is divided by the number of words written. The resulting coefficient then is compared to suggested grade-level norms (Courtis, 1919; Brueckner & Bond, 1955).

Spelling Errors

Errors that students commit on spelling tests and other written work provide an indication of the nature of the student's spelling difficulties. Error analysis reveals the student's error tendencies and enables the teacher to detect excessive or infrequent types of errors. Most spelling errors are of a phonetic nature (Spache, 1940), occur in the middle of the word (Jensen, 1962; Kooi, Schutz, & Baker, 1965), and involve a single phoneme (Gates, 1937; Hildreth, 1962). A few words do not account for a disproportionate number of errors (Swenson & Caldwell, 1948).

Only a few standardized tests specifically analyze spelling errors. The *Spelling Errors Test* (Spache, 1955) calls for a response to 120 dictated words and permits the examiner to classify the responses according to 13 common error types. The *Larsen-Hammill Test of Written Spelling* (Larsen & Hammill, 1976) is comprised of two subtests — Predictable Words and Unpredictable Words. The test yields a comparative analysis of the student's ability to spell phonetic and nonphonetic words.

Proofreading

Standardized proofreading tests include the *Every Pupil Achievement Test* (Robinson, 1970), the *California Achievement Tests* (Tiegs & Clark, 1970), the *SRA Achievement Series* (Thorpe, Lefever, & Haslund, 1963), the *Northumberland Standardized Test: II English* (Burt 1925), and the *Metropolitan Achievement Tests* (Durost, Evans, Leake, Bowman, Cosgrove, & Reed, 1970). Each of these tests measures recognition processes.

Proofreading skills should be examined in both isolation and context. Some informal proofreading measures are to:

1. Present alternative spellings of a word and have the student select the correct spelling.
2. Introduce different words and have the student decide which words are spelled correctly or incorrectly.
3. Mark words in a sentence and have the student indicate which, if any, of the marked words are misspelled.
4. Have the student mark and correct misspelled words in a sentence, paragraph, etc.

Phonics

In evaluating phonic skills, the analysis should involve sound-symbol associations and not symbol-sound associations. Two standardized tests that meet this requirement are the *Gates-Russell Spelling Diagnostic Test* (Gates & Russell, 1937) and the Spelling subtests of the *Durrell Analysis of Reading Difficulty* (Durrell, 1937). Informal tests corresponding to this principle include the *Diagnostic Test* (Teachers Manual, 1956) and the *St. Louis Spelling Test* (Kottmeyer, 1959).

Dictionary Skills and Spelling Rules

There is a lack of formalized instruments for examining dictionary skills and spelling rules. Therefore, these elements must be examined informally. Dictionary skills can be assessed by directly observing the student locate unknown spelling words in the dictionary. The student's knowledge of spelling rules can be examined by having each student spell nonsense and real words that require the use of a specific rule (see Brueckner & Bond, 1955).

Evaluating Student Progress

Annual goals often are evaluated by administering a standardized test at the beginning of the year and again at the end of the year. This procedure, however, is generally not appropriate for measuring student performance on specific short-term objectives. Daily work products, observation over time, number of trials per lesson, criterion-referenced testing, and applied behavioral analysis are means by which short-term objectives can be measured (see Hersen & Barlow, 1976; Hudson & Graham, 1978; Moran, 1975). For instance, the student's spelling tests and words misspelled on writing assignments may be kept in a spelling folder. Periodically, the teacher should analyze the contents of the folder to determine spelling mastery, error patterns, phonemic skills, etc. This information then may be used to determine if the student is making adequate progress in meeting specific short-term objectives.

Methodological Procedures

The outline in Figure 3 illustrates the basic components of the spelling model. Spelling practices supported by research and those not supported by research are capsulized in Figure 4. Only practices supported by empirical data were incorporated into the model here. Readers interested in a more thorough discussion of research supported practices are referred to Fitzsimmons and Loomer (1977).

Spelling Vocabulary

The beginning step in teaching spelling vocabulary is to determine which words to teach. Many students already know a few words in each lesson (E. Horn, 1960; Swenson & Caldwell, 1948). The student's learning, therefore, should be directed toward words he or she cannot spell correctly. This focuses spelling instruction on acquisition rather than maintenance.

Use of the test-study method indicates which words require study. Through this technique, the student first is given a pretest to determine which words in a particular lesson are unknown to him or her. The test administrator pronounces each word, uses it in an oral sentence, and pronounces it again (Brody, 1944; Cook, 1932; Foran, 1934; Nisbet, 1939). After unknown words are identified, the student studies them. The pretest is then given a second time and the teacher notes which words, if any, are spelled incorrectly. Misspelled words are incorporated into future lessons.

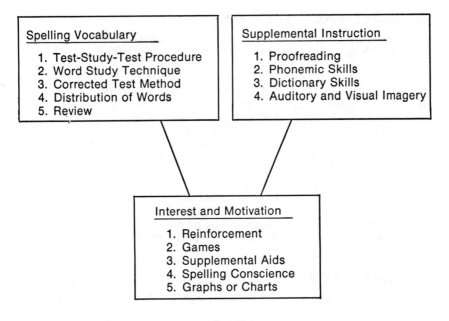

FIGURE 3
Components of the Spelling Model

Words to be studied should be presented in a list or column form. This is advantageous because it focuses specific attention upon each and every word. If the student does not know the meaning of the word or if the word is a homonym, the teacher may wish to embed the word within a sentence.

Each student must be taught an efficient, systematic technique to study unknown spelling words. Letting students devise their own individual methods is not advisable. An effective word study method can be established by developing a worksheet that specifies the study pattern in a step-by-step manner. Initially, the student uses the worksheet, under teacher supervision, to learn each unknown spelling word. Gradually, the worksheet is faded out as the study method becomes internalized.

An effective word study method concentrates on the whole word and requires careful pronunciation, visual imagery, auditory and/or kinesthetic reinforcement, and systematic recall (i.e., distributed learning and over-learning). Figure 5 presents a variety of word study techniques that, for the most part, meet these stipulations. These authors suggest that the student be taught either the Fitzgerald Method or one of the two methods by E. Horn. If these techniques prove ineffective for a particular student, the Gilstrap Method may be more suitable. Or, a teacher may wish to use one of the other word study techniques (e.g., Fernald Method, Cover-and-Write Method, etc.) with a specific student.

PROCEDURES SUPPORTED BY RESEARCH

1. The test-study-test method is superior to the study-test method (Blanchard, 1944; C. Edwards, 1931; Fitzgerald, 1953; Gates, 1931; Hibler, 1957; T. Horn, 1946; Kingsley, 1923; Montgomery, 1957; Yee, 1969).
2. Learning spelling words by a synthetic approach is a better technique than learning words by syllables (T. Horn, 1947, 1969; Humphry, 1954).
3. It is more efficient to present words for study in a list or column form than in sentence or paragraph form (M. Edwards, 1953; Hawley & Gallup, 1922; E. Horn, 1944, 1954b; McKee, 1924; Strickland, 1951; Winch, 1916).
4. The single most important factor in learning to spell is the student correcting his or her own spelling test under the teacher's direction (Beseler, 1953; Christine & Hollingsworth, 1966; T. Horn, 1946; Louis, 1950; Schoephoerster, 1962; Thomas, 1954; Tyson, 1953).
5. Spelling games stimulate student interest (Fitzgerald, 1951a; E. Horn, 1960; T. Horn, 1969).
6. Sixty to 75 minutes per week should be allotted to spelling instruction (E. Horn, 1960; T. Horn, 1947; Larson, 1945; Rieth, Axelrod, Anderson, Hathaway, Wood, & Fitzgerald, 1972).

PROCEDURES NOT SUPPORTED BY RESEARCH

1. Writing spelling words in the air is a valuable aid in learning new words (Petty & Green, 1968).
2. Studying the "hard spots" in words improves spelling ability (Masters, 1927; Mendenhall, 1930; Rosemeier, 1965; Tireman, 1927).
3. Students should devise their own method for studying spelling words (Fitzgerald, 1951a; E. Horn, 1944, 1954b, 1960; T. Horn, 1969).
4. Student interest in spelling is secondary to rewards received for achievement in spelling (Columba, 1926; Diserens & Vaughn, 1931; Forlano, 1936; E. Horn, 1960, 1967; D. Russell, 1937; Thorndike, 1935).
5. Writing words several times ensures spelling retention (Abbott, 1909; Petty & Green, 1968; E. Horn, 1967).

FIGURE 4
Research on Spelling Procedures

The single most effective technique in learning to spell is followed when the student (under the teacher's direction) corrects his or her own errors immediately after taking a spelling test. The corrected-test method allows the student to (a) see which words are difficult, (b) locate the part of the word that is troublesome, and (c) correct errors. Examples of this technique include the following:

1. Teacher spells word orally. Student corrects word in writing (Hibler, 1957).
2. Teacher spells word, emphasizing each letter as student points to each letter as it is pronounced (Allred, 1977).
3. Teacher spells word and student marks through each incorrect letter and writes correct letter above it (Hall, 1964).

Fitzgerald Method
(Fitzgerald, 1951a)

1. Look at the word carefully.
2. Say the word.
3. With eyes closed, visualize the word.
4. Cover the word and then write it.
5. Check the spelling.
6. If the word is misspelled, repeat steps 1-5.

Horn Method 1 (E. Horn, 1919)

1. Look at the word and say it to yourself.
2. Close your eyes and visualize the word.
3. Check to see if you were right. (If not, begin as step 1.)
4. Cover the word and write it.
5. Check to see if you were right. (If not, begin at step 1.)
6. Repeat steps 4 and 5 two more times.

Horn Method 2 (E. Horn, 1954c)

1. Pronounce each word carefully.
2. Look carefully at each part of the word as you pronounce it.
3. Say the letters in sequence.
4. Attempt to recall how the word looks, then spell the word.
5. Check this attempt to recall.
6. Write the word.
7. Check this spelling attempt.
8. Repeat the above steps if necessary.

Visual-Vocal Method
(Westerman, 1971)

1. Say word.
2. Spell word orally.
3. Say word again.
4. Spell word from memory four times correctly.

Gilstrap Method (Gilstrap, 1962)

1. Look at the word and say it softly. If it has more than one part, say it again, part by part, looking at each part as you say it.
2. Look at the letters and say each one. If the word has more than one part, say the letters part by part.
3. Write the word without looking at the book.

Fernald Method Modified

1. Make a model of the word with a crayon, grease pencil, or magic marker, saying the word as you write it.
2. Check the accuracy of the model.
3. Trace over the model with your index finger, saying the word at the same time.
4. Repeat step 3 five times.
5. Copy the word three times correctly.
6. Copy the word three times from memory correctly.

Cover-and-Write Method

1. Look at word. Say it.
2. Write word two times.
3. Cover and write one time.
4. Check work.
5. Write word two times.
6. Cover and write one time.
7. Check work.
8. Write word three times.
9. Cover and write one time.
10. Check work.

References to Other Techniques

Aho, 1967
Bartholome, 1977
Clanton, 1977
Glusker, 1967
Hill & Martinis, 1973
Phillips, 1975
Stowitschek & Jobes, 1977

FIGURE 5
Word Study Techniques

4. Teacher writes word correctly next to misspelled word. Student writes word correctly (Kauffman, Hallahan, Haas, Brame, & Boren, 1978).

5. Teacher writes exact imitation of student's error and then writes word correctly. Student writes word correctly (Kauffman et al., 1978).

The prevailing practice of presenting all the spelling words at the beginning of the week is not suitable for handicapped students. To present and test a few words daily is preferable. Also, the teacher should intersperse known and unknown words in each spelling test (Neef, Iwata, & Page, 1977). Each newly mastered spelling word should be tested a few days after the initial presentation and then periodically throughout the school year. This helps ensure spelling maintenance and growth.

Many students evidence difficulty in identifying misspelled words, but this skill can be improved through practice (Valmont, 1972). A good way to begin is to provide time to proofread written assignments and stress the importance of spelling consciousness. Proofreading skills may be improved through exercises similar to the following:

1. Have the student locate incorrect spellings in a short list of words (Hardin, Bernstein, & Shands, 1978).

2. Provide practice in detecting words that don't look right in other students' writing assignments (Rudman, 1973).

3. List the number of misspelled words in a composition and have the student search for and correct errors (Valmont, 1972).

4. Underline words that may be misspelled and have the student check their accuracy (Personkee & Yee, 1971).

Phonic skills can be developed through application of a wide variety of activities (see Hanna et. al., 1971; Hillerich, 1976). Specifically, these skills can be taught inductively, in isolation or context, and/or by association. Each of these techniques should be used selectively with handicapped students in teaching sound-symbol associations, prefixes, suffixes, and base words. To illustrate, a student initially might learn to associate a particular sound (e.g., $/t/$) with its corresponding symbol (t). Later, the student might be asked to write the appropriate beginning letter (t) in response to a dictated word (tap).

E. Horn (1960) indicates that spelling rules should be (a) taught inductively rather than deductively, and (b) developed in connection with words to which the rule applies. Moreover, only one rule should be taught at a time. Both the positive and negative aspects of the rule should be highlighted. The rule also should be systematically reviewed and applied.

An important element in spelling instruction is dictionary training. Students need to know how to use the dictionary for many purposes. Dictionary training activities may include alphabetizing words, approximating the location of a given word in the dictionary, using guide words, dividing words into syllables, and so forth.

Students also may require training in visual and auditory imagery. To be effective spellers, students must be able to easily and correctly perceive the words to be spelled. Hudson and Toler (1949), Mason (1961), and Radaker (1963) indicate that auditory and/or visual training may result in improved spelling achievement.

Interest and Motivation

Positive attitudes are crucial to spelling improvement. As most teachers know, effectiveness of instructional procedures depends greatly upon the student's interest and motivation. Regardless of the quality of the program, progress will be restricted if the student is not motivated to spell words correctly or is not interested in spelling. Since attitudes and methodology are intrinsically bound together, techniques designed to foster positive attitudes should be an integral part of the total spelling program.

How does the teacher promote positive attitudes toward spelling? First, the student must develop a desire to spell words correctly. Spelling consciousness can be stimulated by: (a) showing the student the importance of correct spelling in practical and social situations; (b) providing the student with an efficient method of word study; (c) limiting the spelling vocabulary to words most likely needed in the student's present and near future writing endeavors; (d) encouraging pride in correctly spelled papers; and (e) requiring study of only those words that the student is unable to spell.

Of the sources available to the teacher for promoting positive attitudes, probably none other is as important as the student's awareness of progress or success (E. Horn, 1960). Many handicapped students experience considerable frustration in learning to spell. To minimize the effects of persistent failure, the teacher should dramatize each student success using charts, graphs, verbal praise, and so on. The experience of noting progress may be motivating for both student and teacher.

Whenever possible, the student should maintain the chart or graph himself or herself (Wallace & Kauffman, 1973). For example, the student might first record on a graph the number of words spelled correctly on the pretest, and later add to the graph the number of words spelled correctly on the posttest. This exercise provides a visual representation of the student's progress in learning how to spell new words.

For some handicapped students, the dramatization of success is not, in and of itself, enough to overcome undesirable attitudes. The teacher may have to build into the spelling program rewards for good performance.

Studies by Benowitz and Busse (1970, 1976), Benowitz and Rosenfeld (1973), and Thompson and Galloway (1970) reveal that material incentives are successful in improving spelling achievement. If material incentives are used, they should be combined with verbal praise. As the student's attitudes and achievement improve, the material incentives should be slowly phased out. Motivation inspired by intrinsic reinforcement is ultimately preferable to material rewards.

Games and special devices are also often suggested as a means of improving spelling attitudes. Research evidence indicates that certain games may be of some benefit (E. Horn, 1960). Nevertheless, they should supplement rather than supplant direct instruction. Teachers either may develop games of their own or locate games developed by others (see Fitzgerald, 1951a; Hildreth, 1962). Games like hangman, crossword puzzles, scrambled words, spelling bingo, and spelling baseball are enjoyable to most students.

ADDITIONAL CONSIDERATIONS

In designing an appropriate spelling program, the proposed methods, materials, reinforcers, and daily activities should be realistic with respect to the instructional time available. It is recommended that 60 to 75 minutes per week be allotted to spelling instruction. Although a few students may require additional time, most students do not benefit from extended periods of study in spelling (Fitzsimmons & Loomer, 1977).

The time allocated for daily spelling instruction can be supplemented and maximized by the advantageous use of tutors or paraprofessionals. Research indicates that tutors are effective in improving tutees' spelling progress (Bandle, 1949; Lovitt, 1975; Stillberger, 1950).

Additionally, the instructional process may be enhanced by enlisting the cooperation of the student's parents. The involvement of parents as "equal partners" in making decisions related to their handicapped child is implicit in PL 94-142 (Hudson & Graham, 1978).

Of final concern is the effect of dialect upon spelling achievement. Many handicapped students are members of minority groups that converse in a dialect other than "standard" English. Although students from minority groups may spell things the way they hear or say them, under no circumstances should the teacher attempt to change their dialect with the hope that acquisition of standard English will improve their spelling achievement. Instead, it is recommended that students pronounce words affected by their dialect and carefully note how they are spelled.

CONCLUSION

The model presented in this article is intended to provide teachers with a valid, flexible, and systematic guide to spelling instruction. The authors hope that teachers will adapt the model to their own particular students and situations. For instance, in a mainstreaming program, each of the participating teachers might bear responsibility for specific aspects of the spelling curriculum. In this way, the efforts of both special and regular educators are coordinated and the likelihood of spelling success maximized.

Finally, spelling instruction in the present program is direct and not incidental. Nonetheless, spelling is an integral part of the writing process and not a discrete, separate skill. The language arts are highly interrelated, and students need a lot of practice using their spelling skills in context (i.e., writing).

REFERENCES

Abbott, E. On the analysis of the memory consciousness in orthography. *University of Illinois Psychological Monograph 11*, 1909.

Aho, M. Teaching spelling to children with specific language disability. *Academic Therapy*, 1967, *3*, 45-50.

Allen, D., & Ager, J. A factor analytic study of the ability to spell. *Educational & Psychological Measurement*, 1965, *25*, 153-161.

Allred, R. *Spelling: The application of research findings.* Washington, DC: National Education Association, 1977.

Archer, C. Shall we teach spelling by rule? *Elementary English*, 1930, 7, 61-63.

Ashbaugh, E. *The Iowa spelling scales.* Iowa City: Bureau of Educational Research and Service, 1921.

Ayer, F. *Ayer standardized spelling test.* Austin, TX: Steck, 1950.

Ayer, F. An evaluation of high school spelling. *School Review*, 1951, *59*, 233-236.

Baker, G. *A comparison of traditional spelling with phonemic spelling of fifth and sixth grade students.* Unpublished doctoral dissertation, Wayne State University, 1977.

Bandle, G. *The influence of group cooperation on spelling achievement.* Unpublished master's thesis, University of Iowa, 1949.

Bartholome, L. Using the typewriter for learning: Spelling. *Balance Sheet*, 1977, *58*, 196-200.

Bedell, R., & Nelson, E. Word attack as a factor in reading achievement in the elementary school. *Educational & Psychological Measurement*, 1954, *14*, 168-175.

Beers, J. *First and second grade children's developing concepts of tense and lax vowels.* Unpublished doctoral dissertation, University of Virginia, 1974.

Beers, J., & Henderson, E. A study of developing orthographic concepts among first grade children. *Research in the Teaching of English*, 1977, *11*, 133-148.

Benowitz, M., & Busse, T. Material incentives and the learning of spelling words in a typical school situation. *Journal of Educational Psychology*, 1970, *61*, 24-26.

Benowitz, M., & Busse, T. Effects of material incentives on classroom learning over a four-week period. *Journal of Educational Psychology*, 1976, *68*, 57-62.

Benowitz, M., & Rosenfeld, J. Three types of incentives and classroom learning of middle and lower-class children. *Psychology in the Schools*, 1973, *10*, 79-83.

Beseler, D. *An experiment in spelling using the corrected test method.* Unpublished master's thesis, Central Washington State College, 1953.

Blair, T. ERIC/RCS. *Reading Teacher*, 1975, *28*, 604-607.

Blanchard, G. *An experimental comparison of the test-study and the study-test methods of teaching spelling in the eighth grade.* Unpublished master's thesis, Fordham University, 1944.

Block, J. But will they ever lern to spel korectly? *Educational Research,* 1972,, *14,* 171-178.

Boder, E. Developmental dyslexia: A diagnostic screening procedure based on three characteristic patterns of reading and spelling. *Journal of Learning Disabilities,* 1971, *4,* 297-342.

Brody, D. A comparative study of different forms of spelling tests. *Journal of Educational Psychology,* 1944, *35,* 129-144.

Brueckner, L., & Bond, G. *Diagnosis and treatment of learning difficulties.* New York: Appleton-Century-Crofts, 1955.

Burt, C. *Northumberland standardized tests: 11 English.* London: University of London Press, 1925.

Camp, B., & Dolcourt, J. Reading and spelling in good and poor readers. *Journal of Learning Disabilities,* 1977, *10,* 46-53.

Christine, R., & Hollingsworth, P. An experiment in spelling. *Education,* 1966, *86,* 565-567.

Clanton, P. *The effectiveness of the letter-close procedure as a method of teaching spelling.* Unpublished doctoral dissertation, University of Arkansas, 1977.

Clymer, T. The utility of phonic generalizations in the primary grades. *Reading Teacher,* 1963, *16,* 252-258.

Cohen, L. *Evaluating structural analysis methods used in spelling books.* Unpublished doctoral dissertation, Boston University, 1969.

Columba, M. *A study of interests and their relations to other factors of achievement in elementary school subjects.* Washington, DC: Catholic University, 1926.

Cook, W. Shall we teach spelling by rules? *Journal of Educational Psychology,* 1912, *3,* 316-325.

Cook, W. The measurement of general spelling ability involving controlled comparisons between techniques. *University of Iowa Studies in Education: 6,* 1932, *6,* 1-112.

Courtis, S. *Measurement of classroom products.* New York: General Education Board, 1919.

Davis, L. *The applicability of phonic generalizations to selected spelling programs.* Unpublished doctoral dissertation, University of Oklahoma, 1969.

Dieterich, D. Diserroneosospellingitis or the fine (language) art of spelling. *Elementary English,* 1973, *49,* 245-253.

Diserens, C., & Vaughn, J. The experimental psychology of motivation. *Psychological Bulletin,* 1931, *28,* 15-65.

Dunwell, S. *Report on WRITE: Computer assisted instruction course in written English usage.* Poughkeepsie, NY: Shared Education Computer Systems, 1972.

Durost, W., Evans, W., Leake, J., Bowman, H., Cosgrove., C., & Reed, J. *Metropolitan achievement tests.* New York: Harcourt Brace Jovanovich, 1970.

Durrell, D. *Durrell analysis of reading difficulty.* Yonkers: World Book, 1937.

Edwards, C. *A comparative study of two techniques of spelling instruction.* Unpublished master's thesis, University of Iowa, 1931.

Edwards, M. *An evaluation of the Casis school instructional program in spelling.* Unpublished master's thesis, University of Texas, 1953.

Fitzgerald, J. *The teaching of spelling.* Milwaukee: Bruce Publishing Co., 1951. (a)

Fitzgerald, J. *A basic life spelling vocabulary.* Milwaukee: Bruce Publishing Co., 1951. (b)

Fitzgerald, J. The teaching of spelling. *Elementary English,* 1953, *30,* 79-84.

Fitzsimmons, R., & Loomer, B. *Spelling research and practice.* Iowa State Department of Public Instruction and University of Iowa, 1977.

Fleming, C. *Kelvin measurement of spelling ability.* Glasgow: Robert Gibson & Sons, 1933.

Foran, T. *The psychology and teaching of spelling.* New York: Catholic Educational Press, 1934.

Forlano, G. *School learning with various methods of practice and rewards.* New York: Columbia University, 1936.

Frasch, D. How well do sixth graders proofread for spelling errors? *Elementary School Journal,* 1965, *65,* 381-382.

Gates, A. An experimental comparison of the study-test and test-study methods in spelling. *Journal of Educational Psychology,* 1931, *22,* 1-19.

Gates, A. *A list of spelling difficulties in 3,876 words.* Unpublished manuscript, 1937.

Gates, A., & Russell, D. *Diagnostic and remedial spelling manual.* New York: Columbia University, 1937.

Gentry, J. *A study of the orthographic strategies of beginning readers.* Unpublished doctoral dissertation, University of Virginia, 1977.

Gilbert, L., & Gilbert, D. The improvement of spelling through reading. *Journal of Educational Research,* 1944, *37,* 458-463.

Gilstrap, R. Development of independent spelling skills in the intermediate grades. *Elementary English,* 1962, *39,* 481-483.

Glusker, P. An integrational approach to spelling. *Academic Therapy,* 1967, *3,* 51-61.

Gold, V. *The effect of an experimental program involving acquisition of phoneme-grapheme relationships incorporating criterion referenced tests with evaluative feedback upon spelling performance of third grade pupils.* Unpublished doctoral dissertation, University of Southern California, 1976.

Graves, D. Research update: Spelling texts and structural analysis methods. *Language Arts,* 1976, *54,* 86-90.

Grottenthaler, J. *A comparison of the effectiveness of three programs of elementary school spelling.* Unpublished doctoral dissertation, University of Pittsburgh, 1970.

Guiler, W., & Lease, G. An experimental study of methods of instruction in spelling. *Elementary School Journal,* 1942, *42,* 234-238.

Hahn, W. *Comparative efficiency of the teaching of spelling by the column and contextual methods.* Unpublished doctoral dissertation, University of Pittsburgh, 1960.

Hahn, W. Phonics: A boon to spelling. *Elementary School Journal,* 1964, *64,* 383-386.

Hall, N. The letter mark-out corrected test. *Journal of Educational Research,* 1964, *58,* 148-157.

Hanna, P., Hanna, J., Hodges, R., & Rudorf, E. *Phoneme-grapheme correspondences as cues to spelling improvement.* Washington, DC: U.S. Government Printing Office, 1966.

Hanna, P., Hodges, R., & Hanna, J. *Spelling: Structure and strategies.* New York: Houghton-Mifflin, 1971.

Hardin, B., Bernstein, B., & Shands, F. The "Hey what's this?" approach to teaching spelling. *Teacher,* 1978, *94,* 64-67.

Hawley, W., & Gallup, J. The list versus the sentence method of teaching spelling. *Journal of Educational Research,* 1922, *5,* 306-310.

Hersen, M., & Barlow, D. *Single case experimental designs.* New York: Pergamon Press, 1976.

Hibler, G. *The test-study versus the study-test method of teaching spelling in grade two: Study I.* Unpublished master's thesis, University of Texas, 1957.

Hildreth, G. *Teaching spelling: A guide to basic principles and practices.* New York: Holt, Rinehart & Winston, 1962.

Hill, C., & Martinis, A. Individualizing a multisensory spelling program? *Academic Therapy,* 1973, *9,* 77-83.

Hillerich, R. *Spelling: An element in written expression.* Columbus, OH: Charles E. Merrill Publishing Co., 1976.

Hillerich, R. Let's teach spelling — not phonetic misspelling. *Language Arts,* 1977, *54,* 301-307.

Hodges, R. Theoretical framework of English orthography. *Elementary English*, 1977, *49*, 1089-1105.

Horn, E. Principles of methods in teaching spelling as derived from scientific investigation. In *Eighteenth Yearbook, National Society for the Study of Education.* Bloomington: Public School Publishing Co., 1919.

Horn, E. *A basic vocabulary of 10,000 words most commonly used in writing.* Iowa City: University of Iowa, 1926.

Horn, E. Research in spelling. *Elementary English Review*, 1944, *21*, 6-13.

Horn, E. Phonics and spelling. *Journal of Education*, 1954, *136*, 233-235, 246. (a)

Horn, E. What research says to the teacher. *Teaching Spelling*, 1954, *3*, 32. (b)

Horn, E. *Teaching spelling.* Washington, DC: American Educational Research Association, 1954. (c)

Horn, E. Spelling. *Encyclopedia of educational research.* New York: Macmillan, 1960.

Horn, E. *Teaching spelling: What research says to the teacher.* Department of Classroom Teachers, American Educational Research Association of the National Education Association, 1967.

Horn, T. *The effects of the corrected test on learning to spell.* Unpublished master's thesis, University of Iowa, 1946.

Horn, T. *The effect of a syllabic presentation of words upon learning to spell.* Unpublished doctoral dissertation, University of Iowa, 1947.

Horn, T. Research critiques. *Elementary English*, 1969, *46*, 210-212.

Horn, T., & Otto, H. *Spelling instruction: A curriculum-wide approach.* Austin: University of Texas, 1954.

Hudson, F., & Graham, S. An approach to operationalizing the I.E.P. *Learning Disability Quarterly*, 1978, *1*, 13-32.

Hudson, J., & Toler, L. Instruction in auditory and visual discrimination as a means of improving spelling. *Elementary School Journal*, 1949, *49*, 459-466.

Humphry, M. *The effect of a syllabic presentation of words upon learning to spell.* Unpublished master's thesis, University of Texas, 1954.

Ibeling, F. Supplementary phonics instruction and reading and spelling ability. *Elementary School Journal*, 1961, *63*, 152-156.

Jensen, A. Spelling errors and the serial-position effect. *Journal of Educational Psychology*, 1962, *53*, 105-109.

Jobes, N. *The acquisition and retention of spelling through imitation training and observational learning with and without feedback.* Unpublished doctoral dissertation, George Peabody College for Teachers, 1975.

Kauffman, J., Hallahan, D., Haas, K., Brame, T., & Boren, R. Imitating children's errors to improve spelling performance, *Journal of Learning Disabilities*, 1978, *11*, 33-38.

King, L. *Learning and applying spelling rules in grades three to eight.* Contributions to Education, No. 517. New York: Bureau of Publications, Columbia University, 1932.

Kingsley, J. The test-study method versus study-test method in spelling. *Elementary School Journal*, 1923, *24*, 126-129.

Knoell, D., & Harris, C. A factor analysis of spelling ability. *Journal of Educational Research*, 1952, *46*, 95-111.

Kooi, B., Schutz, R., & Baker, R. Spelling errors and the serial-position effect. *Journal of Educational Psychology*, 1965, *56*, 334-336.

Kottmeyer, W. Teacher's guide for remedial reading. St. Louis: Webster, 1959.

Kyte, G. Maintaining ability grouping in spelling. *Phi Delta Kappan*, 1949, *30*, 301-306.

Lambert, C. *Seven-plus assessment: Spelling.* London: University of London Press, 1964.

Larsen, S., & Hammill, D. *The Larsen-Hammill test of written spelling.* San Rafael, CA: Academic Therapy Publications, 1976.

Larson, T. *Time allotment in the teaching of spelling.* Unpublished master's thesis, University of Iowa, 1945.

Louis, R. *A study of spelling growth in two different teaching procedures.* Unpublished master's thesis, Central Washington State College, 1950.

Lovitt, T. Applied behavior analysis and learning disabilities. Part II: Specific research recommendations and suggestions for practitioners. *Journal of Learning Disabilities,* 1975, *8,* 504-518.

Mason, G. Word discrimination drills, *Journal of Educational Research,* 1961, *55,* 39-40.

Masters, H. *A study of spelling errors.* Unpublished master's thesis, University of Iowa, 1927.

Mendenhall, J. *An analysis of spelling errors: A study of factors associated with word difficulty.* New York: Columbia University, 1930.

Miller, L., & Graham, S. Reading skills of LD students: A review. *Alabama Reader,* 1979, *6,* 16-25.

Miller, L., & Carpenter, D.   Analyzing errors in written spelling (submitted for publication).

Monson, J. Is spelling spelled rut, routine, or revitalized? *Elementary English,* 1975, *52,* 223-224.

Montgomery, M. *The test-study method versus the study-test method of teaching spelling in grade two: Study II.* Unpublished master's thesis, University of Texas, 1957.

Moran, M. Nine steps to the diagnostic prescriptive process in the classroom. *Focus on Exceptional Children,* 1975, *6,* 1-14.

McElwee, G. *Systematic instruction in proofreading for spelling and its effects on fourth and sixth grade composition.* Unpublished doctoral dissertation, University of Wisconsin-Madison, 1974.

McKee, P. *Teaching and testing spelling by column and context forms.* Unpublished doctoral dissertation, University of Iowa, 1924.

Neef, N., Iwata, B., & Page, T. The effects of known-item interspersal on acquisition and retention of spelling and sight word reading. *Journal of Applied Behavior Analysis,* 1977, *10,* 738.

Nisbet, S. Non-dictated spelling tests. *British Journal of Educational Psychology,* 1939, *9,* 29-44.

Oswalt, W. *The effect of proofreading for spelling errors in spelling achievement of fifth grade pupils.* Unpublished doctoral dissertation, Temple University, 1961.

Otto, W., & McMenemy, R. *Corrective and remedial teaching.* Boston: Houghton-Mifflin, 1966.

Personkee, C. The use of nonsense words to test generalization ability in spelling. *Elementary English,* 1972, *49,* 1233-1239.

Personkee, C., & Knight, L.   Proofreading and spelling: A report and a program. *Elementary English,* 1967, *44,* 768-774.

Personkee, C., & Yee, A. *Comprehensive spelling instruction: Theory, research, and application.* Scranton: Intext Educational Publishers, 1971.

Peters, M. *Success in spelling. A study of factors affecting improvement in spelling in the junior-school.* Cambridge: Institute of Education, 1970.

Petty, W., & Green, H. *Developing language skills in the elementary schools.* Boston: Allyn & Bacon, 1968.

Phillips, V. *The effect of a mode of presentation of spelling on reading achievement.* Unpublished doctoral dissertation, University of Illinois, 1975.

Radaker, L. The effect of visual imagery upon spelling performance. *Journal of Educational Research,* 1963, *56,* 370-372.

Read, E., Allred, R., & Baird, L. *Continuous progress in spelling: Intermediate teacher's manual.* Oklahoma City: Individualized Instruction, Inc., 1972.

Rieth, H., Axelrod, S., Anderson, R., Hathaway, F., Wood, K., & Fitzgerald, C. Influence of distributed practice and daily testing on weekly spelling tests. *Journal of Educational Research,* 1972, *68,* 73-77.

Rinsland, H. *A basic vocabulary of elementary school children.* New York: Macmillan, 1945.

Robinson, A. *Every pupil achievement test: Spelling.* Emporia, KS: Bureau of Educational Measurement, Kansas State Teacher's College, 1970.

Rosemeier, R. Effectiveness of forewarning about errors in response — Selective learning. *Journal of Educational Psychology,* 1965, *56,* 309-314.

Rowell, G. A prototype for an individualized spelling program. *Elementary English,* 1972, *49,* 335-340.

Rudman, M. Informal spelling in the classroom: A more effective approach. *Reading Teacher,* 1973, *26,* 602-604.

Russell, D. *Characteristics of good and poor spellers.* New York: Columbia University, 1937.

Russell, K. *An evaluation of the effect of word analysis exercises on spelling achievement.* Unpublished doctoral dissertation, Boston University, 1954.

Schell, L. B+ in composition: C- in spelling. *Language Arts,* 1975, *52,* 239-257.

Schoephoerster, H. Research into variations of the test-study plan of teaching spelling. *Elementary English,* 1962, *39,* 460-462.

Schoolfield, L., & Timberlake, J. *Phonovisual method book.* Washington, DC: Phonovisual Products, 1949.

Schwartz, S., & Doehring, D. A developmental study of children's ability to acquire knowledge of spelling patterns. *Developmental Psychology,* 1977, *13,* 419-420.

Shubik, H. *An experimental comparison of the test-study and the study-test methods of teaching spelling in third grade.* Unpublished master's thesis, Fordham University, 1951.

Simon, D., & Simon, H. Alternative uses of phonemic information in spelling. *Review of Educational Research,* 1973, *43,* 115-137.

Spache, G. A critical analysis of various methods of classifying spelling errors. *Journal of Educational Psychology,* 1940, *31,* 111-134.

Spache, G. Validity and reliability of the proposed classification of spelling errors. *Journal of Educational Psychology,* 1941, *31,* 204-214.

Spache, G. *Spelling errors test.* Gainesville, FL: Reading laboratory and Clinic, University of Florida, 1955.

Stillberger, E. *Individual differences of achievement in spelling.* Unpublished master's thesis, University of Iowa, 1950.

Stowitschek, C., & Jobes, N. Getting the bugs out of spelling — Or an alternative to the spelling bee. *Teaching Exceptional Children,* 1977, *9,* 74-76.

Strickland, R. *The language arts in the elementary school.* Boston: D. C. Heath, 1951.

Swenson, E., & Caldwell, C. Spelling in children's letters. *Elementary School Journal,* 1948, *19,* 224-235.

Teacher's Manual. *Portland speller.* Portland, OR: Portland Public Schools, 1956.

Templin, M. Phonic knowledge and its relation to the spelling and reading achievement of fourth grade pupils. *Journal of Educational Research,* 1954, *47,* 441-454.

Thomas, R. *The effect of the corrected test on learning to spell, grades four, five, and six.* Unpublished master's thesis, University of Texas, 1954.

Thompson, E., & Galloway, C. Material reinforcement and success in spelling. *Elementary School Journal,* 1970, *70,* 395-398.

Thompson, M. *The effects of spelling pattern training on the spelling behavior of primary elementary students.* Unpublished doctoral dissertation, University of Pittsburgh, 1977.

Thorndike, E. *The psychology of wants, interests, and attitudes.* New York: Appleton-Century-Crofts, 1935.

Thorpe, L., Lefever, D., Haslund, R. *SRA achievement series.* Chicago: Science Research Associates, 1963.

Tiegs, E., & Clark, W. *California achievement tests.* Monterey: McGraw-Hill, 1970.

Tireman, L. *The value of marking hard spots in spelling.* Unpublished master's thesis, University of Iowa, 1927.

Tovey, D. Sound-it-out: A reasonable approach to spelling? *Reading World,* 1978, *17,* 220-233.

Turner, E. Rules versus drill in teaching spelling. *Journal of Educational Psychology,* 1912, *3,* 460-461.

Tyler, I. *Spelling as a secondary learning.* New York: Columbia University, 1939.

Tyson, I. *Factors contributing to the effectiveness of the corrected test in spelling.* Unpublished doctoral dissertation, University of Iowa, 1953.

Valmont, W. Spelling consciousness: A long neglected area. *Elementary English,* 1972, *49,* 1219-1221.

Wallace, G., & Kauffman, J. *Teaching children with learning problems.* Columbus, OH: Charles E. Merrill Publishing Co., 1973.

Warren, H. *Phonetic generalizations to aid spelling instruction at the fifth-grade level.* Unpublished doctoral dissertation, Boston University, 1969.

Warren, J. *Phonetic generalizations to aid spelling instruction at the fifth-grade level.* Unpublished doctoral dissertation, Boston University, 1970.

Westerman, G. *Spelling and writing.* San Rafael: Dimensions, 1971.

Winch, W. Additional researches on learning to spell. *Journal of Educational Psychology,* 1916, 7, 93-110.

Yee, A. Is the phonetic generalization hypothesis in spelling valid? *Journal of Experimental Education,* 1969, *37,* 82-91.

Hargis points out that teachers are taught much more about word attack skills than word recognition. Word recognition is the process of learning to instantly recognize printed words. Word recognition has its own set of understandings and techniques. These include imagery level, which makes some words three times as easy to learn as others. Specific principles of repetition apply to retarded children, who require about three times as many repetitions to learn words. Hargis has developed an extensive analysis of this subject, including suggestions for teachers on how to develop and select instructional materials.

Word Recognition Development

Charles H. Hargis

In considering reading skills, teachers seldom recognize the distinction that should be made between *word recognition* and *word identification*. Yet, skills in these two areas are distinct and should receive separate instructional consideration.

The term *word recognition* as used here refers to the process of learning to instantly recognize printed words. This differs from terms that suggest word identification or the identification of words by decoding or analytic processes. This latter is often referred to by terms such as *word attack, word identification, phonic analysis,* and *decoding.*

Distinguishing between word recognition and word identification has to do with the familiarity of printed words. Word recognition implies familiarity. Word recognition development is the process of becoming familiar with specific printed words, in whatever context they may occur.

The more efficient reading becomes, the more efficient the word recognition process is. "Word calling" behavior is associated with poor recognition skill. Word callers overly depend on the word identification process to figure out how to say (call) the word. Reading is a laborious word-by-word "sounding out" procedure, with the child calling the word only after being sure of a pronunciation. Over-dependence, or an almost exclusive emphasis, on word identification skills causes word callers to attend to the spelling-sound constituents of printed words so that they don't gain sufficient familiarity with words themselves. Also fostering this "word-calling" behavior is the excessive use of oral reading as the main reading activity. Accuracy in pronunciation — rather than improved word recognition or comprehension — seems to be the criterion measure of success in oral reading activities.

SIGHT WORDS

Often, word recognition activities are compartmentalized in a separate place in the reading curriculum. Certain sets of words are usually emphasized in these activities. The words are usually called sight words or service words. They are composed of a relatively small number of common high-frequency words. The Dolch Basic Sight Word List (1941), the one most commonly associated with sight word teaching, is subsumed in virtually all other such word lists. These words occur with high frequency in all spoken or printed discourse. They constitute over half the total number of different words used in primary level basal readers (Mangieri & Kahn, 1977).

A great number of these words are phonically irregular (e.g., *are, were, some, said, their, have*). Others have complex letter-sound associations that will not be introduced until some time later — frequently after the first-grade level. Since the use of even rudimentary sentences is not possible without having to use some of these words, they are usually introduced as sight words so that students can begin doing some reading.

Children who have reading problems seem to have inordinate difficulty in learning to recognize these common sight words. They show inconsistency from day to day in recognizing these words, and confusion occurs between many of the words.

IMAGERY LEVEL AND DIFFICULTY

Remarkably little research has been done on what characteristics of words pose obstacles to their recognition. Some research has been directed at the identification problems of words by their configuration, phonic characteristics, and length (Hargis & Gickling, 1978; Wolpert, 1972). But much more interest has been paid to skill deficits in the learner.

Only recently has interest been expressed in another characteristic of words that has turned out to be significantly related to learning recognition: the imagery level of words. Imagery level or concreteness of a word has to do with how readily a mental image can be formed of the referent the word represents. Concrete nouns can have the highest imagery level. They are words like *car, dog, house,* and *tree.* Low imagery nouns are words like *time, idea, fun,* and *belief.*

Other parts of speech can have various levels of imagery as well, but verbs, adjectives, or adverbs, do not have a mental image distinct from the things they operate with or modify. The verb *run,* though concrete for a verb, requires some animate nouns to illustrate its meaning. Adjectives also require nouns, and adverbs require verbs or adjectives.

Still other quite common words that make up sentences serve primarily syntactic functions. They are sometimes called structure words. Structure words include prepositions, articles, auxiliary verbs, relative pronouns, and conjunctions. These words have very low imagery. One simply does not form a mental image of *some, at, where, been, these,* and so on.

Several research projects have been conducted to determine any differences in the difficulty of learning to recognize words by levels of imagery (Hargis & Gickling, 1978; Gickling, Hargis, & Radford, 1982; Hargis, 1978). Groups of both handicapped and nonhandicapped children have been presented high imagery and low imagery nouns and some common structure words. All the students included for study were performing on a pre-reading level. None could read any of the words to be taught. All the words were taken from Stone's Revised Word List (Spache, 1964). Each of the words was placed on a 3″ x 5″ word card. These words were presented in the same way and received the same amount of teaching time. Findings of the research projects point out quite clearly that high imagery significantly enhances the development of word recognition. This is true for the nonhandicapped as well as the handicapped. The high imagery nouns were found to be almost three times as easy to learn as the low imagery nouns and structure words.

In these experiments all the words were presented in isolation on cards, with no connected reading activities at the time. Subsequent research has demonstrated the facilitating effect that the context of a phrase or sentence has on learning lower imagery words. But much work on developing word recognition skill is done with isolated drill activity, often using flash card drills or games in which the words are isolated. Low imagery words are exceedingly difficult to learn without the context that discourse provides. Isolated word drill is an extremely inefficient, often frustrating, method of learning words other than high imagery nouns. Imagery level is truly an important consideration if words are presented in isolation. In observing more than occasional instances of children who received much of their remedial reading work through isolated drill activities with the Dolch words, seldom do these children make even modest progress in learning the words. And the teachers are invariably confused by the day-to-day inconsistency in performance toward mastering the words.

The meaning and concreteness of many of these words must be provided by their context in connected discourse and in association with other words. The phrase *these apples* makes the use of *these* far more concrete, and each repetition in such an association represents a much larger step toward mastery.

For high imagery words, however, the child's realm of experience enables many isolated words to appear meaningfully. These images include stop signs, other traffic signs, names of familiar restaurants, stores, restroom signs, and so forth. Picture dictionaries capitalize on high imagery nouns and picture combinations. No child or adult, of course, would expect to find a sign saying *these, were, before, will,* or *some.* Unfortunately, children who have the greatest reading problems will likely receive less meaningful repetition in discourse and more repetition in isolated drill.

REPETITION IN CONTEXT

Gates (1931) did the primary work in studying the extent of repetition needed in learning to recognize words. This important but neglected work provides the general guidelines for supplying repetition of words by levels of intelligence. Table 1 illustrates the average minimum number of repetitions a child needs in printed discourse. Gates pointed out that this need for repetition was independent of any exposure to the words a child might get in isolated drill, either as a part of word identification skill exercises or word recognition drill.

The number of repetitions required for mastery probably varies when considering individual words. Imagery level or concreteness may have a facilitating effect in context, and even exposure of high imagery words in isolation is beneficial. The old sight words or service words will get plenty of repetition almost unintentionally in discourse. Most of them have such utility in forming sentences that they have to appear with regularity. In fact, as was mentioned earlier, the Dolch words constitute over half the word occurrences in primary basal readers. Words occurring with low frequency, however, will require systematic attention in regard to repetition.

TABLE 1
Mean Number of Word Repetitions Required by IQ Levels

Repetitions	IQ
20	120-129
30	110-119
35	90-109
40	80-89
45	70-79
55	60-69

Adapted from Gates (1931).

INTRODUCTION RATE

In his early work Gates provided guidelines for the rate at which words could be successfully introduced, as well as the number of repetitions they would require. He found that one new word in 60 was a sufficiently manageable rate for most beginning readers to deal with. At that time (the 1920s), the available primary reading material introduced new words in the range of 1 in 10 to 1 in 17 running words. This range obviously had been too difficult, and teachers had to take rather heroic steps to provide enough supplementary teacher-made materials to aid students in reading their books at all.

Gates' research had considerable impact in regard to word introduction rates. Beginning in the 1930s, basal readers generally conformed to his guidelines for introduction. The provision for repetition he suggested, however, has not been managed. Words do not consistently receive systematic minimum repetition, and the repetition is not adequate for slow and disabled readers. Some words receive more than adequate repetition simply because they are structure words with utility such that they must be used repeatedly. Systematic and informal tabulation of repeated use of words finds some with zero repetitions in the same story in which the word was introduced and only two repetitions in the same book. More repetitions of words is the mean figure, but at least 30 percent of the words receive inadequate repetition for slower students.

Too many words remain unfamiliar, thereby increasing the load of unknown words beyond the limits acceptable for instructional purposes. Many teachers with problem readers find themselves in the same predicament as teachers of the 1920s. To make a book readable for a child, they have to provide sufficient supplementary teacher-made material to reach the necessary rate of repetition for many words that have remained unfamiliar. Teachers of reading disabled students are annoyed and frustrated at the lack of materials these students can read.

Some beginning reading instructional materials provide for repetition based on repeating patterns of letter-sound associations. This is well and good, but it should not overshadow, as it seems to, the requirement for consistent repetition of the words themselves.

THE INSTRUCTIONAL LEVEL

Controlling the introduction of words in reading material is one thing, and providing repetition is still another. A word may remain unfamiliar long after too many new ones have been introduced. Betts (1946) addressed the question of how many strange words a child can deal with in a reading activity and still maintain sufficient on-task behavior and comprehension for instructional purposes. He described the idea of the instructional level and the independent level. He also described the level of difficulty to be avoided, which he called the frustration level. Generally speaking, at the instructional level a child can encounter from two to four percent new or unfamiliar words. With teaching assistance, material of this difficulty can permit a comprehension level of about 75 percent and sufficient on-task time. If the material exceeds the four-percent limitation, comprehension falls off dramatically, as does on-task behavior. For reading material that requires no teaching assistance and can be used independently or recreationally, the child should encounter fewer than two percent unknowns.

ASSESSMENT

Like Gates' work on introduction and repetition, Betts' work was of fundamental importance. The reader at this point might say, "Yes, I know all about the instructional level, but I can't *find* anything for my students at their instructional level, and when I do, it is so much below their age level that they reject it as babyish." Other teachers respond, "Yes, this is a good idea, but what if the child can't read or can hardly remember any word consistently — even his name?"

Finding out what the student does know is a fundamental requirement. This may be difficult. First, finding the words that the student recognizes will be helpful. The teacher should take the words the student has had some contact with, then make a word recognition test from books or from drill work the student has used. The words can be placed on flash cards or word lists. The student then is to look at the words and see if he or she can name them. The teacher should identify those that the student immediately recognizes and those identified with hesitancy. These words will form the basis for preparation of the instructional reading material.

The focus is on what the child *knows*. The reading material that will have to be provided must be composed largely of knowns. According to instructional level guidelines, this must be 96 percent knowns — which can seem like a formidable challenge if the child turns out to know only nine words or even fewer! The child does need to begin reading connected discourse. In some cases, the format has to be appropriate for a teenager.

Where does one find materials written in such a restricted vocabulary and also provide about 50 repetitions for each new word? Well, the fact is that you cannot. Teachers who have students like these will find that they have to make much of the material for these children themselves. Format can be handled by making type size, spacing, and paper similar to that generally used by age peers, but other considerations may pose more of a challenge.

PREPARATION OF READING MATERIALS

When a child knows only a few words, writing connected discourse can present problems. A large pool of words from which to draw makes writing a story or selection much easier. With only a few words, the only way the instructional level guidelines can be followed is to use repetition. Consider the following selection:

I see a Trans Am.
I see a motorcycle.
I see a bike.
The Trans Am has four wheels.
The motorcycle has *two* wheels.
The bike has *two* wheels.
I have a bike.
I want a motorcycle.
I want a Trans Am.

In this selection, the student could recognize all but the word *two*. The context in the selection, however, was powerful enough that he was able to identify *two* with no assistance.

At a much simpler level, selections like the following may be necessary:

I see a *chair*.
I see a *table*.
I see a *car*.
I see a *bike*.
I see a *dog*.

If a child doesn't know any words with consistency, the use of repetition will have to be even more vigorously applied. In the selection above, even the vertical alignment of the words is used to provide visual context to help identify the words. The words *I* and *a* were selected because the letter names are also the words. The word *see* was not known, but it was introduced to the student, and vertical alignment assisted in its subsequent identification. The high imagery nouns were still unfamiliar, but the student had access to word cards with the item pictured, and the other items were labeled in the room. Thus, the known context was not provided entirely by words.

In any case, the meaningful repetition of words is an effective step toward subsequent selections that can rely more on internal context and be a little more varied. Success is critically important to working with children with chronic reading problems, and the material itself is directly related to success or failure.

The words to be identified for introduction in these selections should serve specific purposes. The words should have real utility. They should appear with high frequency so that their acquisition makes the child more independent. Another purpose is to help the student get ready to read in a specific book or series.

Teachers will have a hard time continuing to make all the student's reading material. Therefore, when possible, the words introduced in teacher-made material should be the same as those used in the commercial material the child is to begin reading. The student can be placed in the book when he or she has a sufficient stock of words to read it. Additional words can be included in the teacher-made materials to spark interest. For instance, *Trans Am* was included in the selection illustrated earlier because of the child's specific interests. It points out a case of a child who was basically a nonreader learning a word because of his interest in a particular automobile.

WORD IDENTIFICATION

Experience has shown that the most important word identification skill is the use of context. Other word identification skills are most beneficial when coupled with the use of context in predicting what an unknown or unfamiliar word is. A child may be getting only word analysis skill work during reading instruction (primarily letter-sound association at this level). If the child is not yet reading connected discourse, he or she cannot apply the skill with context. A teacher working with children like this is often heard to say, "He knows his sounds, but he still can't read!"

Children must have the opportunity to read at an instructional level or they cannot effectively apply word identification skills. Too many hard words decrease the likelihood of efficient use of word identification skills. Consequently, *effective word identification development is contingent upon word recognition development.*

Often, unfortunately, if children have pronounced reading difficulties, they are more likely to receive isolated word identification skill work and virtually no opportunity to read in connected discourse. As a consequence, the word identification skills do not generalize to real reading and they remain only fragmented items with little utility. Far too many students reach adolescence without significant reading skills because of this.

CATCHING UP

If a student is beyond the primary grades and still has had little achievement in reading, the problem or deficiency may seem to constitute an insurmountable obstacle. One procedure, however, can provide at least a partial solution to the problem. This strategy involves a fairly rapid way (relatively speaking) of increasing the stock of words in a student's word recognition vocabulary. Another important feature of this procedure is that it is a reading activity that need not cause further failure and frustration.

The first step is to identify a book or selection that is both comprehensible and short. What is meant by comprehensible is that it is understood when read to the student. The passage should be within the student's listening capacity. Short, in this instance, means no more than 15 minutes of teacher time to read it. Listening capacity of a student for a given selection can be determined by reading a portion of it to him or her (approximately 250 words) and then asking the student questions that generally reflect its content. If comprehension is at least 70 percent, the passage is at or within the student's capacity level. Helpful, but not critical, is that his activity be interesting to the student.

The next step is to tape record the selection. During the taping, the teacher should provide cues on the recording to indicate from what page the recording is being read and when the pages are being turned.

In actual procedure, the student simultaneously listens to the recording and follows the printed text. The student is permitted to "read" and listen to the tape as many times as necessary to learn to recognize all the words in the selection. The reason for using a relatively short selection is to allow listening to it with sufficient repetition to learn to recognize all the words.

The Gates' (1931) guidelines for word repetition in connected discourse provide a good rule of thumb for the number of times the student will have to listen to the tape before he or she can read it independently. These guidelines, however, must be used with due consideration to the number of repetitions words may receive within the selection itself. If a word were repeated five times within the selection, the average student would require about seven repetitions of the tape to learn to recognize that word. Of course, the number of repetitions of individual words within any selection varies enormously. High utility structure words are repeated quite naturally. *A, an, some,* or *the,* for example, appear in a majority of sentences in any selection.

Also, one can only guess how helpful initial listening/reading of the selection may be if the selection is of considerably greater difficulty than the student's instructional level. Much time during the first repetitions will be devoted to keeping the place, being lost, or trying to not get lost. In contrast, without any pressure the student is permitted to spend reading time in this activity until he or she feels comfortable about mastering the selection.

Mastery is demonstrated by the student's ability to read the passage aloud to the teacher without the aid of the tape. Carol Chomsky (1978) mentioned cases that took 20 repetitions covering about a month's time. Limiting the tape to only 15 minutes still requires quite a large number of reading periods to get enough repetition to learn troublesome, infrequently occurring words.

When the student attempts to read the material aloud without the tape, the teacher should listen with complete sympathy and no correction. The procedure, after all, is to be used with children who are chronic failures in reading and they need to gain confidence so they will stay with the task.

In regular reading activities, known context, teacher assistance, and word identification skills will help the child cope with new and unfamiliar words. In the activity just outlined, the tape provides the necessary aid in dealing with the large load of unfamiliar words. The tape almost represents a teacher or tutor at hand to provide the word when one is not recognized. It does this far more efficiently than choral reading or the reading circle does, especially since the student is in control as he or she pushes the levers on the tape recorder. Also, the student listens to one efficient reader at a normal oral reading rate. The student can also repeat as many times as needed.

One of the best features of this system is that it assures success in a reading activity when only failure has been known before. Success and the ability to complete a task are greatly reinforcing.

The number of new words the child can learn to recognize through this procedure will provide a substantial resource in gaining access to more reading material. The number of different words that can appear in a 10- or 15-minute selection varies enormously, of course, but by the third grade level several hundred different words may be used, including most of the Dolch words.

With this activity, the potential for catching up is very good for older students who are rather far behind their potential for reading achievement. Nevertheless, this activity should be considered as only an interim or supplementary activity. In spite of how much it may help problem readers at first, it does nothing to help the student use context in identifying unfamiliar printed words. This kind of prediction will be the most important word identification skill for further growth in reading. Also, reading with tapes is paced by oral reading. Silent reading rate is held down to that of oral. This is all right at beginning reading levels, but it is not a practice to be maintained for long. Initially, children who have experienced chronic failure find this failure-free activity quite reinforcing. But the feelings of success and confidence that it initially inspires may well turn to boredom with continued use.

SUMMING UP

Increased fluency in word recognition marks the real improvement in reading skill. Several conditions for improving word recognition skill have been presented to this point. The first had to do with imagery level of words and their mode of presentation. Students are likely to benefit from the isolated presentation of low imagery words. The only words likely to be learned with reasonable facility in isolated presentation are high imagery nouns. These are the concrete nouns that can be pictured. Other, lower imagery words can be learned with more facility if they are presented in connected discourse. The words *some, these, that, is, happy, are,* and *big,* for example, take on considerable meaning from the association with high imagery nouns in connected discourse.

These dogs are happy.
That dog is big.

Some dogs are brown.
Some dogs are white.

Pictures that clearly illustrate the discourse have further facilitating effect on learning the words, because concreteness and meaning are enhanced.

The second condition for improving word recognition is adequate repetition in context. Gates' (1931) guidelines for repeating words still provide important objectives for minimum repetition of words in connected discourse. About 25 percent of the school-age population will not be served adequately by the amount of repetition provided by available reading programs.

The third condition is the appropriate rate of introduction of new words. Gates found that one new word in 60 was appropriate for most students. But an interaction between repetition rates and introduction rates must be considered. New words will be about as strange in a good many of their subsequent appearances as they were when they were first introduced.

How can this problem be managed? The question was addressed by Betts when he formulated the notion of the instructional level. Preparing or finding material at the instructional level is the fourth condition for improving word recognition development. With the instructional level, the student should encounter new or still unfamiliar words within the range of two to four percent in connected discourse. In other words, 96 to 98 percent of the connected discourse must be composed of familiar words. This ratio of knowns to unknowns is important because it permits the student to stay on task and maintain adequate comprehension. Some juggling may be required to keep the number of new and still unfamiliar words within this percentage range.

Instructional level reading not only permits the student to make progress in word recognition development, but it also provides sufficient useful context to aid in identifying new and unfamiliar words. It is a level that can foster prediction and use of context. Additionally, the student can benefit from application of other word identification skills when they are coupled with this context.

Regardless of the word identification program the teacher employs, these four considerations on word recognition development are important. Word identification programs differ widely in approach and emphasis. Some skills presented may or may not be a part of various programs, or they may be placed in different order in the teaching sequence. Whatever program is used, the students will undoubtedly benefit more from it if these four conditions regarding word recognition are given primary consideration.

A different emphasis in assessment must be taken to deal with word recognition development. The emphasis must be placed on known words. After all, to meet the instructional level objectives, at least 96 percent of connected discourse must be familiar. When working with students who have little reading ability, finding even a few words may require considerable reaching.

When a teacher discovers that a student knows scarcely any words, this is not an insurmountable problem. Repetition of the very few knowns can accomplish the requirements for the instructional level. Pictures, for picturable words, or labels on actual objects can be used if familiar context cannot be provided in printed discourse.

For older students who have a potential for acquiring reading skill but still have none, the tape-recorded selection method can be a big lift. This method is a failure-free device to help far-behind older children to make a big increase in word recognition level. For a morale and confidence boost after chronic failure, it has considerable value. It also can provide a large stock of words in a student's word recognition vocabulary that are a big asset in either preparing or finding reading material at an appropriate instructional level.

The importance of word recognition development with students with severe reading problems cannot be overemphasized. Such systematic attention to word recognition is probably not as essential for typical learners. The fact that careful attention to word recognition development is more necessary for children with learning problems may be due in part to a greater focus on word identification skill deficits. If those deficits are emphasized, it will usually be at the expense of other aspects of reading development rather than in a balanced complementary combination. Subskills and sight word teaching that are fragmented and isolated from real reading almost never produce much progress.

REFERENCES

Betts, E. A. *Foundations of reading instruction.* New York: American Book Co., 1946.

Chomsky, C. If you still can't read in third grade: After decoding, what? In S. J. Samuels (Ed.), *What research has to say about reading instruction.* Newark, DE: International Reading Association, 1978.

Dolch, E. W. *Teaching primary reading.* Champaign, IL: Garrard Press, 1941.

Gates, A. I. *Interests and ability in reading.* New York: Macmillan, 1931.

Gickling, E. E., Hargis, C. H., & Radford, D. *Word recognition development among retarded and nonretarded prereaders as a function of high versus low imagery nouns.* Manuscript submitted for publication, 1982.

Hargis, C. H. *Word recognition development as a function of imagery level.* Paper presented at the meeting of the Linguistic Society of America, Champaign-Urbana, July, 1978.

Hargis, C. H., & Gickling, E. E. The function of imagery in word recognition development. *Reading Teacher,* 1978, *31,* 870-875.

Mangieri, J., & Kahn, M. S. Is the Dolch list of 220 words irrelevant? *Reading Teacher,* 1977, *30,* 649-651.

Spache, G. D. *Good reading for poor readers.* Champaign, IL: Garrard Publishing Co., 1964.

Wolpert, E. M. Length, imagery values and word recognition. *Reading Teacher,* 1972, *26,* 180-186.

The authors examine written language skills in the mildly handicapped and suggest a model for understanding the teaching of written expression. The article emphasizes the importance of motivation in writing.

Some areas of writing not often thought of include essay exams and note taking. An article such as this is highly valuable because of its practicality.

Written Language for Mildly Handicapped Students

Edward A. Polloway, James R. Patton, and Sandra B. Cohen

The ability to communicate in written form has frequently been referred to as the highest achievement in language for people in all modern cultures. Effective written communication requires application of conceptual and organizational skills in situations ranging from the concrete to the abstract. Unlike a more strictly defined skill area such as spelling, writing demands, foremost, a psychological rather than a mechanical commitment in order to produce excellence.

Written communication builds upon the language skills of speaking, listening, and reading. Ironically, perhaps for this very reason, writing has failed to receive its due from educational theorists, researchers, and practitioners. Thus, even though considered an honored and respected ability, it paradoxically has often been overlooked as an important curricular domain, and as a result, a high prevalence of poor writers can be found both throughout the grades and in adult society. Riemer (1969) emphasized the significance of writing for higher education, business, and various professions and decried the American educational system for failures in the pedagogy of writing. He stated:

> American adults don't write because they are the victims of a system intensely determined to make them readers, not writers, and because there is not true and proper curriculum designed to develop writing. (p. 43)

Lack of curricular attention to writing has also been a particular problem in special education. The emphasis on teaching handicapped students to be good readers and efficient mathematicians has frequently left behind equally important concerns for the "second R."

Without question, all language domains are complex. This is certainly no less so for writing. As a curricular domain, writing includes the initial efforts of young children to scribble and spell their names, as well as the advanced compositional skills of the accomplished author. The breadth of written communication allows many avenues for theoretical and instructional approaches to develop. Within this broad spectrum, we have selected for discussion a singular component of writing skill development: the conceptual-expressive aspect of written language. Essentially the concern is for the ultimate goal of writing, which is effective communication. The more conceptual aspects of writing, however, can never be fully separated from tool subjects such as spelling and handwriting. Research and discussions on handwriting (Graham & Miller, 1980) and spelling (Graham & Miller, 1979) have led to the belief that writers can efficiently monitor written expression only when some degree of legibility is evident (Cohen & Gerber, 1982).

Hammill and Poplin (1978) specified the objectives of writing instruction as including the goals of:

1. teaching the minimal competencies required for success within the school curriculum;
2. teaching the abilities requisite for successful post-school adjustment; and
3. providing an opportunity for self-expression.

If these goals can be achieved, the student will have acquired not only a significant practical skill but also a vehicle for organizing and directing thought to further personal ideation. The close relationship between writing and thinking was succinctly stated by Loban, Ryan, and Squire (1969):

> To write clearly, students must think clearly. To write competently, students must think competently. To write with power and imagination, students must think with power and imagination: think/write, write/think — these processes can not be disjoined. When a student has learned to write better, he has learned to think better. (p. 319)

In addressing the topic of written language and exceptional learners, our concern here is for those who are commonly referred to as mildly handicapped — students identified as learning disabled (LD), mildly retarded (EMR), and emotionally (or behaviorally) disordered (ED). Categorical emphases, however, are of limited significance since in written language programming, as in other curricular areas, individual needs must predominate and group generalizations regarding teaching methodology are of questionable value. In terms of chronological ages, the population of greatest concern is that group placed under increasing demand for communication skill development by regular classroom requirements and post-school survival. For many mildly handicapped persons, acquiring a reasonable degree of facility in written language may contribute substantially to community self-sufficiency and independence, vocational flexibility, and success in higher education.

No longitudinal investigation of the written language abilities of mildly handicapped students has been reported that is comparable, for example, to the work of Loban (1963) with nonhandicapped children. Therefore, although texts frequently refer to the deficits of EMR, LD, and ED students within this domain, empirical data on the nature and specifications of these problems is quite limited. Among the studies that have been reported, the results are generally predictable. Myklebust (1973), for example, researched the writing output of four age groups of reading disabled students and found common deficiencies in linguistic output (evaluated in terms of total words used and number of sentences written), syntactical competence, and the ability to use abstractions.

A more recent study by Poplin, Gray, Larsen, Banikowski, and Mehring (1980) did provide an initial basis for considering the deficits of LD students. Comparing a group of disabled and nondisabled students at three grade levels (3-4, 5-6, and 7-8) across the five principal subtests of the *Test of Written Language,* they reported greater deficits in areas reflecting conventional aspects of grammar and spelling as contrasted with those more reflective of ideation and the conveyance of learning.

Also, Hermreck (1979) compared compositions of learning disabled and nonhandicapped students in several grades and found differentiated word totals. In fact, non-LD students wrote an average of 42 percent more words per composition than did their handicapped peers.

Deficits shown by some handicapped students in grammatical skills can be explained somewhat by the data reported by Deshler (1978). Specifically, disabled learners detected only one-third of the errors they made. On the basis of these data, one may justifiably assume that problem learners need strategies to monitor writing performance.

Despite the scarcity of research on conceptual and expressive writing deficits of handicapped students, clinical and anecdotal data certainly verify their prevalence. Wiig and Semel (1980), for example, stated that pre-adolescents and adolescents with language disabilities often have a series of specific difficulties that interfere with performance in decoding and encoding language. They suggested that common problems may be present in semantics (e.g., narrow word meanings, minimal semantic elaboration, and restricted variety in word use), syntax (e.g., limited use of complex sentences, tense and time markers), and memory (e.g., inefficiency in word retrieval and deficits in retention). These problems are especially significant for students as they face the written language demands a the upper elementary and secondary levels. Similarly, Davis (1975) characterized the writing of college students with learning disabilities as being: (a) rigid with limited variety in sentence patterns, word selection, and style; (b) poorly organized in controlling ideas and developing thoughts and arguments; (c) lacking in comparisons, elaborations, or conclusions.

In another study with learning disabled college students, Wells (1973) highlighted a number of relevant problems that demonstrate the possible resultant effects (i.e., when students get older) of having deficits in written expression. Among the points she specified, the following illustrate the seriousness of the issue: (a) a number of students in college classrooms had debilitating problems with written expression; (b) writing skills were required in a majority (70 percent) of the freshman courses surveyed; (c) learning disabled students faced a high probability of experiencing failure in their classes; (d) many of these students were relegated to remedial programs in which their eventual progress was limited; and, (e) much confusion existed as to the best methods for identifying, diagnosing, and working with these students.

Students with written language deficits apparently face a variety of specific difficulties. To assist the practitioner in successfully planning and implementing appropriate instruction, it is important to understand the nature of the act of written communication, the assessment of writing skills, and empirically and experientially supported techniques for remediation of writing deficits.

A MODEL FOR WRITTEN LANGUAGE

To approach the remediation of various written language skill deficits without an initial analysis of the nature and process of writing itself would be questionable pedagogical practice. Although for many mature writers, aspects of this process may be automatic or at least semi-automatic, students with difficulties in writing may evidence problems at a more conscious, functional level. Hall (1981) termed three stages of a writing task as *pre-writing, writing,* and *post-writing*. These are incorporated within Figure 1, a conceptual model of the written language process. It has been developed from the perspective of the learner/writer and therefore is concerned with input to the student, task demands on the student, and output by the student. The major components of the model have direct implications for basic instructional principles, assessment, and remediation.

Input

This consideration refers to the provision of stimulation to the student. It summarizes the various ways the educational and home environment can be manipulated to influence the would-be writer. The basis for its consideration is simply, as Petty and Bowen (1967) noted, that "input must precede outgo." Without stimulation, we can not anticipate response. Through the verbalizations of others (as in speeches and lectures), opportunities to

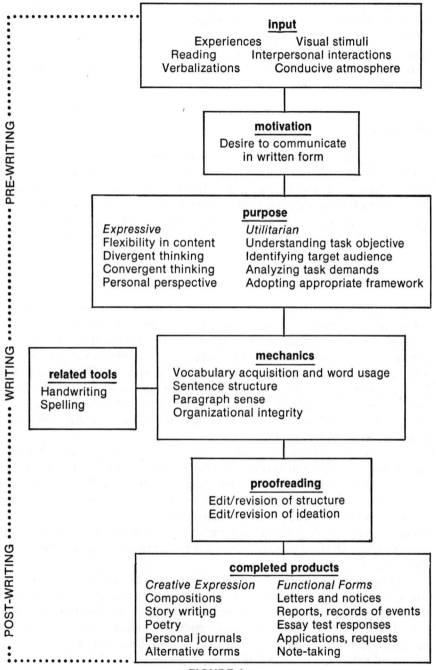

FIGURE 1
A Model of Written Language

experience the environment through diverse means (e.g., field trips, athletics, classroom activities), encounters with reading, interpersonal interactions of a verbal or nonverbal nature, and continuous and varied auditory/visual stimuli (e.g., multi-media, television, radio, movies, charts, photographs, pictures), the student can develop both an interest in a given topic and the degree of familiarity or experience necessary for effective communication.

Motivation

This aspect of written expression stems directly from the various forms of input. Students have to develop the felt need to communicate. Clearly, a poor attitude toward writing is among the most important considerations in instruction (Alley & Deshler, 1979; Mercer & Mercer, 1981; Smith, 1974). In addition to antecedent stimulants, this can be achieved through event consequences such as increased personal interaction and positive feedback.

Purpose

Establishing purpose serves as the basis for organizing writing and creates an awareness of writing as a natural process of communication (Golden, 1980). For handicapped learners, two general purposes for writing can be identified: *expressive* and *utilitarian*. These represent variant forms of writing that are separated in this model to highlight their different objectives. Expressive or creative writing emphasizes the personal communication of experiences and thoughts in an original way, and utilitarian or functional writing conveys information in a more structured form, as with letters and reports (Mercer & Mercer, 1981).

Despite this oversimplified distinction, the two purposes need not be oppositional. The two forms can be teamed to facilitate the acquisition of abilities (Cohen & Plaskon, 1980). In addition, as noted by Petty and Bowen (1967), utilitarian writing can become more creative as it becomes more individualistic, novel, and unusual. Thus, although the instructor initially should differentiate between the two forms in assisting handicapped students to set purpose, the relationship between them ultimately may become far less disparate.

By helping the writer set and refine purpose, the teacher is encouraging students to be more attentive to the demands of the topic, to be more reflective of ways to achieve goals, and to become actively involved in each of the writing stages necessary for an acceptable product. These concerns — attention, reflection, and active learning — have frequently been identified as major deficiencies in the learning repertoire of mildly handicapped students (see, for example, Epstein, Hallahan, & Kauffman, 1975; Ross, 1976; Torgeson, 1977; Wong, 1979).

In expressive writing, the specification of purpose entails several critical features. First, the writer must appreciate the inherent flexibility in selecting and developing content for the theme. Such an awareness stems directly from the open atmosphere of the classroom. Next, the ability to think in a divergent fashion must be tapped as the writer explores the specific ideas and topics of interest within the overall boundaries of the assignment. Convergent thinking then provides the vehicle for organization by narrowing the scope of the topic and allowing for the selection of relevant information. Finally, the constant input of a personal perspective ensures an eventual product that will be unique and original.

In utilitarian writing, the shift in focus dictates a parallel change in the writer's understanding regarding purpose. Understanding the task objective is requisite to further consideration. Clearly the writer must be able to appreciate the rationale behind, for example, a well-written letter of request or an autobiographical sketch as part of an application procedure. Second, the writer must have an awareness of the target audience so that the appropriateness of form can be matched to the characteristics of the reader(s). As Golden (1980) stated:

> Since purposeful writing can not occur in a vacuum, writers are, in varying degrees, aware that someone will read their message or poem. (p. 758).

Although the audience is also a concern in creative expression, it is far more critical in functional writing.

Following from these initial points, an analysis of task demands then requires the writer to consider questions of length, specific conventions tied to a given product (e.g., the parts of a formal letter), and the possible need for any number of concerns such as persuasion, specificity in request, factual detail, and general overview. Finally, these aspects can provide a basis for selecting an appropriate framework, such as a list, an outline, or a narrative, that will best enhance the purpose of communication.

Mechanics

The mechanical aspects of writing are of varying importance depending upon the nature of a specific assignment or task. The specific items outlined in Figure 1 summarize the basic mechanics common to semantically, syntactically, and organizationally sound written products. Each of these categories subsumes a host of subskills related to the development of writing competence.

Vocabulary acquisition and *word usage* are the basic semantic foundations for writing. Two instructional goals predominate in vocabulary acquisition: to encourage students to make use of the variety of words they already possess in their oral receptive and expressive lexicon, and to help students learn and use new words particularly as they aid in the written discussion of a given topic. Teachers must be alert to spelling deficits as they can contaminate written vocabulary; and students should be aided in developing compensatory means to facilitate the use of specific words.

Word usage is concerned with the appropriate construction of meaningful phrases and sentences based on selections from a student's vocabulary. The key instructional objectives should encompass the needs to: (a) curtail the redundant use of common words; (b) increase the use of descriptive words; (c) alternate synonyms for common thoughts in a passage; (d) select words that most precisely fit the meaning of the sentence; (e) avoid awkward word combinations; and (f) maintain consistency with the purpose of the writing task and the intended audience.

Sentence structure, used here as a generic term referring to the range of specific grammatical skills, is allied with the major syntactical concerns within sentences including appropriate verb tense, noun-verb agreement, noun-pronoun agreement, correct forms for other morphological structures, capitalization, and punctuation. In addition, the need for variety in the forms and functions used should be emphasized. Fragments and run-ons should be avoided, with form varying from simple to compound and complex. The writing function should emphasize the use of a blend of declarative, interrogative, imperative, and exclamatory sentences.

Paragraph sense refers to the transition in writing from syntactically accurate sentences to well-written compositions or reports. It taps the student's ability to organize thoughts in a coherent fashion that conveys a central message to the reader. In a developmental sense, the following sequential abilities must be learned: (a) paragraphs must express a single concept or main idea; (b) initial, topical sentences should provide a lead-in for the reader; (c) subsequent sentences should provide further support to the concept being discussed; and (d) final sentences in longer paragraphs should serve a summary or transitional function.

Organizational integrity is concerned with the overall product. The focus is on how the mechanics and the writing style manage to achieve the identified purposes. Students must be alert to: (a) the manner in which ideas are sequenced; (b) consistency between the discussion and conclusions; (c) clarity of the message communicated; (d) retention of personal style (when appropriate); and (e) relevance of detail to the stated purpose.

Proofreading

Classified in the conceptual model as an essential aspect of the postwriting stage, proofreading basically entails the process of editing and revising for both content and structure. Frequently, the importance of this concern may not be apparent to handicapped learners, because of an emphasis on task completion. In other instances, problem learners may associate editing with a failure syndrome, as a result of over-correction of previous writing assignments. Lovitt (1975) noted that many writers consider revision as simply changing punctuation marks and misspellings. To move beyond this limited concept of proofreading, students must be taught specific steps to follow in reviewing their own written work samples.

An emphasis on proofreading should also offer far greater advantages to the writer than the repetitive completion of worksheets. As Poplin et al. (1980) noted, the benefits of this emphasis would include the more meaningful nature of the exercise because of students' greater familiarity with the words and ideas they created and the increased potential for generalization of skills.

Completed Products

After revisions of the post-writing stage, students will have developed a completed product. Returning to the distinction between expressive and utilitarian purposes, these products can be classified to a certain extent as creative or functional. Creativity is typically most evident in original compositions, poetry, personal journals, and other vehicles for individual ideation. Functional products include social and business letters, class reports, minutes of meetings and other records of events, various forms of applications, and essay test responses that allow some flexibility in writing output. Note-taking, also an important functional skill, dictates its own mechanics and is necessary for survival in the regular classroom. The need for accurate, useful notes becomes increasingly vital to students as they enter the upper levels of school, where the lecture format is the presentation of choice in many classes.

Writing achievement in one form (either expressive or utilitarian) does not necessarily imply parallel performance in the other, although much transference occurs. Thus, instructional attention must be given specifically to each type of writing, while planning for and expecting a certain level of generalization.

ASSESSMENT

Since written language is by definition a permanent product, one may be tempted to assume that it is easily assessed. In reality, though, it is a complex process and is plagued by a number of inherent problems, including the following:

1. There is no established sequence of skills for written expression comparable, for example, to the content area or arithmetic.
2. There is a paucity of formal instruments available to both the writing teacher and researcher.

3. Of the formal instruments that do exist, there remain two key concerns: (a) they tend to focus on assessing the "mechanical" aspects of written expression to the exclusion of the other components; and, (b) they typically follow a contrived multiple-choice format that does not require any productive writing on the part of the student and limits the demonstration of student performance.
4. There is some disagreement as to how to most appropriately judge or assess the quality of students' writing. (Hogan & Mishler, 1979)

A basic question emerges from this mire of confusion: Why even attempt to assess written expression? Cohen and Plaskon (1980) have suggested certain eminently important reasons: ". . . to identify students who are experiencing problems; to chart individual child progress; and to identify a student's strengths and weaknesses" (pp. 307-308). Bearing in mind the caveats listed at the beginning of this section and the impetus provided by Cohen and Plaskon, the need to examine more closely the assessment of written expression is obvious. In so doing, a summary of the state of the art is well warranted, recognizing that new developments are ongoing.

Formal Assessment of Written Expression

Unfortunately, some of the instruments (e.g., *Peabody Individualized Achievement Test* and *Wide Range Achievement Test*) most frequently used in the schools to obtain achievement levels on mildly handicapped students do not yield information on a student's written skills. The formal devices used for assessing written language fall within two major categories: achievement-oriented tests and diagnostic tests.

Many standardized *achievement-oriented* tests contain sections that assess various components of written expression. These tests, for the most part, assess the mechanical aspects (word usage, capitalization, punctuation, grammatical structure) of written expression by way of a contrived format. The following example illustrates the type of format often used. It requires the testee to choose the sentence that contains improper word usage.

Item	Answer
1. When will you arrive?	① ② ③ ④
2. The boys and girls play together.	
3. She swam yesterday.	
4. No mistakes.	

Two assumptions are made about a student's performance on this type of item: (a) there is a close relationship between performance on this contrived sampling and actual writing ability; and (b) the student is able to read at the approximate grade level of the test being given (Cohen & Plaskon, 1980). Both of these points must be acknowledged when interpreting results from a test like this. Table 1 lists many of the formal achievement-oriented devices from which information on writing skills can be obtained.

Although *diagnostic* instruments in the area of written expression are few, five tests can be of assistance: the *Picture Story Language Test* (Myklebust, 1965), the *Test of Written Language* (Hammill & Larsen, 1978), the *Sequential Test of Educational Progress* (Educational Testing Services, 1958), the *Brigance Diagnostic Inventory of Essential Skills* (Brigance, 1977, 1980). Although potentially valuable on their own, these devices are particularly useful when used to supplement informal techniques. Table 2 presents pertinent information on each of these measures.

Even though some problems are associated with using formal devices, they can assist diagnostically inclined teachers if these professionals recognize the limitations of the tests, use them for diagnostic purposes only, and augment them with appropriate informal techniques in order to maintain as complete a picture as possible.

Informal Techniques for Assessing Written Expression

Teachers constantly use informal procedures to acquire information on students. Various types of informal techniques include checklists, rating scales, interviews, questionnaires, observations, and students' work samples. The advantages of informal techniques have been hailed by a number of professionals for a variety of reasons including their relevance to instructional needs and the amenability to administration by teachers themselves. For a more detailed discussion of the merits of informal techniques, the reader might want to refer to McLoughlin & Lewis (1981) or Wallace & Larsen (1978).

How can informal procedures be utilized to assess written expression? Once the major components of written language have been delineated, checklists or rating scales can be readily developed to correspond to the subcomponents of this skill. For instance, having identified punctuation as a subcomponent of written expression, the teacher can construct a simple checklist for a group of students in a class, to be used as a record of individual correct or incorrect use of the various forms of punctuation (e.g., period, comma).

Recently, new formats for informally recording information about students' written expressive abilities have been suggested. Techniques that provide an overall profile or analysis of these abilities have been developed independently by Burns (1980) and Wallace and Larsen (1978). Both of these devices include the elements of composition and mechanics. An example of a checklist format that can easily be used by teachers, *Checklist of Written Expression Skills,* has been constructed by Poteet (1980) to informally assess the areas of penmanship, spelling, grammar, and ideation.

TABLE 1
Representative Achievement-Oriented Tests

Test	Grade/Age Appropriateness	Subtests Related to Written Expression	Features
Woodcock-Johnson Psycho-Educational Battery (Woodcock & Johnson, 1977)	(A) 3-0 to 8-0+	1. Dictation 2. Proofing	Both of these subtests assess skills in punctuation, capitalization, spelling, and usage.
Test of Adolescent Language (TOAL) (Hammill, Brown, Larsen, & Wiederholt, 1980)	(A) 11-0 to 18-5	1. Writing/Vocabulary 2. Writing/Grammar	1. Student writes sentence using one stimulus word. 2. Student must combine two sentences into one new sentence.
Stanford Achievement Test (SAT) (Madden, Gardner, Rudman, Karlsen, & Merwin, 1973)	(G) 1.5 to 9.5 Language Subtests 3.0 to 9.5	This test assesses: capitalization punctuation usage	This test has six levels. Subtests vary from level to level.
California Achievement Test (CAT) (Tiegs & Clark, 1970)	(G) 1.5 to 12.0	1. Language Mechanics 2. Language Usage and Structure	1. Student must capitalize and punctuate sentences and paragraphs. 2. Student must fill in a blank space in a sentence with the appropriate selection from four choices.
Metropolitan Achievement Test (MAT) (Durost, Bixler, Wrightstone, Prescott, & Balow, 1971)	(G) K to 9.5 Language Components 3.5 to 9.5	Language a. punctuation b. capitalization c. usage	This test includes six different levels.
Iowa Tests of Basic Skills (ITBS) (Hieronymus & Lindquist, 1974)	(G) ⁓ to 8	Language a. spelling b. capitalization c. punctuation d. usage	This test has seven levels.
SRA Achievement Series (Thorpe, Lefever, & Hasland, 1974)	(G) 2 to 9	Language Arts a. usage (includes capitalization & punctuation) b. spelling	Two editions in this series: primary & multilevel. Subtests vary according to which edition is used.

Weiner (1980) has produced an informal device (*Diagnostic Evaluation of Writing Skills* — DEWS) containing 41 criteria for assessing a student's writing. These 41 criteria can be collapsed into the following categories: graphic (visual features), orthographic (spelling), phonologic (sound components), syntactic, semantic, and self-monitoring. The criteria were selected based on the common types of errors displayed by learning disabled students. A rating scale format requires the teacher to qualitatively assess performance.

Affleck, Lowenbraun, and Archer (1980) have developed a scale whereby the teacher rates a student's performance as poor, adequate, or excellent on written dimensions such as content, vocabulary, selection and usage, sentence usage, paragraph usage, capitalization, punctuation, handwriting, and spelling.

In addition to the procedures mentioned above, a variety of specialized techniques can be informally used to assess written expression. These methods tend to provide an index of the productivity and quality of a student's writing skills. Five of these procedures are presented in Table 3.

Sequential Assessment of Written Language

To facilitate the sequential assessment of written expression, a more rigorous consideration of the various components of the conceptualization in Figure 1 is warranted. As has been noted, much of the commercially available instrumentation assesses the mechanical aspects of written expression, basic skills at the writing stage. This is not surprising since skill areas such as capitalization, punctuation, and syntax are rule-governed. As a result, these areas can be more easily evaluated. If students are to develop adequate writing skills, however, skills at the pre-writing and post-writing stages, as well as those at the writing stage, must be attended to. Here are some items that teachers might consider for gathering information about students at each stage of the model.

Input

1. Students' educational backgrounds (e.g., previous teachers, experiences with writing);
2. How students spend their vacations, weekends, etc.;
3. What books students have read;
4. What students talk about when they are at home with peers; and,
5. An individual student's learning style or how he/she learns more efficiently.

Motivation

1. The value or importance of writing as students perceive it;

TABLE 2
Representative Diagnostic Tests

Test	Age/Grade Appropriateness	Type of Administration	Norm- or Criterion-Referenced	Subtests	Type of Derived Sores	Features
Picture Story Language Test (PSLT) (Myklebust, 1965)	(A) 7 to 17	Individual and/or Group	Norm	(3 scoring areas) 1. Productivity Scale 2. Syntax Scale 3. Abstract-Concrete Scale (Semantics)	1. Age Equivalent 2. Percentile Ranks 3. Standard Scores	Student is shown a picture and then asked to write a story about what is seen.
Test of Written Language (TOWL) (Hammill & Larsen, 1978)	(A) 8-6 to 14-5	Individual	Norm	*Principal Subtests* 1. Vocabulary 2. Thematic Maturity 3. Spelling 4. Word Usage 5. Style *Supplemental Subtests* 1. Thought Units 2. Handwriting	1. Grade Equivalent 2. Standard Scores 3. Written Language Quotient	Student is shown a series of three pictures and then asked to write a story based on these pictures. The sample obtained is used to determine scores for Vocabulary, Thematic Maturity, Thought Units, and Handwriting. The other subtests are presented separately.
Sequential Test of Educational Progress (Educational Testing Services, 1958)	(G) 4 to Junior College	Individual and/or Group	Norm	1. Organization 2. Conventions 3. Critical Thinking 4. Effectiveness 5. Appropriateness	Grade Equivalent	Student is asked to identify errors in actual writing specimens of children and then to select the appropriate revision.

Brigance Diagnostic Inventory of Basic Skills (Brigance, 1977)	(G) K to 7	Individual	Criterion	1. Capitalization 2. Punctuation 3. Parts of Speech	None	This instrument is used most effectively when a student's responses can be analyzed in greater depth and used for educational planning, no normative data are available.
Brigance Diagnostic Inventory of Essential Skills (Brigance, 1980)	(G) 7 to 12	Individual	Criterion	1. Quality of Writing 2. Capitalization 3. Punctuation 4. Addresses Envelope 5. Letter Writing	None	(See comments above) In addition to the subtests that fall under "Writing," this instrument also contains other subtests under the categories of "Spelling" and "Vocational."

TABLE 3
Representative Informal Procedures for Assessing Written Expression

Technique*	Description	Methodology	Example	Comment
1. Type-Token Ratio	Measure of the variety of words used (types) in relation to overall number of words used (token)	$\dfrac{\text{Different words used}}{\text{Total words used}}$	type = 28 token = 50 ratio = $\dfrac{28}{50}$ = .56	Greater diversity of usage implies a more mature writing style.
2. Index of Diversification	Measure of diversity of word usage	$\dfrac{\text{Total number of words used}}{\text{Number of occurrences of the most frequently used word}}$	total words = 72 number of times the word *the* appeared = 12 index = 6	An increase in the index value implies a broader vocabulary base.
3. Average Sentence Length	Measure of sentence usage (number of words per sentence)	$\dfrac{\text{Total number of words used}}{\text{Total number of sentences}}$	total words = 54 total sentences = 9 words per sentence = 6	Longer length of sentences implies more mature writing ability
4. Error Analysis	Measure of word and sentence usage	Compare errors found in a writing sample with list of common errors		Teacher can determine error patterns and can prioritize concerns.
5. T-Unit Length (Hunt, 1965)	Measure of writing maturity	1. Determine the number of discrete thought units (T-units) 2. Determine average length of T-unit: $\dfrac{\text{Total words}}{\text{Total number of T-units}}$	"The summer was almost over and the children were ready to go back to school." *Quantitative:* *(1; 2; 5 + 10)*	This technique gives the teacher information in relation to productivity and maturity of writing skills.

Technique	Description	Methodology	Example	Comment
		3. Analyze quantitative variables: a. no. of sentences used; b. no. of T-units; c. no. of words per T-unit *Note:* Use the following convention for summarizing this information (no. of sentences; no. of T-units; no. of words per T-unit) 4. Analyze qualitative nature of sentences	*Qualitative:* 1. compound sentence 2. adverbs: of degree — "almost" of place — "back" 3. adjective — "ready" 4. infinitive — "to go" 5. prepositional phrase adverbial of place — "to school"	

More detailed descriptions of these techniques are in Cartwright (1969) and Polloway & Smith (1982).

2. Students' interests, as ascertained by administering interest inventories that explore educational, extracurricular, and community interests, as well as preferences in hobbies, books, movies, and the like;
3. Career goals (to gain information that will be useful for pointing out the relevance of particular writing skills); and,
4. Reinforcement preferences.

Expressive Purpose

1. Can students establish a purpose when they write?
2. Are they able to brainstorm (use divergent thinking)? (Give students the titles of a story and let them generate possible story plots);
3. Can they progressively narrow down the scope of a topic (use convergent thinking)? (Provide varied information on a given topic and require students to state the basic theme); and
4. Can they generate written samples that reflect their own thinking?

Utilitarian Purpose

1. Can students understand why they are writing something? (Asking students to state their objective);
2. Do they realize to whom they are writing? (Have them describe relevant reader characteristics related to the topic); and,
3. Do they recognize the major components of their task? (Have students articulate or list the specific parts of a letter, keeping in mind both to whom and for what purpose they are writing).

Mechanics

Both formal and informal techniques, as previously discussed, may be useful for assessing students' written expressive ability in the areas of vocabulary acquisition, word usage, and sentence structure. Student-produced writing samples, however, are preferable to contrived samples.

More directive efforts may be required to assess students' abilities in paragraph sense and organizational integrity. To assess paragraph sense, a teacher might survey writing samples and look for the following in the student's paragraphs:

1. One main idea;
2. A topic sentence that focuses attention on the main idea;

3. Supporting sentences that detail information relevant to the topic;
4. A summary or transitional sentence when appropriate; and,
5. Indentation and a new line for beginning a new paragraph.

With regard to the organizational integrity of the total product, it is important to consider the following:

1. Logical sequencing of ideas throughout the composition, essay, or letter?
2. Internal consistency (Do conclusions follow from the discussion? Do specific points made relate to the general topic?);
3. Clarity of thought; and,
4. Continuity of movement rather than abrupt changes in sub-topics or style.

Proofreading

To a great extent, many of the formal assessment devices available actually require proofreading skills. They are often restricted, however, to the skill of editing for structural errors rather than editing for content problems. To determine if students are able to effectively use proofreading and editing skills, evaluation should focus on the following questions:

1. Can students identify specific mechanical errors within a sentence or a paragraph?
2. Can they identify organizational and ideational problems within a composition?
3. Can they effectively use strategies for proofreading (e.g., a sequential list of self-check statements);
4. Can they evaluate whether the objectives or purposes of the completed written draft have been met? and,
5. Can they transfer these skills from contrived exercises to actual written assignments?

Completed Product

Final products can be evaluated relative to the goals and directions established by the writing task. In addition, some general guidelines are:

1. Does the written product communicate the message originally intended?
2. Does the student comply with the accepted syntactical conventions of the language system?
3. Does the student utilize the correct form and procedure appropriate for creative or utilitarian purposes?

4. Is the writing style consistent with acceptable standards associated with the particular product?
5. Does the writing show evidence of a unique, personal perspective?

The successful blend of information from informal and formal techniques within a structured conceptualization of written language will enable the teacher to overcome some of the inherent problems in assessment noted earlier in the section. The result should be a clear profile of an individual's skills and difficulties, which can then provide a basis for selecting appropriate instructional strategies.

INSTRUCTIONAL STRATEGIES

A written language methodology and curriculum designed distinctly for handicapped students is not being proposed in this discussion. Rather, as Polloway and Smith (1982) have stated:

> In general, teachers will need to organize their curriculum specially around regular class language activities to the extent that students participate in general education programs. Regardless of the situation, however, methods of teaching written expression to exceptional children more often reflect close ties to, and adaptations of, general curriculum than any other language area (Haring & Bateman, 1977; Kirk & Johnson, 1951; Wallace & McLoughlin, 1976). (p. 350)

Therefore the teacher's task is to begin from a foundation of sound instructional strategies for written communication and make modifications that will be effective for individual needs of handicapped learners.

Input

The basis for beginning writing and written language instruction is *stimulation*. Students must be provided with input that fosters the formulation of their own ideas. Teachers should capitalize on the other language domains to enhance this process. For example, opportunities to talk about personal experiences and listen to others' encounters can provide a basis for writing purpose and content. Reading interesting stories can also develop the student's desire to communicate feelings about the ideas expressed by the author (Polloway & Smith, 1982). Dawson and Zollinger (1957) outlined an instructional language experience-type approach that provides a means of integrating the various language arts.

Petty and Bowen (1967) have emphasized the importance of ensuring an appropriate climate for writing. They noted several aspects of such a climate that would provide an atmosphere conducive for writing: the attitudes and personality of the teacher (characterized by an open and friendly rather than a rigid demeanor), the establishment of frequent opportunities for writing, and students' awareness of the potential outlets for their work. Handicapped students in particular need to develop a sense that writing is an enjoyable rather than a punitive activity. The above points can be summarized as the need for writing stimulation within the context of a positive, supportive atmosphere.

Motivation

Closely tied to the discussion of input is the topic of motivation. The preeminent concern is the development of intention to communicate, the desire to share one's thoughts with a given readership. Without attention to motivation, an individual's writing will likely reflect only minimal personal perspective and creativity and will fail to realize the basic goals of functional writing tasks.

Ideally, motivation should be a function of one's own internal needs to communicate and to express feelings, ideas, and needs. As Tway (1975) noted in reference to nonhandicapped children: "No one can really motivate anyone else to write; motivation must come from within. Teachers can only stimulate" (p. 193). Tway also suggested that motivation could best be developed by showing a basic respect for a student's expression, by establishing real purpose in writing, by endowing writing with a special sense of importance and enjoyment, and by ensuring the writer that a specific goal is in sight.

In the case of exceptional learners, however, motivational problems are often intensified because of the failure set that many students have acquired through previous writing experiences. Alley and Deshler (1979) emphasized this point by noting that the feelings of students toward writing should be the first consideration of teachers. As Lerner (1981) stated, children who have experienced a dearth of success:

> . . . soon learn to beat the game by limiting their writing vocabulary to words they know how to spell, by keeping their sentences simple, by avoiding complex and creative ideas, and by keeping their compositions short. (p. 344)

Given this general tendency of some writers, Brigham, Graubard, and Stans (1972) questioned the basic assumption that ". . . writing flows from the writer" (p. 442) and that emphasis must be placed in building motivation just through stimulation. The option they proposed, in one of the initial efforts of applied behavior analysts in this domain, was to identify a series of objective aspects of writing, place reinforcement contingencies on them, and thus improve compositional skills through the sequential reinforcement of specific skills. The ABA methodology and results of this study and related ones are further discussed in succeeding sections.

Based on the valid identification of students' interests, structuring a writing program on these interests seems justifiable, keeping in mind that what appeals to some students may not appeal to all their classmates. If teachers truly are concerned about individualizing the programs of their students, capitalizing on students' interests makes good pedagogical sense.

Purposeful Writing

In their list of basic principles for improving writing ability, Otto, McMenemy, and Smith (1973) noted that ". . . writing is always done for a particular purpose and a particular audience, both of which the writer should be aware of at all times" (p. 390). Consistent with this statement, students must come to realize the essential reason for the writing tasks in which they are engaged, whether they are flexible assignments with an emphasis on self-expression or highly structured tasks with an emphasis on adopting a particular form.

Initial instruction with beginning writers can successfully help them set purpose and complete instructional exercises designed to emphasize task objectives. Short, specific assignments are valuable for sharply defining the student's task and, therefore, enabling a focus on the purpose of the assignment. For example, exercises with a creative purpose could include writing a paragraph on the descriptive properties of an interesting classroom object, on the qualities of friendship, on one's favorite movie. Utilitarian exercises could include composing an invitation to a party, an announcement of a school movie, a covert note to a friend, a brief article for the school newspaper, or a postcard to be sent to a relative.

The importance of short assignments when students are first beginning to write can not be overstated. By presenting children with lengthy tasks or by setting aside an inordinate amount of time for them to write, the teacher may inadvertently create an association in the child's mind between writing and boredom, thus generating general disinterest and destroying purpose. A brief period of 15-20 minutes should be sufficient (Polloway & Smith, 1982).

Setting purpose continues to have importance for advanced writers as well. A direct instructional approach to writing at this point should emphasize the specific steps listed in Figure 1, initially with the teacher leading the student through them (via visual and verbal prompts) and subsequently with the student working independently (self-instruction). For expressive writing, students should be encouraged to ask themselves these types of questions:

What interests me most about this topic?
What information do I know about this topic?
What else do I need to learn about it?
How can this information be related?

How can it best be organized?

What are my personal opinions about the subject?

How can I convey my personal feelings in my writing?

For utilitarian writing, students should consider these questions:

What is my objective in this task?

Who am I writing for? What do they know about this topic?

What do they want to know?

How can I make sure I convey the necessary and correct information?

Do I need to do research on the topic to be familiar with it?

How should I arrange and organize my writing to be most effective in meeting my objective?

Mechanics

The discussion on written mechanics focuses on the areas of vocabulary development and structural skills (e.g., sentence and paragraph sense and overall organization). Inherent in this framework are the specific writing craft skills noted in Figure 1. The semantic concerns related to increasing vocabulary and the mechanical concerns related to writing form must both be given instructional consideration.

Vocabulary

A key concern in enhancing written communication skills is to increase the size of writing vocabulary and to increase the frequency with which these new words are used. The basis for instruction is to expose students to a multitude of verbal forms and then assist them in incorporating the words into their compositions. Specific objectives should include acquiring a store of synonyms for commonly used words, developing a familiarity with a variety of descriptive words, and using unusual words and original phrases as alternatives to more typical lexical options.

Teachers should be aware that many otherwise capable students may tend to avoid using words they can not spell, thus reducing the quality of their writing. Only when they can be convinced to not worry about spelling and concentrate on ideas can a true appreciation of their abilities be obtained (Johnson & Myklebust, 1967). Similarly, when working with students for whom English is a second language, the primary concern should be with qualitative aspects rather than with correct spelling.

Cohen and Plaskon (1980) have stressed that mildly handicapped students should develop a vocabulary that can be used accurately: "Although the objective is to expand the child's facility with words, it must not be gained at the expense of writing fluency. A functional goal of providing [them] with word skills which allow them to successfully manipulate a limited core of words is advisable" (p. 295). They therefore suggested teaching word clusters that can center on topical themes. The clusters they listed included words for naming and describing common actions, personal attributes, and time, as well as facility with use of prefixes, suffixes, synonyms, and common idiomatic expressions.

A host of instructional exercises can be developed to assist in building vocabulary. For example, Van Allen (1976) suggested the use of a *word wall* that can be devoted to lists of words that might be helpful to students in writing. The list could include high frequency words, common descriptors, words of the senses, and specialized words tied to holidays or to specific units being studied. It could also be modified and individualized by developing a notebook of words for each student.

For individual writing assignments, the entire class could initially generate a list of key words to be written on the board. In this way, the conceptual break required to select and revisualize specific words could be avoided, and at the same time students would be provided practice in use of these words.

Several studies have reported on the value of reinforcement contingencies on vocabulary development. Maloney and Hopkins (1973) reported that points awarded to students in grades 4-6 contingent on the number of different objectives and action verbs used and the variant ways that sentences were begun enhanced these three aspects of composition and also resulted in the submission of papers subjectively rated as more creative by blind reviewers. Glover and Gary (1976) indicated that students' writing could be improved by developing vocabulary usage through the identification of "unusual uses" for a variety of nouns. Four measures of creativity (fluency, flexibility, elaboration, and originality) improved as a result of applying this technique. Kraetsch (1981) reported data on a single-subject design study indicating that oral instructions to a student to write "as many words and ideas as you can" had a significant effect on written output as measured by the quantity and diversification of words and the quantity of sentences produced. In all three studies, vocabulary was shown to improve, along with other aspects of writing, through reinforcement strategies.

Structure

The most significant question in teaching structural skills is how to build the appropriate skills without stifling students' interest in using written means for expression and communication. Sink (1975) contrasted two approaches to this question: the *teach-write* and the *write-teach* approaches. The former, representing the traditional pedagogy in composition, emphasizes instruction in skills as a basis for successful written expression, and the latter places more stress on initial writing, giving rise to instruction on specific skills (see Table 4).

TABLE 4
Assumptions of Two Approaches to Instruction

Teach-Write	Write-Teach
1. Stress on form over ideas.	1. Stress on ideas over form.
2. Curriculum-centered.	2. Student-centered.
3. Emphasis on the mechanical act of writing.	3. Emphasis on the personal act of writing.
4. Structure as initial basis for writing.	4. Ideation as the initial basis, later shaped to structure.
5. Skills analyzed in isolation.	5. Isolated skills analysis viewed as interfering with spontaneity.
6. Once student possesses skills, he/she will want to write.	6. Child already wants to write and just needs stimulation.

Adopted from: Sink, D. M. Teach-write/Write-teach. *Elementary English*, 1975, *52*, 175-177.

A substantial body of related research has been reported with nonhandicapped students. Sherwin (1969), in his review of 50 years of research on the relationship between formal instruction in grammar and skill in writing, concluded that this type of instruction ". . . is an inefficient and ineffective way to help students achieve proficiency in writing" (p. 135). He cited a 1962 dissertation by Harris, deemed to be the most methodologically sound of the research reviewed, which concluded that such an approach may have a relatively harmful effect on the correctness of children's writing. Although Sherwin (1969) also concluded that writing alone does not teach writing, he summarized his review by nothing that the most important features of instruction are ". . . motivation, selective criticism, discussion, practical explanation, and revision" (p. 168).

Definitive research with exceptional learners on this question has not yet been reported, but the write-teach approach has received more widespread support. Cohen and Plaskon (1980), for example, encouraged the use of spontaneous daily written expression opportunities as a basis for instruction in conventional skills. In a similar vein, Poplin et al. (1980) concluded from the limited data relative to this question:

> Until otherwise proven, meaningful experiences with immediate, reasonable, and knowledgeable feedback still seem to offer the most effective method of improving mechanical, conventional knowledge of the writing process without interfering with and stifling the all-important ability to "get across" in writing what the student intends to communicate. (p. 52)

Given the limited support for the traditional approach to teaching grammar, the most appropriate instructional approach would appear to be one that provides *feedback* on a small number of selected structural errors in a given assignment. Errors to be corrected should be chosen based on their value to the student's communicative efforts. In addition, assignments should be evaluated in terms of their consistency with the student's oral language abilities. This can give the writer a basis for error awareness, which generally must precede accurate transcription. This awareness can be achieved by leading through a series of tasks requiring students to initially select the grammatically accurate sentence from several choices and eventually to identify specific errors within a sentence or paragraph. "Listening" for errors then becomes the basis for proofreading.

The value of feedback mechanisms on a student's writing has been documented in a variety of research studies. For example, the use of these mechanisms tied to structural skills was reported to be effective by Hansen and Lovitt (1973, cited by Hansen, 1978). They indicated that feedback on mechanics was more effective than was feedback on content in influencing both mechanics and content in a positive way.

Strategies designed to increase fluency have also been found to have a positive effect on structure (Brigham, Graubard, & Stans, 1972; Van Houten, Morrison, Jarvis, & MacDonald, 1974). Van Houten and his colleagues reported that feedback on the number of words written, accompanied by the posting of highest scores and instruction to exceed these scores, resulted in a doubling of the rate of words written in addition to an increase in the mechanical aspects of the compositions of second and fifth graders.

The most important focus within the mechanics of written language should be the sentence. By stressing well-developed sentences, teachers will be training handicapped students to think clearly and then to express themselves in complete thoughts in order to successfully communicate. Many handicapped students may rely on simple, repetitive, "safe" sentence structures, resulting in less fluent writing products. Others may experiment unsuccessfully with variety and be identified as producing awkward constructions (Hall, 1981). For either of these two sub-groups of poor writers, the instructional focus must be on teaching students to expand sentences within acceptable structural patterns. Several approaches to sentence expansion have been developed. Teachers should select a particular strategy based upon: (a) understanding the technique; (b) student needs; and (c) student language abilities.

Fennimore (1980) reported on instructional activities developed to facilitate sentence understanding and variety. She referred to these as sentence extension activities since the basic premise of the instruction was to enhance students' oral and then written sentences by enlarging the repertoire of words and forms available to them. For example, the sentence, "The boy ran" was extended by having the class identify lists of alternatives to *boy* and *ran*, adverb and adjective modifiers within the subject, modifiers of the verb, prepositional phrases to indicate where the boy ran, and so forth. This type of exercise can then become incorporated into compositional efforts that may stem from the original brief sentence form.

Sentence expansion or extension is the basis for the *Phelps Sentence Guide Program* (Phelps-Teraski & Phelps, 1980). This systematic program involves a structured questioning process to which students respond in complete sentences. Logical extensions would then include instruction on nouns (e.g., *Who* did it?), verbs (e.g., *What* was done?), descriptors (e.g., What kind?), and objects (e.g., To what? For what?). By combining oral and written language, these sub-skills and other related ones can be taught within the context of the meaning of a sentence in lieu of being presented as specific semi-isolated items in a grammar instructional sequence.

Paragraph Sense

As noted earlier, paragraph sense builds from a student's competence in using basic paragraph components in a sequential and logical manner. As Otto, McMenemy, and Smith (1973) stated, "The most important concept for students to attain relative to paragraph development is that written communication is essentially a matter of making assertions and elaborating upon them" (p. 394). Therefore, specific teaching techniques should be adapted that assist students in stating their basic premises and then expanding their thoughts in an organized fashion.

To develop good paragraphing skills, students should be provided given exercises on sequencing sentences that they can read without difficulty, as well as feedback on their own efforts. Again, the value of short assignments as a basis for such writing should be noted. Particularly in the case of students who have limited ability to develop lengthy, creative pieces, emphasis should be placed on consistent usage of simple rules for paragraph building within the context of functional tasks.

Organizational Integrity

The concept of organizational integrity refers to the overall sequence, clarity, and flow of writing beyond the paragraph level. Essentially, it is the final concern of the writer and the one that relates most closely to the setting of purpose during the pre-writing period. Within the written language model presented in this article, it serves as the basis for pulling together the objectives established before writing, with the mechanics utilized during the composition stage as a basis for the reviewing/editing process of post-writing. Therefore, it is most closely tied to the process of proofreading.

Proofreading

Proofreading is a critical skill upon which the quality of a finished product hinges, particularly when teachers are using the write-teach approach. To expect that most students will automatically edit and revise their work would be naive. As noted earlier, many exceptional students may come to view proofreading as an aversive rather than a positive process. Even those who are willing to revise must develop that ability; they must be shown *how* to proofread (Hillerich, 1979). The teacher's role, therefore, is one of modeling the specific techniques inherent in the proofreading process and delineating its advantages to the finished product.

The instructional goal is to have students learn the basic steps necessary to revise their writing and to later apply them independently. The questions listed below, incorporating suggestions by Dankowski (1966) and Burns (1980), provide an outline of self-evaluation procedures for writers to follow:

1. Does each sentence make sense?
2. Is every word spelled correctly?
3. Are all punctuation marks used correctly? Are any needed marks omitted?
4. Are all words capitalized that should be?
5. Have I used descriptive words and phrases to express my ideas?
6. Are any of the points I made vague and in need of clarification?
7. Are there more specific, precise ways to say anything in my paper?
8. Overall, is the paper organized in a clear way to make the reader's job an easy one?
9. Have I met the objectives I set for the paper?
10. Have I chosen a good title (when applicable)?

The entire proofreading process may be too involved for students with writing difficulties to tackle at one time. Therefore, although complete evaluation would require consideration of all aspects, one or two should be selected for a given assignment until students refine both their writing and editing skills. As time and skill development progress, more of the proofing guides can be added.

Editing and revision are generally considered to take place after writing, but they also occur at times during the writing process. Frequent conceptual breaks in mid-sentence or mid-paragraph (such as to check spelling), however, should be discouraged, to minimize interference with ideation.

Organizing proofreading instructional exercises in the classroom can be done in a variety of ways. One effective technique to help students develop an initial orientation toward proofreading is to have them practice verbalizing the various steps. Consistent with this approach, Hansen (1978) suggested that students work on the editing process by reading their stories aloud to the teacher during individual conferences, to learn to listen for inconsistencies.

The concept of the directed writing activity (DWA) (Blake & Spannato, 1980), modeled after the directed reading activity, includes a series of sequential steps that students follow in order to reach a desired communication objective. Blake and Spannato listed the following steps: *pre-writing*, to include topic selection and information collection; *framing*, the development of questions about the topic and the inventory of what is known or needs to be known; *writing,* organized according to questions identified previously with transition between thoughts; *revision of the content and the grammar; editing,* as for punctuation and capitalization; and development of the *final draft,* to incorporate all the revisions and editing changes.

Completed Products

Some considerations unique to specific types of written products should be stated. For simplicity, these are discussed under the two major areas of creative expression and functional forms.

Creative Expression

Development of ideation in written compositions and related products has unique significance to exceptional learners. As Polloway and Smith (1982) stated concerning this expressive component of written language:

> Although instruction often centers on teaching skills and developing cognitive abilities, it would be self-limiting to overlook the affective side of written composition — its ability to serve as a vehicle for thought and ideas that handicapped students might otherwise withhold. The potential gains that adolescents with learning, emotional, or behavioral problems can achieve are especially noteworthy. Therefore, instruction in this area and the subsequent development of skills can be both a means as well as an end in itself. (p. 342)

A major objective for teachers of mildly handicapped learners, then, should be to provide ample opportunity for expressive writing.

An emphasis on creative expression in writing deemphasizes over-correction regarding mechanical aspects. Creative writing favors the content over the craft. Tiedt (1975) noted that teachers should appreciate the ideas expressed reasonably coherently by writers rather than focusing on omissions, misspellings, poor handwriting, or missing punctuation marks. She stressed the need to be most concerned with the positive aspects of the student's writing. If, instead, students learn that *how* they write is more valued than *what* they write, the result will likely interfere with the expressive and communicative process (Golden, 1980).

Johnson and Myklebust (1967) provided an excellent outline of a progression of ideation reflected in the varying content of students' products. Basically, their idea sequence follows from the concrete to the abstract. The first stage, *concrete-descriptive,* emphasizes the use of a simple descriptive sentence or a series of such sentences about common things in the child's environment (e.g., The girl is running to the store.). The second stage, *concrete-imaginative,* stresses inferences from some stimulus or experience. In this stage, students would be encouraged to draw generalizations, to imagine what is happening, and to then respond accordingly.

A shift in emphasis to abstractions characterizes the other two stages in the Johnson and Myklebust progression. The third level, *abstract-descriptive*, places greater stress on the concepts of times and sequence, with students urged to write stories with logical order, appropriate transitions, and the development of plot and characters. The final level, *abstract-imaginative*, is based on open-ended types of questions and propositions upon which students base their perceptions. Stylistic improvements such as figures of speech can be incorporated, too, at this stage.

Given a logical progression through which to lead children in writing, teachers can enhance ideation and productivity using the basic strategies discussed earlier under "Input" and "Motivation." In addition, teachers should have access to a variety of appropriate topics for compositions to instill interest and stimulate thinking. The reader is referred to books by Carlson (1970), Petty and Bowen (1967), and Polloway and Smith (1982) for suggestions. The value of contingencies placed on writing (as noted earlier) to yield creativity should also be considered.

Many other vehicles are available to the teacher for encouraging the student's expression. Examples include story-writing, poetry, and developing diaries or journals as independent writing activities.

Story writing can take on a variety of forms as a tool to motivate composition writing. An interesting approach (Collins, 1980), called class-mating, was developed to increase writing motivation in secondary students by having them develop stories to be read by elementary-aged children. Collins indicated that this strategy provided an audience for writing and enabled teachers to emphasize the need for grammatical accuracy in standard English for "published" work.

Teachers often shy away from teaching *poetry*, because of the language limitations of their students. As Rich and Nedboy (1977) noted in discussing the creations of young adolescents, however, the question is not whether it is truly poetry since the mark of success is not in the creation of a literary product ". . . but in the use of poetry writing as a vehicle for reaching a variety of other goals" (p. 94). Similarly, Nathanson, Cynamon, & Lehman (1976) commented:

> Teaching poetry to exceptional children of any chronological age, of any intellectual level, or of any handicapping condition enables the classroom teacher to expand his or her own potential beyond the purely functional approach to curriculum development. (p. 90)

Personal diaries or *journals* have been a popular instructional adjunct ever since the report by Fader and McNeill (1968) confirmed the value of such an approach. This technique is based on having the student write for a designated length of time or a designated number of pages without teacher evaluation. The student selects the topics, which range from simple copying exercises to truly creative expression.

In a related vein, Tsimbos (1980) described how journals could be used with children for whom English is a second language. In this program, students were required to write a minimum number of words per day without regard for correctness. The teacher then read these and gave responses limited to specific English vocabulary words or ideas that would assist the student in better expression. Essentially, the program provided a basis for communication in English between student and teacher.

Functional Forms

Utilitarian writing dictates greater concern for structure than does creative expression but nevertheless should provide an opportunity for a personalized form of communication. The most common types of functional writing include letters, notices, invitations, reports, and applications. Each of these carries with it a given format and, thus, specific procedures for instruction. In each case, the initial emphasis on short, specific assignments should be adhered to, to promote appropriate production.

Two other areas of functional writing warrant special attention because of their particular importance to adolescents with writing difficulties: note-taking and essay exam writing. These skills become more important as students enter higher grades. Although both areas relate more closely to study skills than to written expression, they demand attention because they are typically neglected in formal instruction.

Note-taking. For just a moment, consider how you developed your own personal note-taking skills — whether you created your own system, were given formal instruction, or viewed someone else's format and adopted it. Regardless of which of the above mechanisms might apply, at some time in all students' educational careers, they must become "note-takers." School failure or success may depend in part on whether a student becomes efficient or remains inefficient at this task.

Note-taking skills become necessary, for example, when listening to a speaker, watching a film, or reading a textbook. Alley and Deshler (1979) have categorized note-taking into three specific skill areas:

(1) outlining — the sequential arrangement of main features of a book, a subject, or a lecture;
(2) formal notetaking — the concise but comprehensive statement of essential matter read or heard; and
(3) informal notetaking — the brief, spontaneous recording of material to assist the memory or for subsequent reference or development. (p. 129)

The value of these skills lies in the fact that they greatly assist students organizationally, an important concern for many mildly handicapped students. The following list of suggestions offers a few ideas for teachers in helping students become better note-takers:

1. Preparation
   a. Make sure all necessary materials are ready. This may include specially prepared paper (e.g., with a specific note-taking format).
   b. If available, obtain ahead of time a skeletal outline of the lecture from the instructor.

2. Instruction
   a. Give practice at taking notes.
   b. Provide feedback on the quality and quantity of notes.
   c. Teach the use of various shorthand conventions, abbreviations, or personal codes (e.g., $\overline{s}$ for without, $\overline{c}$ for with).
   d. Emphasize that students are *not* to write down every word.
   e. Provide training in how to recognize key words (e.g., "most important") or key behaviors (e.g., writing a phrase on the board) of instructors.

3. Aids
   a. Have students use small pocket-size notebooks for a variety of reasons (e.g., "things to do today," assignments, questions to ask the instructor).
   b. Encourage the taping of lectures in order to augment poor in-class note-taking skills.
   c. Have students check their notes with those of others.

Essay Test-taking. Although techniques are available for maximizing students' performance on various types of tests, our attention is directed to essay situations that require written expressive skills to a greater extent than other formats. To students with problems in written language, the essay test can be devastating. The conventions of writing already discussed in this article still apply, but a few additional suggestions are offered:

1. Nurture a positive, success-oriented attitude toward the impending test situation.
2. Encourage students to use their time effectively, both prior to the test when preparing and during the test itself.
3. Have students perform triage on the essay questions — responding first to the questions to which they know the answers, and postponing the more difficult ones.
4. Instruct students on recognizing and understanding certain "task-demand" clue words such as *compare, elaborate,* and *list.*

5. Encourage students to outline the answer to each essay question before giving any written response. This helps not only the testee but the examiner as well.

6. Incorporate the use of mnemonic aids in test preparation and test taking (for example, the taxonomic breakdown of Kingdom, Phylum, Class, Order, Genus, Species may be remembered more readily through the mnemonic phrase, "*King Peter Comes Of Good Stock*").

7. Use alternative means of evaluation with students who encounter great difficulty with written form, as their performance on essay-type tests may not accurately reflect their competence or knowledge.

CONCLUDING REMARKS

Finally, several areas warrant the attention of practitioners and researchers interested in enhancing the professional state-of-the-art in written language instruction for the handicapped. These areas include: clarification of writing characteristics typically found to be strengths and weaknesses within sub-groups of the mildly handicapped population; refinement of informal assessment inventories that have a primary focus on the various facets of written expression; resolution of the relative merits of reinforcement strategies versus stimulation exercises as a basis for motivating variant groups of handicapped learners; and development of detailed, direct instructional systems for teaching writing that parallel recent efforts, for example, in reading and arithmetic.

REFERENCES

Affleck, J. Q., Lowenbraun, S., & Archer, A. *Teaching the mildly handicapped in the regular classroom* (2nd ed.). Columbus, OH: Charles E. Merrill, 1980.

Alley, G., & Deshler, D. *Teaching the learning disabled adolescent: Strategies and methods.* Denver, CO: Love Publishing Co., 1979.

Blake, H., & Spannato, N. A. The directed writing activity: A process with structure. *Language Arts*, 1980, *57*, 317-318.

Brigance, A. H. *Brigance diagnostic inventory of basic skills.* Woburn, MA: Curriculum Associates, 1977.

Brigance, A. H. *Brigance diagnostic inventory of essential skills.* North Billerica, MA: Curriculum Associates, 1980.

Brigham, T., Graubard, P., & Stans, A. Analysis of the effects of sequential reinforcement contingencies on aspects of composition. *Journal of Applied Behavior Analysis*, 1972, *5*, 421-428.

Burns, P. C. *Assessment and correction of language arts difficulties.* Columbus, OH: Charles E. Merrill, 1980.

Carlson, R. K. *Writing aids through the grades.* New York: Teacher's College Press, 1970.

Cartwright, G. P.   Written expression and spelling. In R. M. Smith (Ed.), *Teacher diagnosis of educational difficulties.* Columbus, OH: Charles E. Merrill, 1969.

Cohen, S. B., & Gerber, M. M.   Assessment of written expression and handwriting skill. In A. F. Rotatori & R. Fox (Eds.), *Assessment for regular and special education teachers: A case study approach.* Baltimore: University Park Press, 1982.

Cohen, S. B., & Plaskon, S. P.   *Language arts for the mildly handicapped.* Columbus, OH: Charles E. Merrill, 1980.

Collins, J. L.   Class-mating: A strategy for teaching writing in urban schools. In G. Stanford (Ed.), *Reading with differences.* Urbana, IL: National Council of Teachers of English, 1980.

Dankowski, C. E.   Each pupil has his own editor. *Elementary School Journal,* 1966, *66,* 249-253.

Davis, V. I.   *Including the language learning disabled student in the college English class.* Paper presented at 26th Annual Meeting of the Conference on College Composition, St. Louis, 1975. (ERIC Document Reproduction Service No. ED 114 823)

Dawson, M. A., & Zollinger, M.   *Guiding language learning.* Yonkers-on-Hudson, NY: World Book Co., 1957.

Deshler, D. O.   Psychoeducational aspects of learning-disabled adolescents. In L. Mann, L. Goodman, & J. L. Wiederholt (Eds.), *Teaching the learning disabled adolescent.* Boston: Houghton-Mifflin, 1978.

Dunn, L. M., & Markwardt, F. C.   *Peabody individual achievement test.* Circle Pines, MN: American Guidance Service, 1970.

Durost, W. N., Bixler, H. H., Wrightstone, J. W., Prescott, G. A., & Balow, I. H.   *Metropolitan achievement test.* New York: Harcourt, Brace, Jovanovich, 1971.

Educational Testing Services, *Sequential test of educational progress.* Palo Alto, CA: Author, 1958.

Epstein, M. H., Hallahan, D. P., & Kauffman, J. M.   Implications of the reflectivity-impulsivity dimension for special education. *Journal of Special Education,* 1975, *9,* 11-25.

Fader, O. N., & McNeill, E. B.   *Hooked on books: Program and proof.* New York: Berkeley Publishing, 1968.

Fennimore, F.   Attaining sentence verve with sentence extension. In G. Stanford (Ed.), *Dealing with differences.* Urbana, IL: National Council of Teachers of English, 1980.

Glover, J., & Gary, A. L.   Procedures to increase some aspects of creativity. *Journal of Applied Behavior Analysis,* 1976, *8,* 79-84.

Golden, J. M.   The writer's side: Writing for a purpose and an audience. *Language Arts,* 1980, *57,* 756-762.

Graham, S., & Miller, L.   Handwriting research and practice: A unified approach. *Focus on Exceptional Children,* 1980, *13*(2), 1-16.

Graham, S., & Miller, L.   Spelling research and practice: A unified approach. *Focus on Exceptional Children,* 1979, *12*(2), 1-16.

Hall, J. K.   *Evaluating and improving written expression: A practical guide for teachers.* Boston: Allyn & Bacon, 1981.

Hammill, D. D., Brown, V. L., Larsen, S. C., & Wiederholt, J. L.   *Test of adolescent language.* Austin: TX: Pro-Ed, 1980.

Hammill, D. D., & Larsen, S. C.   *Test of written language.* Austin, TX: Pro-Ed, 1978.

Hammill, D. D., & Poplin, M.   Problems in writing. In D. D. Hammill & N. R. Bartel (Eds.), *Teaching children with learning and behavior problems.* Boston: Allyn & Bacon, 1978.

Hansen, C. L.   Writing skills. In N. G. Haring, T. C. Lovitt, M. D. Eaton, & C. L. Hansen (Eds.), *The fourth R: Research in the classroom.* Columbus, OH: Charles E. Merrill, 1978.

Haring, N. G., & Bateman, B. *Teaching the learning disabled child.* Englewood Cliffs, NJ: Prentice-Hall, 1972.

Hermreck, L. A. *A comparison of the written language of L.D. and non-L.D. elementary children using the inventory of written expression and spelling.* Unpublished master's thesis, University of Kansas, 1979.

Hieronymus, A. N., & Lindquist, E. F. *Iowa tests of basic skills.* Boston: Houghton-Mifflin, 1974.

Hillerich, R. L. Developing written expression: *How to raise — not raze — writers.* Language Arts, 1979, *56*, 769-777.

Hogan, T. P., & Mishler, C. J. Judging the quality of students' writing: Where and how. *Elementary School Journal,* 1979, *79*, 142-146.

Hunt, K. W. *Grammatical structures written at three grade levels.* Research Report No. 3. Champaign, IL: National Council of Teachers of English, 1965.

Jastak, J. F., & Jastak, S. R. *Wide range achievement test.* Wilmington, DE: Guidance Associates, 1965.

Johnson, D. J., & Myklebust, H. R. *Learning disabilities: Educational principles and practices.* New York: Grune & Stratton, 1967.

Kirk, S. A., & Johnson, G. O. *Educating the retarded child.* Cambridge, MA: Houghton-Mifflin, 1951.

Kraetsch, G. A. The effects of oral instructions and training on the expansion of written language. *Learning Disability Quarterly,* 1981, *4*, 83-90.

Lerner, J. W. *Learning disabilities: Theories, diagnosis, and teaching strategies* (3rd ed.). Boston: Houghton-Mifflin, 1981.

Loban, W. D. *The language of elementary school children:* NCTE Research Report No. 1. Champaign, IL: National Council of Teachers of English, 1963.

Loban, W., Ryan, M., & Squire, J. R. *Teaching language and literature: Grades seven-twelve* (2nd ed.). New York: Harcourt, Brace & World, 1969.

Lovitt, T. C. Applied behavior analysis and learning disabilities: Part 2. *Journal of Learning Disabilities,* 1975, *8*, 504-518.

Madden, R., Gardner, E. F., Rudman, H. C., Karlsen, B., & Merwin, J. C. *Stanford achievement test.* New York: Psychological Corporation, 1973.

Maloney, K. B., & Hopkins, B. L. The modification of structure and its relationship to subjective judgments of creative writing. *Journal of Applied Behavior Analysis,* 1973, *6*, 425-433.

McLoughlin, J. A., & Lewis, R. B. *Assessing special students.* Columbus, OH: Charles E. Merrill, 1981.

Mercer, C. D., & Mercer, A. R. *Teaching students with learning problems.* Columbus, OH: Charles E. Merrill, 1981.

Myklebust, H. *Picture story language test.* Los Angeles: Western Psychological Services, 1965.

Myklebust, H. R. *Development and disorders of written language: Studies of normal and exceptional children.* New York: Grune & Stratton, 1973.

Nathanson, D., Cynamon, A., & Lehman, K. Miami: Snow poets: creative writing for exceptional children. *Teaching Exceptional Children,* 1976, *8*, 87-91.

Otto, W., McMenemy, R. A., & Smith, R. J. *Corrective and remedial teaching.* Boston: Houghton-Mifflin, 1973.

Petty, W. T., & Bowen, M. E. *Slithery snakes and other aids to children's writing.* New York: Appleton-Century-Crofts, 1967.

Phelps-Teraski, D., & Phelps, T. *Teaching written expression: The Phelps sentence guide program.* Novato, CA: Academic Therapy, 1980.

Polloway, E. A., & Smith, J. E. *Teaching language skills to exceptional learners.* Denver, CO: Love Publishing Co., 1982.

Poplin, M., Gray, R., Larsen, S., Banikowski, A., & Mehring, T. A comparison of components of written expression abilities in learning disabled and non-learning disabled children at three grade levels. *Learning Disability Quarterly*, 1980, *3*, 46-53.

Poteet, J. A. Informal assessment of written expression. *Learning Disability Quarterly*, 1980, *3*(4), 88-98.

Rich, A., & Nedboy, R. Hey man . . . We're writing a poem: Creative writing for inner city children. *Teaching Exceptional Children*, 1977, *9*, 92-94.

Riemer, G. *How they murdered the second R*. Toronto: W. W. Norton, 1969.

Ross, A. O. *Psychological aspects of learning disabilities and reading disorders*. New York: McGraw-Hill, 1976.

Sequential test of educational progress. Palo Alto, CA: Educational Testing Service, 1958.

Sherwin, J. S. *Four problems in teaching English: A critique of Research*. Scranton, PA: International Textbook (for National Council of Teachers of English), 1969.

Sink, D. M. Teach-write/Write-teach. *Elementary English*, 1975, *52*, 175-177.

Smith, R. M. *Clinical teaching: Methods of instruction for the retarded*. New York: McGraw-Hill, 1974.

Thorpe, L. P., Lefever, D. E., & Haslond, R. A. *SRA achievement series*. Chicago: Science Research Associates, 1974.

Tiedt, I. M. Input. *Elementary English*, 1975, *52*, 163-164.

Tiegs, E. W., & Clark, W. W. *California achievement test*. Monterey, CA: CTB/McGraw Hill, 1970.

Torgeson, J. K. The role of nonspecific factors in the task performance of learning disabled children: A theoretical assessment. *Journal of Learning Disabilities*, 1977, *10*, 27-34.

Tsimbos, L. Journal writing for non-native speakers of English. in G. Stanford (Ed.), *Dealing with differences*. Urbana, IL: National Council of Teachers of English, 1980.

Tway, E. Creative writing: From gimmick to goal. *Elementary English*, 1975, *52*, 173-174.

Van Allen, R. *Language experiences in communication*. Boston: Houghton-Mifflin, 1976.

Van Houten, R., Morrison, E., Jarvis, R., & MacDonald, M. The effects of explicit timing and feedback on compositional response rate in elementary school children. *Journal of Applied Behavior Analysis*, 1974, *7*, 547-555.

Wallace, G., & Larsen, S. C. *Educational assessment of learning problems: Testing for teaching*. Boston: Allyn & Bacon, 1978.

Wallace, G., & McLoughlin, J. *Learning disabilities: Concepts and characteristics*. Columbus, OH: Charles E. Merrill, 1976.

Weiner, E. S. Diagnostic evaluation of writing skills. *Journal of Learning Disabilities*, 1980, *13*, 43-48.

Wiig, E. H., & Semel, E. M., *Language assessment and intervention for the learning disabled*. Columbus, OH: Charles E. Merrill, 1980.

Wong, B. Research and educational implications of some recent conceptualizations in learning disabilities. *Learning Disability Quarterly*, 1979, *2*,(3), 63-68.

Woodcock, R. W., & Johnson, M. B. *Woodcock-Johnson psychoeducational battery*. Boston: Teaching Resources, 1977.

This article recommends a functional approach to teaching math for the mildly handicapped. The concept has proved to be highly successful in practice. It involves eight carefully sequenced steps. The first is motivation, a purpose — a functional need to solve a problem. After motivation is developed, the student has an understanding and a need to know the answers.

The other steps are quite simple and are all related to keeping the problem simple and purposeful. The student is required to estimate the answer and then compare his or her answer with the estimate. Generous use of concrete materials is suggested. The article offers many practical examples so others will know how to implement such a program.

Mathematics for Handicapped Learners: A Functional Approach for Adolescents

Stuart E. Schwartz and Diane Budd

James, a typical high school student in a program for educable mentally retarded pupils, was frustrated by the task of learning to measure. His classroom teacher, an experienced and creative person, had used many different activities and reinforcement methods in an attempt to teach Jim to measure, but Jim had made no progress for months.

The work-study teacher took Jim to the area vocational school one day and after a visit around the center, Jim decided he wanted to be a carpenter's helper. In response to Jim's questions, the carpentry teacher replied, "No, you don't have to be a good reader to be a carpenter, but you've got to be able to measure."

Jim returned to class and told his teacher of his need to learn to measure. The teacher continued to use the same methods as before but applied these to functional carpentry tasks. Jim now has *a reason to learn,* and he and his teacher succeeded in two weeks' time.

321

*   *   *

Andrea, a hard-of-hearing teenager, was not interested in school, was simply putting in her time, and was failing math. She had been required to memorize math facts for the four basic math functions.

The girl knew she wanted to get married and rear children someday. When the math teacher told his class of academically deficient students that they were no longer going to study math but, rather, the use of numbers in home and child care, Andrea became excited. She began to hear about home budgets, buying food, banking, and other *useful* topics. For the first time in a long while, Andrea liked school — well, at least she liked math class, because she had *a reason to learn.*

*   *   *

Hundreds of additional true stories about mildly handicapped adolescents and their frustrations with arithmetic can be told. Educators have long been concerned about the best content and procedures in mathematics instruction for mildly handicapped learners. This article deals with *functional mathematics* for adolescents with mild learning handicaps. It suggests content, materials, and procedures. First, however, a definition of functional math for handicapped students is necessary. *Functional math refers to the study of uses of mathematics needed for vocational, consumer, social, recreational* and *homemaking activities.* Functional math includes the application of those uses. Therefore, a functional math program is designed to teach mildly handicapped pupils two important concepts: (a) how math will help them be successful adults, and (b) how to use math to be successful adults. Functional math involves not only the teaching of arithmetic computational skills; it means teaching the use of arithmetic to solve everyday problems.

WHY FUNCTIONAL MATH?

One current topic that pervades newspapers, magazines, television news shows, and conversation throughout our nation is the spiraling rate of unemployment. The *Statistical Abstract of the United States* (U.S. Department of Commerce, 1979) showed an overall unemployment rate of 5.8% for American workers during 1979. For the teenaged population (16-19 years) the unemployment figure was 16.1%. One only has to read daily newspapers to realize that unemployment problems continue to exist. A large percentage of the nonhandicapped population appears to be having great difficulty obtaining and maintaining employment. This situation is magnified for handicapped youth who, as a group, experience even greater unemployment or underemployment (Martin, 1972). In order to compete with nonhandicapped peers in the job market, they must become equipped with as many technical and employability skills as possible.

The principle of normalization advocates that handicapped persons attain as normal an existence as possible in the community. Academic skills, especially mathematics, provide the foundation for subsequent learning in both technical skills (e.g., carpentry, engine repair) and employability skills (e.g., budget management). Functional mathematics is a vital part of the continuum of skills leading to normal life.

As reflected in the *Dictionary of Occupational Titles* (U.S. Department of Labor, 1977), many occupations require the use of various levels of mathematics. Even in the rare instances when a job does not require math, the worker must know basic functional math in order to compute hours, wages, deductions, vacation and sick leave hours, and other payroll-related tasks. This need is also reflected in work-study programs that contain both on-the-job training and regular academic curriculum. The regular academic curriculum should relate to the needs of the student on the job and, therefore, should include functional math as a necessary component (Rigger & Rigger, 1980).

The concepts contained in career education also support the necessity to teach functional mathematics to handicapped youth. According to Brolin and Kokaska (1979), nine global competencies are required for the daily living skills deemed necessary for successful, independent living in society. The first of these nine is labeled "Managing Family Finances." Within this competency are five subcompetencies: (a) identify money and make change, (b) make wise expenditures, (c) obtain and use bank and credit facilities, (d) keep basic financial records, and (e) calculate and pay taxes. A review of these subcompetencies suggests that financial use of mathematics is a prerequisite for independent living and occupational skills that make up such a large part of successful adult adjustment. Each one of these functional mathematic subcompetencies can be analyzed and broken down into sequential tasks to be taught to the handicapped individual. The tasks may then easily become part of the student's individual education program.

Clark (1980) also sees career education as a means of making academics such as mathematics more meaningful and relevant. For instance, teaching subtraction and addition as they occur in the correct balancing of a checkbook or a savings account makes math relevant and meaningful. When learning tasks relate to recognized present needs or to perceived future needs, the tasks would seem more important to learn.

The concept of failure is a widely noted problem among handicapped learners. If a handicapped youth, however, has a good understanding of functional mathematics, that student will probably more often succeed in school and society. This skill may help diminish the fear of failure. For instance, if a student can become a wise consumer who makes appropriate personal expenditures, the student may be able to transfer that knowledge to the job situation and be more confident and competent when making decisions concerning business expenditures.

Vitello (1976) has reported that mentally handicapped youth have difficulty understanding math concepts contained within symbols. Several studies have indicated that functional math makes symbols and abstract information (such as one yard, one foot) more concrete, relevant, and meaningful (Sengstock & Wyatt, 1976). For example, one often-used lab exercise in industrial arts involves constructing a tool tote according to planned specifications. This competency includes the concrete use of measurement skills and results in a product that makes those skills more meaningful to the student.

Buffer and Miller (1976) contend that functional mathematics stimulates and motivates underachievers and, therefore, achievement levels are improved by using a functional approach. Presenting such stimulation and motivation is the key reason for stressing the need for a functional mathematics program for handicapped students. Too often students have found the assignment of page after page of computations to be abstract and meaningless. Development of math skills based on relevant, concrete reasons provides the motivation for youth to see math as meaningful.

A FUNCTIONAL MATH TEACHING SEQUENCE

A number of authors (Krause, 1978; Peterson, 1973) have suggested math curricula for mildly handicapped learners. These curricula often contain the skills and methods for doing the basic arithmetic functions (addition, subtraction, multiplication, and division). The time required to teach these abstract skills is often lengthy. Mildly handicapped adolescents may not know why they are doing what they are doing, how an answer was obtained, or what an answer to a problem means. A *functional* math curriculum provides the answers to these problems.

Figure 1 depicts an eight-step sequence that is useful in initiating teaching strategies for a functional math curriculum. Methods for all these steps are discussed in the following paragraphs. The reader should consider the concreteness, realism, and functionalism of each step. Following that discussion is an outline of suggested content for a functional math curriculum.

Step 1: Become Motivated

The purpose of the initial phase of this functional math sequence is to help students become aware of how math will help them be better or more successful adults. School content must be relevant to the student's everyday needs (McDowell & Brown, 1978) and to the student's perceived future needs. The entire career education movement that has been sweeping our schools strongly supports the need for motivation in terms of occupational and daily living skill preparation. If teachers are able to convince students of the math

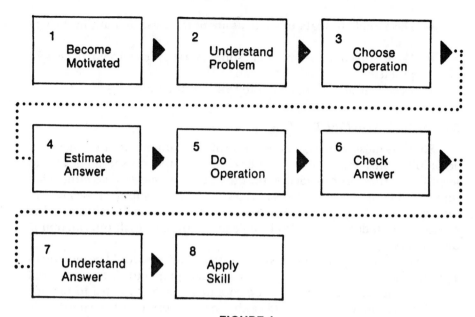

FIGURE 1
Functional Math Teaching Sequence

content's relevancy to present and future life, motivation to learn and gain skills should follow (Finn & Brown, 1977).

This first step should help create an excitement for learning. The teacher who convinces students that they can use the functional math skills that are about to be taught is probably halfway to the goal of having excellent achievement among students.

Some Suggested Strategies

- Take students on field trips to various places of employment and have students analyze how math contributes to job success.
- Discuss the uses of math in the home.
- Establish a class store or business and discuss the need for arithmetic skills.
- Provide games reflecting real life situations that require math to solve problems.
- Ask guest speakers, such as employers, to address the need for math skills among employees.
- Use instructional materials that demonstrate math usage for realistic problem solving.
- Visit vocational education classes and ask the vocational teachers to point out math skills needed for success.

- Have graduates talk to students about their use of math in the real world.
- Have students use math to solve everyday classroom or school problems.
- Relate all math instruction to real life situations.

Step 2: Understand the Problem

Students must understand the nature of the math puzzle or problem. To accomplish this, terminology must be clear, and students should be able to identify information provided within the problem and to determine what information is missing. Students must identify the question(s) posed within the problem. Then, thorough analysis of the question(s) being asked is needed. The students must also be able to determine which information is unnecessary.

If a teacher were to avoid or skip this step, students would be moving to a problem-solving component without adequate preparation. Students need to understand what is being asked before they can be expected to provide meaningful answers. They should be able to tell, at this point, what valuable information will be provided once an answer is determined.

Some Suggested Strategies

- Provide learning activities that define all new or difficult vocabulary. Be sure that the students understood all terminology.
- Use realistic problems for all discussions.
- Present problems and ask students to repeat those problems, exactly as they heard or read them. Then present the problems and ask students to repeat the problems using their own words.
- Provide activities that allow students to identify which parts of the information presented *are not* needed in order to solve the problem.
- Provide activities that allow students to identify which parts of the information presented *are* needed in order to solve the problem.
- Have students make up realistic math problems and present them to the class. Have classmates tell what they think the problems require.
- Provide exercises that require students to tell what the problems are asking. (Don't require students to mathematically solve problems at this time.)
- Use instructional materials that provide realistic problems, and have students verbally and schematically analyze those problems.

Step 3: Choose the Operation

Once students fully understand what the math problem is asking, the choice of which operation to use should be a somewhat easier step. But the students must first know what operations exist, what their symbols are, and what the operations actually do. Specifically, the students should know that addition exists and that addition combines items or groups of items. This example would be true for subtraction, multiplication, and division as well.

Knowledge of the existence of operations, recognition of symbols, and understanding of what the operations do is usually taught in early grades —before initiating a functional curriculum. The teacher has to determine if students have this prerequisite knowledge, and if a student is deficient in any of these skills, they should be addressed before proceeding with Step 3.

Some Suggested Strategies

- Begin with simple thought problems. Have students state what question is being asked (Step 2). Tell the students what operation would solve the problem and explain why.
- Repeat the first strategy but have students choose the operation to solve the problem.
- Have students create math problems that can be solved by using a specific operation.
- Design worksheets that present problems and require the students to draw lines to the correct operation names and symbols.

Step 4: Estimate the Answer

This step is included to help students logically determine if their choice of operation is correct. It also assists students in checking their answers when the operation is completed.

After the student selects an operation, the teacher might assume that the student knows approximately what to expect as the outcome of the problem. This step may also allow the teacher to determine if the student knows approximately what the answer will be or at least can accurately predict the expected direction (larger/smaller) of the answer.

If a student is unable to provide estimated answers that are, at a minimum, in the expected direction of the answer, he or she may not adequately understand the operation. Difficulty with the estimation may also indicate a lack of understanding of the problem or that, even though the choice of operation may have been correct, the wrong numbers were selected for that operation.

Some Suggested Strategies

- Teach students techniques for rounding off numbers.
- Introduce educational games that require students to guess (estimate) answers.

- Provide learning exercises that require only a choice of operation and answer estimation.
- Develop class exercises that give possible answers to questions and have students choose the most probable answer. Begin this activity with obvious answers, and then move up to more difficult choices.

Step 5: Do the Operation

In Step 5 the students actually do the operation using skills acquired in earlier grades. In traditional math classes students are often asked to immediately do an operation (+, −, ×, ÷) before having been formally taught the first four steps and given a chance to utilize them. This fifth step should follow the other four in sequence so the teacher is sure the students understand the mathematics exercises.

If any students need assistance with the operational procedures, the teacher can provide individual or group instruction, but only the students who need help should be included in this instruction. A good option is to provide electronic devices, tables of problems and answers, or manual materials. The focus in a functional curriculum is to provide meaningful, relevant math experiences. When certain students are unable to do operations fairly easily, they may tend to concentrate more on the operation than on why they are using the particular operation and what it should tell them. If students have learned all steps before this one, they should not be penalized for lack of skill with the operation but should be assisted in Step 5 so they will be able to proceed to Step 6. A device such as a battery-operated, hand-held calculator may be of great help in reducing the emphasis on the operation itself. Our society does not stigmatize people for using calculators; students can be taught to use calculators without fear of personal embarrassment.

The functional math program does not support the idea of presenting page after page of problems that simply provide practice in doing the operations. A math operation should take place to solve a *realistic* problem so that the operation is meaningful.

Some Suggested Strategies

- Provide a review of skills for doing the basic math functions with whole numbers, decimals, fractions, and percentages.
- Teach students how to use devices like tables or calculators to do operations. Such functions as entering numbers and copying readouts may require practice to improve students' accuracy.
- Be sure that adequate space immediately adjacent to written problems is available for doing operations.

Step 6: Check the Answer

After Step 5 has been accomplished, students must learn to check their answers. The aim is to ensure that numbers were copied correctly, that operations were performed correctly, and that the answers are logically correct.

To check the accuracy of their answers, students should be advised to repeat the operation in a different manner. If initially computed manually, for instance, the operation could be done on a calculator as a check. Or it could be checked again manually with numbers in reverse order (for addition and multiplication). Other procedures, such as multiplying the divisor by the answer to determine if it equals the dividend, could also be used.

To logically check answers, students should be taught to determine if their answers approximate their own estimates, as taught in Step 4. Step 7 will help this process as well.

Some Suggested Strategies

- Provide devices like calculators, rods, chips, or abaci for checking answers.
- Require students to show two ways to obtain their answers.
- Have students check other students' answers for accuracy and logic.

Step 7: Understand the Answer

After determining an answer in the form of a numerical response, the students should be taught to label and state its meaning. As stressed throughout, the usefulness of the math is critical, and without a label and statement of meaning, the numerical answer is a useless abstraction.

The label applied to the answer should actually evolve from Step 2, in which students establish what useful information is to be derived. Concluding the meaning of the answer may require discussion, including direct teacher questions like, "Just what does the answer mean to tell you?" Prompting and a refresher of Step 2 may be needed.

Some Suggested Strategies

- Remind students of their responses at the Step 2 stage.
- Develop and maintain a master list of possible labels for answers.
- Have students both write and verbally state the meanings of their answers.
- Use materials that require labels for all answers.

Step 8: Apply the Skill

This step applies the entire process to realistic, meaningful problems to reinforce the problem-solving skill and to demonstrate the usefulness of the skill. Practicing the first seven steps is important. If any step is skipped, the entire sequence may be threatened. Therefore, repetition or rehearsal of the complete process is vital.

As students practice the sequence, they should begin to realize how their ability to solve math problems has improved. Since realistic problems are involved, convincing students that this ability will be helpful to them should be easy.

Some Suggested Strategies

- Require students to practice the entire sequence of Steps 1-7 using material and problems that are realistic and relevant.
- Be creative in developing problems.
- Have students develop problems based on their real life needs.
- Use a worksheet for problem solving. The worksheet shown in Figure 2 is useful in ensuring that students use all steps in solving functional math problems.

FUNCTIONAL MATH CONTENT

The outline of content suggested here is not exhaustive but is suggested as a starting point in a functional math program. Some content, such as number recognition and usage, does not require actual problem solving, just the application of meaning and use of the numbers.

Consumer Skills
    Making change
    Determining cost of sale items utilizing percentages (e.g., "25% off")
    Determining tax amounts
    Doing cost comparisons
    Buying on "time"
    Balancing a checkbook
    Determining total cost of purchases

Homemaking Skills
    Measuring ingredients
    Budgeting for household expenses
    Calculating length of cooking and baking time when there are
        options (e.g., for a cake using two 9″ round pans vs. two 8″
        round pans)
    Measuring material for clothing construction
    Doing cost comparisons

1. Will knowing how to do this math help you someday?

   Yes _____ How? _____

   No _____ Ask your teacher how this math will help you.

2. Read the problem. What question is being asked?

   _____

   _____

3. What will the answer tell you?

   _____

   _____

4. Circle the one or ones you will use.

   $+$ $-$ $\times$ $\div$

5. Estimate your answer. Use a label.

   _____

6. Do your math.

7. Put your answer here. Use a label.

   _____

8. Check your answer. Does your check agree with your answer?

   Yes _____ No _____ If yes, go ahead. If no, redo your math.

9. Is your answer close to your estimate?   Yes _____ No _____

   If yes, go ahead. If no, think: Was your estimate wrong? Or is your answer wrong?

10. What does the answer tell you? _____

    _____

FIGURE 2
Problem-solving Worksheet

Health Care
    Weighing oneself and others
    Calculating calorie intake
    Determining when to take medication

Auto Care
    Calculating cost of auto parts
    Measuring spark plug gaps
    Determining if tire pressure is correct
    Figuring gas mileage

Home Care
    Determining amount of supplies (paint, rug shampoo) to buy
    Determining time needed to do projects
    Measuring rods and drapes
    Finding cost of supplies
    Finding cost of repairs

Vocational Needs
    Calculating payroll deductions
    Determining money owed
    Knowing when to be at work
    Doing actual math for various jobs

MATERIALS

A cursory examination of publishers' catalogs of educational materials reveals many math materials; but a more in-depth look at secondary level materials shows that only a small portion of these materials presents math concepts in functional ways. Many materials give information in abstract ways that are difficult for handicapped students to comprehend (Budd, 1979).

In reviewing math materials for handicapped youth, teachers must be concerned with a variety of criteria. One area of concern is the actual academic content. Does it represent functional mathematics? Does it reflect competencies needed for independent living in the real world?

Another concern is the reading level of that content. Are comprehension and vocabulary levels appropriate for the handicapped individual? Many materials are considered to have a low reading level if the level is listed as 5.0 or 6.0, but this may be altogether too complex for some handicapped students (Dunn, 1973). Some publishers do specify lower reading levels. Still, teachers should review these materials firsthand, looking specifically at the length and complexity of sentences and the number of syllables in words to ascertain if the stated reading level is accurate. Short, simple sentences and monosyllabic words are generally reflective of a lower reading level. If the teacher still has some doubt as to the actual reading level, the educator may use the "Fry Readability Chart" (Fry, 1977) or other reputable measures to determine the actual reading level.

Math problems are stated in many ways. If the reading level is too complex, it compounds the task and causes the student to have to decipher the words rather than solve the math problems. Beattie and Schwartz (1979) used the Fry system to examine a random sample of books used in special education classes. The results showed that the students, who were at an average second grade reading level, were confronted with sixth grade reading level textbooks. If the material does not reflect the stated reading level, the teacher may wish to review other materials or attempt to reconstruct the reading content so it is at an appropriate level.

Another concern regarding math materials for handicapped students is the availability of that material in both visual and auditory formats. Many visually impaired students have enough residual vision to be able to see an overhead projection of large, dark print. Hearing impaired students also benefit from visual presentation of math concepts. Some learning disabled students seem to do better if math is presented auditorially immediately after visual presentation of the same material.

The method and format used to present the material is also worthy of examination. For instance, a material that uses three dimensional money facsimiles or real money (as opposed to flat, two-dimensional pictures of money) may be better suited for functional mathematics presentations. Flat, pictorial representations alone have rarely been validated as effective teaching devices (Trace, Cuvo, & Criswell, 1977).

Materials that include real objects are usually functional materials. *Real-Life Math* (Schwartz, 1977) is one example. This functional math kit includes real-looking checks, checkbooks, banking supplies, business forms, and business posters. Functional materials help provide the interest and motivation necessary for secondary level handicapped students.

As educators review math materials for handicapped students, they should carefully examine the illustrations. Many times, handicapped role models are not represented well in materials. Handicapped youth may relate better to handicapped models who are functioning in the real world than to nonhandicapped models. Often, minority people are not well represented in materials. The Educational Products Information Exchange (EPIE) Institute (1975) has produced a comprehensive materials assessment instrument that should assist educators as they consider many of these important points.

Some handicapped students learn certain mathematical skills and concepts better through the use of active games rather than traditional approaches (Taylor & Watkins, 1974). Teacher-made games may be utilized. For instance, a mock industrial facility might be created in one corner of the classroom. Students may role play the employees of the industry and do the math those employees would do. Also, teachers might construct self-correcting games that involve knowledge of math concepts, such as one with a gameboard that can be traversed only as participants provide correct answers to math problems.

The following list suggests math materials that appear to present mathematical information in a functional way. The authors are not endorsing or judging these products, and the list is not intended to be all-inclusive. It is provided as a starting point for teachers.

ACCENT/CONSUMER EDUCATION

Follett
Chicago, IL

These booklets present some of the math concepts and social skills needed to function within our society. Topics include understanding consumer credit, budgeting and buying, and insuring life, income, and property.

CONSUMER EDUCATION

Interpretive Education
Kalamazoo, MI

This series acquaints the student with methods of wise shopping. It includes tags and labels, shopping values, bargain hunting, and reading ads.

IT'S YOUR MONEY

Steck-Vaughn
Austin, TX

A consumer guide to money management is the subject of this two-volume worktest. Exercises concentrate on taxes, budgeting, and credit buying.

MATHEMATICS IN DAILY LIVING

Steck-Vaughn
Austin, TX

This four-book consumable series helps build competency in basic math skill through adult topics.

MONEY MATTERS

Janus Book Publishers
Hayward, CA

This new workbook series allows students to apply skills in a functional way. Topics include budgeting, checking accounts, comparative shopping, and ad reading.

PACEMAKER PRACTICAL ARITHMETIC SERIES

Fearon-Pitman
Belmont, CA

Practical problems and exercises reinforce arithmetic skills. The series has three worktexts.

REAL-LIFE MATH

Hubbard, Inc.
Northbrook, IL

A multi-media program, this kit presents banking and business skills. Activities include student simulation of business and banking transactions while practicing basic arithmetic computations.

SEQUENTIAL MATH

Harcourt, Brace, Jovanovich
New York, NY

This material can be used individually by either readers or nonreaders to reinforce math skills.

TARGET MATH SERIES

Mafex, Inc.
Johnstown, PA

The focus of this series of worktexts is on math concepts needed for independent living. Topics include using the bank, credit, time cards, spending money, math for family finances, and other functional math concepts.

ASSESSMENT IN MATHEMATICS

According to PL 94-142, each handicapped student is entitled to an Individualized Education Plan (IEP). This means that each handicapped student is to have specific annual goals and short-term objectives for each subject, including mathematics competencies. It sometimes becomes a difficult task because of the wide range of abilities and aptitudes among the mildly handicapped population. Consequently, teachers should begin this task by determining the current level of mathematical competence for each student. Then, planning for individualized instruction in mathematics may ensue. Determining the present level of math skill can be accomplished in several ways. One method is to use commercially produced math assessment instruments; another is to use teacher-made, criterion referenced texts.

Commercially-produced Assessment Instruments

At this time there seems to be a paucity of test instruments in mathematics, especially at the secondary level. In reviewing the tests available, they appear to generally reflect the content of regular elementary and secondary math programs. They are also normed on the performance of typical children. These instruments can be useful for global information about mathematical competency and for determining certain diagnostic information.

Some of the commercial tests may be useful in ascertaining the students' present level of math functioning at the beginning of the school year. The *Key Math Diagnostic Arithmetic Test* (Connolly, Nachtman, & Pritchett, 1971), for example, can be used to test in three areas: content, operations, and applications. This instrument has been found to be especially well suited to the needs of educable mentally retarded students (Peterson, 1973).

Another instrument, the *Stanford Diagnostic Mathematics Test* (Beatty, Madden, & Gardner, 1976), is a group-administered test that measures mathematical concepts and skills and covers four levels ranging from grade level 1.5 to high school. It can be useful in diagnosing specific strengths and weaknesses (Salvia & Ysseldyke, 1978).

Diagnosis: An Instructional Aid in Mathematics (Guzaitis, Carlen, & Juda, 1972) is a criterion referenced system designed to assess specific mathematical skills. It appears to help the classroom teacher in planning appropriate instruction (Boros, 1972).

These tests may be useful in gaining global information or concluding appropriate student placement, but they do not really measure the student's practical use of those mathematical concepts. Such tests also contain items that may be too difficult and complex for many handicapped students. Often the handicapped student has not been exposed to the same experiences as the children on whom the test was normed; consequently, the test may not be suitable for use with a handicapped population (Algozzine & McGraw, 1979).

Informal Mathematics Evaluation

Teachers may find this second option more appropriate for individualizing instruction. It entails developing and using informal criterion referenced assessments. They can be developed from any amount of information to be taught in a course or in a weekly lesson. Often, they are used as pretests; then, the same or a matched assessment can be used as a posttest, to reflect the competencies developed as a result of the instruction.

Results from these tests can reveal if the instruction has been appropriate or if changes or modifications are needed. If the assessment shows that the student has not attained competency in a certain area, the teacher can review methods, materials, and objectives to determine if instruction has been appropriately planned and presented. In developing assessments teachers should keep in mind that the test should be easy to administer and score, have items clearly stated and correct, be well organized and sequenced, have items that adequately evaluate student competency, and have appropriate criterion referenced questions.

A sample criterion referenced, teacher-made assessment item is provided in Figure 3. It closely follows the format of Figure 2 so that the teacher can readily make a determination of students' strengths and weaknesses in the suggested functional math sequence.

Annual Goal: Banking and Consumer Skills

Specific Goal: Student will correctly compute new account balance after writing a check.

Problem:

    You now have $21.75 in your checking account. If you write a check for $9.70 to pay for a new shirt, how much will you have left in your checking account?

---

1. Do you think you will need to do problems like this when you're an adult?

    Circle one: Yes   No   Maybe

2. What does the problem ask:

    Check one: _____ How much you spent for the shirt.

                    _____ How much you will have after buying the shirt.

                    _____ How much you started with in your account.

(Continued next page)

FIGURE 3
A Sample Teacher-made Assessment Item

3. Circle the operation you need to use.

$+$ $-$ $\times$ $\div$

4. Check the answer you think is about right.

_____ $12.00

_____ $30.00

_____ $21.00

5. Do your math work here:

Answer _____

6. Check your answer here.

Check one: _____ Same

_____ Different

7. What does your answer tell you? _____

_____

_____

FIGURE 3
A Sample Teacher-made Assessment Item (continued)

CONCLUSION

The goal of providing a meaningful, realistic math program to handicapped learners is shared by the vast majority of educators. The approach suggested here should help teachers evaluate and modify their math programs to provide a more functional math curriculum that is both meaningful and realistic to handicapped adolescents.

The reasons to learn math, stressed by a functional math program, should help pupils become excited and motivated to learn. Realism in content, learning activities, and materials is also important toward instilling in pupils the desire to learn. With a focus on the *use* of math for satisfying one's real life needs, pupil motivation should follow. As handicapped adolescents request more work and ask or demand to be taught new skills so they can solve realistic problems, teachers will know that these pupils are being well prepared for their futures.

REFERENCES

Algozzine, R., & McGraw, K. Diagnostic testing in mathematics: An extension of the PIAT? *Teaching Exceptional Children*, 1979, *12*, 71-77.

Beattie, J. R., & Schwartz, S. E. Readability of special education math books. *The Pointer*, 1979, *23*, 43-46.

Beatty, L. S., Madden, R., & Gardner, E. F. *Stanford diagnostic mathematics test*. New York: Harcourt Brace Jovanovich, 1978.

Boros, D. K. (Ed.). *Seventh mental measurements yearbook*. Highland Park, NJ: Gryphon Press, 1972, pp. 842-890.

Brolin, D. E., & Kokaska, C. J. *Career education for handicapped children and youth*. Columbus, OH: Charles E. Merrill Publishing Co., 1979.

Budd, D. M. *Secondary programs for exceptional students: A survey of resources*. Orlando, FL: Florida Learning Resource System, 1979.

Buffer, J. J., & Miller, P. W. The effects of selected industrial arts activities on educable mentally retarded students' achievements and retention of metric linear concepts. *Journal of Industrial Teacher Education*, 1976, *15*, 7-16.

Clark, G. M. Career education: A concept — A challenge. In S. E. Schwartz (Ed.), *Institute on career education for the handicapped*. University, AL: Project Retool, 1980.

Connolly, A., Nachtman, W., & Pritchett, E. *Manual for the key math diagnostic arithmetic test*. Circle Pines, MN: American Guidance Service, 1971.

Dunn, L. M. (Ed.). *Exceptional children in the schools: Special education in transition*. New York: Holt, Rinehart & Winston, 1973.

Educational Products Information Exchange (EPIE) Institute. *EPIE career education SET* (Vol. 1 & 2). New York: Author, 1975.

Finn, P., & Brown, J. Career education and the mathematics classroom. *Mathematics Teacher*, 1977, *70*, 489-496.

Fry, E. Fry's readabilty graph: Clarification, validity and extension to level 17. *Journal of Reading*, 1977, *21*, 242-252.

Guzaitis, J., Carlin, J. A., & Juda, S. *Diagnosis: An instructional aid (mathematics)*. Chicago: Science Research Associates, 1972.

Krause, E. F. *Mathematics for elementary teachers*. Englewood Cliffs, NJ: Prentice-Hall, 1978.

Martin, E. W. Individualism and behaviorism as future trends in educating handicapped children. *Exceptional Children*, 1972, *38*, 517-525.

McDowell, R. L., & Brown, G. W. The emotionally disturbed adolescent: Development of program alternatives in secondary education. *Focus on Exceptional Children*, 1978, *10*, 1-15.

Peterson, D. *Functional mathematics for the mentally retarded.* Columbus, OH: Charles E. Merrill Co., 1973.

Rigger, T. J., & Rigger, S. W. Mathematics for vocational rehabilitation of secondary EMH students. *Journal of Special Education*, 1980, *16*, 117-126.

Salvia, J., & Ysseldyke, J. E. *Assessment in special education and remedial education.* Boston: Houghton Mifflin Co., 1978.

Schwartz, S. E. *Real-life math.* Chicago: Hubbard Publishers, 1977.

Sengstock, W. L., & Wyatt, K. E. The metric system and its implications for curriculum for exceptional children. *Teaching Exceptional Children*, 1976, *8*, 58-65.

Taylor, G. R., & Watkins, S. T. Active games: An approach to teaching mathematics skills to the educable mentally retarded. *Arithmetic Teacher*, 1974, *21*, 674-678.

Trace, M. W., Cuvo, A. J., & Criswell, J. L. Teaching coin equivalence to the mentally retarded. *Journal of Applied Behavior Analysis*, 1977, *10*, 85-92.

U.S. Department of Commerce. *Statistical abstract of the United States.* Washington, DC: Bureau of the Census, 1979.

U.S. Department of Labor. *Dictionary of occupational titles (4th ed.).* Washington, DC: U.S. Government Printing Office, 1977.

Vitello, S. J. Quantitative abilities of mentally retarded children. *Education & Training of the Mentally Retarded*, 1976, *11*, 125-129.

The author poses the question of whether science is an appropriate subject for the mildly handicapped. She emphatically concludes that these students can learn to solve problems by studying science, that relevant science can be of real value. Keller advocates a hands-on approach, encouraging students to manage equipment — and also raising their self-esteem. She presents a number of science activities for teachers, specifying what materials are needed and how to teach these materials. The article concludes with some examples related to outdoor education.

Science for the Handicapped

W. Diane Keller

Traditionally, science for the handicapped has been infrequent if not nonexistent. Many educators have believed that handicapped children could not manipulate science equipment or that the content itself was inappropriate for this population. Few materials, equipment, or methodologies have been developed for teaching science not only as appropriate for handicapped students but as a unique vehicle for providing valuable educational experiences.

The movement toward providing science activities for handicapped students has sometimes placed burdens on teachers who are not experienced with this concept. The discussion here is an attempt to help bridge the gap and move science education for the handicapped into a more prominent place in the classroom curriculum. The ideas are directed primarily at special education teachers with little formal science training and regular classroom teachers who lack training in adapting materials for handicapped students.

WHY SCIENCE FOR THE HANDICAPPED?

Questions often asked are: Is science content not irrelevant for this population? Considering the hands-on, experimental nature of science classrooms, how can handicapped students participate without disrupting the entire class? Do the benefits of teaching science to handicapped students merit the expenditure of energy necessary to adapt materials for them?

Questions like these have stimulated educators to look closely at the benefits of teaching science to handicapped students. Upon examination, one realizes that science activities can offer many special opportunities for these students. Science activities represent a valuable way for handicapped students to learn how to solve problems. Like everyone else, handicapped students are faced with persistent life problems. Armed with the problem solving skills learned in science classes, they can more readily find out other information they need to know. Therefore, problem solving and inquiry are essential components of the curriculum design. Based on the idea that scientific processes are important tools for handicapped students to use in solving lifetime problems, science content taught in classrooms must be relevant to everyday life. This is of primary importance when considering that science instruction in the school setting is probably the only concentrated instruction in science that many handicapped students receive during their lifetimes. Thus, learning about inquiry methods and problem solving steps in the school setting represents an important survival tool for handicapped students.

Can handicapped students manipulate scientific equipment? The answer is yes. Instructors have found that most handicapped students not

only are able to handle scientific equipment, but that a hands-on approach can alleviate persistent problems of classroom motivation.

An additional benefit from activity-centered learning experiences is that the students' self-esteem is enhanced as they work alongside peers in hands-on activities. Handicapped students learn that their unique skills are valued and that they can associate with other students in a competent way.

Science activities can also be a means of developing appropriate interpersonal skills. Small-group activities, as well as experiences in larger groups, provide opportunities for handicapped students to learn to function as useful members of a team. They often learn (sometimes to the teachers' surprise!) that they can participate in group situations without causing disruptions.

Communication among students, which is necessary for performing activities, fosters growth of vocabulary skills, and it establishes concepts in a meaningful context. The activity becomes the "teacher." Students begin to learn from experience rather than simply being "told" information. This also provides another bit of support for independence. And appropriate actions are reinforced.

As individual handicapped students share experiences with peers and achieve successful results, they acquire self-reliance and feelings of independence. Manipulation of equipment supports the development of small motor skills. Hand-eye coordination is enhanced. Feelings of classroom failure begin to disappear. Knowledge of what is expected and feelings that "I can perform" increase along with appropriate behavior. Successful experiences are accompanied by a lesser tendency for handicapped students to rely on adults or other authority figures for reinforcement, assistance, or performance of activities because the students have discovered that they can perform for themselves.

What teacher has not heard students say that the material they are studying has no meaning for them, that the content they are expected to learn seems useless? Establishing relevancy is a challenge for teachers. This is of particular importance for teachers of handicapped students, since the students often have short attention spans and many times do not generalize well. Science activities can be of special benefit in that regard. Most handicapped students learn best when the relevance of the material relates to their immediate or future needs. Many opportunities exist for tying science content to problems in everyday life. For instance, health care, food concepts, clothing management, appliance maintenance, lawn or garden care can all be successfully integrated into existing science programs. The connection between present activities and future benefits can readily be established. The issue of relevancy is then closer to being solved.

Why teach science to the handicapped? Because science does not involve hit-or-miss lessons. It is more than the product. It includes the *process of learning* as well. It can help handicapped students, and all students, solve persistent life problems. The science class offers a unique opportunity for helping students learn to identify, address, and successfully develop problem solving behaviors that they need to cope with life problems.

In the process of learning to solve problems, establishing successful peer relationships, identifying and solving persistent life problems, and perceiving the relevance of the materials presented, students develop a sense of control over their own destiny. They come to feel that they are less at the mercy of others and that they are able to influence the direction and destiny of their own lives.

CLASSROOM SETTINGS FOR TEACHING SCIENCE

In the past, instruction of handicapped students has often taken place in self-contained classrooms, and science activities have not always been included in the curriculum design. Today, a variety of science material is available from which to choose. Much of this material has been designed for use in self-contained classrooms as well as other settings.

With implementation of the Education for All Handicapped Children Act of 1975 (PL 94-142), many handicapped students now have the opportunity to study science in regular classrooms. Teachers may need reassurance that hands-on activities in the existing program are still appropriate with the new composition of their classes. With relatively minor modifications many activities can be made appropriate for handicapped students.

Additional science preparation and instruction can take place in resource rooms. Resource teachers can be of valuable service when efforts are coordinated with regular classroom teachers. Cooperating resource room and classroom teachers might, for example, introduce concepts and vocabulary words in the resource room prior to the learning activity in the regular classroom. In this way handicapped students can become familiar with concepts and vocabulary and establish a meaningful context for science concepts (Callahan, 1980).

Science instruction can occur in self-contained classrooms, regular classrooms, resource rooms or any combination. The setting should be determined by what is least restrictive and most appropriate for the handicapped student. The important consideration is that science instruction take place and that activities be modified to suit the most appropriate setting.

LEARNING PROBLEMS

Handicapped students, like the general population, are a diverse group with a wide range of interests, abilities, and social development. Therefore, any curriculum design must be adaptable to the needs of a diverse population. Not all handicapped students have learning problems, but certain learning characteristics are exhibited by many students who are handicapped. These should be taken into account when adapting or developing new materials:

- Establishing a frame of reference for this population is more difficult than for the average student. Activity materials should be familiar, realistic, and tangible.
- These students may not be proficient in the extemporaneous generation of ideas. Activities designed to promote extemporaneous expression must provide a concrete, familiar frame of reference.
- Reading skills may be deficient. Enlarged print, low reading levels, short phrases, audiotapes, and similar things should be considered and available if students are not to be penalized for their difficulties in reading.
- Language skills may be deficient. Functional language rather than technical language should be used whenever possible.
- Mathematical skills may vary widely. Instruction must be provided as a part of the science activity if mathematical skills are necessary for successful completion of the activity.
- Deficiencies in short-term memory or retention may be present. Slow pacing, redundancy, and activities developed in small, discrete units provide assistance in assimilating and remembering information.
- Information is not always learned incidentally, so all desired outcomes should be specifically designated.
- Abstract reasoning and ideas should be avoided. Activities should begin with concrete references.
- Fine distinctions are difficult for many handicapped students. When similar activities are used, their differences must be made obvious.

- Transfer of learning from one situation to another may be difficult. Therefore, instructional activities must be tied to a corresponding real-life situation to establish relevancy.
- Social skills may not always be at a level commensurate with chronological age. Activities involving group interaction should be encouraged — but with no assumptions about development levels of the students.

SCIENCE AS PART OF A TOTAL CAREER

Factors in addition to PL 94-142 and other legislation are causing changes in science education. One of these is career education. Many segments in American society are revealing a growing dissatisfaction with current programs in education. A cry for relevancy is directed at the sciences as well as all instructional areas. Career education is, in part, a response to that cry. A distinction must be made between career and vocation to understand fully the significance this movement can have for science education. *Career* can be defined as the entire amount of work done in one's lifetime, with *work* meaning a conscious effort aimed at producing benefits for oneself or others. In contrast to the encompassing definition of career, *vocation* can be defined as one's primary work role at any given time. Under these definitions, career includes a variety of activities. It encompasses one's vocation, one's leisure activities, and activities necessary to maintain daily existence. These latter activities are often called *daily living skills.*

Career education, then, can be composed of all these activities. The concept takes on a broad meaning covering a person's lifetime activities. Viewed in this light, career education is highly significant to science education of the handicapped. If one considers science education as an opportunity to equip individuals with problem solving skills for persistent life problems, career education and science education have the same concerns. In fact, career education offers a vehicle for establishing the relevancy of science concepts taught in the classroom. Instead of establishing a curriculum based on traditional textbook content, science activities can be based on topics that pertain to one's life. For instance in studying life sciences content about the human body, the units could include health care, personal hygiene, or rearing children.

Example activities used later in this article include a strong career education component. Career education is emphasized on the basis that science activities have significance for the totality of a student's problem solving needs. Problems occur throughout a student's career, and the skills learned in science activities can be applied when encountering new problems. Questions and decisions involving vocations, leisure activities, health care, and other areas of life can be incorporated in teaching science content. Thus, skills learned in science class can be useful throughout a student's total career.

ADAPTING SCIENCE MATERIALS FOR HANDICAPPED STUDENTS

To state that teachers should adapt or use developed materials to meet the needs of handicapped students is not enough. Teachers also need to know how to go about adjusting the educational climate of the classroom. This will help ensure that an educational program most nearly normal and relevant to the needs of special children will be used.

Although materials have been designed for handicapped students, teachers may not be able to find pre-existing curriculum materials that are appropriate for individual classrooms. Teachers may have to adapt their existing programs. To facilitate this process, the following suggestions and strategies are offered, using the learning characteristics presented earlier as a guide. Examples of materials developed in the BSCS "Me In The Future" program (Bishop & Callahan, 1979) illustrate specific suggestions.*

1. *Activity materials should be familiar, realistic, and tangible.* The materials should be checked for relevancy. Teachers must establish a frame of reference so students can understand the concepts from the perspective of everyday experiences. An example of how abstract concepts may be brought into a student's frame of reference is given below, from *Science and Homes and Furnishings* (Biological Sciences Curriculum Study, 1980a). In a similar way, any science class could relate abstract concepts to everyday problems. Sentence length, vocabulary level, and repetition should be noted in examining the activity.

WHAT CLEANS BEST?

Pre-activity

Focus: *Taking care of your things can mean cleaning them.*

Your home is where you live. Your home can be big or small. It can be old or new. Homes can be very different from each other.

All homes cost money to live in. Taking care of things makes them last longer. Taking care of your home can save you money. Taking care of furniture, wall coverings, and floor coverings can save you money.

One way to take care of a floor is to use a sealer and wax. In the last activity you saw that waxing makes your floor look better. In this activity you will see that sealing and waxing a floor also makes it easier to clean.

---

*"Me In The Future" is a science program with a career education focus. It has been developed by the Biological Sciences Curriculum Study for use with students who are academically unsuccessful because of mental retardation, learning disabilities, or motivational problems. With the career emphasis, "Me in the Future" is divided into four major areas: Metrics; Science and Vocations; Science and Leisure Activities; and Science and Daily Living Skills.

The right cleaner can also make your floors easier to clean. Different stains need different cleaners. That makes it easier to take care of the floors in your home.

To learn more about cleaning floors, go on to the activity.

Activity

Focus: *Special cleaning jobs need special cleaners.*

In Activity 4 you prepared a floor tile in two different ways. Half the tile did not get any covering. The other half of the tile was covered with sealer and wax.

Today, you are going to put some dirt on that tile. Then you will see if using coverings (sealers and waxes) make tiles easier to clean.

GET READY

Get these materials from the kit:

Beakers, 250 ml, 2	Spoon, plastic
Pencil, wax	Tile from Activity 4
Soap, liquid	Worksheet 5

Get these materials from your teacher:

Paper towels
Shortening, vegetable
Water

GET SET

1. Put 200 ml of water in one beaker. Use warm water if you can. Use the wax pencil to mark the beaker with *W* for water.
2. Put 200 ml of water in another beaker. Add one teaspoonful of liquid soap to that beaker. Stir in the soap. Use the wax pencil to mark the beaker with **S** for soap.
3. Take the two beakers and all the other materials to the place where you left the piece of tile from Activity 4.
4. Remember, the half of the tile with an **X** is the half that has sealer and wax.

GO

1. Use your finger to make a grease (shortening) mark on each half of the tile.
2. Wipe your finger off with a paper towel.
3. Take a clean paper towel. Dip it in the glass of water. Try to wash the grease off the **left** side of the tile. Does it come off?
4. Take another clean paper towel. Dip it in the glass of water. Try to wash the grease off the **right** side of the tile, the side with the **X**. That side was sealed and waxed. Does the grease come off? Does it come off any easier than the side with no wax? Does waxing a floor make it easier to clean?
5. Take another paper towel. Dip it in the soapy water. Try to wash of the **left** side of the tile again. Did you get off any more of the grease that time? Does soapy water work better than just plain water to clean grease?
6. Take another clean paper towel. Dip it in the soapy water. Wash the right side of the tile again. Did you get off any more grease that time?

Does soapy water work better than just plain water to clean off grease? Is it easier to clean a sealed and waxed piece of tile than it is to clean a piece of tile that has no wax? If you had a tile floor in your home and wanted to keep it clean, what would you want to do to take care of it? You should be able to answer all those questions now.

Answer Questions 1, 2, and 3 on Worksheet 5.

[worksheet not included here]

You have seen that using wax and sealer makes floor tiles easier to clean. You learned that it takes soap and water to clean off grease.

Those are two things you can do to keep your floors and others parts of your home clean and looking good. There are many other cleaners made for the home. When you buy a cleaner or wax, read the label carefully. The label tells you how to use the product.

Now, put the materials away. Show your worksheet to your teacher.

CHECKLIST

_____ 1. Clean up your area.
_____ 2. Put your materials away.
_____ 3. Hand in your worksheets to your teacher.

Post-activity

Focus: *Different spills need different cleaners.*

Sealers and waxes can protect floor coverings. Sealers and waxes can make floors last longer. They can save you money.

Sealers and waxes can also save time and work. It is easier to clean floors that have been waxed. Marks and spills come off easier. Marks and spills come clean quicker.

Different things clean off different spills. For some stains, such as grease, you need soap and water.

If you spill something on a floor, you might try to clean the floor with just water. You don't want to take up the wax and sealer every time something spills. You might have to strip the wax and sealer for a really tough stain. Stripping a floor (taking off all the old wax and sealer) and putting new wax down takes time. Stripping and rewaxing a floor is hard work. Stripping and rewaxing may be the only way to clean off a tough stain.

Many floors are covered with rugs or carpets instead of tile. A stain on a rug or carpet must be cleaned in a different way. In the next activity you will learn how to take care of a rug or carpet.

Cleaning floor coverings is a part of taking care of your home.

Knowing how to take care of your home means knowing how to save money, time, and work.

2. *Activities should be structured so that students are given concrete references for generation of extemporaneous ideas.* In the following example, students are asked to solve a problem. Many handicapped students have difficulty in separating steps in problem solving as well as in generating possible solutions. When adapting materials, teachers can list the steps to be followed in solving problems. This eliminates asking students to generate solutions that might require prior knowledge they do not possess. In the following example, relating to Activity 5, problem solving steps are highlighted and possible solutions to the problem given.

STEP 1: FIND THE PROBLEM

Elliott's problem is to decide which cleaners to use on the different areas of his apartment.

What are the parts of the problem?
1. What kinds of things should be cleaned?
2. What kind of cleaner is needed for each thing?

STEP 2: THINK OF POSSIBLE SOLUTIONS

After identifying the problem and its parts, you should observe and describe all the facts that are important to each part of the problem. Then organize all the information you know about the problem. Use that information to think about all the ways you might solve the problem. When you think about all the possible solutions, you are "brainstorming" to try to figure out ideas or answers to the problem.

Elliott has come up with three possible solutions or ways to clean his apartment. Here they are:

Solution 1:	Solution 2:	Solution 3:
1. tile floor cleaner	1. wax	1. paint
2. vacuum	2. bleach	2. heavy duty cleaner
3. soap and water	3. paint	3. wax

STEP 3: CHOOSE A SOLUTION

The third step is to pick the most likely solution. Look over all the possible advantages and disadvantages to each solution. Remember all the parts of the problem, and pick the best answer based upon the information you have gathered.

---

3. *Handicapped students may be deficient in reading and language skills.* Enlarged print, a simple reading level, short phrases, and audiotapes could be considered in helping ensure that student are not penalized for inadequacies in reading printed materials.

Clear instructions and redundancy can be built into activities to facilitate short-term memory. Note in the following crafts activity from *Science and Crafts* (Biological Sciences Curriculum Study, 1980b), that easily read language, short sentence length, functional words, clear instructions, and redundancy have been incorporated to help students successfully complete an activity that includes several steps.

Activity

Focus: *You will use something in your environment in a craft activity.*

Everything around you is part of your environment. That includes the air you breathe, the people in the room with you, the furniture in the room, and any plants and animals that may be near you.

Your environment is all the living and nonliving things around you.

Look around the room.
The chairs, the desks, the people, and the pencils, paper, and tacks are all part of your environment.

Look outside.
The trees, the flowers, and the clouds are also part of the environment.

Most people go through the day without really **looking** at what is around them.

Let's take a closer look at something you probably see every day. Let's use it to make an interesting design.

GET READY

Get these materials from the kit:
    Carbon paper

Get these materials from your teacher:
    Iron   Newspaper
    Leaves   Paper, blank sheet

GET SET

Arrange the materials in front of you.

GO

Pick up a leaf and look at it carefully.

What color is the leaf?
Did you see its shape?
Did you see any lines on the leaf?

The closer you look at the leaf, the more things you can see. That is also true about your environment. When you look closely at the whole environment, you see a lot of things you didn't see before.

Now that you have looked closely at the leaf, let's use it to make a design.

You already know that heat can change things. Scientists often use heat to change things in their experiments. Have you ever put butter in a hot pan? What happens? The butter changes from something solid or hard into a liquid. The heat changes the butter. The heat **melts** the butter. In this experiment you will use heat to melt the ink on carbon paper. You will use pressure to put the melted ink onto a leaf. Then you will use the leaf to make a print. Now that you know how it works, let's make a design.

1. Plug in the iron and set it at low.
2. Take a piece of newspaper and cover your work area.
3. Lay the leaf on the newspaper.
4. Cover the leaf with the sheet of carbon paper. (Be sure the ink side of the carbon paper is touching the leaf.)

Before you go on, make sure you have put the materials in this order:

Iron
Carbon paper
Ink side   [illustrated]
Leaf
Newspaper

5. Now take the iron and press the carbon paper. The ink on the paper should be ironed (melted) onto the leaf. (Keep ironing until the leaf is covered with ink.)
6. Set the iron aside — out of the way. Leave it plugged in. You will need it later.
7. Take the carbon paper off the leaf and throw it away.
8. Now let's use the leaf to make some designs.
9. Move the leaf to one side. Put a piece of blank paper on top of the newspaper.
10. Set the leaf on the clean paper, ink side down.
11. Lay a piece of newspaper over the leaf.

Before you go on, make sure you have put the materials in this order:

Iron
Newspaper
Plain paper   [illustrated]
Leaf
Ink side down
Newspaper

12. Take the iron and press over the leaf. Press for 30 seconds.
13. Remove the newspaper and the leaf. Look at the design the leaf made.
14. If you like, you can move the leaf around on the paper. Repeat steps 10, 11, and 12. Make more leaf prints and new designs.
15. When you have finished printing, unplug the iron, let it cool, and put it away.

Clean up your work area.

You may use this print to decorate your home or give it to a friend.

Post-activity

Focus: By using knowledge of the methods of science and everyday materials, crafts can be a good way to spend your leisure time.

You have learned that by using what you know of the way scientists work, you can "turn" some things you might see every day into craft materials. In this activity you used a leaf you got from your teacher. There are many different kinds of leaves in your environment. Any of these could also be used to make a print. By choosing different leaves with different shapes, you can make lots of different designs.

If you know what things to look for, and how to use the methods of science to change them, crafts can be an enjoyable way to spend your leisure time.

CHECKLIST

_____ 1. Clean up your area.
_____ 2. Put your materials away.
_____ 3. Hand in worksheets to your teacher.

---

4. *Transfer of learning from one situation to another is sometimes difficult for handicapped students.* Learning activities should be tied to real-life situations as closely as possible. Relevance is established if students find the information useful. For example, in studying anatomy, hygiene, disease prevention, or other life science topics, students are more interested and receptive to activities if the information can be used in everyday situations.

5. *Social skills may be developmentally behind chronological age.* Group activities provide opportunities for students to interact successfully with peers. These activities should allow each student to participate as a

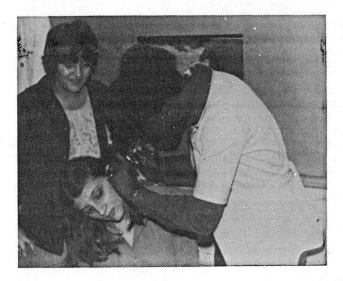

team member, but the success of any activity should not be tied to any particular set of social skills.

Development of small motor skills can be enhanced through science activities. Opportunities for hands-on experiences should be made available whenever possible.

From this, one can see that a variety of strategies may be called upon in adapting materials for handicapped students. Teachers may find that in giving consideration to materials for students mainstreamed into regular classrooms, regular students also benefit from the measures taken to promote student success. Once materials have been adapted for student use, teachers must evaluate the success of the materials and the context in which they are

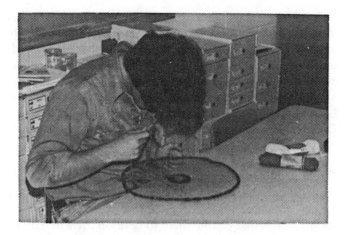

being used. The following suggestions summarize considerations for teachers as they adapt science materials for special students.

- Check the relevancy of the content for the target population you are going to serve. Does it meet the present and future needs of this target population, and are the goals established in concert with the teacher, the student, and the parent?
- Understand the basic underlying assumptions of the target population. What disabilities are present, and what disabilities are imagined? If your experience with the target population is so limited that you cannot separate what you perceive as a potential disability from what disabilities really exist, ask for assistance. Talk to the special education director of your district, the resource room teacher, or your principal and gain their help so you will be able to determine what assumptions are essential regarding the student's ability to perform in the classroom setting. Evaluate the resources available for making the proper adaptations. Remember that re-inventing the wheel is not necessary. Programs that have previously been developed may have much to offer as a basis for adaptation. These may be free of charge to you or obtained inexpensively.
- Use as many people resources as are available to you. They could include the resource room teacher, other science teachers, parents, peer tutors, and local associations for the advancement of handicapped individuals or for provision of science information to the citizenry at large.
- Build your system so that feedback on the effectiveness of your adaptations can be measured and appropraite modifications accomplished. To do everything correctly the first time is difficult, and beginning efforts to meet the needs of the handicapped should be

undertaken with an eye toward continued improvement of the program. For this improvement to be significant, it has to be based on the failures as well as the successes of previously tried methods.

● Keep in mind that handicapped individuals can learn and that they are quite capable of benefiting from an instructional program, especially if that instructional program is broadly designed to meet the needs of all children regardless of handicapping condition (Callahan, 1980).

SUMMARY

The contribution that science education can make to the total education of handicapped students should not go unrecognized. All students have the right to opportunities that enable them to develop their potentials as much as possible. "Teachers who have been reluctant in the past to try science activities because of the potential disruptive behaviors may feel the activity approach is nearly impossible today with handicapped children in the classroom. It is imperative for science educators to band together to encourage teachers not only to maintain the level of activities in their present science program but to increase the level and variety of activities" (Piper, 1980). Unique experiences in science activities offer students the chance to develop a sense of control over their own destiny. The opportunities in science education merit the attention of educators as they strive to provide appropriate educational plans for all students.

REFERENCES

Biological Sciences Curriculum Study. Science and homes and furnishings. In *Me in the future.* Boulder, CO: Author, 1980. (a)

Biological Sciences Curriculum Study. Science and crafts. In *Me in the future.* Boulder, CO: Author, 1980. (b)

Bishop, J. L., & Callahan, W. P. Using *Me in the Future* with regular students in the mainstream science classes. *BSCS Journal*, Nov. 1979, *2*(4).

Callahan, W. P. Personal interview, University of Northern Iowa, Cedar Falls, 1980.

Keller, W. D. *Objective cluster bank index: Science* (Vol. 6). In E. L. Meyen, *Instructional based appraisal system.* Bellevue, WA: Edmark Associates, 1979.

Piper, M. K. A science activity teaching plan. *School Science & Mathematics*, 1980, *80*.

Keller puts forth a convincing argument that outdoor education can be used to teach most subjects to most types of children of most ages. Outdoor education, whether in urban or rural locations, has many unique advantages. It is almost always self-motivating, and it helps students learn group values.

This article projects the types of equipment needed, makes organizational suggestions, gives scheduling ideas, and in general outlines what is necessary to start and operate such a program. Several examples of active outdoor education programs are presented. The reader will become aware of how outdoor education can be used to teach almost everything from science to art.

Outdoor Education
For the Handicapped

W. Diane Keller

Providing outdoor experiences for the handicapped is not a new idea. Handicapped people have had many opportunities to participate in camp activities like swimming, fishing, and nature walks. Outdoor experiences, though, are not the same as outdoor education. Although both occur in an outdoor setting, they are not synonymous. Outdoor education differs in that *it is designed to use the outdoors to give students unique, educational experiences.*

This article is about outdoor education, and "outdoor" as used here means outside the classroom, encompassing activities in both urban and wilderness environments. Outdoor education makes available to students the most favorable environment in which the concepts they are studying can be learned. The experiences are hands-on and "real"; the stimuli for learning come from the environment. This may be in contrast to the classroom, where experiences often have to be contrived to stimulate the actual environment.

Situations in which concepts may be best taught outdoors cross all curricula. Studies may include the interrelationships among organisms in a particular environment (science); local pioneer history (social studies);

measurement used in determining volume, area, or weight (mathematics); or geometric design (art).

Outdoor education is still in its infancy as a part of the regular curriculum of today's schools. Attempts to define it often seem vague and confusing because the definitions vary with the educators and schools using it. Outdoor education is defined here as *the teaching of those things in the outdoors that can best be taught in that setting.* For this article, outdoor education will encompass the following ideas:

- The activities occur outside the classroom.
- Students experience the activities "first hand."
- The environment is the teacher.
- The total educational experience may include pre- and post-activities that may or may not occur in the regular classroom.

This article discusses:

1) what outdoor education offers handicapped students;
2) what outdoor education offers teachers of handicapped students;
3) possible outdoor education programs for the handicapped;
4) suggestions for beginning a local outdoor education program.

BENEFITS FOR HANDICAPPED STUDENTS

Outdoor education offers many opportunities for handicapped students. First, *outdoor education can give students an opportunity to understand and learn from a natural environment.* Handicapped students often have difficulty generalizing classroom information to specific situations. Providing a learning experience in the outdoors where it normally happens allows students to learn from a "real" situation that requires no generalization or application to a specific situation because the situation presents itself directly to the student. For example, students studying designs used in modern architecture can go into the urban environment, observe the structures, and see how the designs fit into the settings. This is in contrast to classroom discussion of the buildings. When students observe or participate in the actual event, generalization is not necessary. The learning is direct.

Second, *students can experience the relationship between self and the environment.* Outdoor education activities enhance a sense of awareness and dependency upon the environment. Allowing students to experience this interaction between people and environment can teach in clear, simple terms. Students who are camping learn they get cold or uncomfortable if they do not prepare bedding properly. Thus, they learn responsibility. In nature classes students can observe and learn about animal behavior directly rather than have it described to them. As they let the environment teach, they can learn through a multiple of stimuli. Students can actually move into the physical environment of an animal like a frog. The smell of the watery surroundings, the temperature of the water, the texture of the sandy or muddy bottom, and the other animals and plants all act on students' senses to let them know about the frog and its habitat.

Students in urban settings can also experience the environment through the various senses, and can learn through direct contact. The harshness and stress of a busy city street can be experienced through smell, sight, hearing, and touch. Students involved in map studies can understand them better when actually figuring out and traveling bus routes rather than simulating the experience within the classroom. Although the examples are quite different, in each case the environment is the teacher. The student has the opportunity for direct environmental contact and is allowed to learn from the experiences contained within the particular surroundings.

Third, *outdoor education can remove negative classroom stimuli, replacing these with multiple stimuli conducive to learning.* Many factors limit the success of students within the classroom. Handicapped students in particular may have a low expectancy for class success. They might have found that their environment demands responses that they cannot give. Being involved in a new, outdoor setting can sometimes remove the negative stimuli and allow the student to learn without the barrier of low self-expectancy.

Often, students learn information outdoors when the same information presented inside a classroom seems vague and difficult to understand. For example, inner-city children sometimes have problems understanding information about plants and animals when it is presented in the classroom, whereas taking them into the outdoors makes the information observable, relevant, interesting, and easy to understand because it allows them to experience and know information rather than be told about it. And any degree of learning helps reduce the expectancy to fail — a positive cycle.

Students who have difficulty behaving satisfactorily in the classroom benefit especially from the removal of classroom stimuli. This may be most important with students who find the classroom physically restrictive. In the outdoors they have more room to move about, more space to work off excess energy. They can exhibit appropriate social behavior and at the same time learn content and group sharing skills. The author has found being outdoors of particular benefit when working with inner-city, junior-high students. Verbal and physical movement had to be contained while in the classroom; the outdoors allowed more room for responses to be made in a variety of acceptable ways.

A further advantage to removing classroom stimuli is that the outdoor setting offers a multiple of stimuli, and each student has a chance to learn via various stimuli. This may be important for a child who cannot read but who can understand auditory or visual signals. Each person in the outdoors is allowed the chance to succeed in a nonacademic setting. While certain factors, like reading ability, may be limiting in the classroom, these factors may not be so limiting in the outdoors, where individuals often find that in utilizing any of many stimuli, they can perform as well as other people.

Fourth, *outdoor education strengthens social skills.* Many handicapped students lack social skills. Outdoor education experiences can be organized to make mutual dependence necessary for tasks to be performed. If *all* students in a group lack the total skills needed for success, the handicapping conditions can be less limiting, because all students are needed to contribute to the welfare of the group. Relays, housekeeping, and team sports are examples of situations in which all students must contribute to achieve group success. Being needed and part of a group gives students positive feedback as they participate successfully in social activities.

Fifth, *outdoor education enhances self-reliance and self-identity.* The environment makes demands and elicits actions. If the proper action is not taken, the behaviors meet with negative reinforcement. If the proper action is taken, positive reinforcement ensues. For example, if insect repellent is not used, the individual incurs insect bites — negative reinforcement. In the outdoors students recognize and experience challenges of varying degrees. They learn to solve problems. As they meet challenges and overcome obstacles, they develop a sense of self-reliance. Self-identity and self-esteem rise accordingly. Being outdoors provides numerous situations for coming together and solving problems. In this setting, too, situations can be manipulated to emphasize what can be done rather than what cannot be done. This allows greater opportunities for developing self-reliance.

Students who have never been outdoors overnight or alone for a time in the woods learn self-reliance in an outdoor setting. Urban children in particular achieve a sense of accomplishment and increased self-esteem from coping with and solving problems in wilderness settings. Individuals who may not perceive themselves as being able to enjoy outdoor athletic activities achieve self-esteem and self-reliance as they learn to function successfully outdoors. Hiking, skiing, sledding, and preparing meals are examples of activities that lead to increased self-esteem and the ability to depend on oneself.

Sixth, *content and problem solving can be successfuly learned in the outdoors.* The environment constantly presents problems that must be solved. The problems cannot be ignored, because they do not go away. Food getting, shelter, and getting from one place to another all present challenges. Both individual and group skills can be used in finding solutions.

Individuals can decide which skills to use and in doing so decide what is best for them. Regardless of the method chosen, they must solve the problem, because the environment leaves no room for camouflage. The environment does not go away or lessen its demands. Human participants have to develop creative skills in formulating solutions and solving problems.

Seventh, *outdoor education offers recreation to students.* It promotes students' physical and emotional health. The recreation aspect makes learning fun. It contributes to students' growth by providing positive reinforcement. It nurtures a healthy approach to the world.

BENEFITS FOR TEACHERS

Outdoor education also presents advantages for teachers. First, *it provides a setting that aids individualization.* By its very nature, the outdoor experience is individualized. The environment acts on each student in a different way, so the individual learning experiences are unique. Different problems present themselves to each student; and different solutions are found for common situations by different students. Since each situation offers personalized learning possibilities, students can attack problems in their own manner and at their own speed. Thus, rather than having to spend time devising a situation for each student, the teacher is free to facilitate each students' efforts to solve problems.

Second, *barriers between authorities and students are more easily overcome in the outdoors.* Outdoor education helps teachers transcend these "walls" that exist between students and authority figures. It promotes rapport between students and teachers. This happens initially because most handicapped students are relatively unfamiliar with the outdoors. They feel afraid or unsure of success in this new setting. As a result of their discomfort, they look to the teacher for assurance and support. The teacher becomes an ally in solving problems. The teacher is no longer the enforcer of learning, because the environment has this role. The teacher is free to respond to students as a *facilitator* of their success in the outdoors.

If sleeping quarters are not properly prepared, discomfort results. If a meal is not made, there is no food. If the distance to a destination is improperly calculated, the trip may prove unduly long and tiring. The setting often gives negative feedback, and the teacher is needed as a helper and friend in solving problems. Thus, the image of a teacher as an authoritarian figure is reduced, and negative stimuli can be broken down.

Third, *outdoor education tends to stimulate student interest and make students want to learn.* In the outdoors most students are eager to learn. Many times they are willing to learn the same information outdoors that they have resisted inside the classroom. Outdoors, much information is seen as relevant and interesting. Also, the feedback is immediate.

Knowledge of muscles and conditioning is helpful when hiking several miles. Knowledge of edible plants is important when planning a meal that must be gathered from the land. Information about measurement and map reading is needed to figure distance. Geometric shapes take on importance when constructing a building. Students more readily learn information that is needed and immediately useful. The teacher does not have to provide the motivation, because it is inherent in the outdoor experience.

Fourth, *outdoor education lends itself to student innovation and creativity.* In the outdoors students recognize problems, ask questions, and formulate solutions. They are able to try out many possible solutions in a less restricted setting than the classroom. The outdoors offers more space for movement, more tolerance for noise, and more acceptance of possible error. Student interactions do not have as many limitations as in the classroom. They are free to try various solutions, many of which would be too large, too loud, or otherwise impossible in the classroom. The outdoor setting relieves the teacher from these classroom dilemmas.

As a qualifying note — even though outdoor education has much to offer educators, it is not a replacement for textbook learning. It is, instead, a practical application of what can be learned from books. It can be an effective means of reinforcing what has already or will be presented in the classroom.

EXAMPLES OF OUTDOOR EDUCATION PROGRAMS

Programs may be used with children having a variety of handicapping conditions. The individual programs may vary with the type of individuals served, but certain major outcomes should be expected from each program:

- The individual comes to experience a unity with nature.
- The individual comes to value himself or herself and others as they interact.
- The individual discovers the value of group action.
- The individual learns new skills in caring for his or her own needs.
- The individual learns the satisfaction of solving problems physically.

The total outdoor education experience should include pre- and post-activities that may occur indoors as well as outdoors. Greater interest and understanding of the total experience should result.

Walden-In-The-Woods

The state of New York is one area where leadership has been shown in the field of outdoor education. State funds have been allocated to support programs. Educational experiences in both manmade and natural environments outside of the classroom have been encouraged.

Walden-In-The-Woods is a program that has been successful with learning disabled students. It is a full-time outdoor education program located at the Madden Outdoor Education Center in Kent, New York, serving local school districts with a variety of courses including forest ecology, geology, and aquatic life. Students at Walden-In-The-Woods have experienced failure in the regular classroom. Participants of the program are boys who meet the following criteria:

- The student is able to function in the program without special support services that could not be provided in an outdoor setting.
- The student wants to participate in the program.
- The student is able to participate without endangering the safety of himself or others.
- The student is 11-15 years of age.

The goals and success of this program have been described by Christenson (1977):

> The goal is to provide them [students] with a program in which they will meet with multiple successes in the academic, social, emotional, and vocational areas. Outdoor education is an alternative vehicle we use in order to accomplish this. Past experience demonstrated to us that this program works and is highly successful for some students. To us, it is the right program at the right time for these particular students.
>
> Our outdoor program meets the special needs of most of our students more fully than do the existing school programs in the district for the middle and junior high school age learning disability student, and, therefore, it may be a viable alternative for others to consider.

Emily Griffith Boys' Home Program

Another outdoor education program, which has been successful with emotionally handicapped boys, is provided by the Emily Griffith Boys' Home at Denver, Colorado. The program lasts approximately nine months, full-time, and utilizes outdoor experiences in assisting boys from 13 to 17 years old to learn to function successfully so they later can return to regular school or everyday activities. Outdoor education activities are a major part of the school curriculum because they remove students from the alienated regular school setting, raise students' self-concept, increase their interest in school, and promote better staff-student relations. The activities include situations of relatively low stress such as grassland outdoor experiences, to somewhat higher stress situations including a Colorado mining town simulation.

In a three-week outdoor study of ancient Indian culture in the Arizona desert, students receive opportunities to reflect on ancient and modern culture and learn skills about surviving successfully in their own world at the same time.

Students learn to be responsible for themselves, that they are responsible for much of what happens to them. A high stress winter survival experience is one of the culminating experiences of the curriculum. Backpacking and outdoor living are also part of the experience, along with many other outdoor activities.

Students in the Emily Griffith program learn to solve problems under stress situations of gradually increasing difficulty. Each of the situations illustrated provides challenges in the outdoors that must be met by the students. The teaching staff views these experiences as an integral part of the

Each of the activities presents problems that must be solved by the students — some individually and some in groups.

The experiences sometimes build in the necessity of teamwork for success.

The program also allows for reflection upon what the experiences mean and to allow the students to incorporate this learning into their own lives.

educational process. Toward the end of the second semester, the students must demonstrate that they have successfully learned how to function in an acceptable manner in society. They must show that they have learned to assume responsibility for their own actions and have acquired the ability to determine their own direction.

Outdoor education experiences play an important role in helping students acquire the skills that will enable them to return to the regular world. Gains that have been attributed to the outdoor education program include increased responsibility for self, increased reading and comprehension skills — and, even, better penmanship skills (Christenson, 1979).

Breckenridge Outdoor Education Center

School districts that are not able to provide the necessary facilities for the outdoor education programs they would like sometimes contract with

Ski touring is available for the visually handicapped in the winter.

private institutions for such services for their handicapped students. The Breckenridge Outdoor Education Center (BOEC) in Breckenridge, Colorado, is a private institution that has been successful in working with mentally retarded and with physically handicapped students. BOEC offers a variety of courses planned for all seasons. Some of these are skiing, skating, and camping in winter; and horseback riding, swimming, and canoeing in milder seasons. Although school districts may contract with BOEC for outdoor activities, other handicapped persons of all ages also participate in some of the courses. This offers a good opportunity for increased interaction among participants.

BOEC uses wilderness experiences as an educational vehicle whereby people learn about themselves. The experiences help reduce social and physical isolation, and they enhance participants' independence and increased self-concept.

Programs like those of the Emily Griffith Boys' Home and BOEC might be used by school districts that are unable to provide adequate services for reasons involving finances, appropriate staff, adequate sites, or housing. Districts might also choose such programs to enhance interaction among various age groups.

Specially developed trails are used for ski touring. Deep paths are made so that direction can be determined easily.

Another winter activity, pulk skiing, is available for mobility restricted persons. A pulk is an orthopedically designed Norwegian sled.

Trained staff is available for working with individuals of varying age ranges and of various handicapping conditions.

SUGGESTIONS FOR DEVELOPING
AN OUTDOOR EDUCATION PROGRAM

Probably the most common outdoor education program serving handicapped populations would be found in the mainstreaming situation in local school districts. As outdoor education becomes more a part of regular curricula in school districts across the United States, educators who are unable to contract with a private agency and who do not have an outdoor education program within their own school system might benefit from the following suggestions in developing programs to meet their own circumstances:

1. *Use immersion activities.* Completely involve the student in the environment to be studied. This helps remove negative barriers that handicapped students often experience in educational activities. Provide adequate time for the immersion experience to occur.

2. *Let the environment do the teaching.* In outdoor education programs, teachers often find themselves in the position of allies. As students request assistance, teachers can facilitate the learning experience while letting the environment act as the teacher.

3. *Pace the activities for the appropriate ages and handicapping conditions of the students.* This helps ensure success and positive learning experiences.

4. *Build in success.* Be sure each student has a number of positive experiences. This is beneficial in overcoming negative self-image and self-confidence problems.

5. *Consider the outdoor experiences as an integral part of the educational curriculum,* complementing the pre- and post-academic activities.

Factors that should be considered when planning an outdoor educational program include cost, salaries of personnel, food, insurance, transportation, and features of the site — its closeness to populated areas, distance from the school, accessibility, its topography, possible hazards to health, and the physical facilities.

The classroom teacher's role is essential to the success of an outdoor education program. The students should receive careful preparation prior to the outdoor experience. Planning is important to assure continuity between the classroom and the outdoor experiences. Ideas the teacher might discuss before the class goes outdoors are, in addition to the outdoor activity itself:

cooperation
using the senses effectively
how the outdoor experience relates to classroom learning
rules
individual and group responsibilities.

If possible, the classroom teacher should be personally familiar with the outdoor setting so that the pre-experiences in the classroom can better complement the outdoor activities. And attention should be given to the possibility of interdisciplinary studies that could include social studies, language arts, science, mathematics, physical education, home economics, industrial arts, art, drama, music. The teacher should always be aware of the potential for utilizing activities for multiple purposes. After the students return to the classroom, they should receive sufficient additional experiences to complement the outdoor activity and for reflection on the total experience.

To assist in planning and implementing an outdoor education program, national organizations and resource people within the community can be of assistance. Possible sources for aid include:

American Camping Association (Bradford Woods, Martinsville, IN 46151)
Boy Scouts of America (2 Park Avenue, New York, NY 10016)
Bureau of Outdoor Recreation (Department of the Interior, Washington, DC 20025)
American Red Cross
Local chapter of the March of Dimes
County Health Department
Parks and Recreation Department (City or County)
YMCA; YWCA
Civic organizations
and parents.

Suggested Outdoor Activities

An outdoor education program could encompass a variety of activities that are compatible with the indoor academic program. General topics might include:

Social Studies — ancient culture of the area; local industries like logging, mining, or agriculture; local history; local customs; geography of the area.

Science — natural history of the area; weather; geology; astronomy; archaeology.

Mathematics — maps; measurement (volume, distance, weight); using a compass; geometric shapes; basic mathematical skills (addition, subtraction, multiplication, fractions).

Language Arts — poetry; composition; logs or journals; story telling; ballads and local folk tales.

Physical Education — hiking; survival skills; first aid; outdoor safety; good body conditioning; outdoor sports.

Homemaking — cooking and meal planning; choosing proper clothing for outdoor conditions; caring for clothing when outdoors; cleaning cooking utensils properly; housekeeping in living quarters.

Industrial Arts — using tools in the outdoors properly; taking care of tools; safety; strength of materials; durability of materials.

Drama, Art, Music — plays and skits; singing; painting and sketching; using natural materials for crafts; assuming the role of pioneers for a day.

Activities should be geared to the age and the handicapping condition(s) of participants. If the outdoor education program is to continue throughout the entire school career of the student, common themes can be introduced and built upon in accordance with the various grade levels. For example, "environmental interactions" might be a theme throughout the total program: Kindergarten or early elementary children might participate in activities that principally make them aware of the environment. Late elementary or junior high students might examine and analyze the various parts of the environmental system. High school students might concentrate on what is happening, how humanity influences that interaction, and how it affects them individually. The basic theme is constant throughout the entire program, but is more fully developed as the child progresses in grade level and ability.

Elementary Grade Activities

Suggested activities for students in the elementary grades can focus on the following (interdisciplinary topics should be used when possible):

Social Studies — pioneer tools and customs; Indian homes and customs; simple maps; local business (e.g., agriculture, mining); local almanac tales.

Science — senses (listening, feeling, smelling); identifying birds as to color, shape, size, sound, nesting habits, how they fly, etc.; types of soil; animal homes and tracks; various kinds of seeds.

Mathematics — counting legs on a spider, petals in a flower, needles in a pine cluster, points on a leaf; shapes.

Language Arts — telling local legends; acting out animal behavior (e.g., fox, frog); pretending to be a tree; reciting a short poem; describing a living thing observed in nature.

Physical Education — walking a log; taking a walk along a nature trail; jumping over stacked logs; playing volleyball; running in a relay.

Homemaking — setting a table; replacing utensils after they are clean; observing various types of foods prepared; trying one edible wild food (teacher assistance needed); making a bed.

Industrial Arts — observing pioneer tools, Indian tools, modern, local tools; making a tool from a twig or stone; cleaning and putting away a tool properly.

Drama, Art, Music — acting like a pioneer for two hours; drawing or sketching something from nature; singing songs; observing shapes or sounds in nature; making a collage.

Junior High Activities

Following are some examples of subjects and activities suitable for students in late elementary or junior high school:

Social Studies — visiting an old cemetery; acting as a pioneer one day; Indian lore and customs; local topography; historical land use of the area.

Science — local plants and animals; aquatic studies; night hikes to study nocturnal animals; plant and animal communities; population counts of local plants and animals.

Mathematics — measuring diameter and circumference of trees, depth of local water, size of buildings, distance between two objects (e.g., a lake and the sleeping area); calculating the amount of water needed for the evening meal.

Language Arts — writing a short story about something observed; writing a poem; keeping a journal; telling about a local custom or about someone who once lived in the area (could be fictitious).

Physical Education — relay race; volleyball; morning hike; swimming; a long hike with the group.

Homemaking — meal planning; local edible vegetables; foods grown by local people; housekeeping chores (sleeping area, kitchen area); estimating food needed for group for one meal.

Industrial Arts — fashioning an Indian tool; using only pioneer tools for one day; learning safety rules using pioneer tools; building a small bridge of stones or logs.

Drama, Art, Music — singing; collage of natural materials; painting with natural dyes; skit; sounds and shapes in nature.

High School Activities

High school students might benefit from the following:

Social Studies — visiting local law enforcement agencies; examining various different buildings with unique histories or features; comparing food prices in two stores; studying building shapes.

Science — wilderness trip; astronomy facilities; wild life of the area (compared with home environment); constructing an imaginary animal home; observing how humans have affected and changed the environment.

Mathematics — using a compass and following a trail; using a map to follow a trail; estimating then measuring the length of 10 different items; estimating and measuring the weight of trash from one meal; a geometric treasure hunt.

Language Arts — keeping a journal; writing a short story about something observed; writing a poem; making a list of everything seen alive in nature within 30 minutes; writing a letter home during a several-day camp experience.

Physical Education — wilderness trip; relay scavenger hunt; pitching a tent; building a campfire; following a cross country trail.

Homemaking — preparing one meal as a team; cleaning the eating area after a meal; participating in cleaning up the sleeping area; making an eating utensil from a natural object.

Industrial Arts — demonstrating knowledge of safety with tools; making a meal or tool using materials available to Indians; examining or discussing use of blacksmith in the area; observing and using modern tools for gathering water or needed chores.

Drama, Art, Music — participating in a play about the activities for the parents (post-activity); making a craft gift; singing; painting using native materials; sketching natural shapes and designs.

Schedules, Equipment, and Preparation

Because most school districts that presently have outdoor education programs focus on a one-week concentrated outdoor event, this is the model used for the following examples of schedule, equipment, and checklist.

Another model that should be seriously considered by schools is the integration of outdoor activities into the regular curriculum throughout the school year. With this model students receive intermittent, continuing reinforcement for learning, and the outdoor experiences are tied in closely with academic studies in the classroom.

Outdoor education schedules must be carefully planned to allow adequate time for the planned group activities, as well as for time alone. Large groups should be divided into smaller groups to facilitate personal interaction. Individual group schedules may have to be staggered to ensure the opportunity for each individual to participate in all of the activities. A format for a possible several-day outdoor experience in wilderness surroundings is given as Figure 1.

Following is a suggested equipment list to give each student before a several-day camp experience, such as the one given in Figure 1.

Bedding
   sleeping bag or
   a couple of blankets

Clothing
   jeans (two or three pairs, old)
   heavy and light shirts
   two pairs of shoes suitable for
      the outdoor climate
   hat or cap
   daily change of socks
      and underwear
   warm jacket or sweater
   raincoat
   pajamas
   gloves and scarf
      (if cold weather)

General
   flashlight
   notebook and pencil

Toilet Articles
   toothbrush and toothpaste
   soap
   towel and washcloth
   lip balm
   sunscreen
   comb
   toilet paper
   deodorant
Optional
   bird or animal books
   camera
   compass
   binoculars

Do not bring:
   radio
   money
   knives
   matches

Teachers should prepare their own equipment list to include any special supplies such as props and/or costumes for skits, art supplies, identification keys, measuring instruments, microscope, athletic equipment — any equipment and material needed for the planned activities. Teachers might also take extra bedding or clothing to cover possible lacks in the students' provisions.

	MONDAY	TUESDAY	WEDNESDAY	THURSDAY	FRIDAY	SATURDAY
7:30 a.m.	Elementary: Rise and prepare for breakfast / Jr. High & High School: Rise and prepare breakfast					
8:00	Elementary: Breakfast / Jr. High & High School: Breakfast and Clean-up					
8:30			: Shapes in Nature / : Make Natural Dyes / : Aquatic Life (microscopes)	: Water Life / : Edible Plants / : Poetry/Story Writing	: Forest Life / : Measure Trees / : Pioneer Life For a Day	Prepare / to / Leave
10:00	Free Time and Snacks					
10:30		: Elem.: Plant Homes / : Jr. High: Map Making / : H.S.:"Camouflage" Simulation Activity	: Nature Rubbings / : Indian History / : Immersion Activity —"Be" a Frog or Aquatic Animal	: Immersion Activity —"Be" a Water Animal / : Make a Pioneer or Indian Meal / : Crafts/Dyes/ Textures	: Measure Tree Sizes / : Aquatic Study / : Make and Use a Pioneer Tool	Leave / for / Home
12:00	Elem.: Lunch and Nap / Jr. High: Lunch and Free Time / High School: Lunch Preparation and Clean-up					
1:00 p.m.	Orientation + / Elem.: "Sounds" Walk / Jr. High: Nature Walk / H.S.: Nature Walk	: Count Kinds of Plants / : Visit Local Cemetery / : Designs in Nature	: Count Petals in Flowers / : Study Indian Tools and Food / : Build a Simple Rock or Log Bridge	: Edible Plants / : Orienteering / : Geometric Shapes	: Leaf Prints / : Crafts / : Pioneer Games	
2:00	Free Time and Snacks					
3:00	Elem.: Collage of Natural Things / Jr. High: Habitat Study / H.S.: Habitats & How Humans Alter Them	: Natural History of Area / : Pioneer Study / : Manmade Alterations in Local Geography	: Nature Stories / : Indian Artifacts (archaeology) / : Physical Education Activities	: Textures in Nature / : Social Service Project / : Population Study	: Pioneer Life / : Craft Fair / : Write a Pioneer Skit	
5:00	Help Prepare Dinner, Eat, and Clean Up					
7:00	Elem.: Songs / Jr. High: Scavenger Hunt / H.S.: Treasure Hunt	: Star Gazing / : Pioneer Games & Square Dance / : Songs	: Folk Dancing / : Indian Games / : Story Telling	: Indian Games / : Astronomy (telescope) / : Square Dancing	: Pioneer Games / : Campfire Songs / : Skit	
8:00 / 8:30 / 9:00	Elem.: Prepare for Bed / Jr. High: Prepare for Bed / H.S.: Prepare for Bed					

Adjustments can be made in the time allotted for food preparation, eating, and clean up, depending upon the age group and handicapping conditions.

FIGURE 1
Format Example for Outdoor Experience

Following is a teacher checklist that should be consulted before leaving the school:

Permission Slips	Each student should have turned in a signed parental permission slip before leaving for the outdoor trip. The information should include physician's name and phone number, special medication, allergies, or specific medical problems, and a phone number for emergencies.
Equipment	In addition to equipment needed for the planned activities, extra recreational equipment might be included for volleyball, softball, badminton, and similar sports.
First-aid Kit	A well supplied first-aid kit is essential. Extra sunscreen, lotion, insect repellent, lip balm, and similar items could also be part of the kit.
Special Medication	Any special medicines for students should be labeled and packed carefully, and accompanied by appropriate instructions.

Other items should be added to this list to fit the individual programs.

After the outdoor education activities have been completed and the students have returned to the classroom, the teacher should provide adequate follow-up activities. Without proper reinforcement, the value of the outdoor experience may be lost. This is especially true if the home or community environment does not provide reinforcement for behavior changes that took place during the outdoor experience.

Urban Outdoor Education

Although the examples given here for outdoor activities have centered on wilderness or nature type experiences, these are not the only, or necessarily the most effective, types of outdoor activities. Urban areas offer many opportunities for outdoor education, including interdisciplinary studies. A few possible topics are:

structural design
urban pollution
   (air, noise, water)
urban land use
effect of urban living
   on people

law enforcement/
   the legal system
museums
multi-cultural experiences

Evaluation

Evaluation is an important part of an outdoor education program. It provides feedback about the value of the curriculum, strengths and weaknesses of the program, and its effects on the students. Evaluative techniques might include surveys, anecdotal records, sociograms, interviews, comparison of pre- and post-academic and behavioral achievements.

SUMMARY STATEMENT

The contribution that outdoor education can make to education is currently being recognized by many educators. All students have the right to opportunities that enable them to develop their potentials as much as possible. The possibilities that outdoor education offer to handicapped students should not be overlooked as educators strive to plan more effective educational designs.

REFERENCES

D. Christenson. Personal interview, Emily Griffith Boys' Home, Denver, 1979.

G. Christenson. Walden-in-the-Woods. *Communicator* (Journal of the New York State Outdoor Education Association), Fall-Winter, 1977.

Werber, B. Personal interview, Breckenridge Outdoor Education Center, 1979.

Brolin reviews the progress of American schools toward including career education as a major part of the curriculum. He cites references indicating that special education is short of the mark in career education. He then proposes the Life-Centered Career Education (LCCE) Model, which is a competency based approach. Career education is distinguished from traditional education and differentiated from vocational education, which is more occupation oriented.

The LCCE model is the career education program that probably has the broadest adoption rate in the U.S. It emphasizes the acquisition of 22 major competencies under three major categories: (1) daily living, (2) personal-social, and (3) occupational skills. The 22 major competencies make up a comprehensive program, which is spelled out in enough detail for readers to determine if they want to explore this curriculum further.

Life-Centered Career Education For Exceptional Children

Donn E. Brolin

Approximately 10 years have elapsed since career education entered the national scene (Marland, 1971). Introduced as a major educational reform, it has gradually gained momentum. School systems throughout the country have adopted it in their programs. The basic tenets of and the need for career education have become increasingly more apparent to educators and others concerned about educational services to students. Creation of a U.S. Office of Career Education in 1974 gave the necessary impetus to the movement, and under the able leadership of its first and present director, Kenneth B. Hoyt, at least some facet of career education has become an integral part of curricula in the majority of American schools.

In the case of exceptional children, career education has sustained an even more pronounced effort. Backed by endorsement from the national special education teacher organization, the Council for Exceptional Children (CEC), special educators and those concerned about their students' career development have responded to the need to redirect curricula so that it is more relevant and practical to community living and working needs required in the real world. Extensive overviews on career education for exceptional individuals have been written by Brolin and Kokaska (1979), C. Johnson (1979), and Kolstoe (1981). Recent examples of effective career education practices have been set forth by D. Johnson (1979), Evenson and Spotts (1980), Gillet (1980), Borba and Guzicki (1980), Lamkin (1980), Ellington (1981), Brolin (1982), and others.

Many national and state conferences on career education for exceptional children have been conducted during the past several years. Curriculum materials, inservice models, and special mini-grants from special education and career education departments at the state level have assisted educators in implementing career education concepts. A new CEC division, the Division on Career Development (DCD), was organized in 1976 and is growing in stature and significance by providing leadership to the field. In the past three years 10 states have organized their own DCD units so that career education will become a substantial force in services to exceptional students at the grass roots level. Many other states are close to becoming official units at the time of this writing.

Despite general acceptance of the career education concept and need, exceptional students still are not receiving the amount and type of career education that will result in their successful community adjustment as adults. Heller (1981, p. 582) identified the following deficiencies as presently existing in programming for exceptional students at the secondary level: (a) school organization being too much along departmental and subject matter lines, (b) orientation of training programs toward the younger handicapped child, (c) too heavy an emphasis placed on vocational programs by special educators without any alternatives or future planning, and (d) the attitude of special educators and others that exceptional individuals don't require much attention at the secondary level. And, Sitlington (1981, p. 596) noted that ". . . vocational education programs: (a) usually do not begin until 11th grade, which is often too late for the handicapped student, (b) by definition are concerned primarily with specific skill training, with little emphasis on career awareness and exploration, and (c) have in-class components that are often too difficult for the handicapped learner." In addition, 13 advocacy groups calling themselves the Education Advocates Coalition has cast doubts on progress of the Education for All Handicapped Children's Act of 1975 (PL 94-142), calling the response to its mandate a "national disgrace" (*Guidepost*, 1980).

Career eduation offers an organized K-12+ approach to correcting the deficiencies presently inherent in curricula for exceptional (and other) students. As Kolstoe (1981) noted, "Career education offers a service delivery that has great potential for the 1980s" (p. 11).

Several models that have emerged in special education deserve attention by educators interested in the career education approach: (a) Clark's (1979) School-Based Career Education Model, (b) Larson's (1981) adaptation of the Experience-Based Career Education Model (EBCE), and (c) the work of this writer and his colleagues in developing the Life-Centered Career Education (LCCE) Model during the decade of the 1970s. Actually, the three models can be nicely integrated by school personnel who desire an even more comprehensive approach to curriculum development for their students.

This article presents the Life-Centered Career Education (LCCE) Model, a competency-based approach. Readers interested in the Clark and Larson models are encouraged to contact these individuals directly for further information about their career education concepts and methods.[1] Before presenting the LCCE Model, a brief review of career education is given so that readers unfamiliar with its basic tenets will be better able to understand the total concept.

THE CAREER EDUCATION CONCEPT

At the Helen Keller Centennial Conference in 1980, Kenneth Hoyt noted that "... the career education concept, formally begun in 1971, has survived for a full decade — three times as long as the typical educational reform movement. During this period of time, it has developed and specified its basic goals and demonstrated its ability to deliver career education to the general population of K-12 youth. It is a concept that holds great implications for persons with visual handicaps — both youth *and* adults" (Hoyt, 1980, p. 8). At that conference, he described *career education* as:

> ... making *work* a personally meaningful and productive part of the total lifestyle of all persons ... that *work*, as used in career education, is defined as "conscious effort, other than that aimed primarily at coping or relaxation, to produce benefits for oneself and/or for oneself and others." Furthermore, the word "Career," as used in career education, is defined as "the totality of work one does in his/her lifetime." (p. 2)

Considerable confusion has existed for years about interpretation of the word "career" in career education. Many educators define the term synonymously and narrowly with "job" or "occupation," whereas others (like myself) view one's career as consisting of numerous roles, including work activities that are nonoccupational. Donald Super (1976) defined *career* as:

> ... the sequence of major positions occupied by a person throughout his preoccupational, occupational, and postoccupational life; includes work-related roles such as those of student, employee, and pensioner, together with

---

[1] Dr. Clark is with the University of Kansas, Lawrence; Dr. Larson is with Iowa Central Community College, Ft. Dodge.

complementary avocational, familial, and civic roles. Careers exist only as people pursue them; they are person-centered. (p. 20)

This definition, written for the U.S. Office of Career Education, clearly distinguishes career education from vocational education, which is primarily an occupationally-oriented program (except for the homemaking aspect). Unpaid work such as volunteer work, productive use of leisure time, the unpaid work of the fulltime homemaker, and the school work of the student are all within the realm and goals of career education.

The Council for Exceptional Children (1978) supports the broader view of career education, based on the work of its study group, by defining it in the following manner:

> *Career education* is the totality of experiences through which one learns to live a meaningful, satisfying work life . . . providing the opportunity to learn, in the least restrictive environment possible, the academic, daily living, personal-social, and occupational knowledges and skills necessary for attaining their highest levels of economic, personal and social fulfillment. This can be obtained through work (both paid and unpaid) and in a variety of other societal roles and personal life styles . . . student, citizen, volunteer, family member and participant in meaningful leisure-time activities.

Brolin and Kokaska (1979, p. 104) offered the following key concepts consistent with the above conceptualization of career education:

- It extends from early childhood through the retirement years.
- It focuses on the full development of all individuals.
- It provides the knowledge, skills, and understandings needed by individuals to master their environment.
- It emphasizes daily living, personal-social, and occupational skills development at all levels and ages.
- It encompasses the total curriculum of the school and provides a unified approach to education for life.
- It focuses on the total life roles, settings, and events and their relationships that are important in the lives of individuals, including work.
- It encourages all members of the school community to have a shared responsibility and a mutual cooperative relationship among the various disciplines.
- It includes learning in the home, private-public agencies, and the employment community, as well as the school.
- It encourages all teachers to relate their subject matter to its career implications.
- It includes basic education, citizenship, family responsibility, and other important education objectives.
- It provides for career awareness, exploration, and skills development at all levels and ages.

- It provides a balance of content and experiential learning, permitting hands-on occupational activities.
- It provides a personal framework to help individuals plan their lives, including career decision-making.
- It provides the opportunity for acquiring a saleable occupational entry-level skill upon leaving high school.
- It requires a lifelong education based on principles related to total individual development.
- It actively involves the parents in all phases of education.
- It actively involves the community in all phases of education.
- It encourages open communication between students, teachers, parents, and the community.

Career education is not intended to replace traditional education but, rather, to redirect it to be more relevant and meaningful for the student and to result in the acquisition of attitudes, knowledges, and skills one needs for successful community living and working. It is not meant to be the only education students receive, but it should be a substantial part of the curriculum.

Career education requires the integration or infusion of career education concepts into the content of various subject matter. It ". . . brings meaningfulness to the learning and practice of basic academic skills by demonstrating to the students and teachers alike the multitude of ways in which these skills are applied in work and daily living. A career education emphasis brings observable, experiential relevance to social studies, health, and science curricula, assisting students in perceiving the relationship between educational subject matter and the larger world outside the classroom" (Lamkin, 1980, p. 11). To achieve this, teachers have to find new ways of providing career relevant experiences within a career education context. Hands-on, experiential activities that facilitate the career development process so that students learn about the world in which they live and will work as adults are key ingredients in the career education curriculum approach.

As indicated by Wimmer (1981, pp. 615-616), "If one assumes that the goal of the educational program for a handicapped student is to prepare the student for independent living and social and vocational success, it would seem that instruction should be planned around a career development theme." Nevertheless, Meyen and White (1980, pp. 120-121) noted that although most educators would agree on the basic need for and the tenets of career education, its implementation in a comprehensive sense has spread somewhat slowly across the country. They identified the following factors as reasons:

- Rarely does career education exist as a specific service or separate programming option. Career education programming may indeed exist in a school district (infused into the regular curriculum or even as a few separate courses), but few districts have career education as a visible programming option.

- Career education content does not fall into a precise developmental sequence or hierarchy.
- There is no normative reference base for comparing individuals on career education concepts and skills. Continuous instructional planning requires ongoing evaluation. . . . The general absence of evaluation procedures and instruments in career education makes continuous evaluation difficult.

Meyen and White also believe that career education's short history and the lack of teacher experience in individualizing career education are additional barriers: "Teachers continue to write IEP objectives for the student in curriculum areas for which well-established curricula already exist" (p. 122). Wimmer (1981, p. 613) stated that, "The major problem seems to lie in the basic assumption of some educators that the handicapped student must either adjust to the traditional structure of the secondary school or be taught in a totally separate environment."

I agree with the above writers about the problems in implementing the career education concept and process in many school systems. Unfortunately, the easier way is often selected when deciding upon a curriculum for the year. But schools that have adopted a comprehensive career education approach have demonstrated that students are happier and more successful if they receive this type of education. As a result, most of the educators seem to be more satisfied with their efforts, too!

The remainder of this article focuses on a curriculum approach that has evolved during the 1970s with the assistance of hundreds of special educators and other school personnel who have felt the need to change their curricula to a more career education-oriented approach. The result has been a competency-based approach entitled *Life-Centered Career Education (LCCE)*. The curriculum model has been adopted by several hundred school systems throughout the country and is available from the Council for Exceptional Children (CEC) in the form of two products, *Life-Centered Career Education: A Competency-Based Approach* (Brolin, 1978) and *Trainer's Guide for Life-Centered Career Education* (Brolin, McKay, & West, 1978).

DEVELOPMENT OF THE LCCE APPROACH

Initial efforts in developing the life-centered curriculum began in 1970, with a federal grant from the U.S. Office of Education, Bureau of Education for the Handicapped (now Office of Special Education) to design a more vocationally-oriented secondary and special education teacher training program model at the University of Wisconsin-Stout. The project officer encouraging this effort was Bill Heller, presently Dean, College of Human Development and Learning, University of North Carolina at Charlotte. Dr. Heller was then, as he still is today (Heller, 1981), concerned about the lack of trained personnel to carry out vocational (and career) functions at the secondary level.

Although the primary effort of the Stout project was to identify competencies that secondary teachers of educable retarded students needed to prepare their students for adult functioning, it became necessary to also determine what kind of skills (or competencies) the students needed to acquire for success after schooling would be completed. This work continued with another BEH (OSE) project from 1974-1977 to develop a career education, competency-based curriculum and an inservice training program for school personnel for implementing the program. Entitled PROJECT PRICE (Programming Retarded In Career Education), the effort involved 12 school districts throughout the United States and over 300 school personnel. The final products were extended to other disability groups at the conclusion of the project, with the assistance of CEC.

Thus, the LCCE Model has evolved from several years of developmental work and includes the involvement of several hundred educators and many special/career education experts. Research conducted on these two projects in the 1970s (Brolin & Thomas, 1972; Brolin, 1973; and Brolin, Malever, & Matyas, 1976) has resulted in this competency-based approach to assist educators in infusing career education into curriculum.

THE LCCE CURRICULUM MODEL

The LCCE Curriculum Model promotes the students' acquisition of 22 major competencies falling into three major categories: (a) daily living, (b) personal-social, and (c) occupational skills. These competencies represent what research, practitioner experience, and expert opinion have deemed essential for successful career development. The three curriculum areas (categories), competencies, and subcompetencies are presented in Figure 1.

The LCCE Model interfaces the 22 competencies with two other important dimensions of career education: (a) school, family, and community experiences, and (b) four stages of career development — awareness, exploration, preparation, and placement/follow-up/continuing education. Figure 2 presents a three-dimensional model to illustrate the interaction of these components and the LCCE approach. It views career education as a process for systematically coordinating all school, family, and community components to facilitate each individual's potential for economic, social, and personal fulfillment (Brolin, 1974).

Curriculum Area	Competency		
	1. Managing Family Finances	1. Identify money and make correct change.	2. Make wise expenditures.
	2. Selecting, Managing, and Maintaining a Home	6. Select adequate housing.	7. Maintain a home.
	3. Caring for Personal Needs	10. Dress appropriately.	11. Exhibit proper grooming and hygiene.
Daily Living Skills	4. Rearing Children, Enriching Family Living	14. Prepare for adjustment to marriage.	15. Prepare for rearing children (physical care).
	5. Buying and Preparing Food	18. Demonstrate appropriate eating skills.	19. Plan balanced meals.
	6. Buying and Caring for Clothing	24. Wash clothing.	25. Iron and store clothing.
	7. Engaging in Civic Activities	28. Generally understand local laws and government.	29. Generally understand federal government.
	8. Utilizing Recreation and Leisure	34. Participate actively in group activities.	35. Know activities and available community resources.
	9. Getting Around the Community (Mobility)	40. Demonstrate knowledge of traffic rules and safety practices.	41. Demonstrate knowledge and use of various means of transportation.
	10. Achieving Self Awareness	43. Attain a sense of body.	44. Identify interests and abilities.
	11. Acquiring Self Confidence	48. Express feelings of worth.	49. Tell how others see him/her.
	12. Achieving Socially Responsible Behavior	53. Know character traits needed for acceptance.	54. Know proper behavior in public places.
Personal-Social Skills	13. Maintaining Good Interpersonal Skills	58. Know how to listen and respond.	59. Know how to make and maintain friendships.
	14. Achieving Independence	62. Understand impact of behaviors upon others.	63. Understand self organization.
	15. Achieving Problem Solving Skills	66. Differentiate bipolar concepts.	67. Understand the need for goals.
	16. Communicating Adequately with Others	71. Recognize emergency situations.	72. Read at level needed for future goals.
	17. Knowing and Exploring Occupational Possibilities	76. Identify the personal values met through work.	77. Identify the societal values met through work.
	18. Selecting and Planning Occupational Choices	82. Identify major occupational needs.	83. Identify major occupational interests.
Occupational Guidance and Preparation	19. Exhibiting Appropriate Work Habits and Behaviors	87. Follow directions.	88. Work with others.
	20. Exhibiting Sufficient Physical-Manual Skills	94. Demonstrate satisfactory balance and coordination.	95. Demonstrate satisfactory manual dexterity.
	21. Obtaining a Specific Occupational Skill		
	22. Seeking, Securing, and Maintaining Employment	98. Search for a job.	99. Apply for a job.

FIGURE 1
Life-Centered Career Education, Curriculum Areas, Competencies,
and Subcompetencies

Subcompetencies

3. Obtain and use bank and credit facilities.	4. Keep basic financial records.	5. Calculate and pay taxes.		
8. Use basic appliances and tools.	9. Maintain home exterior.			
12. Demonstrate knowledge of physical fitness, nutrition, and weight control.	13. Demonstrate knowledge of common illness prevention and treatment.			
16. Prepare for rearing children (psychological care).	17. Practice family safety in the home.			
20. Purchase food.	21. Prepare meals.	22. Clean food preparation areas.	23. Store food.	
26. Perform simple mending.	27. Purchase clothing.			
30. Understand citizenship rights and responsibilities.	31. Understand registration and voting procedures.	32. Understand Selective Service procedures.	33. Understand civil rights and responsibilities when questioned by the law.	
36. Understand recreational values.	37. Use recreational facilities in the community.	38. Plan and choose activities wisely.	39. Plan vacations.	
42. Drive a car.				
45. Identify emotions.	46. Identify needs.	47. Understand the physical self.		
50. Accept praise.	51. Accept criticism.	52. Develop confidence in self.		
55. Develop respect for the rights and properties of others.	56. Recognize authority and follow instructions.	57. Recognize personal roles.		
60. Establish appropriate heterosexual relationships.	61. Know how to establish close relationships.			
64. Develop goal seeking behavior.	65. Strive toward self actualization.			
68. Look at alternatives.	69. Anticipate consequences.	70. Know where to find good advice.		
73. Write at the level needed for future goals.	74. Speak adequately for understanding.	75. Understand the subtleties of communication.		
78. Identify the remunerative aspects of work.	79. Understand classification of jobs into different occupational systems.	80. Identify occupational opportunities available locally.	81. Identify sources of occupational information.	
84. Identify occupational aptitudes.	85. Identify requirements of appropriate and available jobs.	86. Make realistic occupational choices.		
89. Work at a satisfactory rate.	90. Accept supervision.	91. Recognize the importance of attendance and punctuality.	92. Meet demands for quality work.	93. Demonstrate occupational safety.
96. Demonstrate satisfactory stamina and endurance.	97. Demonstrate satisfactory sensory discrimination.			
100. Interview for a job.	101. Adjust to competitive standards.	102. Maintain postschool occupational adjustment.		

Source: Adapted from *Life-Centered Career Education: A Competency-Based Approach*, by D. E. Brolin (Reston, VA: Council for Exceptional Children, 1978).

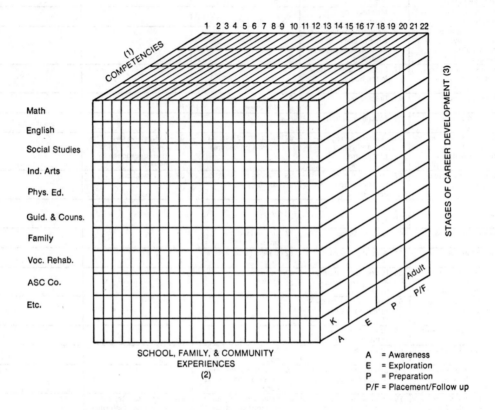

Math
English
Social Studies
Ind. Arts
Phys. Ed.
Guid. & Couns.
Family
Voc. Rehab.
ASC Co.
Etc.

(1) COMPETENCIES

1 2 3 4 5 6 7 8 9 10 11 12 13 14 15 16 17 18 19 20 21 22

STAGES OF CAREER DEVELOPMENT (3)

Adult
P/F
P
E
K
A

SCHOOL, FAMILY, & COMMUNITY
EXPERIENCES
(2)

A   = Awareness
E   = Exploration
P   = Preparation
P/F = Placement/Follow up

FIGURE 2
Career Competency Based Model for Infusing Education into Curriculum

Source: Adapted from *Career Education for Handicapped Children and Youth,* by D. E. Brolin and C. J. Kokaska (Columbus, OH: Charles E. Merrill, 1979).

The Competencies

All the competencies and their 102 subcompetencies were subjected to rigorous review by hundreds of school personnel throughout the country. They endorsed our contention that these competencies generally reflect the major outcomes that should be expected for students if they are to be prepared successfully for community living and working. Clark and White (1980) have described the LCCE Model as the "adult adjustment approach" because of the focus on skills and competencies needed for a person's life career.

Daily Living Skills

Nine Daily Living Skills (DLS) relate to avocational, family, leisure, and civic work activities. Inspection of these competencies should also reveal the occupational implications for career development. Students who have interests and abilities in certain DLS areas (for example, family finances) might also be counseled toward occupations related to those competencies.

Personal-Social Skills

Seven Personal-Social Skills (PSS) are important to family, community, and occupational functioning. These competencies relate to helping the student understand self, build confidence, solve problems, become independent, interact successfully with others, make decisions, conduct self properly in public, and communicate adequately with others. Past experience and research have clearly indicated that a lack in these competencies poses serious problems for exceptional students after they leave school and attempt to secure and maintain employment.

Occupational Skills

Six occupational competencies fall under the curriculum area entitled Occupational Guidance and Preparation. Two of the competencies pertain to learning about the world of work; they entail exploring work possibilities (occupational awareness) and making occupational choices (decision-making). Three competencies relate to building specific vocational skills (work habits, physical capacities, entry-level job skill), and one competency focuses on the process of seeking, securing, and maintaining a job. Occupational awareness, work habits, and physical-manual skills can be developed throughout a K-12 program.

Again, this competency-based approach does not deemphasize basic academic instruction. It does, however, require that instruction be directed so that students can learn the competencies. Therefore, school personnel must determine how they can infuse career education concepts and competencies into their curricula.

School, Family, and Community Experiences

A comprehensive curriculum approach like LCCE requires close working relationships with three groups — the student's family, community agencies and organizations, and business and industry. This brings a realistic, meaningful aspect to the student's education, because it relates directly to performing occupational and daily living activities.

School Personnel

The LCCE curriculum approach advocates a changing role for special education teachers involved with students who can be placed in regular classes and programs. The special educator should become more of a consultant/advisor to school personnel who are teaching the student competencies and other topics. The special educator also has to work closely with parents, community agencies, and industries, integrating and coordinating career development efforts to benefit each student. Further, the special educator should serve as a resource specialist to regular classroom teachers relative to instructional techniques and materials, student information, disability information, career development planning, and the like.

The Family

The LCCE approach promotes greater utilization of the student's family in providing career development experiences in the home and community. Because personal-social development is so important, the special educator can be of invaluable assistance in helping families establish a psychological climate that will facilitate those important competencies. Daily living and occupational competencies can be developed through job duties in the home, family projects, and meaningful leisure and recreational pursuits. Family involvement and cooperation can greatly increase the school program's effectiveness in helping students attain the necessary levels of career development.

The Community

Innumerable resources for career development are available in the community. Civic groups are always looking for special projects to undertake. School programs that have used the Experience-Based Career Education

(EBCE) approach have been surprised at how readily business and industry open their doors to students if they feel the school is advocating a solid program. Many public and private agencies and organizations are also willing to lend support and should be utilized more frequently for career awareness, exploration, and preparation experiences.

Utilization of these three groups is critical to successful career education programming. In the past, school personnel have tended to use family and community resources sparingly. These resources must be used more substantially if the career development needs of exceptional students are to be truly met.

Career Development Stages

The LCCE Model conceives of students passing through four distinct stages of career development: career awareness, career exploration, career preparation, and career placement/follow-up/continuing education. The stages are described below.

Career Awareness

Awareness of the world of work is awakened early in elementary school. Children begin to learn what kinds of work (paid and unpaid) people do and the reasons they do it. The students begin acquiring their own sense of identity, seeing themselves as potential workers and, in essence, begin to form a work personality. Developing positive attitudes about work and increasing awareness of the types of work habits and abilities needed for success are important at this stage. Career awareness activities infused into the elementary curriculum add an exciting dimension to student learning and motivation. Most teachers do some of this now, but in many instances it is probably not being done enough or in an organized manner that relates to competency attainment and career development.

Career Exploration

The junior-high years mark the beginning of career exploration. This is a hands-on stage in which students explore occupational areas, avocational interests, leisure and recreational pursuits, and all other areas related to the 22 competencies and career development. Vocational evaluation should begin at this time and be provided periodically throughout the remaining school years. Community resources take on an important role; students should have the opportunity to explore first-hand the real world and its requirements. A variety of experiences must be incorporated into the students' learning so that they begin thinking more seriously about their own unique set of abilities, interests, and needs and how they relate to a future adult role. If career exploration experiences are carefully planned during the junior-high period, relevant career preparation can be undertaken in senior high.

Career Preparation

This facet of career education should begin at the high-school level and should contain a heavy experiential component. Students having the potential to acquire most or all of the 22 competencies receive relevant courses such as home economics, math, business, health, driver's education, social studies, physical education, and various vocational courses appropriate to their level of interests, needs, and abilities. The use of community resources is also extremely important. The EBCE model mentioned previously provides a methodology for involving business and industry in a meaningful job experience program followed by longer term on-the-job training. Students absolutely must be directed in the daily living and personal-social skills areas, along with the occupational.

Career Placement/Follow-up/Continuing Education

This is a generally neglected component of our services to exceptional children. Career placement occurring near the end of the last semester, or perhaps later, should include not only the placement on a job for pay but also the opportunity to assume responsible nonpaid adult roles relating to avocation, family living, civic and leisure/recreational endeavors. The family takes on a particularly important role at this stage. Therefore, the special educator has to work closely and supportively with the family to assure everyone that the student has acquired a sufficient adult competency level in most or all of the daily living and personal-social skills. A period of follow-up after the student leaves the school is important, and continuing education may be necessary some time after that if the student has difficulties or desires further training.

TEACHING THE COMPETENCIES

The LCCE Curriculum approach requires school personnel to give attention to the students' career development needs by initiating competency-based instruction in the early elementary years and following through until the student leaves the educational program. Some competencies, or some of their subcompetencies, must be taught during the elementary years, whereas others are included during the junior-high and senior-high years. The LCCE Curriculum does not specify when this instruction should begin. Rather, it is left to the discretion of school personnel who are the implementers, since they can best make that determination based on their own situation (personnel, resources, administrative posture, type of students, and so forth).

In teaching the competencies, educators should use a variety of instructional techniques and methods. These may include: games, role playing, puppetry, simulated businesses, occupational notebooks, careers of the month, field trips, learning packages, collages, job dictionaries, arts and crafts, card games, What's My Line? occupational games, values clarification exercises, guest speakers, job analysis activities, work samples, special work assignments, and others.

The Career Education Personnel Preparation (CEPP) Project at the University of Missouri-Columbia provides inservice training for Missouri educators relative to the LCCE approach. Educators undergoing training are asked to prepare a competency unit for teaching one of the subcompetencies. Examples of teacher-developed competency units for one subcompetency in each of the three curriculum areas are presented on the following pages.

The LCCE Curriculum also offers a suggested IEP (individualized education program) structure for recording a plan for specific educational services for each student. Annual goals can be chosen from the 22 competency areas and other categories. The specific educational services can be developed from the competency units and other sources. The short-term objectives can be selected from the 102 subcompetencies, as well as other sources. Thus, an IEP can be constructed from the LCCE competencies, and competency units can be evaluated at least in part by a Competency Rating Scale (CRS), which was also an outcome of the project.

Thus, the LCCE Curriculum allows educators to establish goals, criteria for success, and a method of recording the necessary individualized plans and the outcomes of those plans. Although these components are designed so they can be used separately, the combination of an IEP, competency unit, and CRS can be considered a complete planning, instructional, and evaluation package. Interested readers should obtain a copy of the LCCE Curriculum/program guide from CEC to review the competency units for each of the 102 subcompetencies, the IEP format, and the CRS. The publication also contains a list of instructional materials and resources that relate to the competencies. Detailed suggestions on teaching the competencies are presented in Chapters 4-6 of *Career Education for Handicapped Children and Youth* (Brolin & Kokaska, 1979).

IMPLEMENTING THE LCCE CURRICULUM

The LCCE approach attempts to remedy the three difficulties noted earlier by Meyen and White (1980) relative to implementing career education across the country. First, although career education is not and should not be a separate course, it can become a visible programming component by virtue

EXAMPLE #1   (Nancy Seckel, Teacher)

Domain: Daily Living Skills
Competency: #9 — Getting Around the Community
(Mobility)

Subcompetency: #40 — Demonstrate Knowledge of
Traffic Rules and Safety Practices
Subject: Social Studies, Spelling, English (a good time
to schedule this lesson would be during Na-
tional Safety Week in October)

OBJECTIVES	ACTIVITIES/EVALUATION PROCEDURES	MATERIALS/RESOURCES
1. The student will recognize traffic signs, signals, and markings, and will know safety rules.	Announce a safety week.	
	1. (Monday) Pass out and discuss the red booklet on signs and the yellow card on rules. On appropriately colored poster-board, have each student make one sign and one rule. Tape all of these on the classroom walls and leave up all week.	Booklets, pamphlets, handout materials*
	Have the weekly spelling lesson made up of words such as: diamond, triangle, octagon, pennant, square, rectangle, circle, pentagon, directional, warning, regulatory, pedestrian, crossing, railroad, signals.	Library books
		Film
		Guest speaker
		Bicycle
	English assignment for the week will be to read a library book concerning safety and make a book report.	*Encourage students to put these handouts and others on a bulletin board in their homes for ready reference. This might keep the students from throwing the handouts in a drawer or the trash as soon as they get home.
	Announce a coloring contest.	

2. The student will know bus safety rules.

2. (Tuesday — the last activity of the day) Pass out pamphlets on school bus safety. Have students color them with colored pencils or colored felt-tip pens. After they finish coloring, discuss each rule in the pamphlet. Pass out Safety Place Mats, and serve refreshments of red Kool-Aid®, cupcakes with yellow and green icing, representing caution signs.

3. The student will be able to demonstrate proper use of hand signals in bicycle safety.

3. (Wednesday) Demonstrate appropriate hand signals for bicycle safety. Have all students stand beside their desks and as you say, "left turn," "right turn," "slow," or "stop," the students are to give the appropriate signals.

Continue this for a few minutes until all students seem to be proficient in using these signals.

4. The student will be aware of the State Law, the bicycle safety rules, and bicycle maintenance.

4. (Thursday) Pass out poster and yellow pamphlet on bicycling. Teacher could bring a small bicycle to classroom and show items requiring periodic safety checks. Review all points in the yellow pamphlet and give oral quiz.

(Friday) Have Safety Officer from Missouri State Highway Patrol come to classroom, to show safety film and discuss safety laws and rules. Request that book reports be turned in, and administer spelling test on safety words discussed on Monday.

EXAMPLE #2 (Elaine Keely, Teacher)

Domain: Personal-Social Skills   **Subcompetency:**   #44 — Identify Interests and Abilities
Competency: #10 — Achieving Self-Awareness   **Subject:**   Social Studies

OBJECTIVES	ACTIVITIES/EVALUATION PROCEDURES	MATERIALS/RESOURCES
1. The student will be able to describe himself/herself as an individual with definite likes and dislikes.	Hold a class discussion of values exhibited in certain situations. Role play what he/she would do in a given situation. Have class members participate in forced-choice group activity based on 15 likes/dislikes.	"Growing Up in America" 3" x 5" cards with description of the character and situation to be played.
2. The student will be able to communicate his/her unique self, including hobbies, interests, skills, and physical characteristics for own or others' review.	Have student answer a series of questions on tape. These questions are to be in the areas of hobbies and interests, likes/dislikes, physical characteristics, and social preferences.	List of 15 questions beginning: "If given a choice between _____ and _____, I would do _____. (All who choose the first one go to the other side of the room.) Cassette player/recorder and recorded tape with series of questions or statements.
3. The student will be able to demonstrate or report on a favorite hobby or job he/she feels capable of performing.	Have student demonstrate how to perform some part of his/her job or hobby if demonstrable, or report on his/her job or hobby if not demonstrable.	Materials from hobbies depending on individuals' choices or job tools or reports.

EXAMPLE #3 (Sharon Bullard, Teacher)

Domain: Occupational Preparation and Guidance

Competency: #18 — Selecting and Planning Occupational Choices

Subcompetency: #85 — Identify Requirements of Appropriate and Available Jobs

Subject: "I Guess" Game

OBJECTIVES	ACTIVITIES/EVALUATION PROCEDURES	MATERIALS/RESOURCES
1. The student will be able to recognize the requirements for various occupations	Have students play the "I Guess" game (two or more required)	"I Guess" game board Picture cards Occupational choice description cards:
2. The student will use short-term memory skills in learning the occupation requirements.	a. Place 15 picture cards in pockets. b. Place description cards face down. c. Designate one person as the "reader." From the top of the stack, the reader reads aloud the job description.	Telephone Lineperson Medical Assistant Secretary Farm Worker Truck Driver Fireperson Baggage Handler House Painter Auto Body Painter Upholsterer (furniture) Air Service Clerk Welder Auto Maintenance Worker Bus Driver
3. Students will work together in a game playing situation to improve social skills.	d. Have the player(s) give the answer and the number of the pocket which he/she thinks contains the matching word. e. Ask reader to turn over the card in that pocket and allow the player(s) to see it. The card is replaced if incorrect; if correct, it is given to the player who made the correct response. If a player chooses the "I Guess" pocket and the correct picture is *not* in it, the player is out of the game. Most cards wins.	

of its three dimensions — the 22 competencies, school-family-community collaboration, and the four distinct stages of career development. Second, career education content can be developmentally sequenced with the competencies and stages, which requires determination of what will be taught, when, and by whom. Third, the Competency Rating Scale (CRS) can give a criterion-referenced base for comparing students on career education concepts and skills (competencies). Although the CRS is a general referent, combining it with other instruments such as the Social and Prevocational Battery and the Brigance makes continuous career education evaluation possible.

Implementing the LCCE approach must begin with several educators who are willing to provide the leadership to make change happen in their school or district. Convincing other educators that change is needed is not easy. Three important areas have to be addressed in order to implement such a comprehensive approach: (a) a series of planning and implementation steps, (b) in-service training to other personnel, and (c) a Career Education Plan for the school or district, involving all possible relevant school, family, and community personnel.

Steps in Planning and Implementation

Several years of developmental work with school systems across the country clearly revealed that any educational innovation is practically impossible to implement without careful planning and extensive involvement and input from many different groups of decision-makers. Our experience identified the following as necessary steps in implementing the career education approach:

1. Enlist the support of school district leadership personnel (e.g., administrators, teacher and community groups).
2. Gain approval from the Board of Education to begin organizing for a career development-oriented curriculum in the district or in pilot schools.
3. Appoint a District-Wide Career Education Steering Committee (and necessary subcommittees) to plan, implement, and manage the curriculum development activities for career education.
4. Review literature and programs on career education to determine a philosophy and model.
5. Develop an acceptable definition/conceptualization of career education so everyone will have a common frame of reference.
6. Develop an acceptable career education model.
7. Conduct needs assessment studies to determine the relative status of the current program, students, and staff.

8. Prepare an inservice training program and identify persons within the school district who are competent to serve as trainers.
9. Develop workshop, student, and program evaluation procedures.
10. Conduct inservice training program.
11. Develop a comprehensive Career Education Plan for implementing the curriculum.
12. Gain approval from the administration and Board of Education to implement the plan.
13. Secure facilities and resources for implementing the plan.
14. Implement the plan in terms of priorities and guidelines.
15. Conduct formative and summative evaluations of the implementea program.
16. Change and modify the Career Education Plan as needed.

Space limitations do not permit a detailed explanation of the above steps. This brief listing, however, gives a general idea of the implementation process. The *Trainer's Guide for Life-Centered Career Education* (Brolin, McKay, & West, 1978) provides detailed information, guidelines, and forms for conducting the above activities.

Inservice Training

The LCCE Model requires the involvement of a wide range of school personnel, family and community representatives. Inservice training should interface as many of these individuals as possible.

The LCCE Inservice Training Program involves a group process approach. A 20-session model was devised on the following topics: orientation to workshop and other participants; use of group process techniques; handicapping conditions; concepts and procedures for appropriate educational programming; career education; instructional strategies; competency units; resources and materials; personal-social skills; daily living and occupational skills; community resources; family involvement; individualized education program; student assessment; career education programming; review of student competency assessment data; instructional goals and responsibilities; instructional goals and resources; community assistance and administrative goals; and future actions and workshop evaluation. The last six sessions involve the participants' developing a Career Education Plan.

Effective inservice training takes considerable time and effort. All school personnel may not be involved or need to be involved in every session. This determination depends upon each school district's unique situation.

The Career Education Plan

A Career Education Plan is important because it is solid evidence that a number of people have provided input and contributed to its development.

It is a commitment to change and outlines how, when, where, and by whom career education will be done. It requires the involvement of administrators, teachers, family, and community resources to be truly effective.

The following outline is recommended for writing the plan:

I.   School District Philosophy
II. Definition of Conceptualization of Career Education for Handi-
     capped Student
III. Career Education Goals/Objectives
IV. Instructional Goals/Objectives
V.   Community Involvement Goals/Objectives
VI. Administrative Goals/Objectives
VII. Implementation

An example of a Career Education Plan written similarly to the above outline was done by the School District of West Allis-West Milwaukee, Wisconsin. Interested readers may want to contact Dr. Robert J. Buehler, Director/Supervisor of Special Education, for a copy of their plan.

A FINAL NOTE

The LCCE Curriculum approach offers educators the opportunity to increase their effectiveness with exceptional children. It is not intended to replace most of what is being done now but, rather, to add a more relevant and practical aspect to the students' education — namely, competency education for community living and working. Although much of what is advocated is hopefully being taught already, the LCCE Curriculum organizes it and makes sure that all important competency areas are covered within a K-12+ continuum.

Many school districts throughout the country have implemented LCCE, and at least one state — Washington — has adopted it as their curriculum guide. Examples of LCCE curricula exist in St. Louis, Missouri; Jamestown, New York; Dallas, Texas; Independence, Kansas; Minneapolis, Minnesota; Flat River, Missouri; Racine, Wisconsin; Ames, Iowa; Joliet, Illinois; Las Vegas, Nevada; San Diego, California; Cleveland, Ohio; Bellevue, Washington; and many others. Sheltered workshops and institutional settings have also adopted the LCCE approach. And recently it has been related to postsecondary services through a special federal project of this writer, the Lifelong Career Development (LCD) Project.

Educators must break away from traditional practices and examine their contributions to the educational process. The world in which we live is becoming more complex every year. A primary goal of education is to assist students to become competent. LCCE, with its emphasis on the competencies needed to work and live effectively, can be the point of departure to accomplish this goal. We must help exceptional children become competent by expanding their options through a well organized and humanistic career development process.

REFERENCES

Borba, C. E., Guzicki, J. A. Project Invest: Instructional network for vocational education and specialized training. *Career Development for Exceptional Individuals*, 1980, 3(2), 83-87.

Brolin, D. E.   Career education needs of secondary educable students. *Exceptional Children*, 1973, *39*, 619-624.

Brolin, D. E. *Programming retarded in career education.* Working paper no. 1, Project PRICE. Columbia, MO: University of Missouri-Columbia, September 1974.

Brolin, D. E. (Ed.).   *Life-centered career education: A competency-based approach.* Reston, VA: Council for Exceptional Children, 1978.

Brolin, D. E. *Vocational preparation of persons with handicaps.* Columbus, OH: Charles E. Merrill, in press.

Brolin, D. E., & Kokaska, C. J. *Career education for handicapped children and youth.* Columbus, OH: Charles E. Merrill, 1979.

Brolin, D. E., Malever, M., & Matyas, G. *PRICE needs assessment study.* Working paper no. 7, Project PRICE. Columbia, MO: University of Missouri-Columbia, June 1976.

Brolin, D. E., McKay, D. J., & West, L. W.   *Trainer's guide for life-centered career education.* Reston, VA: Council for Exceptional Children, 1978.

Brolin, D. E., & Thomas, B. (Eds.).   *Preparing teachers of secondary level educable mentally retarded: Proposal for a new model.* Final report. Menomonie, WI: University of Wisconsin-Stout, August 1972.

Clark, G. M.   *Career education for the handicapped child in the elementary classroom.* Denver: Love Publishing Co., 1979.

Clark, G. M., & White, W. J. *Career education for the handicapped: Current perspectives for teachers.* Boothwyn, PA: Education Resources Center, 1980.

Council for Exceptional Children. *Position paper on career education.* Reston, VA: CEC, 1978.

Ellington, C. Teaching prevocational skills to handicapped students. *Career Development for Exceptional Individuals*, 1981, *4*(1), 35-37.

Evenson, J., & Spotts, R.   Experience-based career education for handicapped students. *Career Development for Exceptional Individuals*, 1980, *3*(1), 12-16.

Gillet, P.   Career education and the learning disabled student. *Career Development for Exceptional Individuals*, 1980, *3*(2), 67-73.

Guidepost. Handicapped children denied services. Washington, DC: American Personnel & Guidance Association, May 1, 1980, p. 1.

Heller, H. W.   Secondary education for handicapped students: In search of a solution. *Exceptional Children*, 1981, *47*(8), 582-583.

Hoyt, K. B. *Career education for persons with visual handicaps.* Paper presented at the Helen Keller Centennial Conference, Boston, Massachusetts, June 24, 1980.

Johnson, C. M.   Career education for exceptional individuals: An overview. *Career Development for Exceptional Individuals*, 1979, *2*(1), 12-29.

Johnson, D. R.   Project explore — A vocational assessment model for youth with special needs. *Career Development for Exceptional Individuals*, 1979, *2*(1), 40-47.

Kolstoe, O. Career education for the handicapped: Opportunities for the '80s. *Career Development for Exceptional Individuals*, 1981, *4*(1), 3-12.

Lamkin, J. S. *Getting started: Career education activities for exceptional students (K-9).* Reston, VA: Council for Exceptional Children, 1980.

Larson, C. Personnel communication regarding the EBCE-MD model. Ft. Dodge, IA: Iowa Central Community College, January 1981.

Marland, S. *Career education now.* Speech presented before the annual convention of the National Association of Secondary School Principals, Houston, Texas, 1971.

Meyen, E. L., & White, W. J. Career education and P.L. 94-142: Some views. In G. M. Clark & W. J. White (Eds.), *Career education for the handicapped: Current perspectives for teachers.* Boothwyn, PA: Educational Resources Center, 1980.

Sitlington, P. L. Vocational and special education in career programming for the mildly handicapped adolescent. *Exceptional Children,* 1981, *47*(8), 592-598.

Super, D. E. Career education and the meanings of work. *Monographs on Career Education.* Washington, DC: U.S. Department of Health, Education, and Welfare, Office of Education, June 1976.

Wimmer, D. Functional learning curricula in the secondary schools. *Exceptional Children,* 1981, pp. 610-616.

3

Issues in Curriculum Development

Richard J. Whelan

The articles in this section address important, but certainly not all, issues germane to curriculum for exceptional children and youth. Curriculum is a comprehensive, broad term. It may be defined as organized and monitored experiences provided to pupils by educators in a school setting. Curriculum is a formal tool by which society attempts to develop and change the behavior of its children and youth. The purpose is to impart knowledge, skills, and feelings necessary to function as contributing participants in society. Is it any wonder that over time curriculum is associated with many issues, some strident, some demanding action now, some requiring long-range planning, and some specific to subgroups within the overall school age population (e.g., the handicapped). As a term or label, curriculum is so broad that it elicits many different interpretations and general questions encompassing broad areas of concern. Just three general questions are:

1. To what ends (goals) must experiences (means) be directed?
2. What experiences should be selected for organization and monitoring?
3. Is there recognition that experiences must enhance the development of several types of learning before the pupil can acquire and maintain curriculum goals?

One can readily see that these questions can give rise to a multitude of issues. Obviously, curriculum must serve the goals that society deems important. But what are these goals, and who decides that they are appropriate and correct? Is it local school boards, state legislatures, Congress, individual citizens, advocacy groups — or is it a consensus reached after participation by all? Surely, all can agree on certain common goals, such as acquisition of arithmetic, reading, and writing skills. But can agreement

403

exist on values — morality, cooperation versus competition, culture — or should the school-based curriculum even be concerned with teaching values?

When a curriculum is used to impart a predetermined set of values, the assumption is that adults have validated ones to pass on so that youngsters will not make unnecessary mistakes. Other ways young people acquire values are: (a) learning on their own, (b) selective modeling, and (c) active participation in exploring and choosing from among alternatives (Simon, Howe, & Kirchenbaum, 1972). Once goals or ends are set, experiences must be devised to reach them. Selection of experiences also gives rise to many issues. Should experiences be indirect or direct? To learn about the interaction among elements, should a pupil read about them (indirect) or actually mix (direct) them (Bruner, 1963)? The cost of providing the experiences, classrooms versus laboratories, also gives rise to issues for resolution.

Types of learning to be acquired also influence curriculum. A set of experiences that does not promote learner progress is obviously useless for attaining curriculum goals. Thus, one must recognize that mastery of learning types is necessary to bring about changes of behavior — the purpose of curriculum (Gagne, 1965). For instance, repetition may be used for learning some performance or task, but other learning may require recall skills before a change in behavior is observed.

Curriculum, then, even though its definition is relatively simple, is highly complex. Curriculum planning, implementation, and evaluation have been beset by issues for many, many years. This is true for regular education, and even more so for special education. For example, in the 1950s special education curriculum for the exceptional was thought to have several features (Frampton & Gall, 1955):

1. It must prepare the handicapped to live in a nonhandicapped society.
2. Principles of curriculum development are the same for all children and youth, handicapped or not.
3. It must be adaptable to both group and individual needs.
4. Special instructional devices and procedures are often required to impart the curriculum to the handicapped (e.g., braille, speech reading).
5. Wherever possible, curriculum for the handicapped should be the same as for the nonhandicapped, and it should be provided in regular education settings.

Though one can give a nod of agreement to these five features, each one can also give cause for disagreements. If the nonhandicapped do not want to accept the handicapped, what purpose is served by preparing the handicapped to live in a general society? Wouldn't it be better to teach the handicapped to live and work among their own kind? The answers to these questions impact upon curriculum and the environment in which it is to be taught — e.g., segregated versus nonsegregated settings. What choices do the handicapped have in this policy issue? One response could be: "I want to live and work with my handicapped peers, but I also want access to all privileges that the nonhandicapped enjoy." Is this response reasonable or not? Are there other responses?

Are — or even *should* — principles of curriculum planning be the same for all children and youth? For example, if the assumption is that all types of learning should be mastered, should they be sequenced from simple to complex? Or can two or more types be worked on at the same time? The answers to these questions, of course, have an influence on the experiences the curriculum provides.

Individual versus group learning has posed a dilemma for educators. A general set of experiences tends to increase group performance variance. Experiences geared to individual mastery tend to decrease variance in a group. How does a teacher truly meet individual needs in a group of 15? With an aide? A tutor? A machine? Does teaching toward the individual do injustice to the learning that comes from group interaction?

Advances in technology have allowed the handicapped to participate more fully in learning experiences. Yet, issues arise here, too. Is technology the master or the tool? Are its costs justifiable on the basis of observed benefits?

The fifth feature is closely related to the first. But the assumption is that the curriculum for the nonhandicapped has inherent goodness. That assumption, of course, is debatable. Is integration desirable for both the handicapped and nonhandicapped? Which group benefits the most from it? The least?

Issues regarding curriculum are of several types. Some involve policy. What does society want for *all* its children and youth? How many dollars will it pay to attain its wants? Others are technical issues. What is the best way to get from point A to B to C? In any event, the label "curriculum" clearly is not neutral. It elicits various meanings in and reactions from people. Recognizing that it is a value-laden label can only help to (a) identify issues, (b) clarify them, and (c) pose solutions for the improved education of all children and youth.

The intent of this section is to identify some specific curriculum-related issues regarding the education of handicapped children and youth. The articles address topical and important issues of the day and, indeed, the future. Additional issues are not addressed. Just three of these issues are briefly introduced below.

1. One area of continuing concern is teacher preparation. Does the content of teacher education programs match requirements inherent in the school's curriculum? If not, what can be done to reduce the

mismatch? For example, the curriculum itself may be inappropriate for the population to be served. In this instance, the teacher preparation may be entirely correct. On the other hand, the teacher education program may be based on the interests of professors rather than on the needs of pupil-based curricula.

2.   If curriculum is viewed as an intervention, more attention must be paid to evaluation of its effects (outcomes). All too often, comprehensive, diagnostic data are used to assign handicapped pupils to interventions that have little or no validity as demonstrated by changes in pupil behavior (Larson, Parker, & Hammill, 1982).

3.   Classification systems may be useful for statistical reporting, but they have questionable value in contributing to curriculum selection for the handicapped. If they did, effective curricula could be identified for each classification (e.g., mentally retarded, visually impaired). In reality, differences within classifications are often greater than differences between classifications or categories of handicapping conditions. Therefore, curriculum selection based only upon classification does not seem to be a fruitful avenue for continued exploration.

The first issue, of course, speaks to closer cooperation between teacher education institutions and schools. And closer cooperation means that special and regular education must become a profession in charge of its destiny. Certification standards, acceptable practices, requirements for continuing education, and the like are usually set by a profession. This is not the case for education, and that state of affairs has resulted in discontinuity between teacher preparation curriculum and that actually used in schools.

As to the second issue, special and regular education is no more immune to fads than is society as a whole. A well packaged and marketed "how to" classroom management program is welcomed unconditionally because so many teachers and administrators are looking for solutions to perplexing behavior problems. Yet, the package probably contains only restatements of what has been known, but not practiced for years. In addition, the "lovely package" rarely, if ever, contains any evidence that its procedures actually work. Again, the question of which interventions work for which set of learner aptitudes requires constant scrutiny and analysis.

Classification or labeling is a science in and of itself. Each category of handicapping condition has its own criteria for classification. The fact that the criteria are inclusive of medical, psychological, and educational analyses, however, does not automatically predict selection of successful recommendation procedures. They may only mean grouping with pupils who carry the same label but not the same performance profiles on curriculum-based assessments. For example, two emotionally disturbed children may attain the same scores on a test, but they might have missed entirely different items.

The items missed or correct are more important for curriculum decisions than is the total score. How often is item analysis used in making an individualized education program (IEP) and placement decision?

In the recent history of special education in the United States, three distinct but interrelated events have had a profound impact. One event has been the rise in influence of advocacy or *lobbying* groups. These groups have pushed and pulled decision makers at all levels to institute appropriate educational and treatment programs for the handicapped. Another has been the use of *legal* remedies (litigation) to attain equal protection and due process for the handicapped when lobbying has been too slow or unfruitful. Courts, for example, have decided in favor of inclusion rather than exclusion of the handicapped, unbiased assessment procedures, and procedural due process rights, to name only a few. A third event has been the use of federal and state *legislation* to institutionalize the gains made from lobbying and litigation. Thus, rights for the handicapped that have been won in other situations have been recognized as national policy through the process of legislation. In addition, legislation on substantive practices has dollars attached to it, providing states and school districts the resources necessary to carry out policy decisions.

The three Ls — lobbying, litigation, legislation — while aiming at improved educational practices for the handicapped, have functioned to solve many issues. For instance, the handicapped must be provided a free, appropriate, public education (FAPE). But the three Ls also raised other issues — or at least brought subliminal ones to the spotlight of attention and controversy. The articles in this section address four of these issues. They describe issues and present possible solutions to them. Not all readers will support the solutions, either because they have taken positions not subject to change, or they want to explore other alternatives before taking a policy stand. The issues are:

1. What is a least restrictive environment (LRE), and how does it influence the curriculum?
2. Although parents have been informally encouraged to show interest in the education of their children for many years, they are now required to have the opportunity to participate in planning the curriculum. How can schools make this partnership productive for children?
3. Are tests biased, does bias exist only in the examiner, or is bias inherent in both? Unless bias can be reduced, eliminated, or at least identified, how can accurate decisions be made concerning curriculum development for handicapped pupils?
4. Education has entered another era of technological promises. Years ago the computer was supposed to assume a substantial burden of instruction — e.g., computer-assisted instruction (CAI). But the

technology never spread. Was this because of high costs? Lack of software? Fear of the new? Will the low costs of microcomputers finally bring a new era to curriculum planning for handicapped children and youth?

As stated previously, the topic of curriculum generates many, many issues. Just a few have been pinpointed here, and a few more follow in the subsequent articles. Before concluding this brief discussion, a definition of what an issue *is* seems appropriate. First, an issue is a point of dispute that elicits statements of different positions. Second, the dispute flows out of or is a byproduct of an action, be it national policy or local selection of a social studies series. One can realize, then, that any decision may generate several issues. Yet, that issues be raised is proper. And even more proper is that the issues be discussed in the light of maximum scrutiny, because optimum solutions can be proposed, tried, and evaluated only with the accompaniment of full and open discussion. The handicapped children and youth of this country deserve and need the best of curriculum opportunities that emerge from enlightened solutions to pressing issues.

REFERENCES

Bruner, J. *The process of education.* New York: Vintage Books, 1963.

Frampton, M., & Gall, E. (Eds.). *Special education for the exceptional: Vol. 1, introduction and problems.* Boston: Porter Sargent Publishers, 1955.

Gagne, R. *The conditions of learning.* New York: Holt, Rinehart & Winston, 1965.

Larson, S., Parker, R., & Hammill, D. Effectiveness of psycholinguistic training: A response to Kavale. *Exceptional Children,* 1982, *49*(1), 60-66.

Simon, S., Howe, L., & Kirschenbaum, H. *Values clarification.* New York: Hart Publishing Co., 1972.

Probably no part of PL 94-142 has generated more controversy than its provision that the handicapped be educated with the nonhandicapped to the maximum extent appropriate. This philosophical policy statement is referred to in the Rules and Regulations pursuant to PL 94-142, under the heading of Least Restrictive Environment (LRE). The concept is more popularly called — erroneously, as it turns out — mainstreaming. The law does not mention by label either LRE or mainstreaming. These are names given to the policy described in the law by regulatory developers and others (professional associations, advocacy groups). Meyen and Lehr address a complex issue and bring their own interpretation to the meaning of the LRE concept. Their plan is probably more in keeping with the intent of the law than are many others. The article also reflects the best that is known of instructional practices.

Least Restrictive Environments: Instructional Implications

Edward L. Meyen and Donna H. Lehr

With passage of PL 94-142, the Education for All Handicapped Children Act of 1975, one could argue that the ultimate in legislative assurances had been achieved for handicapped children and youth. By law, the handicapped must receive a free and appropriate education. Insertion of the word *appropriate* extends the implications of the law beyond the issue of equal rights. It gives both advocates and professionals an agenda for the future as attempts are made to operationally define appropriateness and to strengthen instructional interventions.

The required individualized education program (IEP) is emerging as a useful tool (1) for focusing the attention of parents and educators on instructional needs of the handicapped, and (2) as an accountability measure in the overall issue of due process. The more significant impact of the

409

legislation, however, may center on the response of public schools in implementing the principle of least restrictive environment (LRE). Given the specification of educational goals and short-term objectives based on individual needs of the handicapped child, the most normal appropriate instructional setting must be selected for implementation.

INFERRED MEANING OF LRE

Although PL 94-142 requires adherence to the least restrictive principle and sets forth procedures for determining compliance, it falls short in offering those responsible for implementation clear guidelines as to what constitutes least restrictiveness for particular students. In the absence of such guidelines, local districts, faced with compliance, have moved to operationalize a definition and in the process have oversimplified the principle. The consequence is an emphasis on placement options centering on retention in the regular class — popularly referred to as mainstreaming.

An explanation for this response relates to the nature of least restrictiveness as a concept. In contrast to due process procedures and the required individualized education program, the least restrictive environment principle does not lend itself to the stating of specific procedures. It is not analogous to a procedure or program. In this context it could be argued that LRE is inappropriate to be legislated as an educational practice.

The principle of least restrictiveness represents to a large extent a philosophical position. It evolves from a much broader set of societal applications documented as early as 1918 (see Kaufman & Morra, 1978) in a case involving the right of the federal government to establish a national bank. Although the principle has since been applied to a number of social issues, it was not until the 1970s that it emerged as a primary reference in legal cases pertaining to the rights of children. Educationally it is based on the premise that all children, including the handicapped, should be educated in a manner that does not inhibit their interaction with peers nor employ unusual instructional arrangements. It calls for a pattern of life as close to the expected norm as possible.

Adherence to such a philosophy makes individuals more conscious of their placement decision making regarding handicapped children and youth. It causes them to resist placement outside the regular class except when fully justified as being in the best interest of the student. This is a laudable and defensible position, but when legislated as an instructional practice, the inability to precisely define it in the form of enforceable procedures makes it vulnerable to inappropriate applications, and in some cases decisions are made that are detrimental to the best interests of the students for whom it is intended to serve.

In the absence of an operational definition of the least restrictive environment, examples from the literature that have focused on mainstreaming will be presented. References are being made to mainstreaming only because the term has come to be interpreted as synonymous with least restrictive environments in the public schools. In the context of this paper, it is an appropriate term, but in a broader discussion of least restrictiveness, it would prove to be insufficient. Kaufman, Gottlieb, Agard, and Kukic (1975), in attempting to develop a conceptual framework for mainstreaming, offered the following definition:

> Mainstreaming refers to the temporal, instructional, and social integration of eligible exceptional children with normal peers based on an ongoing, individually determined, educational planning and programming process and requires clarification of responsibility among regular and special education administrative, instructional, and supportive personnel (p. 41).

An analysis of this definition indicates three primary components that must be addressed in implementation: integration, educational planning and programming processes, and clarification of responsibility.

Turnbull and Turnbull (1978), in describing the history of mainstreaming as a judicial preference, have provided a useful discussion that defines and explains mainstreaming. The following has been excerpted from a more comprehensive discussion by the authors:

> . . . Mainstreaming is a method for individualizing an exceptional pupil's education, since it prevents a child being placed in special programs unless it is first determined that he cannot profit from regular educational placement. It simultaneously addresses the requirements of an appropriate education — an individualized education — and nondiscriminatory classification. It promotes the concept that curriculum adaptations and instructional strategies tailored to the needs of exceptional children can occur in regular classrooms, as well as in special classrooms. . . (p. 140).

> . . . Mainstreaming is also preferred because it is widely and forcefully advocated by many educators. They argue that the handicapped child will learn more, and more easily, by being educated with the nonhandicapped child. They contend that there are serious doubts about the educational efficacy of special (separate) programs; and they say that the nonhandicapped child needs the educational and experiential benefits of coming into contact with handicapped children (p. 141).

The intent of these definitions is difficult to challenge. The problem in reviewing such definitions is that one begins to assume that the practices that occur during implementation are equivalent to the intent of the definition. As previously mentioned, LRE (or mainstreaming) essentially represents a philosophical position. Attempts by districts to operationalize the beliefs embedded in LRE too often result in placement decisions based on assumptions that are not sound.

For example, it is assumed that the goals and short-term objectives of an IEP combined with information on available options constitute sufficient information upon which to make a decision on the least restrictive setting for a given student. In the case of the severely handicapped, this may operate reasonably well since there is no strong expectancy that the severely handicapped should be retained in regular classes. There is, however, a support base for LRE placements appropriate to the needs of the severely handicapped using other configurations of options. For the mildly handicapped the popular logic of the least restrictive concept argues for placement in the regular class, and the weight of the IEP evidence must be exceedingly convincing to result in a placement decision other than the regular class. In other words, for the mildly handicapped the burden of proof appears to rest with those who would propose placement options other than the regular class, whereas minimal attention is given to demonstrating that the regular class does in fact meet the needs of the individual. In contrast, for the severely handicapped the burden of proof lies more directly with those who would recommend regular class placement.

LEAST RESTRICTIVENESS FOR THE MILDLY HANDICAPPED

Selection of the least restrictive environment should be based on knowledge of conditions that offer the highest probability for remedying academic performance-related deficits and not conditions that are socially least restrictive. The inclusion of social benefits for the mildly handicapped or "value" enrichment for their nonhandicapped peers is not sufficient compensation for ineffectual instruction. The thesis of this article is that many of the required conditions are currently not likely to exist in the typical regular classroom setting and by their omission the regular class becomes highly restrictive.

The position being promulgated here is that least restrictiveness for the mildly handicapped is not necessarily a temporal question. Rather, it is a question directed to the future — e.g., will intensive remedial instruction for a short duration commencing at the time of identification result in the individual's maintaining him/herself more independently in least restrictive environments in the future?

Most schools are implementing least restrictive placements in the context of a "now" orientation without giving sufficient attention to the conduciveness of the setting for the needed remediation. The authors have difficulty accepting the logic that the reality circumstances of the regular classroom will better prepare the mildly handicapped for adult life when what those individuals need to accomplish is to overcome the academic deficits they are currently experiencing. To couch the instructional needs of the mildly handicapped in the broader context of the social and developmental arena may be counter-productive. It does make the selection of the least restrictive environment easier but does not address the individual's immediate and/or long-term instructional needs. From our perspective, the goal should be to prepare the mildly handicapped for a less restrictive life. This does not necessarily mean that least restrictiveness in a social context is appropriate to remedial instruction.

INSTRUCTIONAL DIFFERENCES PRESENTED BY THE MILDLY HANDICAPPED LEARNER

An obvious characteristic of students identified as mildly handicapped is the variance they reflect across most behavioral dimensions relevant to school performance. What causes a student to be classified as mildly versus moderately or severely handicapped typically depends upon the criteria applied by those responsible for making such decisions. Thus, the variability is probably accented to a degree by the inconsistency of criteria used to define these groups.

In examining eligibility criteria developed by state educational agencies, a characteristic common to most mildly handicapped individuals appears to be an inability to profit sufficiently from nonspecialized instructional programs (those regularly offered to students). We can infer from this observation that if instructional problems of the mildly handicapped could be remedied, they would not further be considered handicapped (for school purposes) or in need of special programming. This is particularly true of the mildly learning disabled, mentally retarded, and behaviorally disordered. It excludes the speech impaired, who need treatment even though the speech problem may not interfere with academic performance. The same would be true of students with mild sensory impairments. It is reasonable to argue, however, that academic performance represents the primary factor distinguishing the majority of students considered mildly handicapped from their nonhandicapped peers. The mildly handicapped present primarily instructional problems, and decisions related to what constitutes the least restrictive environment should hinge on the type of remedial instruction required and the conditions essential to optimally benefit from such instruction. Based upon what we know about the nature of instructional problems that persist as a learner characteristic, instruction, it seems reasonable to project, must be intense if the learner's deficits are to be corrected.

In examining the literature on the mildly handicapped from the perspective of instructional implications, a small group of characteristics (each of which has been empirically researched) emerges. Upon further examination these characteristics (detailed below) translate into instructional needs which, from the perspective of the authors, are not receiving sufficient attention in implementation of the least restrictive environment concept for the mildly handicapped.

1. *Task Oriented Behavior.* A number of studies have been conducted to determine differences in task orientation between mildly

handicapped students and their nonhandicapped peers. Research conducted by Bryan (1974) and Bryan and Wheeler (1972) led to the finding that learning disabled children spend significantly less time in task oriented behavior and more time in non-task oriented behavior than do average achievers. Krupski (1979) found mildly retarded students to be more distractible, spending less time on task and more time out of their seats than their nonretarded peers. It was reported, though, that these behaviors differed in relationship to the type of task presented to the child.

In a study of behaviors correlated with achievement in high and low achievers, Soli and Devine (1976) found differences between those two groups.. They reported that the behaviors most highly correlated with low achievement were lack of attention, self-stimulation, playing, and complying. For the high achieving group the correlate behaviors were positive peer interaction related to the assigned task, requests for help from the teacher, in-seat behavior, and lack of production of inappropriate noise. Forness and Esveldt (1975) reported similar results when comparing the difference in attending behavior of learning disabled and non-learning disabled children.

2. *Attentional Problems.* Differences between attention patterns of mildly handicapped children and their nonhandicapped peers have been demonstrated by a number of studies. Extensive reviews of the literature can be found in Keogh and Margolis (1976), Hallahan and Kauffman (1975), and Hagen and Kail (1975). Evidence from the classroom, clinical setting, and laboratory setting support the conclusion that mildly handicapped children spend less time attending to task than do their nonhandicapped peers when matched for chronological age.

Some work has been done to determine the nature of attention and its relationship to learning. Keogh and Margolis (1976) cited studies providing evidence for the existence of several components of attention that have differing effects on learning. They reported Dykman's proposal of four components of attention: alertness, stimulus selection, focusing, and vigilance. Hallahan, Kauffman, and Ball are credited with identifying the independence of time attending and shifts in attending. Keogh and Margolis proposed the aspects of attending to be (1) coming to attention, (2) decision making, and (3) maintaining attention. They also suggested an approach to viewing the attentional characteristics which may result in differential educational interventions for the remediation of attentional problems.

3. *Peer-Social Interactions.* A growing body of literature indicates that mildly handicapped students do not interact with nonhandicapped

peers to the same extent that nonhandicapped students interact with their own peer group. Nonhandicapped students have been reported to be less responsive to initiatives from handicapped peers than from their nonhandicapped peers. Bryan (1974) found that while handicapped children were as likely to initiate interaction with their peers, they were more likely to be ignored by them when compared with the nonhandicapped. Gottlieb and Davis (1973) found that when nonhandicapped students were given the choice of handicapped or nonhandicapped peers to serve as game partners, they were more likely to choose the nonhandicapped students. Bryan and Bryan (1978) reported that handicapped peers were viewed as less popular than their nonhandicapped peers as indicated on scales of Attraction and Social Rejection. Bryan and Bryan also investigated the types of communication behaviors demonstrated by the two groups of students. They found that the handicapped peers demonstrated a significantly greater number of "nasty" statements and received a significantly greater number of rejection statements from their nonhandicapped peers.

Many hypothesize that integrating mildly handicapped children into regular classes will improve the attitude of the nonhandicapped toward their handicapped classmates. MacMillian (1977) concluded from a review of the literature that there is no support for this hypothesis and that, in fact, mildly handicapped students in segregated classes are more accepted than those in integrated programs.

4. *Pupil-Teacher Interactions.* While a major controversy surrounds the issue of effects of labeling on handicapped children, the data reported in the literature indicate that lower achievers receive differential treatment in classes. Brophy and Good (1970) found that teachers demanded better performance from students they identified as high achievers and, additionally, they more frequently provided praise to those students for their performance when compared with the perceived low achievers. Bryan (1974) also found differences in the nature of interactions between learning disabled students and their teacher and their non-learning disabled peers and the teacher. The data from this study indicate that as much time was spent interacting with the teacher by both populations, but the learning disabled students were more likely to be ignored by the teacher; when they did receive attention, it was more likely to be of a helping nature than that received by their nonhandicapped peers. Jacobs (1978) found significantly different ratings by teachers who were told to evaluate behavioral and personality characteristics of a child labeled as learning disabled when compared to teachers rating the same child when they were told the child was "normal."

INTENSIVE INSTRUCTION

In advocating intense instruction as essential to the remediation of academic deficits characteristic of the mildly handicapped, "intense instruction" must be defined. To suggest that intense instruction can be measured as a single variable or that all learners respond alike to the same level of intensity would be presumptuous. Intensive instruction is presented as a set of circumstances that impact on the actual interaction of the learner in the instructional situation. Although the authors were unable to locate research studies focusing on the collective features they attribute to intensive instruction, considerable research exists on rate of learning and pupil-teacher ratios.

Time on task is central to the arguments presented in this article, which questions the typical regular class setting as the least restrictive environment for the mildly handicapped. Bloom (1974), in discussing time and rate of learning, built on Carroll's (1963) model of school learning, in which time is considered the critical variable. As a basis for presenting evidence in support of mastery learning strategies, Bloom utilized Carroll's concept of elapsed time as differentiated from the time the learner spends on tasks engaged in the act of learning. He cited research conducted by Anderson (1973), Arlin (1973), and Lahaderne (1967) as illustrating a strong positive relationship between time directly engaged in learning and achievement.

Although it has been widely assumed that class size is related to the effectiveness of instruction for children, few studies have led to conclusions supporting this relationship. Since the reduced pupil-teacher ratio has long been considered a necessary ingredient for education of the mildly handicapped, conclusions drawn from the literature related to this topic are highly significant. Using meta-analysis, Glass and Smith (in Cahen and Filby, 1979) have pooled and analyzed a half century of data to investigate the relationship. The data indicate that, on the average, achievement improves as class size decreases, with a marked improvement when class size is reduced to fifteen or fewer students. Questions remain as to why this occurs. If answers are found, the implications are many for instruction in the regular class.

Porwall (in Cahen & Filby, 1979) concluded that reduction in class size enables an increase in the individualization of instruction. Cahen and Filby have described current studies designed to systematically examine the question of *how* this class size reduction affects instruction. Questions being considered include: Will there be (1) more individualization, (2) improved diagnostic procedures, (3) an increase in direct instruction, and (4) more monitoring and feedback, as a function of reduced class size?

The student's history of interaction with the set of circumstances that may be considered to be related to intensity of instruction is important in determining the most appropriate educational setting for the student. Also, our view of assessing the academic achievement of the mildly handicapped is that the exclusive emphasis given to the current functioning level of the student as determined by achievement tests is limiting. A more useful approach, in addition to establishing the student's level of performance, would be to determine the intensity of instruction per unit of time which contributed to the student's current level of functioning.

We recognize that although this is a researchable hypothesis and possibly practical as an approach in the future, it does present a variety of problems in reconstructing evidence of past instruction for purposes of determining intensity of instruction. For purposes of illustration, however, let's look at an example. We would submit that two students, both fifteen years of age and reading at the third grade level, may differ greatly if one can substantiate how each came to achieve that third grade reading level. The student who was provided intense instruction during the elementary and intermediate grades may well have a more serious problem than the peer who was subjected to a variety of instructional approaches but for whom few expectations were held. The latter student may be considered a good candidate for further remedial instruction with optimism of overcoming specific deficits in reading, whereas the student reading at the same level but who had previously received more intense instruction might be a more appropriate candidate for an instructional program emphasizing coping skills.

The point being made is that for the mildly handicapped, emphasis must be placed on intensity of instruction — not merely elapsed time. We further speculate that for the mildly handicapped student placed in the regular class, greater proportion of time is spent in the context of elapsed time than on task and, consequently, the environment becomes restrictive from the perspective of remediation. At least, it inhibits rather than enhances the student's performance.

Intensive instruction, in summary is characterized by:

1. The consistency and duration of time on task.
2. The timing, frequency, and nature of feedback to the student based on his or her immediate performance and cumulative progress.
3. The teacher regularly and frequently communicating to the student an expectancy that this student will be able to master the task and demonstrate continuous progress.
4. A pattern of pupil-teacher interaction in which the teacher responds to student initiatives and uses consequences appropriate to the student's responses.

For intensive instruction to occur, several conditions must exist. This includes low pupil-teacher ratios, teachers capable of implementing the features of intensive instruction, materials that allow for individualization, the employment of instructional management practices that incorporate the specifying of objectives and careful monitoring of pupil progress, and flexible scheduling that enables instruction to occur within varied time frames.

CONCLUSION

The authors have questioned the manner in which the least restrictive environment principle is being applied to the mildly handicapped. We have taken the position that the needs of the mildly handicapped are primarily instructional in nature and necessitate an intense approach to remediation. We have also argued that conditions in the typical classroom are not currently conducive to the provision of intense instruction, and that decision on least restrictive placements for the mildly handicapped should be based on a determination of settings that offer the highest probability that intense instruction appropriate to the students' needs will occur. The extent to which such conditions will emerge depends greatly upon reorienting the people responsible for educational assessment and decision making regarding appropriate instruction.

Following are examples of options worth exploring.

1. Once a student is identified as mildly handicapped, consideration should be given to placement of the student in a highly intense instructional program for two to three months or until the effectiveness of remediation has been substantiated, and then begin to increase participation in the regular classroom setting. During the intensive instruction period, attention would be given to determining the kinds of conditions necessary for the student to be maximally responsive to instruction. This would aid in the selection of other placement options.

2. The pupil-teacher ratio in mainstreamed classrooms should be reduced to 15 to 1 or lower. If this is not feasible on a full-day basis, a half day might be beneficial.

3. Teachers of mainstream classrooms should be trained to employ techniques related to intense instruction — for example, feedback to students, maintaining on-task behavior, and individualizing instruction.

4. Continuous instruction should be provided; e.g., summer school remedial programs should be offered during the period of time in which the student is progressing toward a performance level that would enhance his/her performance in a regular classroom situation.

5. In making placement decisions on junior and senior high aged students, evaluators should give consideration to the nature of the

student's educational history, and to the extent possible determine the intensity of instruction that contributed to the student's current level of functioning.

6. Use of paraprofessionals in mainstreamed classrooms should increase. Such persons could help implement recommendations of the special education teacher with specific students in the mainstreamed setting.

REFERENCES

Anderson, L. W. *Time and school learning.* Unpublished doctoral dissertation, University of Chicago, 1973.

Arlin, M. N. *Learning rate and learning rate variance under mastery learning conditions.* Unpublished doctoral dissertation, University of Chicago, 1973.

Bloom, B. S. Time and learning. *American Psychologist,* September 1974, 682-688.

Brophy, J. E., & Good, T. L. Teachers' communication of differential expectations for children's classroom performance: Some behavioral data. *Journal of Educational Psychology,* 1970, *61,* 365-374.

Bryan, T. An observational analysis of classroom behaviors of children with learning disabilities. *Journal of Learning Disabilities,* 1974, *7,* 35-43.

Bryan, T., & Bryan, J. Social interactions of learning disabled children. *Learning Disability Quarterly,* 1978, *1,* 33-37.

Bryan, T., & Wheeler, R. Perception of learning disabled children: The eye of the observer. *Journal of Learning Disabilities,* 1972, *5,* 484-488.

Cahen, L. S., & Filby, N. N. The class size/achievement issue: New evidence and a research plan. *Phi Delta Kappan,* March 1979, 492-495.

Carroll, J. B. A model of school learning. *Teachers College Record,* 1963, *64,* 723-733.

Forness, S. R., & Esveldt, K. C. Classroom observation of children with learning and behavior problems. *Journal of Learning Disabilities,* 1975, *8,* 382-385.

Gottlieb, J., & Davis, J. Social acceptance of EMR during overt behavioral interactions. *American Journal of Mental Deficiency,* 1973, *78,* 141-143.

Hagen, J. W., & Kail, R. V. The role of attention in perceptual and cognitive development. In W. A. Cruickshank & D. P. Hallahan (Eds.), *Perceptual and learning disabilities in children (Vol. 2).* Syracuse, NY: Syracuse University Press, 1975.

Hallahan, D. P., & Kauffman, J. M. Research on the education of distractible and hyperactive children. In W. M. Cruickshank & D. P. Hallahan (Eds.), *Perceptual and learning disabilities in children* (Vol. 2). Syracuse, NY: Syracuse University Press, 1975.

Jacobs, W. R. The effect of the learning disability label on classroom teachers' ability to objectively observe and interpret child behaviors. *Learning Disability Quarterly,* 1978, *1,* 50-55.

Kaufman, M. J., Gottlieb, J., Agard, J., & Kukic, M.D. Mainstreaming: Toward an explication of the construct. In E. L. Meyen, G. A. Vergason, & R. J. Whelan (Eds.), *Alternatives for teaching exceptional children.* Denver, CO: Love Publishing Co., 1975.

Kaufman, M. J., & Morra, L. J. The least restrictive environment: A major philosophical change. In E. L. Meyen (Ed.), *Exceptional children and youth.* Denver, CO: Love Publishing Co., 1978.

Keogh, B. K., & Margolis, J. Learning to labor and wait: Attentional problems of children with learning disorders. *Journal of Learning Disabilities,* 1976, *9,* 276-286.

Krupski, A. Are retarded children more distractible? Observational analysis of retarded and nonretarded children's classroom behavior. *American Journal of Mental Deficiency*, 1979, *84*, 1-10.

Lahaderne, A. M. *Adaptation to school settings: A study of children's attitudes and classroom behavior.* Unpublished doctoral dissertation, University of Chicago, 1967.

MacMillan, D. L. *Mental retardation in school and society.* Boston: Little, Brown, 1977.

Soli, S. D., & Devine, V. T. Behavioral correlates of achievement: A look at high and low achievers. *Journal of Educational Psychology*, 1976, *68*, 335-341.

Turnbull, H. R., & Turnbull, A. P. *Free appropriate public education — Law and implementation.* Denver, CO: Love Publishing Co., 1979.

McAfee and Vergason coin the term "integrative power," which simply means that parents and teachers working together in a collaborative relationship can accomplish more for the handicapped than when each works alone. A unique feature of this article is a proposal for an overall school IEP that can be a foundation for individual IEPs. In addition, parents would not only participate in planning, but would also be active in carrying out with teachers the mutually agreed upon programs.

Parent Involvement in the Process of Special Education: Establishing the New Partnership

James K. McAfee and Glenn A. Vergason

Parent involvement in education — and specifically the education of exceptional children — is one of a small set of topics that seem to monopolize professional education literature. Few other subjects have been as extensively and disjointedly probed, prodded, and preached. A manual search of general and special education literature written during the period 1970-1978 uncovered nearly 800 sources in the area of parent-school relationships. Two bibliographies published by the Council for Exceptional Children on parental role in the education of exceptional children list 100 and 112 entries respectively (CEC, 1977a and b). Certainly, there is no dearth of information.

The parents of American school children have always maintained a role in the public education system. The nature and depth of that role have assumed a variety of guises. The parent-school relationship, until post

World War II years, was often personal and based upon a number of socioethnic factors. These factors included the following:

1. Most communities were relatively stable, and parents passed their relationships with schools down to their children.
2. Teachers and administrators were an integral part of the community, and many of them returned to teach in the schools that had provided their own educations.
3. Schools were an integral part of the neighborhood; they often functioned as the recreational and social center of the community.
4. The community had relatively homogenous values, and teachers' values were reflected in the values of the community as a whole.
5. Parents and schools had an understanding or "implied contract." Parents viewed education as the means by which the lives of their children would be improved. Thus, they sent their children to school inculcated with respect for and awe of education
6. The management structure reflected the desires of the community.

The advent of increased mobility fractured the stability and utility of these relationships and axioms. Schools came to be more frequently administered by professional educators who were not identified with the community. Teachers in inner city schools often commuted from the surrounding suburbs. Now, the educational values of the school may not reflect those of the students, their parents, or the community. Children who are bused from various locales meet the same clash of values. The difference in values may be real or perceived, but its effect is supported by differences in attire, appearance, recreation habits, and other variables. Communities have been changing rapidly in socioethnic composition — and values and expectations reflect the egress and influx of socioethnic groups. Educators have discovered that the manner in which they teach is no longer effective. The implied contract is no longer viewed similarly by parent and teacher.

The impact of large numbers of previously segregated exceptional children entering public schools has created similar problems. Educators can no longer sell the majority view to parents and children whose needs, goals, and desires are different. The onus, then, is on educators to develop a new relationship — one suited to the present situation.

Educators and parents have not failed to recognize these new sources of conflict. What educators have done, however, is to attempt to convince parents that the values and expertise of the educational system is more desirable and more effective than anything the parents have to offer. Thus, the majority of parent involvement programs have taken the form of training parents to deal with the special needs of their children.

Luterman (1971), Wilkie (1973), Nardine (1974), McConnell (1974), Sykes (1974), Schopler and Reichler (1971), Kifer (1974) and many others reported significant success in training parents to use special educational and therapeutic techniques with their children. Innovation and creativity mark many of these programs. Nardine (1974) used video tapes to provide parents with direct feedback. McConnell (1974) sent professionals from the Bill Wilkerson Hearing and Speech Center into the homes of preschool communicatively handicapped children; these children evidenced significant academic superiority in their later school years. In another undertaking, parents and their visually impaired children attended a six-day camp together, where both groups were engaged in learning experiences (Sykes 1974). Schopler and Reichler (1971) trained parents in therapeutic techniques for use with their psychotic children; this application resulted in improvement in the children's behavior and in family functioning. Predelinquent children and their parents were trained together to develop negotiation responses, in a program reported by Kifer (1974). Research consistently has supported the advisability of parental involvement in the education of exceptional children (Clements & Alexander, 1975). But this involvement must change to reflect changes in law, culture, technology and knowledge of human behavior.

IMPACT OF PUBLIC LAW 94-142

The Education for All Handicapped Children Act was signed into law on November 29, 1975, but the final Regulations for that Act were not published until August 23, 1977 (Federal Register, 1977). Thus, two years elapsed before educators began to have the opportunity to investigate the full meaning of the legislation. That impact still has not been realized fully in the area of parent-school relationships. This inertia is similar to that experienced after the portentous *Brown v. Board of Education* decision (Abeson & Bolick, 1974). In spite of the enormous publicity and the extensive media coverage of subsequent events, many black parents did not understand. — nor were they able to take advantage of — their newly found power.

A similar response to the parental rights provisions of PL 94-142 should be expected. A vanguard of parents (who are at least partly responsible for the law in the first place) will test their strength. Many others will be unsure of their new role. Educators will feel threatened by this new relationship much as many were by the *Brown* decision. There is, however, a significant difference. The *Brown* decision required schools only to fulfill their obligations as an educational system, whereas the regulations of PL 94-142 are much more extensive. These regulations not only tell educators that equal educational opportunity must be provided, but also how it must be provided, what the specific responsibilities of the school are, how parents are to be involved, what the extent of the educational program must be, and in general expand the school's role as a social agency.

The impact of this law probably will not be contained only in the area of special education. Parents of nonhandicapped children will not long tolerate the unequal conditions created by implementation of the regulations. Probably, there soon will be demands for IEPs for all children, increased parental authority, and perhaps some anger over differential costs. Parents of nonexceptional children can be expected to explore similar rights and privileges for their children. First, however, the current inertia must be overcome.

A recent study by Yoshida, Fenton, Kaufman, and Maxwell (1978) highlighted the current attitudes of special educators concerning parent involvement and, in fact, demonstrated a firm resistance to meaningful parental impact on educational planning. The investigators questioned more than 1,500 planning team members in Connecticut — a state which has expanded the role of parents to include participation at planning team meetings. (The planning teams determine eligibility and programming for special education candidates.) The team members were asked to indicate which parental roles on a planning team they would support. Of 24 possible roles, only 2 received majority support, and both of those were passive (presenting and gathering basic information). The respondents expressed a strong dislike for parental involvement in evaluation, monitoring, or management of school programs. Thus, the study seems to indicate that educators' attitudes do not correspond with the legal doctrines of parent involvement, nor do they demonstrate an adequate understanding of the forces present in the educational lives of children. Some, if not the majority of educational personnel, appear to cling to a belief that parents may be cajoled into accepting and acquiescing to professional expertise. Parents, then, are essentially viewed as partially incompetent junior partners who are to be convinced of the righteousness of education.

The *real* parent-school relationship is not dictated by law. Law may provide an impulse that initiates a change in momentum, but real and meaningful parent involvement grows out of community values, power balances, parent and teacher expectations, economics, and the general social climate existing within the school, the district, the state, and the nation. In spite of an increased legally defined relationship, the chasm continues to widen — a chasm into which the children of America are poured and are expected to survive.

DEFICIENCIES AND PROBLEMS OF CURRENT PRACTICE

Parent involvement programs generally have neglected to account for the following:

1. Parents are the single most important influence on the development of children.

2. People (parents) who are disenfranchised will not actively seek to support the organization (educational system); in fact, they generally will work against it in some way.

3. When the goals and values of two groups are incongruent, an active process must work between them to ensure that both groups will influence a final agreement if those groups have any desire to produce a joint product (in this case, parents and educators producing educated children).

4. Mutual agreements must have some means of enforcement.

5. Merely teaching parents about education does not ensure their support.

6. Neither parents nor educators can be held solely *responsible* for the educational achievement of children.

7. Parent *responsibility* cannot be dictated, but it must be developed if American education is to be improved.

Few programs openly attempt to develop parental *responsibility* for the educational success of their children. Parental responsibility may have developed incidentally in some programs, but this is rarely a specific objective. Merely training parents is insufficient as a means of eliciting responsibility. Northcott (1973) reported the use of a systems approach to parent participation, in which parents and teachers were exposed to various situations wherein trust and interdependence were built. Another program stressing parent involvement and responsibility led to improved achievement of 70 Title I preschool children (Marcovich, 1975).

Such studies, while informative, still do not address the real issues of parent involvement; they merely expose the superficial aspects of parent training and the utilization of parents as "foot soldiers." There have been few bold attempts to place parents in the role of managers. In fact, Kelly (1974) reported that many educators advise that parent-teacher contacts be limited to conferences, and even warn against parent involvement in the child's academic program. Clements and Alexander (1975) stated that although official attitudes toward parent involvement are voiced as affirmative, they actually range from disassociation to pressure on parents to "pay the price" for keeping their children in special programs. (The previously mentioned investigation by Yoshida et al. (1978) certainly provides objective support for that contention.) Even though Clements and Alexander recognized these serious deficits, ironically, the model they offered provides little more than informational and emotional support to parents; it does not afford parents an active and strong role in the educational management of their children.

The issue is not whether parents should be involved, nor the extent of involvement but, rather, how the situation can be structured to best utilize parents in efforts to maximize the educational achievement of children; that is:

1. How can educators structure the contract (whether written or unwritten) between parents and schools so that both sides must pull their weight toward the same goals?
2. How can parents assume their responsibility in educational success of their children?
3. How can education regain the support of the community?

The first task is to analyze the current situation. It is insufficient and dangerous to accept the current dichotomy that educators are responsible for education in school and parents outside of school, and that neither has a right to invade the sanctity of the other's "territory." Not only is it right that territorial boundaries be permeable — it is mandatory.

The Tenth Annual Gallup Poll on Education (Gallup, 1978) revealed a number of interesting and contradictory trends in public attitudes toward education. The respondents (again) listed discipline as the biggest problem facing the schools. But the public failed to see the connection between parent involvement and discipline, since only 1% listed the former as a critical problem and only 4% viewed lack of interest on the part of parents as a significant deficiency. The schizophrenic response pattern was continued when the public was asked, "What should the schools be doing that they are not?" The fourth-ranked response was a need for more parent involvement. The second-ranked response was a need for better teachers — not meaning better trained teachers, but teachers more able to inspire students to set high goals. One has difficulty understanding how parent involvement could rank so high among priorities, with the simultaneous belief that we should look to teachers rather than parents as a source of inspiration for children.

Have parents abandoned their responsibility willingly or have educators convinced them that parents are not needed? The articles by Kelly (1974), Clements and Alexander (1975) and Yoshida et al. (1978) would seem to indicate the latter. Educators may have succeeded in convincing parents that the task of education is best left to educators. Surprisingly, the issue investigated by Gallup that drew the most definitive response tendency was that parents should be held financially responsible for children's vandalism and school attendance. Thus, fortunately, the public has not totally accepted the schism between school and family.

The Gallup Poll just barely scratches the surface of the problems affecting the parent-school relationship. The social and psychological conditions contributing to this situation are complex and highly emotional. Public respect for education has diminished considerably since George Gallup conducted his first survey in 1969. Educators and the public must realize, however, that it was not teachers who demanded that graduation standards be abandoned or that public schools conduct special programs to hold dropouts in school. The public (parent groups in the forefront) has demanded changes to reflect the changing values of the nation. Education has been reactive. Woodring (1978) discussed this phenomenon with eloquence: Public schools are highly visible and, hence, open to constant criticism. If children continue to misbehave in school, educators are blamed for being lax; if children are punished, parents become angry. Educational philosophy has vacillated because parents are confused about what they want and educators have become overly concerned with maintaining a smooth organization rather than educational quality. The purpose of education has been bastardized, expanded, and diluted.

David McClelland (1977), in a report on power, delivered a unique insight that may be applied to the failures of schools to please parents and to live up to the expectations developed for them. He contends that our social programs (public schools included) have been managed by people who were motivated by "N power" — a need to have impact. These people were not satisfied with improvement or achievement; they sought a total, unattainable upheaval whereby all problems would be eliminated in a single swift stroke. Thus, schools were faced with the impossible goals of integrating a society that had been segregated for hundreds of years, of curing poverty, of providing therapy for maladjusted adolescents, and of substituting for parents who were increasingly caught in a whirlwind of change and activity. Such motivation is doomed to failure because impossible goals have been established. The schools have become a supermarket for social services. The role of public education has been an ever widening spiral. Unfortunately, the resources — economic, legitimate, and technological — are not available in sufficient quantities to fulfill all of these new roles. The result is a feeling of frustration and antagonism on the part of both consumers (parents) and providers (educators).

Woodring (1978) suggested that schools go back to doing what they do best and leave other responsibilities to parents and other social agencies. That suggestion, however, does not and will not improve the day-to-day parent-school relationship since neither parents nor schools can turn back the clock to a different time. What is needed is a new model based upon current and forecast conditions.

The impact of Public Law 94-142, discussed earlier, has one other facet that must be considered: PL 94-142 provides a contract that is binding on only one party — the school. Parents have no written, designated, enforceable role. This omission has forced educators to develop IEPs essentially without regard for the most critical factor — parent support. In this case at least, parent support has a far different meaning than parent consent or involvement. Children spend 80% of their time outside of school, but educators are conceptually saddled with the responsibility for the child's total adjustment when, in reality, parents must be held partially accountable. Moral standards and educational attitudes of children cannot be taught in a classroom. Children whose schools are located in communities in mayhem will not improve, in spite of all educational effort, unless their communities and parental responsibility improve (Woodring, 1978). Schools run a distant second to parents in influence on young children and an even more distant third to peers and parents during adolescence (Mussen, Conger, & Kagan, 1969). Yet, we continue to castigate schools disproportionately for the failures of children. Neill (1978) reported a study conducted by the Rand Corporation that concluded:

> Short of drastic changes in the U.S. education system, there appears to be limits on how much public schooling can change students either absolutely or relative to other social influences (family, peers, or the economic system). Federal policy should lower its sights (p. 157).

Another alternative would be to apportion responsibility for educational success (however defined) among those groups who can be held at least partially accountable (parents and educators in the elementary schools, with a possible expansion to students in the secondary schools). Clements and Alexander (1975) rightfully pointed out that the responsibility for education and socialization is a shared one. Our schools often have operated as a secret society. Parents were included only to the extent of getting them to go along with whatever was offered. Educators felt that they could impact on children only if they neutralized parent impact by keeping them ignorant. What resulted was a situation in which parents (especially parents of exceptional children) believed that the schools could take care of everything by themselves. The end product was an estrangement from the system of the people who can have the greatest impact — parents.

In this regard, education may gain a principle from medicine. Physicians may not attempt to cure a person who will not agree to the prescribed treatment. If a patient fails to accept the prescription or diagnostic tests, a doctor may send a registered letter to that patient announcing that he is releasing himself from responsibility. What educators have done is to project an ability to cure the man in spite of himself. In fact, if the studies by Yoshida et al. (1978) and Kelly (1974) are at all indicative of the current attitudes, educators have not only accepted but have sought the messianic task of educating the nation's youth in spite of themselves or their parents. For this, education will continue to pay the price. It may be easier just to accept the harsh public criticism than to undergo the tense and demanding rituals and adjustments of sharing responsibility.

The attitude discussed in the preceding paragraph has a secondary effect. It creates a power struggle between parents and schools. Educators have relied upon expert power as a manipulative device. Parents have been forced into a position of perceived powerlessness. May (1972) terms the power possessed by education and other social organizations "nutrient power": the ability of an individual or a group to provide for the welfare of another individual or group. The resultant powerlessness of the recipient leads to an adversarial position wherein the recipient resents the control exercised by the "benevolent" provider. The provider then becomes a foe simply because of the power differential.

Power, in the American culture, is perceived as innately negative. It is perceived as alien to democratic ideals (McClelland, 1975). The teacher/parent or educator/community relationship, however, is based upon power. We have seen what has happened when the community feels powerless in its attempts to shape its educational institutions. If parents are excluded from management status, they can wield the power of the pocketbook. School bonds are defeated. Property tax revenues are reduced. Either way, there is power equalization or perhaps a swing of power in an opposing direction. The fears of educators result in entrenchment, greater resistance, and a widening power imbalance. Each group seeks to improve its position relative to the other. Positions are hardened, and communication is stifled. Communication is most effective when two individuals or groups view themselves as equal in power (May, 1972); however, neither parents nor schools view the current relationship as equipotential. Distrust abounds, and money is used to balance information and skill.

Two factors influencing the nature of parent involvement have resulted from the massive changes in social patterns during the last 30 years. First, American society currently is made up of a large number of temporary organizations (Bennis & Slater, 1969). The old unwritten contract between parents and schools will no longer work because there is no stability in the relationship. The contract envisioned by the school differs from that envisioned by each parent since backgrounds are so diverse. This heterogeneity of values has resulted in an inability of parents and educators to live up to the expectations of the other. Parents bring old values into a new community and find that these values are not consistent with the views being expressed by others.

Second, parents today are much more educated than were parents of a generation ago. The current corps of parents benefited from the education boom of the 1950s and 1960s. The managerial relationship of a school to educated parents is qualitatively different from that of school to uneducated parents. Once again, the patient-doctor relationship provides a strong analogy. Patients no longer look upon the knowledge possessed by physicians as unfathomable. They wish to be informed about their conditions and the proposed treatment. Many hospitals have developed consent forms explaining in detail the procedures to be used and the possible consequences (Yeager, 1977). Such a movement is taking place in education as well. Parents have greater access to information about education. The media and legislators have been effective at removing some of the occult from the science of education. Educators no longer can sell the public a bill of goods based upon their ignorance. One of the results of this spate of educated parents is the long list of parental rights established by PL 94-142.

If a semblance of stability and reason is going to be restored, educators must adopt new techniques. Risk taking and honesty must become more extensive (Clements & Alexander, 1975).

A MODEL OF IMPROVED EDUCATIONAL EFFECTIVENESS

Are there techniques by which the influences of teachers and parents may be developed and resolved into a unidirectional force leading to improved educational effectiveness? Such techniques not only exist but are used by all people every day. Broadly defined, they include: definition of roles, compromise, negotiation, acceptance of responsibility, and mediation. All social contacts require use and acceptance of these techniques. Citizens of a nation accept the constraint of law because of the security it provides. Parents and educators can develop mutually agreeable role definitions because they perceive that over the long run the gains of such an agreement will far outweigh the losses of territory. Application of the techniques to be outlined will neutralize many of the problems mentioned in this article. The process is continuous and is nurtured by unending effort. It should not be entered into with visions of immediate or complete improvement. The process is people oriented, not systems oriented. As people change, the process will and must change. Thus, the processes discussed below concentrate on behaviors and responsibility rather than systems and resources.

The IEP as a Contractual Agreement

The present structure of IEP development and application is semi-contractual in nature. The school develops an IEP enumerating educational goals and services for the child. The parent consents to the IEP and may certify that consent by affixing a signature. The school then has the obligation (legal or ethical) of executing the promises made in the IEP. The result is (1) a carefully diluted IEP such that the school does not promise anything that may be out of the safe range of delivery possibility; (2) no obligation on the part of the parent to actively support the IEP; (3) a contract binding on only one party — the school; (4) a restriction on productivity. Of these, item two possesses the greatest negative potential. Other writers have recognized the possible ramifications of that phenomenon, especially in efforts to improve the effectiveness of inner city schools. Jackson (1978) states of his own Push for Excellence program that if parents want their children to learn, they must set the stage.

> Parents must pledge to monitor their child's report card . . . At the beginning of the year, the principal must give a "State of the School" address. It should clearly define educational goals, establish rules, set up expectations, and lay out a plan for achieving the goals by the end of the academic year (p. 1935).

Sewell (1978) echoes Jackson by the statement that parents must send their children to school realizing that they (parents) have responsibilities to the school. Poussaint (1978) and Haskins (1978) speak of the responsibility of the school to get parents involved, to go to the length of actively seeking parental involvement in school policy, and the specific educational programs of their children. These statements do not go far enough. They do not address the *hows* of such involvement. This deficiency may result in an attitude such as that encountered in the Yoshida et al. (1978) investigation. The IEP concept can be expanded to serve a more meaningful role in this regard.

If IEP's were developed jointly by parent and educator, rather than merely presented to parents to sign, and if the IEP were to enumerate specific parent responsibilities which, when faithfully followed, would increase the *probability* of academic success and allow for goals set at a higher level, and if the IEP specified a system for updating, monitoring, and negotiating, a true contractual, responsible relationship would exist.

The process involves four major steps. Each of these may be accomplished utilizing a number of specific approaches elaborated upon in the next section. The system is equally applicable to general education. The major steps are:

1. Parents in the community select a group of parents (no more than five) to represent them in meetings and negotiations with a committee of educators selected by the school system. These representatives may be selected from the entire population of parents, or if the process is to be utilized only for special education, just parents of exceptional children should be involved. The former is a much more desirable practice, especially since effective mainstreaming requires integration of general and special education. The efficacy is enhanced greatly if the process includes all education consumers.

2. The two groups develop and adopt a written statement of educational philosophy, goals, and values for the school system. Either group may present a statement as a basis for negotiation, or the groups may decide to generate a statement in concert and work out differences as they go along.

3. These goals and values are contractually agreed upon by both educators and parents, forming the basis for negotiation of IEPs between individual parents and IEP teams. Specific IEPs are developed in a similar manner — that is, parent and educators may submit goals for inclusion. Goals and services are negotiable among all members of the IEP team. There should be *no* IEP planning meetings to which the parents are not invited.

4. Individual parents and IEP teams develop specific plans written as contracts between the school and the parents. After a child has

reached age 13, the IEP team may be expanded to include the student. The conditions under which students participate would follow general guidelines established by the district-wide committee. The depth of involvement would depend upon the individual team's perceptions of the student's ability to accept some responsibility for his or her own educational achievement. Thus, the student will be aware of expectations, will have the opportunity to express thoughts and, more importantly, to commit himself or herself to *responsible* behavior. This commitment would be difficult to obtain without seeking the student's input.

The plan should enumerate goals and target dates, review dates, and assign accountability for each goal or subpart. Parent and student responsibilities should be presented as they bear upon the success of educational goals and may include such things as assuring attendance, responsibility for homework, follow through on disciplinary activities initiated in school, and so forth. Criteria for success would be established for each goal, along with the attendant responsibilities of each person. The signatures of parents and educators would signify that each member agreed to perform in accordance with terms of the IEP contract. Thus, parents would share in the burden of accountability. Schools no longer would be in the lonely position of accountability without sufficient authority or influence, and the community would be less willing to demand services far beyond the resources available. Since parents would now be a part of the system, they should be more understanding of its limitations. Any failure in the program might be traceable to a specific element in the IEP or the incomplete execution of an enumerated responsibility by educator or parent. Parents would gain a role in establishing educational policy that they must have if education is to regain some lost support and educators gain a means for integrating the influences of parents and school. This is an achievement-oriented process —one in which continuous improvement is the goal. Problems will occur every day, but the educational efficiency should improve in recognizable steps.

Some parents may refuse to participate. This occurrence can be dealt with in any number of ways, none of which is entirely sufficient for the student. First, the school system may develop an IEP designed to get around the parent's nonparticipation (i.e., maximize whatever can be accomplished). Second, the school system could appoint a parent surrogate who would protect the interests of the student in IEP development. Finally — and this is a drastic measure — parents who refuse to participate in the education of their children might be deemed negligent, so community sanctions could be sought. Whatever the choice, it should be done within the guidelines set up by the district-wide parent-educator committee. In any event, fewer children will be "lost" because their parents refuse to participate than are presently falling through the cracks that exist because schools and parents have less than desirable means of communication and negotiation.

The model presented here also brings a new, more profound meaning to the IEP. There is no longer a reason for dilution. Adherence means increased productivity and a true contract. Some might argue that this innovation would be an intrusion into the sanctity of the family or that parents should not have a role in determining educational policy. The main argument against this logic is that the nature of child development and our educational programs demand such interaction. The two forces can be either complementary or competitive, but they cannot be maintained separately. How much better it would be if they were at least partly on the same wave length! The following section describes techniques that will enhance the chances of success of such a venture by providing stability for temporary systems, aiding in development of values and goals, and assisting in conflict resolution. The techniques are not presented in any specific order and should be integrated to achieve a comprehensive, coordinated approach.

Putting the Model to Work

Any approach to goal conflict resolution should not be based upon a "horse trading" philosophy. If this is representative of the initial environment, each group will seek to maximize its gain at the expense of the other. It usually is not necessary to have a victor and a victim. In most negotiations, both parties can emerge as benefactors — that is, with more than they started with. In some cases, the major initial gain is a decrease of distracting and time consuming conflict — conflict that prevents development of real effort toward any goal.

Each of the techniques explained below is more applicable under some sets of conditions than others. The techniques are not simple, but they have proven validity and generally long lasting results. In addition, they afford participants a feeling of equipotentiality. Teachers, administrators, and supervisors, as well as parents, must be involved in all training ventures.

Reality Therapy Training

Providing participants of parent-teacher groups with reality therapy (Glasser, 1965) training offers each member a powerful tool for use in dealing with irresponsible behavior. Behavior may be classified as either responsible or irresponsible. Responsible behavior is defined as fulfilling one's own needs without depriving others of the ability to fulfill theirs. Reality is that which makes for the best gain in the long run. Use of the reality therapy model is tantamount to establishing — a basic philosophy of human behavior within which the members of the group may operate. Thus, individuals must view themselves as responsible *to* the group but responsible *for* themselves. Excuses for irresponsible behavior are not acceptable. There-fore, at the meetings in which parents and educators develop the system-wide statement of philosophy, goals and values, reality may be defined in the following manner:

1. Parents have a right and responsibility in the process of education.
2. Parents cannot be excluded.
3. Educators have the expertise needed to develop the achievement of children.
4. The education system must be congruent with the surrounding community.

The remainder of reality is defined by the agreed upon philosophy, including the restrictions imposed by limited resources and state, federal, and local laws.

Responsibility is adherence to established standards or at least to established procedures to change standards. It also means accepting con-sequences when one has behaved irresponsibly. Thus, the peer group defines both reality and responsibility within the larger social context. The peer group also defines consequences for irresponsible behavior. As an example, part of the reality within which the parent-educator group must operate is fiscal. If parents are demanding a new program that will cost two million additional dollars while the community has reduced the revenues available to the education system, the parents are behaving irresponsibly. They have passed the boundaries of reality. A teacher who refuses to modify a particular classroom procedure to accommodate a child's special needs also is behaving irresponsibly, since reality presently requires the inclusion of exceptional children to whatever extent is possible, and certainly a modification of classroom procedure is well within the realm of possibility.

Reality therapy training is potent because it is present oriented, and since behavior control is internalized, it requires low maintenance effort. Acceptance of a milieu of reality and responsibility requires a great deal of initial effort. Participants must understand and accept the basic philosophy supporting the technique. Because the procedure has been eminently suc-cessful with many difficult populations (e.g., juvenile delinquents) and has found its way into presently acceptable systems of management, one has no reason to doubt its applicability in the context of this article.

Participants may not rely upon past prejudice to prevent goal attain-ment. Therefore, parents and teachers cannot define reality in terms of past teacher strikes or school bond defeats. Reality therapy is adult. People are expected to manage themselves. One of the characteristics of our educated society is the resistance of many people to external control. Education is supposed to lead to a greater self understanding, and reality therapy allows participants to maintain that posture. In fact, it bolsters it. The philosophy behind reality therapy is powerful. It provides a sane, dignified alternative to antagonism between parents and teachers. It is not easy but, then, ready mixed recipes have not been altogether effective.

Achievement Motivation Training

Another powerful tool is achievement motivation training. Primarily envisioned and developed by David McClelland (1965, 1977), achievement motivation training attempts to develop a set of behaviors leading to increased achievement. Achievement motivation (symbolized as N ach) is maximized when: (1) goal setting is realistic and involves small steps; (2) the motivational syndrome (a set of specific behaviors) is developed; (3) cognition supports behavior; and (4) the group (peers) supports the behavior change. Some of the propositions of achievement motivation are:

1. The more a person understands the reasons and the possible outcome of a behavior change, the more likely it is to occur.
2. Progress is more likely if written records are maintained.
3. The greater the application of a new motive to real, everyday situations, the more likely the motive is to be increased.
4. Motives that lead to improvements in self-image are more likely to be sustained.
5. Group emotional support for change is necessary.

Application of the above premises to development of a joint parent-teacher effort is not difficult to imagine, nor is it untested. It has been successful in developing entrepreneurship in India and improvement in academic functioning of ghetto school children (McClelland, 1977). Simply stated, parents and teachers in a joint venture must: (1) set attainable goals for themselves (the group) and the system, (2) maintain written records, (3) develop among all members a concept of how specific effort will lead to goal attainment, (4) provide peer support to individuals attempting to modify behavior patterns, (5) select goals which, if attained, lead to improved status for all involved members, and (6) select goals that are reflected in improvement of the everyday lives of the members of the educational system. Achievement motivation training can be viewed as the elaboration and application of the IEP concept to development of the parent-educator management system.

An example of a situation in which achievement motivation principles can be applied may be helpful at this point. Suppose that a parent-educator group realizes that the facilities available (classroom area) are much too small for the number of students. Efforts to improve the situation would be most effective if: (1) goals included adding small increments of classroom space over set periods of time rather than looking for ways to totally eliminate the problem immediately, (2) participants understand the reasons why more space is needed, (3) written records are maintained, (4) credit is given to individuals who make a contribution toward goal achievement, and (5) progress is monitored by the group rather than by a single individual.

Another construct of human motivation lends support and additional insight into the process of achievement motivation training. Porter and Lawler (1968) developed an expectancy theory (VIE), which states simply that motivation as expressed by effort is a function of valence (V - the perceived potency of the goal or the reward), instrumentality (I - the perceived ability of the individual to perform the behaviors required to attain the goal), and expectancy (E - the perceived relationship between goal attainment and reward). Thus, in a parent-teacher effort, developing a contract, either group or individual is important — one in which: (1) established goals are important to both parties (valence), (2) both teachers and parents feel that they have the means to reach the goal (instrumentality), and (3) they feel that effort utilizing that means will result in accomplishment and reward (expectancy).

Each of the three factors may interact with the others in ways that may maximize or minimize the resultant effort. Thus, goals with high valence may be perceived as difficult to attain (instrumentality) and will need to be kept within realistic bounds. Low expectancy (of reward) will diminish effort toward any goal, no matter what its valence. Neglect of any of the factors will reduce the overall effort and result in discouraging performance. Parents and teachers should be cautioned against the desire for one great coup. Selection of goals should be executed with concern not only for the needs of the system but with ample attention to the motivational patterns of the participants.

Negotiation Processes

Despite good faith, lofty motives, and perceived unity of purpose, any group of 10 individuals is bound to encounter points of impasse —situations in which honest disagreement brings progress to a halt. At this point, negotiation processes should be initiated.

Harrison (1973) developed the process of role negotiation as a means by which individuals or groups may deal with conflict. Basically, role negotiation is a behavioral approach which assumes that people have differences and opposing interests. Conflict, competition, and maximization of one's own interests are natural. The alternative to continuous conflict as a consequence of the above phenomena is a negotiated agreement. The agreement is based upon a diagnosis of the rights, powers, privileges, and demands of the incumbents of each role with respect to each other. The targets of change are descriptions of duty, responsibility, authority, and accountability.

At any point in the process, then, parents or teachers may view a choice of goal as particularly favorable to one or the other. To prevent a perceived power imbalance, participants may rely upon role negotiation to reach a compromise. The power content may change but the balance remains intact. The result is an agreement to administer and/or withhold rewards or sanctions for compliance or violation of the new role descriptions. The parties must agree to a quid pro quo bargaining stance, and success depends upon sufficiently potent rewards or sanctions, the willingness of both parties to apply rewards or sanctions, and balance of rewards or sanctions created by third party intervention.

The latter point cannot be sufficiently attended to in this paper but must be addressed at least perfunctorily. The process of negotiation often leads to a need for a third party mediator. A parent-teacher committee should recognize this early in its organizational process and should adopt a set of procedures whereby a competent, experienced, impartial third party may be utilized. The cost will be minor when compared to hours lost in a frustrating deadlock. (Precedent has been established in the hearing officer requirements of PL 94-142.)

Attempts to deal with a particularly knotty problem in the IEP contract development process provides an insightful example of the application of role negotiation. In this example, a mother requests 10 hours of speech therapy per week for her child. The school views this request as beyond its capability. A negotiated alternative to this roadblock would be an offer on the part of the school to provide five hours of therapy per week in exchange for a commitment by the mother to a continuance of a reinforcement program at home. The roles of each participant have been redefined. Each has agreed to alter roles in exchange for a favorable role augmentation on the part of the other. Role negotiation may result in each participant taking on a new role to suit the other, a reciprocal reduction in role demands, or a combination of both. The possibilities are limited only by the creativity and tenacity of the participants.

Similar to role negotiation, *planned renegotiation* (Sherwood & Glide-well, 1973) is an organizational development technique involving cycles of: (1) sharing of information and expectations, (2) commitment to a set of expectations, (3) stability and productivity, and (4) disruption, which is a cue for renegotiation. The major differences between role negotiation and planned renegotiation are that: (1) the latter has built-in cycles and may be preplanned so that both parties can prepare for changes, and (2) the latter allows exploration of alternatives offered by both parties. Thus, the two parties agree to abide by the rules offered by one group for a set period of time, after which the other group has the option of changing the rules. Neither group may prevent renegotiation after one group has held the power.

Renegotiation may result in a change in rules or goals, or existing ones may be extended. In some cases, the parties may agree to go by the standards promulgated by one view for a set period at the end of which the opposing view will reign, or the parties may merely agree to renegotiate. Planned renegotiation may be built into the model (i.e., all rules, roles, goals, etc. adopted must be reviewed and renegotiated at specific intervals), or it may be utilized at irregular periods to meet the need of the moment.

Returning to the example of role negotiation offered above, one can see how planned renegotiation also could be applied. The school might have an alternative to the lengthy therapy desired by the parent. Each party would agree to abide by the demands of the other for a set period of time. At the end of that time they would sit down with data collected under each condition and renegotiate the conditions for the next period. Perhaps in this example the school would be able to demonstrate that its alternative is as effective as the intensive therapy. This evidence then would be offered at a negotiation point, and the IEP would be altered accordingly.

Both role negotiation and planned renegotiation are effective tools to reduce the effects of conflict. They may be utilized simultaneously and in concert with the other techniques discussed above. Countless other techniques, too, might be employed. The major obstacle is the acceptance of new roles for the incumbent. Once that is accomplished, the vision is limitless.

Synthesizing the Techniques

Figure 1 is a graphic representation of the parent-educator management system; and Figure 2 represents a model for the development of IEP contracts. These illustrations are offered only as general guides; the models should be adapted to suit specific needs of the participants. In Figure 1, the atmosphere for the entire process is comprised of reality and responsibility (as discussed previously). The process slows six stages, each of which is subject to recycling and negotiation as needed or at preplanned intervals. Thus, selection of parents and educators for the management team (1) may occur annually, but the restatement of individual goals (4) may occur weekly until a product (5) is generated. The evaluation and feedback stage (6) refers to evaluation of individual goal attainment; this stage may result in a recognition that a new reality exists (e.g. laws have changed, resources have been lost or gained, or community needs and values have been transformed). If such is the case, the new reality must be defined and the process recycled from stage 2. In some systems it may be desirable to integrate assessment of new realities into the evaluation stage. Thus, at times recycling may be as small as a two-stage recycle or as great as a six-stage recycle. The process can be adapted to the need.

Figure 2 represents a similar process but on a micro-cosmic level. Reality is defined by the product of the parent-educator management system — that is, the statement of values, goals, and philosophy. Recycling can occur as a result of changes in needs or abilities of the participants that impinge upon the product (stage 4) as a new reality that may affect the definitions upon which the process is based (stage 1).

Although the figures depict a linear sequence, each stage in actuality may exist concurrently with other stages. Therefore, an IEP may undergo renegotiation even as a new reality enters the picture or evaluation is taking place.

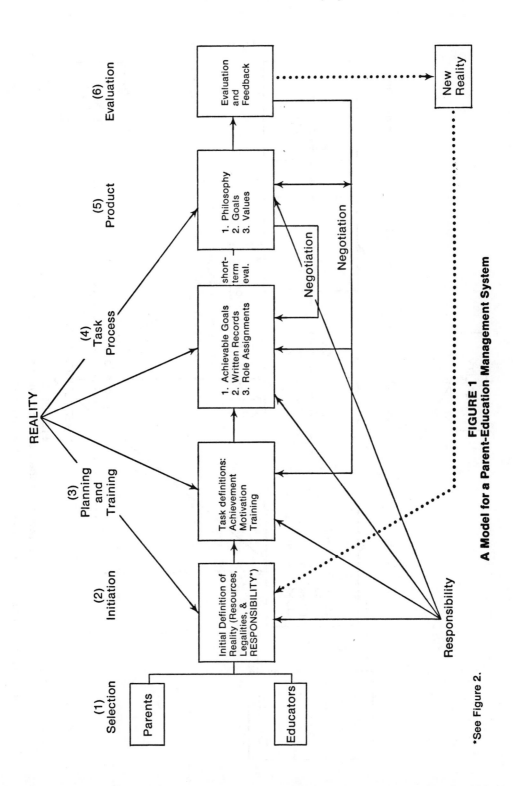

FIGURE 1

A Model for a Parent-Education Management System

*See Figure 2.

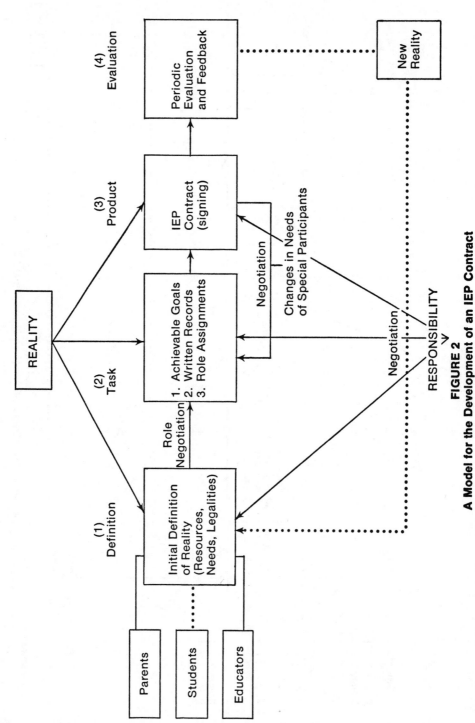

FIGURE 2

A Model for the Development of an IEP Contract

*Originates in wider environment: new resources, change in community, etc.

CONCLUSION

The processes and techniques presented in this paper can lead to what May (1972) termed "integrative power" — the power resulting from collaboration and cooperation. This type of power will not give parents all they want nor will it fulfill all teacher expectations. What will result is a closer approximation of the desires of both sides. Parent-teacher cooperation will result in greater response generalization on the part of children (Johnson & Katz, 1973). Highly educated parents will be more thoroughly satisfied with their relationships with the public schools because the schools will be at least partly of their design (Drucker, 1976). The end result is a development of mutual responsibility.

> All it (the school) can promise . . . is an opportunity to learn under favorable circumstances, with the help of a competent teacher and with a modest amount of essential equipment, including some good books. Whatever the program may be, it is the child who must do the learning. If this can be made clear to parents, their demands on the school may be modified, and perhaps they will accept greater responsibility for their own part in the child's education (Woodring, 1978, p. 517).

No one right path marks the goal of this paper — improved educational output through redefinition of the educator-consumer relationship. American public education must learn to interact efficiently and effectively with its environment. In order to do so, educators must take advantage of the phenomenon of equifinality — the ability of an organization to reach a goal by two or more different paths (Katz & Kahn, 1966). The path outlined in this paper is actually many paths. Utilization must conform to the needs and values of the people in the system to which it is to be applied. That it can be made to succeed is evidenced by the successes of developers of the specific techniques. Patience and realistic expectations are the key cautions. Educators must learn to treat themselves and parents with the same demeanor as suggested for exceptional children: Develop attainable short-term goals and provide sufficient reinforcement of long-range success.

REFERENCES

Abeson, A., & Bolick, N. *A continuing summary of pending and completed litigation regarding the education of handicapped children.* Reston, VA: Council for Exceptional Children, 1974.

Bennis, W. G., & Slater, P. E. *The temporary society.* New York: Harper & Row, 1969.

Clements, J. E., & Alexander, R. N. Parent training: Bringing it all back home, *Focus on Exceptional Children,* 1975, 7, 1-12.

Council for Exceptional Children. *Parent education/parent role — Aurally handicapped, physically handicapped, visually handicapped, multiply handicapped, speech handicapped, emotionally disturbed, disadvantaged: A selective bibliography.* Reston, VA: CEC Information Services and Publications, 1977. (a)

Council for Exceptional Children. *Parent materials — Mentally retarded, learning disabled: A selective bibliography.* Reston, VA: CEC Information Services & Publications, 1977. (b)

Drucker, P. F. Managing the educated. In R. A. Sutermeister, *People and productivity.* New York: McGraw Hill, 1976, pp. 167-178.

Federal Register, 1977, *42,* 42474-42518.

Gallup, G. H. The tenth annual Gallup Poll. *Phi Delta Kappan,* 1978, *60,* 33-45.

Glasser, W. *Reality therapy.* New York: Harper & Row, 1965.

Harrison, R. Role negotiation: A tough minded approach to team development. In W. G. Bennis, D. E. Berlew, E. H. Schein, & F. I. Steele (Eds.), *Interpersonal dynamics.* Homewood, IL: Dorsey Press, 1973, pp. 467-479.

Haskins, K. Mobilizing the parents II. *Phi Delta Kappan,* 1978, *60,* 220.

Jackson, J. L. In pursuit of equity, ethics and excellence: The challenge to close the gap. *Phi Delta Kappan,* 1978, *60,* 191-193.

Johnson, C. A., & Katz, R. C. Using parents as change agents for their children: A review, *Journal of Child Psychology and Psychiatry,* 1973, *14,* 181-200.

Katz, D., & Kahn, R. L. *The social psychology of organizations.* New York: John Wiley & Sons, 1966.

Kelly, E. J. *Parent-teacher interaction: A special educational perspective.* Seattle: Special Child Publications, 1974.

Kifer, R. E. Training predelinquent youths and their parents to negotiate conflict situations. *Journal of Applied Behavior Analysis,* 1974, *7,* 357-364.

Luterman, D. M. A parent oriented nursery program for preschool deaf children . . . A follow up study. *Volta Review,* 1971, *73,* 106-112.

Marcovich, S. J. Seeking to get parents interested in their child's learning, educators in Superior, Wisconsin, rediscovered the kitchen table. *American Education,* 1975, *11,* 9-12.

May, R. *Power and innocence.* New York: Delta, 1972.

McClelland, D. C. Toward a theory of motive acquisition. *American Psychologist,* 1965, *20,* 321-333.

McClelland, D. C. *Power, the inner experience.* New York: Irvington, 1975.

McClelland, D. C. Power, motivation and impossible dreams. *Wharton Magazine,* 1977, *1,* 33-39.

McConnell, F. The parent teaching home: An early intervention program for hearing impaired children. *Peabody Journal of Education,* 1974, *51,* 162-170.

Mussen, P. H., Conger, J. J., & Kagan, J. *Child development and personality.* New York: Harper & Row, 1969.

Nardine, F. E. Parents as a teaching resource. *Volta Review,* 1974, *76,* 172-177.

Neill, G. Washington report. *Phi Delta Kappan,* 1978, *60,* 157-158.

Northcott, W. H. Parenting a hearing impaired child. *Hearing & Speech News,* 1973, *41,* 10-12.

Porter, L. W., & Lawler, E. E. *Managerial attitudes and performance.* Homewood, IL: Dorsey Press, 1968.

Poussaint, A. F. Mobilizing the parents I. *Phi Delta Kappan,* 1978, *60,* 219.

Schopler, E., & Reichler, R. J. Parents as cotherapists in the treatment of psychotic children. *Journal of Autism & Childhood Schizophrenia,* 1971, *1,* 87-102.

Sewell, C. Untitled entry. *Phi Delta Kappan,* 1978, *60,* 200.

Sherwood, J. J., & Glidewell, J. C. Planned renegotiation: A norm setting OD intervention. In W. G. Bennis, D. E. Berlew, E. H. Scheen, & J. I. Steele (Eds.), *Interpersonal dynamics.* Homewood, IL: Dorsey Press, 1973.

Sykes, K. C. Camp Challenge: Program for parents and their preschool children with visual handicaps. *New Outlook for the Blind,* 1974, *68,* 344-347.

Wilkie, J. My baby is deaf. *Volta Review,* 1973, *75,* 103-108.

Woodring, P. A second open letter to teachers. *Phi Delta Kappan,* 1978, *50,* 515-517.

Yeager, R. C. The self-care surge. *Medical World News,* Oct. 3, 1977, 43-54.

Yoshida, R. K., Fenton, K. S., Kaufman, M. J., & Maxwell, J. P. Parental involvement in the special education pupil planning process: The school's perspective. *Exceptional Children,* 1978, *44,* 531-534.

In all of the controversy about bias in testing, few professionals can stand back and offer reasonable criticisms regarding testing or assessment issues. Scannell is one of the professionals who can. As he aptly points out in this essay: "Standardized tests are not perfect tools; their value is influenced largely by the skill with which people interpret and use results." One need not be a statistical research design expert to understand this discussion. What it does is convey information that makes for appropriate consumption and use of test-derived data.

A Positive View Of Standardized Tests

Dale P. Scannell

A few years ago a sage and perceptive connoisseur of popular topics observed that it had been established beyond any reasonable doubt that smoking was the single most important cause of — statistics. The parallel between implications of this statement and the currently popular flurry of anti-test articles is interesting to ponder. Cigarette packages now must carry the warning that smoking is dangerous to your health; and some critics of testing, it seems, will not be satisfied until a similar caveat appears on the covers of all test booklets: "It has been determined by (someone) that testing is dangerous to your personal health and happy existence."

Attacks and counterattacks concerning testing have appeared in a variety of sources — newspapers, weekly popular news magazines, journals of various organizations, and general professional journals (including those that represent the testing professionals). The attacks have been based on a variety of issues but, generally, the counterattacks have only stressed the errors in the attacks. The apologists of standardized tests usually have taken a defensive position, criticizing the critics for misinformation, lack of information, distortion of facts, or of impure motives. The apology for standardized testing represented by this article hopefully will avoid the counterattack mentality by focusing on the positive attributes and potential

443

values of standardized tests within an egalitarian educational system and democratic social order, which the author presumes to be accurately descriptive of United States institutions, in theory if not in practice.

Rather than criticizing the critics of standardized tests — an activity of questionable value — an attempt will be made first to analyze some major reasons for and factors related to the frequency of recent anti-test literature. Although specific features of standardized tests have prompted some of the attacks, it seems likely that tests have been partially victimized by manifestations of general concern about current educational practice. Second, all practices and procedures are based on some premises — as true for the use of standardized tests as for face creams. Thus, some premises concerning education and the role of schools as a social institution will be presented and discussed here — the purpose being to provide rationale for asserting that standardized tests can be useful tools for enhancing educational effectiveness. To the extent that the premises are unacceptable, the case for standardized tests likely will be also.

FACTORS RELATED TO CRITICISMS OF STANDARDIZED TESTS

That standardized testing is a popular target for some professional educators, journalists, and other members of the general public should not be surprising. Testing is a highly visible activity, providing tangible results that will be pleasing to some, unpleasant for others. In some ways and in the minds of some people, testing is a symbol of what the schools are or for which they strive. Since the institution itself has some forcefully vocal critics, testing is bound to come in for its share of the harsh words.

The Public Dichotomy on School Purposes

Over the past 20 years schools often have been criticized for being too impersonal, a factory that processes information into the heads of children with no regard for the personal or human elements of growth and maturation. Concurrently, schools have been faulted for promoting a soft, standardless curriculum that allowed the Russians to be the first into space, that permits illiterates to receive high school diplomas, that emphasizes the socialization of youth to the neglect of academic achievement. To see the evidence of this paradox, one need only review the stated intentions of the private alternative schools that have been started in recent years. In almost equal numbers these form a dichotomy, with the proponents of "back to the basics" or "subject-centered" schools in one camp and' proponents of "humanistic," "social growth," "personalized" schools in the other.

The critics holding to these two extreme positions are withdrawing support of the schools for reasons that are virtually opposite. The schools they criticize and condemn are the same schools, but the perceptions are in direct contrast. It is little wonder that education is characterized by cycles of goals and procedures. Under the circumstances, bizarre, even random, behavior of school personnel could be expected as attempts are made to satisfy a schizophrenic public.

Standardized tests provide tangible results that individuals are not all equal in terms of the characteristics being measured by the tests. Part of the public opinion dichotomy about schooling centers on the issue of whether differences among students should be identified and treated; these attitudes, in turn, are related to what some writers describe as the decline of meritocracy. In the movement to emphasize the equality of rights for all people and to rid society of policies and procedures that discriminate *unfairly* and on the basis of *irrelevant* factors, there has been great difficulty in, and different opinions about, retaining those processes which are based on appropriate and humanistic recognition of individual differences so that each student can be assisted, frequently in different ways, to mature and develop optimally.

One effect of these attitudes as manifested in the schools is the distribution of grades. The use of credit/no credit systems and grade inflation may reflect a growing reluctance of educators to describe differences even when they exist on factors that are readily definable and measurable. There seems to be resistance to recognizing excellence/merit and deficiencies in classroom achievement; reports to parents and the general public often minimize the variability that exists. Thus, results on standardized tests which do point out differences understandably cause alarm, resentment, and attacks on the messenger that brings the bad news. Standardized tests are inimical for those who believe or feel more comfortable in accepting the equality of all people on all characteristics.

The Accountability Trend

Another current social trend is affecting the attitude of some people toward standardized tests. In the past decade the concept of accountability has been applied to schools and individual teachers in forms that vary from rational and professional to the other extreme of witch hunts and an opportunity to "do to schools what we haven't been able to do under other pretexts." Almost all professional educators accept the fact that they are responsible for the wise stewardship of public funds and the careful nurturance of the children who have been entrusted to them by parents. But professional educators are incensed, as any group should be, by unfair and irrational approaches that equate school productivity to assembly line input/output models for purposes of accountability.

All too often, scores on standardized tests have been used as weapons by critics of schools and advocates of accountability. The attackers have demonstrated little understanding of test technology and have magnified their errors by assuming that the only achievements worth considering are those measured by standardized tests. These fallacies have been combined with the graceful avoidance of any consideration of community and social factors that may impinge more stringently on school success than any school variables, including teacher effectiveness or curriculum.

There are compelling reasons to sympathize with beleaguered teachers when critics are upset by results that show 50% of a local class below a national grade level norm (is the definition of the median the villain?); when the critics had been backing a vested interest in health education, consumer education, career education, humanistic education, and other topics added to school responsibilities and now ignore the impact the addition of these curricula has on the time available for the "traditional" subjects; or when the critics ignore factors such as family mobility, single parent homes, corruption in government, and two-breadwinner families, and the effect these social trends have on student interest in and parental support of schools. Standardized tests do provide a potential weapon for an unreasonably critical local community, particularly when school officials do an ineffective or incomplete job of interpreting the results within the milieu of the community.

The Family Educational Rights & Privacy Act and Consumer Advocacy

The preceding point is related to another factor that may contribute to the recent attacks on standardized tests: With the Buckley-Pell amendment guaranteeing the *right to know*, parents and members of the community have been privy to test information that schools, perhaps unwisely, had never released before. "These data are too technical for the layman" and "you may abuse this information because you don't comprehend the limitations" characterized many schools until the law forced them to release the information to those who had the right to receive it. A complete measurement program requires an effective reporting process, and test data are not too technical when presented in appropriate ways. But the point is that parents now have the right to all information about their children, including standardized test data, and the threat of this open system leads some to conclude that standardized tests are too dangerous to continue to use.

The right-to-know legislation is just one manifestation of the consumer advocacy movement that has had a major impact on everyone, with the testing industry being one of the more recent targets. This movement is just one facet of the current social scene affecting schools that impacts on testing and makes good reading in the weekly news magazine.

SOME PREMISES ABOUT EDUCATION AND EDUCATORS

Within the turbulent society that has its effect on schools and standardized testing, some premises about schools and life need to be established before a "case" can be made for standardized tests. These include:

1. Academic, substantive achievement is an important goal of the school;
2. A common set of goals determines at least a major part of the curriculum of American schools;
3. Instruction and curriculum should be based on the best evidence possible;
4. Excellence should be identified and rewarded, and deficiencies should be identified and remediated; and
5. Sincere and rational educators will use information wisely and in the best interests of their students.

1. Academic achievement, including the basic skills and basic disciplines, is an important goal of the schools. Some would argue that this goal defines the *raison d'etre* for schools, the unique role that schools are to play among primary and secondary social institutions. For purposes of this treatise, however, we need not agree that academic achievement is *the* single most important reason for schools to exist, only that academic achievement is *one* of the legitimate goals of the school.

In the United States education has been deemed essential for effective citizen participation required in a democratic society, and essential in fulfilling the basic tenet of our country that we have a collective responsibility to provide opportunity for all people to develop as fully as they are motivated and capable of achieving. The three R's along with the cultural components from history, geography, government, and literature, and a basic introduction to physical and biological science, formed the central focus of the original public schools and have continued to be a major part of the K-12 curriculum. Though schools have been asked to add other subjects and topics and even though short-term priorities have focused on topics outside the core or basic areas, the three R's and the basic disciplines have continued to represent a major component in the curricula within schools of this country, as well as the mark of an educated person and the minimum requirement for intelligent citizenship and personal freedom to seek the level and type of life desired.

2. A common set of goals determines at least a major part of the curriculum of American schools. Although local districts retain autonomy, to a large extent, in establishing curricula and goals for schools, a great deal of commonality is found among the programs in the thousands of districts of this country. Some of the similarity results from the influence of commercially

available instructional materials, but much is attributed to what is known about developmental stages of children and to the similarity of hopes, aspirations, and expectations among people in this country, from farms to urban dwellings, and from the southwest to the northeast corners of the country.

Though we take great pride in local autonomy and protect against moves to centralize control, as well we should, the fact remains that state laws governing age of school entry and leaving are similar and that more similarity than difference exists in the basic curricula. Vocabulary lists include the same words; developmental reading is introduced at the same grade level; grammar, syntax, and punctuation are taught according to the same rules; and math skills are introduced in the same order at about the same grade levels.

Similarities in the content and goals of schools are highly desirable, if not absolutely necessary, in a society with a high degree of population mobility and in a country where citizens tend to identify with national interests more than regional and local interests. The current situation in the United States with regard to these facts suggests that the commonality of basic educational programs will continue, perhaps even expand, in the near future.

3.   Instruction and curriculum should be based on the best evidence possible. Professional educators and many people in the general public long have rejected the idea that all children of a given chronological age or grade level should study the same materials at the same time under the same conditions. The extent to which individualized programs actually are implemented varies considerably from school to school and from classroom to classroom, but most teachers and parents do pay homage to the belief that individuals differ and that programs and instruction should be appropriate for the interests, ability, aspirations, and readiness of individual children. To accept without modification a commercially available program and/or to teach all members of a class in the same way denies the rights of those for whom the program and instruction are not optimal.

Information that will assist curriculum committees, administrators, and individual teachers in planning and implementing programs and daily instruction can be obtained in a variety of ways. These include observation by perceptive professionals, review of cumulative records, locally devised assessment procedures, and comprehensive testing programs using standardized tests. The principle of parsimony should guide selection of the data gathering instrument and technique. When reliable and valid information for a given purpose can be obtained in a casual, inexpensive, and unsophisticated way, that approach should be used. When the decision requires information that cannot be obtained through such means, however, educators should turn to an approach that will provide the type of data required. In all cases the appraisal system should be the least expensive and least disruptive approach that will produce the information required for the decision to be made.

4. Excellence should be identified and rewarded and deficiencies should be identified and remediated. The latter part of this assertion would be closer than the former to universal acceptance in the present society, but both of the concepts — excellence and deficiency — are relative and must be defined operationally as a requisite for the corollary actions — reward and remediation.

Often, we have said and heard that the most important resource of this country is its people. Advances in all societies and in all fields have occurred largely because of the efforts of talented individuals whose talents have been recognized and fostered. The need remains to identify excellence, exceptional accomplishments in science, creative writing, the social sciences, art, music, and the skilled crafts. Individuals must select for themselves the fields they wish to pursue and cultivate, but educators should help all students develop an understanding of their relative strengths and weaknesses and their talents among people in general. Development of a realistic self concept is an important part of maturation and achieving independence and self sufficiency. The identification of excellence, in an absolute sense, is an important social need so that potential leaders and contributors to a better life can be provided the appropriate educational opportunities.

Excellence and deficiencies are important also in a relative sense. When progress and achievement are never recognized and applauded, subsequent performance tends to become less effective. Many studies have shown that laissez-faire or neutral behavior by an authority figure is less effective than either negative or positive reactions to a person's performance. On this basis many instructional strategies include the recognition and reward of correct behavior as a means of enhancing subsequent behavior. As noted above, excellence can be thought of in a relative way. The worst student in a class, who applies a minor part of a process correctly, has achieved excellence and will profit from recognition of that achievement. (This does not imply that average or poor accomplishment in terms of some absolute standard should be treated as achievement of a final goal.)

Teaching involves, in part, assisting children in assessing and accepting their profile of talents and then helping them to set and accomplish reasonable goals. For less talented students, the goals may represent small increments and, for highly talented students, large increments. The evaluation of progress and its reward, in these cases, should be defined individually, but schools have a responsibility for assisting students to continue to develop toward their potential, whatever that may be, on some absolute standard of accomplishment.

Inherent to the identification of excellence is the recognition of deficiencies. When excellence at some level is a goal, anything less must be a deficiency. Schools should insist continually that students strive to accomplish all relevant goals, and educators should accept as a reasonable challenge the guidance and assistance of students in achieving those goals.

For the large majority of school-age children, a reasonable set of goals includes development of the basic skills and learning the basic principles essential for effective citizenship. For those who are capable, educators should not accept performance below that level; the evaluation system should include attention to such basic performance, and those who fail to demonstrate adequate accomplishment should receive the additional help needed to reach that level.

5.   Sincere and rational educators will use information wisely and in the best interests of their students. Teachers, specialists, and administrators have chosen their vocation, in large part, because of their interest in helping children develop into effective and fulfilled adults. They have been trained to collect, interpret, and use information to enhance their work with the children for whom they have educational responsibilities. Almost everyone can cite exceptions to these generalizations, but in the main they apply; to assume otherwise would create the need to replace the present educational system with a new, untried approach that would be built on some noxious and eventually destructive premises. A system built on an assumption that the only safe teachers are those who know virtually nothing about their students is the first step toward a lockstep, sterile social institution.

On the other hand, problems associated with educator/student inter-actions arise more from a lack of appropriate information than from inability to use the information available. If there is a real fear that teachers, counselors, and administrators will accept the information provided by one measure of intelligence or one anecdote (and the evidence does not support this as a general situation), the problem stems from a deficiency, not a surplus, of information.

To deprive teachers of comprehensive information relevant to educational planning and instruction is to deprive students of optimal learning conditions. A goal of an educational system should be to provide teachers with the information necessary for the decisions that must be made on a semester, weekly, and daily basis, and to assure the competence of teachers to interpret and use the information effectively.

Many of the issues associated with educational measurement are not really technical problems but, rather, value judgments related to the philosophy and goals of the community. If a school is supported as a means of providing appropriate opportunities for all citizens to develop optimally in the characteristics associated with the basic skills and disciplines, teachers must have the information needed for individualizing curriculum planning and instruction. On the other hand, if schools are to be custodial institutions with more emphasis on producing homogeneity than on optimal student development, a different approach could be taken with regard to measurement programs. If teachers are viewed as change agents, they need and will use information; if they are custodians, measurement is probably unnecessary.

In recent years standardized tests have been criticized for various short-comings and, in some cases, because they are part of an educational system and philosophy unacceptable to a disenchanted and/or maligned segment of society. Schools are important, highly visible social institutions; most parents and many other citizens take great interest in what schools do and how well they accomplish their purposes. Dissatisfaction with schools and changes in societal values account in part for recent anti-test statements. Attitudes toward standardized tests depend to a large extent on the premises and goals of education that are held to be important. Since tests are merely instruments to be used as part of a broader process of delivering educational services, criticism of standardized tests is inevitable when schools more generally are the focus of criticism. Nevertheless, if certain assumptions about school roles and responsibility are acceptable, standardized tests have a unique contribution to make in improving the effectiveness of education.

THE VALUES AND USES OF STANDARDIZED TESTS

The major values of standardized tests derive from the type of needed information they provide that is not available through other types of assessment procedures. Some decisions that must be made in planning and delivering educational services, and in reporting accomplishments to and obtaining support from the local community, require information uniquely provided by norm-referenced standardized tests. The qualities and characteristics that make this so include:

1. Standardized tests are designed to reflect a national view of the traits measured.
2. Standardized tests provide comparable scores across the various traits measured;
3. Standardized tests provide comparable scores across time (that is, continuity of measurement); and
4. Standardized tests provide data that allow local performance to be compared with that of various reference groups.

Each of these characteristics is important to a number of school decisions and responsibilities, ranging from those made at a district-wide level to those that affect an individual student directly. Within a school system a communication network exists between the school board representing the community, and its central office staff, and personnel in department, building, and classroom positions. The communications relate to the goals and priorities that are translated into educational practices and the accomplishments and needs at each of the levels of the network.

Results from standardized tests and, more importantly, their interpretation, are part of the information in the network. The extent to which standardized tests are good and potentially useful should be judged in terms of whether they provide unique or corroborative information to improve decisions and reporting within the school communications network.

Design Reflects National View of Traits Measured

Group tests of ability (intelligence) sample a domain of skills with educational significance. They are based on theories and empirical research that have passed the test of review and debate within a scholarly community and, thus, the tests reflect definitions that are national, sometimes international, in scope. Rather than attributing to these measures some aura of innateness or inevitability, educators should treat them as measures of achieved or developed skills. These tests assess characteristics necessary for development of cognitive knowledge and provide an indication of maturation level of the characteristics.

Standardized achievement tests sample widely accepted objectives and curricula held to be important for continuous educational development and ultimately effective adult personal and vocational lives. The tests are based on reviews of curriculum guides, commonly used instructional materials, and statements prepared by professional organizations. They are subjected to review by professionals in the disciplines and by classroom teachers. Test items must have good psychometric qualities, and test scores must meet state-of-the-art requirements for validity and reliability.

Establishment of educational priorities and curriculum emphases depends largely on the values and philosophy of the local community, but the process also should be influenced strongly by the nature of the student population, in terms of both talents and prior achievement.

A great deal of information about the talents of local youth can be obtained from information collected by teachers and other school personnel. This type of information is based primarily on personal observations of students during the performance of various educational tasks, and certainly is important in developing a meaningful profile. Observation, however, provides information more directly related to level of performance in complex tasks than to potential; more related to applying a combination of skills and attitudes than to measures of discrete talents.

Locally obtained information about student talents is a good supplement to and a necessary check on the results of standardized tests of ability, but alone they provide an insufficient basis for firm conclusions. Standardized tests provide "cleaner" data in that each subtest focuses on a narrowly defined skill, and intercorrelations with other subtests are known. In addition, results on such tests are not influenced by interpersonal histories, cultural or personal value systems, or any of a number of other factors that influence interpersonal assessment. Although it is desirable, if not essential, that a complete evaluation and action decisions take into account all of the relevant information, measurement of a specific characteristic should be as pure and uncontaminated as possible. Individual, independent measures can be used in various combinations for different purposes, but to be of maximum usefulness, they should contribute unique information.

A national perspective of achievement provided by standardized tests is important in local evaluation and planning even though a perfect correspondence between test content and local curricula seldom exists. Generally, the differences, particularly in the skill areas, are attributable to the fact that local goals cover more topics than the test does. When this is the case, what the test does cover — the most widely accepted goals — is valid as far as it goes, and information from the test is useful in assessing the core topics. In a society that values local autonomy in education, a perfect one-to-one correspondence between test and curriculum would be viewed with alarm.

In the few cases when the tests cover material not included in a school's curricula, local educators might profit from studying the reasons why their program omits nationally common topics or goals. Of course, there is always the possibility that the local program requires an emphasis so different that basic, common topics are omitted, but it seems unlikely that this would be true to the extent that no appropriate standardized achievement test can be found.

Comparable Scores Across Traits Measured

Many educational decisions, ranging from establishment of district-wide priorities to the allocation of time for one day in an individual classroom, require comparisons of student talents and achievements across the major curricular areas. For such comparisons (called profile analysis) to be meaningful, measurements of the various areas must be available in comparable units. Educational measurement lacks absolute scales, but standardized tests are designed to provide comparability across the subtests of a battery; thus, the peaks and valleys of a school or individual student profile are indicative of areas of relative strength and weakness.

At a school district level, decisions are made regarding allocations of funds and personnel to build on district strengths and to remediate weaknesses. A district that is above the 90th percentile in all curricular areas may wish to improve the weakest of its programs. In a district with low overall achievement, priorities must be established to overcome the deficiencies of most serious concern. Standardized tests provide data that allow for — in fact, enhance — the identification of those areas, and when interpreted within the knowledge of district goals and curricular patterns, provide a sound basis for decisions. Establishing district priorities in the absence of comparable measures of performance is a guessing game that is neither necessary nor acceptable when limited resources must be used efficiently to accomplish community educational goals.

At the department and school building levels in most districts, similar decisions must be made and the requirement for adequate data is just as important. Within an English or science department, priorities must be established and comparisons across major curricular topics are necessary. At the classroom level, instructional plans are made at the beginning of the year and modified as additional information becomes available. The plans include gross decisions about the level at which instruction should begin, about the texts, reference, and other instructional materials that would be appropriate, and how instructional time should be allocated to build effectively on talent and prior achievement of individual students.

Locally developed measures and criterion- or domain-referenced tests do not provide comparable scales of measurement. Although talented, sensitive teachers might have some clues as to particular areas of strength and weakness, standardized tests may confirm the "hunches" or, as often happens, show that subjective local appraisal is not entirely accurate.

Profile analysis is an important part of decision processes, for high as well as low achieving districts and students, particularly when budgets are not sufficient to cover all needs optimally. Standardized tests are unique in providing data that promote decisions based on identification of relative levels of accomplishment.

Comparable Scores Across Time

Growth and development may be more important measures of school and individual accomplishment than status measures obtained at some point in time. To assess growth, the measures used must provide continuous scales expressed in comparable units from year to year. Again, because of the lack of absolute scales of measurement, local tests and criterion-referenced tests are insufficient for following progress over time. Grade equivalent, age equivalent, and standard score scales on standardized tests do provide a basis for this important part of an assessment program.

Educational planning and goals usually involve vertical K-12 articulation with the expectation that activities in successive grade levels will guide student development toward accomplishment of goals by the time of high school graduation. Local curriculum sequences frequently differ somewhat in terms of the levels at which certain concepts and skills are introduced and emphasized. Thus, any status measure involving a comparison with national norms must be interpreted in light of local curriculum guides. For example, a district may introduce some topics related to using sources of information a grade or two later than is typical nationally. In such cases, local achievement in that curricular area would be expected to lag behind national performance in the early grades and then show a sudden spurt at the grade level of local emphasis. To know whether such growth occurs, a continuous scale of performance is needed.

Progress over time is a factor of utmost importance in evaluating curriculum and instruction. If deficiencies exist in either the curriculum plan or instructional competence, minimal progress will occur and will be reflected in the testing program results. A one-time occurrence might prompt local attention and review without leading to a definite conclusion that a problem exists; but, if subsequent testing consistently points out the lack of growth at a certain grade level, more serious attention can be given to assessing the reason for the problem. For example, if student progress in mathematics problem solving, as reflected in annual standardized test results, plateaus in grades 5 and 6, the intermediate math curriculum might need revision or teachers of those grades might need inservice education to improve their teaching skills or content knowledge.

The information base required for effective local educational decisions should include growth as well as status measures. Assessment of progress should be combined with the profile analysis of status results as priorities are established and allocations are made. Again, standardized tests are unique in providing sufficient data for these important decisions.

Comparison of Local Performance With Other Reference Groups

Some people minimize the importance of national norms as part of a total school assessment program. They often claim that all local conditions differ in some ways from the typical national condition and that assessment of achievement against some standard of excellence is more important than achievement relative to a norm group. These claims are questionable and, even if true, would hardly be sufficient arguments to justify elimination of norm-referenced standardized tests.

Throughout this presentation, emphasis has been given to the need for careful interpretation of data obtained from standardized tests. The differences between the local school and national averages must be taken into consideration in all serious evaluation programs. Student talent, parental values, levels of financial support, and local curricular patterns have major impacts on the achievements in a given school district, and one reason for giving standardized tests is to obtain thorough, objective, and reliable data regarding talents and accomplishments so that evaluations can be based on solid information rather than on guesswork.

Locally prepared instruments and criterion-referenced tests lack an external referent or standard and, thus, performance on these tests can be interpreted only in terms of subjective judgments about performance levels. Such judgments obviously provide a tenuous basis for local districts to assess how well students are achieving relative to their capabilities and relative to accomplishments under comparable conditions in other communities.

A given level of performance on a test is a fact and can have vastly different meanings in different school systems. A school average score at the 40th percentile on national norms would be regarded as intolerable in a district that has goals virtually identical to those covered on the test, is well above average in per-pupil expenditures, and employs only the most highly qualified teachers. The same level of performance might be lauded in a district with 80% of its student enrollment from low income homes, and which spends 75% of the national average in supporting education and has a 40% annual turnover in its professional staff.

But two additional points concerning the above comparison must be considered. First, graduates from both of these districts are entering the same society. To develop a realistic self concept and reasonable hopes and expectations, students need to know how their accomplishments compare to those of students from other communities (or schools). In a highly mobile society, local norms, or no comparisons at all, fail to provide a sufficient information base for personal assessment and planning. Thus, national norms are helpful for school district evaluation purposes and for helping students to have a better perception of themselves and the nature of the competition they will face in seeking admission for further schooling and for obtaining employment.

Second, because national norms do have limitations in terms of some evaluation needs, many publishers of standardized tests provide special norms useful for particular situations and needs. Achievement norms for students of certain narrowly defined ability levels provide the basis for assessing local performance against that of students with similar ability. Regional norms, norms for large cities, and other variations have been developed to assist communities in selecting appropriate external reference groups for specific types of comparisons. Generally, these special norms are obtained along with the national norms so that different evaluation needs can be served.

Again, education is an important community responsibility, and parents and other citizens take a great deal of interest in the accomplishments of schools they support. With the ever increasing costs for education, community interest in schools likely will grow, accompanied by added demands for substantive reports of school accomplishments. Certainly, a community has the right to know about successes and problems in its schools, and administrators, logically, would want to share such information in a professional way. Pride should be taken when deserved, and accomplishments, when reported objectively, should be an encouragement to citizens for continued support of the schools. Deficiencies, in a relative sense, may be remediable with an increase in support, and how better to convince a community of needs than to report the results of standardized tests properly interpreted.

Education is a unique enterprise, since goals and levels of support are determined by lay citizens while the professionals are expected to implement programs to accomplish the goals and use resources efficiently. Education is truly a shared endeavor, and an appropriate evaluation system can help in strengthening the community/educator partnership needed for continued and improved success.

CONCLUSION

The preceding discussion has emphasized the value of standardized tests for decision making processes within school systems, giving four characteristics of standardized tests that make them unique within the data gathering processes available to schools. Other virtues of standardized tests could be added: efficiency and cost effectiveness as tools for collecting vital information — thus freeing teachers to devote more time to instructional planning and work with individual students; the ability to identify talents and accomplishments that otherwise may go undetected because of a student's poor attitude, motivation, interpersonal skills — or perhaps because of cultural biases that cloud educator sensitivity and objectivity.

Standardized tests are not perfect tools; their value is influenced largely by the skill with which people interpret and use the results. These tests only sample the domain they claim to measure. They are neither complete nor infallible instruments. They do not tap innate student characteristics; they measure the demonstration of acquired talents. They do not measure all the important topics of interest to schools and individuals — thermometers do not measure humidity.

A valuable tool can be misused. Lasar beams are used both to perform delicate operations on the retina of an eye and as weapons of destruction. Educators must select standardized tests appropriate for identified purposes. This responsibility should not be abdicated. Educators must analyze, interpret, and decide how to use results from standardized tests; failure to do so in the past has been a contributing factor to the misuse and concomitant criticism of school practices.

Professionals and the general public probably know more about standardized tests and their limitations than they do about any other source of information concerning student characteristics. Authors and publishers have developed elaborate, detailed reports about the reliability of tests, relationships between scores and other variables, method and rationale used in developing the tests, and limitations of the data. Similar information concerning teacher speculations, anecdotal records, locally developed instruments, and other data gathering techniques would improve the entire decision making process. The availability of these technical data would provide a more adequate basis for comparing the usefulness of standardized tests with other possible data sources.

Educators must continue to seek improvements in the effectiveness and appropriateness of instructional programs. Used by qualified people, standardized tests can make a unique and important contribution. To eliminate the use of standardized tests would be a major step backward, contributing to an educational system in which all individuals would be provided locally determined instruction whether appropriate or not. The technology of scientific appraisal would be replaced by the former technology of the dunce cap and birch rod.

As Taber points out, "The future is here!" for the application of computer technology. Using computers to assist handicapped learners has been a dream for many years, but the high costs of hardware and the unavailability of software precluded wide-scale application. Now, micro-computers are reasonably priced, and programming skills can be trained. Further, a user need not be a programmer. So the microcomputer can now take its place as a tool in service of the handicapped. It follows a long tradition of other tools such as braille, hearing aids, communication boards, braces, and programmed learning.

The Microcomputer — Its Applicability To Special Education

Florence M. Taber

"Computers represent a technology we will be using in the future" was a prediction of the 1960s. The future is here! The most significant advance from the schools' viewpoint, the microcomputer, is with us today — and will be for some time to come. Because of the many possible applications of microcomputers, everyone involved with education should become computer literate. Computer literacy involved the "history, operation, and applications of computers, as well as the social, psychological, and vocational impact of computer-based technology" (Thomas, 1980).

Particularly because of the applications possible with the handicapped, to provide them avenues of communication through which to receive information and express thoughts, special educators should familiarize themselves with the microcomputer. This involves hardware, software, peripherals, and uses. The following discussion offers a "take-off" point — a brief history of the microcomputer, how it operates, how it is used in regular and special education, considerations in purchasing hardware and software, how to create elementary programs, and projections into the future.

HISTORY

To begin to understand the full impact of the microcomputer, one should realize the short time involved in computer development to its present level. This knowledge allows one to recognize how rapidly the technology is changing and to perceive the possibilities for its uses, especially within the area of special education, that are both possible and probable within the next few years.

It is hard to comprehend that in 1964 educators were saying, "Perhaps we should begin to think about computers in education" and in 1972 they were already saying, "Now is the time." By 1977 the influx of computers in the schools had been enormous, although the uses were primarily confined to mathematics, science, and record keeping. Today the educational and education-related uses have expanded to include all areas of the curriculum as well as data management both within the classroom and in the office.

Actually, the computer was first used in the classroom in the 1960s, but at this stage multiple-choice questions simply appeared on the screen and students responded to the questions. True interaction between the computer and the operator was lacking. Then, in the 1970s the microcomputer was developed, allowing interaction between machine and operator — interaction being the capability of the machine to respond based on the input into the machine being used.

Several sources are available to those who are interested in becoming acquainted with the history of the computer and the microcomputer. Among them are *The Mind Tool* (Graham, 1980), *On Computing* (Morgan, 1981) and *Teachers' Guide to Computers in the Elementary School* (Moursund, n.d.).

THE MICROCOMPUTER: DEFINITION AND DESCRIPTION

"A computer is a machine designed for the input, storage, manipulation, and output of symbols (digits, letters, punctuation). It can automatically and very rapidly follow a step-by-step set of directions (called a computer program) that has been stored in its memory" (Moursund, 1980). Simplifying the definition. Moursund stated, "By adding a keyboard to a calculator, giving it some directions, and increasing its speed, it would become a computer. A microcomputer is a very small version of a computer. It combines a microprocessor, or a small central processing unit (CPU), with a silicon chip having memory." Microcomputers are sometimes also called personal computers. They can be used in classrooms, homes, or businesses where the need for this type of computer has been determined through a needs assessment.

Putting the functions of the microcomputer simply, the "brains" are housed in the Central Processing Unit (CPU). The information stored here allows for the manipulation and execution of data.

The input of information enters directly from a keyboard or from external memory. If the information enters from an external source, it is in the form of programs that have been previously written and stored in external memory primarily on a disk or cassette tape. If the information enters the CPU via a keyboard, the keyboard may or may not be housed with the CPU.

To view the program that has been entered into the computer, a video output is connected. A television or video screen is used for this purpose. Figure 1 illustrates these concepts in the simplest terms.

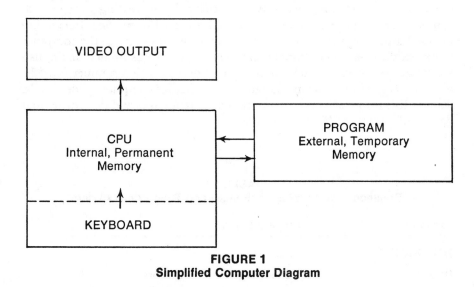

FIGURE 1
Simplified Computer Diagram

The term "memory" has been used a number of times. The CPU that controls the activities of the computer (microcomputer) involves that internal memory and determines how much information the computer can store and manipulate. This has nothing to do with the extent of memory on the disk or tape, which involves external or temporary memory.

The smallest fragment of memory is called a *bit,* and the smallest unit of memory (usually eight bits) is termed a *byte.* When referring to memory, the term *K* indicates the way memory is accessed. For example, 16K means one bit wide but including about 16,000 bytes. The higher the K, the more bytes can be stored in the computer at one time.

Memory can be increased by purchasing various additions. These additions must be compatible with the system's power supply, compatible with the memories presently in use in the computer, and so forth. Therefore, one should get expert advice before purchasing additions, along with advice as to whether the memory chips are ROM or RAM. ROM refers to Read

Only Memory and can program up to 128,000 bits on a chip but is preprogrammed. RAM refers to Random Access Memory. ROM is preprogrammed, cannot be changed, and operates the microcomputer's functions. RAM refers to Random Access Memory and is available to store programs developed by the programmer. Information stored in RAM can be edited, erased, or temporarily stored. In order for programs stored in RAM to become permanent, they must be stored in external memory — or on a disk, cassette tape, or other device external to the CPU. Programs, which are loaded from external memory, are stored in RAM.

Two other distinctions should be made. When purchasing a computer, one is purchasing the *hardware.* When purchasing or creating a program to run on the computer or hardware, one is dealing with *software.* In creating or purchasing software, one must be aware of what language the computer understands. Computer languages are languages just as French or English are languages. Because each language is different, a programmer must be able to speak (write) the same language a particular computer understands. Table 1 lists the most common programming languages and the entities that commonly use them (Moursund, 1981).

TABLE 1
Common Programming Languages and Their Primary Users

Language	Primary Users
FORTRAN	Scientists
BASIC	College Students; Educators
COBOL	College Students; Business
LOGO	Elementary Students
PILOT	Educators
PASCAL	College Students; Government

USES IN EDUCATION

Special educators should look at computer uses in both regular and special education because many of the uses can be employed in both areas, many handicapped individuals are mainstreamed, and because of the state of the art. The uses are already almost limitless, and new uses are being created all the time. Therefore, the more one learns about present uses, the more creative one can be in accommodating the microcomputer to the needs of special education.

How the Microcomputer Assists the Educator

In general, the microcomputer can assist the educator:

— in individualizing instruction;
— in providing a nonthreatening presentation to the learner;
— in teaching process and product through sequential steps;
— in extending the teacher's expertise;
— in simplifying record keeping and other administrative duties.

Individualizing Instruction

Through the computer, students can receive information at their own rates of speed. Through branching, the learner can receive information at the appropriate conceptual and reading levels. In other words, when learners interact with the computer, they branch to more complex material, to more simplified material, or remain at the same level. In this way, each learner can be constantly challenged and yet be successful at the same time.

With multiple terminals hooked to one external CPU, many learners could receive the same program, which can be individualized by the program at different reading and conceptual levels. Little software is available at present, however, that has been programmed to individualize to the needs of particular learners. Most programs that do claim to branch provide additional drill without considering individual levels of presentation or breaking the skill into additional steps. Obviously, if the learner did not comprehend the information the first time, drill is not the answer.

Nonthreatening Presentation

As one young teenager said, "It's okay to make a mistake. The computer doesn't yell at you." She did not mean that the teacher yells at her. She just meant that she did not feel threatened by a machine. Bill James, who designed the Alpha Menu program, based it on the philosophy that the computer should be fun, as it teaches how to use the computer "for communication and environmental control" (Luttner, 1981).

Teaching Process and Product Extending the Teacher's Expertise

The third way the microcomputer can assist the educator is through software that is carefully task-analyzed to teach a process or a product. This leads to the fourth benefit — extending the teacher's expertise. Bagley (1981) supported this use of the microcomputer by stating, "Learners are asked to stretch their knowledge. Subjects who have learned through 'discovery' methods can solve problems that require relating what they knew previously to the principle learned. . . . Paper-and-pencil and linear A/V instructional materials will always have a disadvantage in creating discovery learning."

Not all learning is most effective through the use of a computer, however. The following diagram (Figure 2) should be considered in determining the most effective method to reach specific objectives.

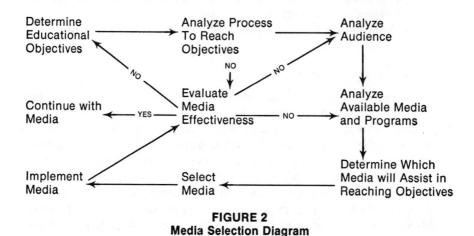

FIGURE 2
Media Selection Diagram

Administrative Applications

Following are just some of the many administrative applications made possible by computers:

assessment and error
   analysis of tests
athletic team statistics
auto parking permits
basic competencies records
business/personnel records
daily attendance
equipment inventory
grade distributions
honor roll
individualized education plans
   (IEPs), developing and testing

library records and reports
rank in class
school calendar
scheduling
student activity records
student deficiency reports
student permanent records and
   transference of same
student progress reports
textbook inventories

General Microcomputer Uses in the Classroom

Numerous uses for the microcomputer within the classroom and with the learner have been discovered. Each classification in Table 2 should be considered and used to its maximum potential.

TABLE 2
Classifications of Microcomputer-Assisted Instruction

Classification	Use
Drill and Practice	To reinforce information learned and for which practice is suggested.
Tutorial	To present information already taught in the classroom but which has to be broken into smaller sequential steps and/or into a lower conceptual level for individual learners.
Simulation	To place a learner in situations that replicate original situations.
Computer-managed Instruction	To instruct the learner in subjects through individualized sequencing.
Problem Solving	To place the learner in situations to solve problems and to receive appropriate consequences. (Having the learner program as well as run previously developed software falls under this category.)
Assessment/ Evaluation	To determine where the learner is regarding a specific objective and for pre- and post-test purposes.
Data Retrieval	To provide feedback to the learner as to progress toward objectives, and to analyze data to create individual learning plans.

Research Findings

A number of conclusions may be drawn from research as indicated by Gleason (1981):

1. The microcomputer assists learners in reaching instructional objectives.
2. A 20% to 40% savings in time learning is realized through comput~ programs as compared to "conventional" instruction.
3. Retention after interacting with programs is as good as or superior to "conventional" instruction.
4. "Students react very positively to good CAI [Computer Assisted Instruction] programs; they reject poor programs."

This last point is supported by Bill James according to Luttner (1981) in her statement, "Functional as a given computer and apparatus may be, if it is not fun for the user, it will not be used," Additional research cited by Joiner, Sedlak, Silverstein, & Vensel (1980) concluded that CAI is more effective with low ability students than with middle or upper ability students.

A number of traditional uses for the microcomputer are well known. Although most are in mathematics and science, some are now appearing in other basic subject areas such as reading, spelling, home economics, and so forth. Eventually, total curricula that could be placed on microcomputer programs would total some 6,000 programs, considering at least 10 curricular areas per each of the 12 grades. Then, if one considers that these programs would have to be developed for at least four major manufacturers of hardware, 24,000 programs would have to be created (Isaacson, 1981).

Novel programs have also been developed. For example, "Sesame Place" (in Ohio) has one of the most original collections of educational computers in the country (Cashman, 1981). Children do not just watch Big Bird and the other characters as they would when watching television, but they interact with them in order to be taught reading, music, logic, creative writing, social studies, and hand-eye coordination. At Sesame Place the keylids have been redesigned with one-inch-square letters lined up in order from A to Z, numbers, and special symbols using color identifiers. Each of these programs is programmed for the Apple II microcomputer, which has 48K bytes of memory and is loaded through a network that enables up to 65 Apple II microcomputers to store and share a common disk. Incidently, this type of redesigning was originally accomplished for handicapped individuals.

MICROCOMPUTERS FOR THE HANDICAPPED

Using the microcomputer to benefit the handicapped is probably the most exciting development for this medium. With various peripherals or additions that can be attached to various computers, especially the Apple, handicapped individuals can receive information that they could not have previously, and they can express themselves where it was impossible before. "People without voices are speaking and people without hands are typing" (Luttner, 1981). Basic living skills such as answering the phone, writing letters, using the radio, and operating other dials are all now possible. For nonverbal students, speech synthesizers take keyboard entries and turn them into speech through a ROM chip. Word boards can also be used by nonverbal students. The following list summarizes uses in special education. Obviously, this is only a beginning. With imagination, this list can become endless!

1. An autocom from Telesensory Systems, Inc. uses a RAM chip containing vocabulary on grid squares on a board that is mountable on wheelchairs or other surfaces. The optical configuration of the autocom allows for changing the size of the squares (Schneider, 1981).

2. The MECC Apple Library Collection has one volume on diskette for special needs students *(Special Needs Volume I)* on spelling. Since typing is often a problem, a box appears over responses, and the student uses the game paddles or any key on the keyboard to respond. The second volume for this population covers speed drill number words, and change. In field testing, one student who is nonverbal uses the "Number Word" program to write letters home to her parents (Loewen, 1981).

3. The Prentke Romich Company has a number of electronic aids that could and probably will be interfaced with the microcomputer *(Electronic Aids for the Severely Handicapped* catalog, 1981).

4. Borg-Warner has an EXPRESS series that includes appropriate controls such as the optical head pointer, manual pointer, or rocking lever to operate the computer keyboard. EXPRESS uses the PRC Apple Keyboard Interface with Borg Warner's Micro System 80 Critical Reading Series on an Apple II computer with 48K bytes RAM using disk input (Borg-Warner Educational Systems, advertisement, 1981).

5. The Alpha Menu by Bill James in San Antonio, Texas, has a program that displays letters, numbers, and punctuation marks in a matrix on a video screen (Luttner, 1981). Then messages can be built at the top of the screen. Quadriplegics have used this system successfully using a light pen, a skate controller, and other devices with a number of switches. Light pens can be attached to the mouth or head to touch letters, which are then added to the message at the top of the screen. The skate controller is a "free moving 'bug'" strapped to the arm or hand. The sticks, switches, and other devices adjust to the users' response time.

   The Alpha Menu program is used on the Apple II plus the standard Disk II drive and monitor. The devices are placed into Apple's game paddle sockets. A hard copy or printout can also be produced if the printer peripheral is used (Luttner, 1981).

6. A system entitled C2E2 (Control, Communications, Education, Entertainment) from the University of Alabama is governed by voice commands and is used to operate various appliances. This system includes the Apple II computer, two Disk II drives, a CRT monitor, a Heuristics Inc. speech interface, a printer, and a "black box" that connects the computer to the appliances (Luttner, 1981).

7. One system was developed for a three-year-old boy who was injured and paralyzed from the neck down as the result of an accident. Later, he and his brother studied BASIC (computer language) and now do their own programming. The modifications necessary were drawn up in an article by Sand (1981).

8. Jay Hewitt at the University of Missouri has developed an Apple-based system that speaks actual words. The operator can speak up to 20 words at a time, selecting from a vocabulary of 5,000 words. The words are located in nested menus so that if two letters are typed, a vocabulary list appears on the screen and the operator has only to select the number of that word — thus minimizing motor coordination and typing skills. A key guard (a plastic frame with finger holes over the top) placed over the keyboard helps avoid pressing more than one key at a time (Luttner, 1981).

9. Chris Thompson at the Trace Center for the Severely Communicatively Handicapped views the Apple as a useful assessment and training tool since most programs can be changed to meet the growing needs of the child (Luttner, 1981).

10. The microcomputer is also being used in homebound programs in which the computer is hooked up through a telephone and the teacher can interact with the student. Here both the teacher and the student have microcomputers that display information and process responses (Joiner et al., 1980).

11. Individualized education plans (IEPs) and data to develop them can be stored on the microcomputer. This information includes goals. objectives, methodologies, costs of services, and resources (Wilson, 1981). The IEPs can be updated and/or transferred instantly.

12. Service bureaus also develop IEPs, maintain curricular data bases and test results, and monitor student progress. These bureaus can be either commercially or publicly supported. An example of a commercial bureau is Gacka Computer-Aided IEPs from Curriculum Associates, Inc., North Bellerica, Massachusetts, and a public bureau is the Child-Based Information System of the Central Susquehanna Intermediate Unit, Lewisburg, Pennsylvania (Wilson, 1981).

13. Control Data Corporation is now developing a system that "monitors a student from initial screening for the handicap through assessment, program selection, IEP development and educational achievement . . . assessed through PLATO terminals" (Wilson, 1981).

14. MCE, Inc., Kalamazoo, Michigan, has developed programs for mildly and moderately impaired youth through adults who assess and teach basic living skills. The branching concept is incorporated; learners, by their interaction with the microcomputer, are branched to higher or lower reading and conceptual levels. These programs have been developed for the Apple II.

15. Speech synthesizers are providing auditory output, and speech can also be employed to run and program.

16. Programs can provide independent living for individuals by operating electrical appliances, answering the phone, and so forth.

This list of uses in special education is only a beginning — and certainly not conclusive. It is intended to stimulate creativity in the special educator. For example, speech synthesizers could be tried with autistic children. Learning at individualized rates and at variable levels is important for anyone, but is especially helpful to the mentally retarded and the learning disabled. The emotionally disturbed may find computers less threatening than traditional teaching. Computers can be especially helpful with the visually impaired or blind (in teaching braille, etc.), hearing impaired (through visuals and synthetic speech), and with the physically impaired (in allowing them nonverbal communication capabilities).

The Maplewood Handicapped Children's Center in Seattle, Washington, stresses the importance of individualization with the media: "The tricky thing about providing a child with a communication device is that you have to find the most appropriate motor movement the child can use. This is of concern for two reasons. First, you don't want the child to be frustrated because the movement is too difficult or too inefficient; and, second, the extended use of an abnormal reflex pattern may actually lead to physical deformity" (in Luttner, 1981). This concern for individualization is applicable to all handicapping conditions — and should be to all teaching situations.

CONSIDERATIONS WHEN PURCHASING HARDWARE

Three major considerations are necessary when purchasing hardware, or the microcomputer: technical, training, and software.

Technical Considerations

Besides warranty, the purchaser must consider the availability of repair facilities. A good deal on a microcomputer will turn into a bad deal if it has to be shipped back for a lengthy time.

The machine's capabilities are of utmost importance. How much memory is available? Some microcomputers get 4K of usable memory, while others get 16K or more. For writing simple programs, not much memory is required. If, however, one intends to use effective software, created or purchased, the memory aspect is extremely important. Most microcomputers use the BASIC language, but the BASIC for one machine is not, at present, compatible with machines from other manufacturers.

Another technical concern involves the device used to load the program from external memory. Tape recorders are readily available, but they are slow to load and are touchy as to whether the heads are clean and the volume is right. Disk drives are popular and are easy and fast to load, but they are considerably more expensive than tape recorders. One must also take care not to mar or bend the disks. Cartridges that are sturdy and yet load quickly are beginning to appear on the market.

The peripherals available, as well as the number of slots for interfacing these peripherals with the microcomputer, must be considered. For example, the Apple has eight peripheral interface slots whereas most microcomputers have fewer. Peripherals such as paddles, printers, speech synthesizers, and so forth are especially important when working with the handicapped.

Training Considerations

Does the company through which the hardware is purchased provide literature on running the computer and how to program it? Is the literature easy to follow or technical enough? Does this company also provide inservice training on computer literacy, running the computer, programming the computer, and how to best utilize it to meet specified needs? Sometimes if the company selling the machine does not provide this service, it can be provided by a private microcomputer consulting firm such as Microcomputer Training and Development Associates (MTDA), 3616 Edinburgh, Kalamazoo, MI 49007.

Software Considerations

Probably the most important consideration in purchasing hardware is the software. What software is available for the machine? Is it educationally effective? Does it satisfy technical requirements? Too much software on the market either does not run or work, or was created by programmers who have ability in their field but know little about educational effectiveness. As indicated by Joiner et al. (1980), "Purchasers of low cost systems, lacking either the skills or time to do their own programming, may find themselves proud owners of equipment that remains idle for lack of sufficient software."

Isaacson (1981) reinforced this opinion by his statement of "the difficulties educational computing face: lack of trained personnel, lack of planning, and lack of the 'fuel' to power the computer — high octane software."

Gleason (1981), in discussing software today, indicated:

1. Production of high-quality programs is expensive; $10,000 per instructional hour is not unrealistic.
2. Companies find that they have to provide extensive training for their production staffs.
3. Programs made for one kind of machine probably will not run on another.

Further support regarding the limited amount of high quality software came from Bagley (1981). She, too, indicated the presence of many poorly designed and poorly written programs on the market, which appear to lack a "systematic approach to instruction."

Holznagel, president of the Association of Educational Data Systems (AEDS) (as reported by Isaacson, 1981), indicated that the available software today falls within three classifications:

1. High octane material   (Little exists)

2. Good ideas, but needs revision   (Some exists)

3. Programs that "knock" badly — poorly designed and implemented, contain bugs, no clear objectives, etc.   (Most programs — especially those that are classroom-designed)

Until the industry becomes standardized or a peripheral is designed to make the various machines compatible, the software available for each machine must be considered *before* purchasing the hardware. To determine the effectiveness of software from both a technical and educational point of view, an evaluation plan is of utmost importance.

EVALUATING SOFTWARE

Programs have to be created with a wedding of educational specialists and computer technologists through a third person who has knowledge in both areas. Isaacson (1981) agreed that a team of educators and technicians is required, and that the educator must have experience in computer programming, psychology of learning, and motivation. He also indicated that education centers, like that of the University of Oregon, are beginning to offer degreed programs in computers in education.

MCE Inc., Kalamazoo, Michigan, has developed programs combining the expertise of special education and computer technology, and has designed programs for the special needs audience using regular and special education principles. It has developed an evaluation form (Figure 3) based on these principles, which the firm believes can be used to evaluate all educational software.

Several organizations that are also evaluating software and can provide information to the reader are:

Trace Research and Development Center
University of Wisconsin
314 Waisman Center
Madison, WI 53706

	EXCELLENT	ADEQUATE	INADEQUATE	NOT RELEVANT
I. INSTRUCTIONAL CONTENT				
1. Is the content consistent with the goals and objectives of the program?				
2. Is the program one of a series in which carefully planned learning objectives have been followed?				
3. Does the instructional guide provide information, suggestions, and materials to assist the teacher in successfully implementing the program?				
4. Are program goals provided that are usable for individualized educational plans (IEPs)?				
5. Are evaluation materials/criteria provided that are usable for individualized education plans?				
6. Are prerequisite skills, vocabulary, and concepts determined and presented?				
7. Is vocabulary defined or paraphrased in text or in the prerequisite skills portion of the "Principles" section of the instruction guide?				
8. Are diagnostic or prescriptive procedures built into the program?				
9. Does the text follow established rules for punctuation, capitalization, grammar, and usage?				
10. Are supplemental materials provided for learner and teacher?				
11. Is the product designed for appropriate age and ability groups?				
12. Is the program compatible with the curriculum?				
13. Is the program compatible with the teacher's needs?				
14. Is the content accurate and complete?				
15. Are examples provided with directions when appropriate?				
16. Are redundancy and drill used effectively?				
17. Is language appropriate in tone and selection?				
18. Are concrete applications for concepts provided?				
19. Is feedback immediate?				
II. INSTRUCTIONAL ADEQUACY				
1. Is instructional design of high quality using accepted learning theory?				
2. Are learners always the target of interaction with the computer — a personalized element?				
3. Are positive responses reinforced?				
4. Are frames that follow incorrect responses nonpunishing?				

From MCE, Inc., Kalamazoo, MI.

FIGURE 3
Evaluation Form

	EXCELLENT	ADEQUATE	INADEQUATE	NOT RELEVANT
5. Is reinforcement variable and random in content and provided on schedules as established by behavior management principles?				
6. Is branching used when the learner demonstrates need for further concept development before proceeding?				
7. Are avenues of communication from the learner to the computer logical and at comprehensible levels?				
8. Is evaluation of each concept appropriate and sufficient?				
9. Are concepts and skills task-analyzed into appropriate steps?				
10. Are color graphics, and animation used effectively to enhance the lesson?				
11. Are sound, inverse print, etc., employed for attention and reinforcement purposes and not distracting?				
12. Is syllabication provided for new and unfamiliar words?				
13. Is sentence length dependent on need and learner levels?				
14. Is the learner always provided with frames that allow for progression through the program?				
15. Does the program provide suitable directions for the learner?				
III. TECHNICAL ADEQUACY				
1. Will the program run to completion without being "hung up" because of unexpected responses?				
2. Are the programs difficult or impossible to be inadvertently disrupted by the learner?				
3. Can learners operate the programs independently?				
4. Is the amount on each frame appropriate?				
5. Is the length of each section appropriate?				
6. Are words and lines spaced for ease of reading?				
7. Is variation of type and organization of textual materials appropriate for a clear presentation?				
8. Are inappropriate responses considered and handled appropriately?				
9. Is the educational technology (i.e., microcomputer) the best available for presenting this subject matter?				
IV. OVERALL EVALUATION				
1. How would you rate this program in its entirety?				

Comments: _____

FIGURE 3
Evaluation Form (continued)

Dresden Associates
P.O. Box 246, Dept. CN-1
Dresden, ME 04342
Phone: (207) 737-4466

MECC Users Newsletter
2520 Broadway Drive
St. Paul, MN 55113
Phone: (612) 376-1117

Minnesota Educational Computing Consortium
2520 Broadway Drive
St. Paul, MN 55113

J E M Research
Discovery Park
University of Victoria
P.O. Box 1700
Victoria, BC V8W 2Y2

Association for Educational Data Systems
1201 - 16th Street NW
Washington, DC 20036

Micro SIFT Project
Northwest Regional Educational Laboratory
710 S.W. Second Avenue
Portland, OR 97204

In addition to the foregoing, evaluation is being implemented on the regional level. For example, the Michigan Association for Computer Users includes members who voluntarily review and evaluate acquired programs. The results are then published by the Association two to three times yearly.

CREATING SOFTWARE

The importance of software evaluation should not deter the special educator from learning about and doing some computer programming, for the following reasons:

1. Some programs on the market can be altered to fit individual needs of a learner. Other programs have security systems that do not allow access. These are usually programs that have been carefully planned and sequenced, and altering them would have an effect on educational effectiveness.

2. Effective software is in need of development. To have many high quality educational programs, the educator should gain some expertise in programming, in order to program and in order to evaluate existing software.
3. Because many areas in the curriculum have not yet been approached in programming, educators are forced to create programs.

A note of "warning": The desire to create programs may be present, but programming can be like eating a favorite chip — once you start, it's hard to stop, and your temporal concepts deteriorate!

To gain knowledge in microcomputing, one might:

1. Learn from a course in BASIC at the local or nearby college.
2. Take a course from a business that sells computers.
3. Enroll in inservice education.
4. Read books and try out your new knowledge on your own.
5. Find a high school student or friend who can spend a few hours a week with you.

Programming

Programs consist of lines of data, comments or information, and commands. Lines are numbered, and the program executes the lines in consecutive order (e.g., 100, 110, 120, etc.). The elementary programmer, especially, should leave at least 10 lines between each one line programmed, in order to add lines of data as necessary. The programmer can go back and do that because the computer will execute the lines in consecutive order regardless of the order in which they are programmed. After typing a line, the Enter or Return key is pressed, which places that line in memory.

If a mistake is made while typing in a line, the back arrow key (⬅) can be pressed to the place of error, or one can type that line number with nothing else. Let's say you spelled a word wrong. Just backspace to the point over the letter you want to change, and finish typing the line correctly. If you are on another line and notice a mistake in a line above, when you start a new blank line, type the line number on which you made the mistake and press Return (or whatever key this is on your machine). The line is erased from memory. If you want that line left in but with corrections made, just retype it.

Following is a very simple program example that will be discussed:

```
110  REM TO PRINT YOUR NAME
120  PRINT "PLEASE TYPE YOUR NAME."
130  PRINT "TYPE IT NOW."
140  INPUT A$
150  PRINT "YOUR NAME IS ", A$;"."
160  END
```

Line 110 starts with the word REM, which stands for Remark. REM statements are not part of the program but are there to help the programmer with organization; they serve the same purpose as an outline. Lines 120 and 130 begin with PRINT and have statements within quotation marks. These statements will be printed out in the program. Line 140 begins with INPUT, indicating that the viewer is to type in something — in this case his/her name. The A$ means the computer expects the person to type in a series, which in this case is a name. The line 150 tells the computer to print out the statement, "Your name is _____." The blank represents the person's name as typed in line 140. The last line, 160, is a command that tells the computer to end the program. If you want to check the program, type LIST, and the program as you have entered it will appear on the screen.

Next, you will probably want to see your program. Type RUN, and this would appear:

```
PLEASE TYPE YOUR NAME.
TYPE IT NOW.
?        (The program will wait for your name.)
YOUR NAME IS _____
```

If you want to save this program and put it into external memory, type in SAVE. On a disk, the program will then be placed in memory on that disk. If placing it into memory on a tape cassette, you would press the keys on the tape recorder that allow you to record information first. If you do not want to save a program, type NEW, and it will be erased forever.

Other kinds of statements one must become familiar with are IF . . . THEN and FOR . . . NEXT statements, which command the computer to do something if certain things are true and do something else if not true. Also, one will become familiar with GO TO statements, which command the computer to go to a particular line. Obviously, the exact command and ways of entering data differ from machine to machine. All are similar, however. Table 3 lists a few of the BASIC commands and how they are executed by four of the major microcomputers (Li, 1981).

Educational Planning

To educationally plan a program, the educator must write out each frame exactly as it will appear on the screen. Each frame must also be numbered in the order on which it will appear on the screen. The educator must provide information as to exactly what is correct, incorrect, or inappropriate on a question frame when input or interaction with the person is expected. Figure 4 is an example of a flowchart for educationally planning a program. Of course, each program will have a different flowchart depending on that program.

TABLE 3
Basic Commands for Four Microcomputers

COMMAND	MICROCOMPUTER			
	APPLE II	**TRS 80**	**ATARI**	**PET**
CLEAR, or erase	CLEAR	CLEAR	CLEAR	CLR
LOAD, or bring in program from memory	LOAD	CLOAD	CLOAD	LOAD
SAVE, or place into memory	SAVE	CSAVE	CSAVE	SAVE
NEW, or delete a program	NEW	NEW	NEW	NEW
LIST, or list all lines in a program	LIST	LIST	LIST	LIST

MICROCOMPUTERS IN THE FUTURE

Educators had better get ready for a new wave in education, because education as we know it today will soon be as antiquated for communication as the quarter picture show or the Pony Express. "Technology will have a dramatic and far-reaching impact on schooling. In the near future, it may *not* be necessary for the child to go to 'school' to learn many of the basics in education" (Gleason, 1981). Home-based and community learning centers may be common. "Computers will not replace teachers, but change the role of teachers from that of transmitters of information to the far more significant role of planning and providing those higher learning experiences" (Gleason, 1981).

The sky is the limit when creative educators team up with creative computer technologists. In special education our job must involve the fast developing uses of technology to assist the handicapped:

— in their quest for effective communication

— in their quest for education

— in their quest for normalization!

REFERENCES

Bagley, C. The experts' views of computer-based instruction. *NSPI Journal* (National Society for Performance in Instruction), March 1981, pp. 38-39.

Cashman, M. Sesame Place joins moppets, micro, and muppets. *Apple*, 1981, *2*(1), 21-22.

Electronic aids for the severely handicapped (catalog). Shreve, OH: Prentke Romich Co.

Gleason, G. Microcomputers in education: The state of the art. *Educational Technology*, 1981, *21*(3), 7-18.

Graham, N. *The mind tool.* St. Paul, MN: West Publishing Co., 1980, Ch. 2.

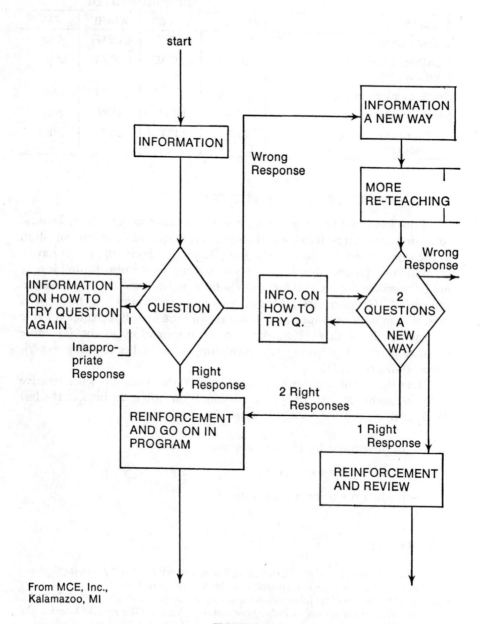

From MCE, Inc.,
Kalamazoo, MI

FIGURE 4
Microcomputer Education (MCE) Flowchart

Isaacson, D. What's holding back computer use in education? *Classroom Computer News*, 1981, *1*(5), 28-29.

Joiner, L. M., Sedlak, R. A., Silverstein, B. J., & Vensel, G. Microcomputers: An available technology for special education. *Journal of Special Education Technology*, 1980, *3*(2), 37-41.

Li, T. Whose basic does what? *BYTE*, Jan. 1981, pp. 318-327.

Loewen, D. Microcomputers and special needs students, *Users*, 1981, 7(5), 5.

Luttner, S. Computers for the handicapped. *Apple*, 1981,*2*(1), 26-29.

MCE Inc., Kalamazoo, MI.

Moursund, D. *Teacher's guide to computers in the elementary school.* La Grande, OR: International Council for Computers in Education, c/o Computing Center, Eastern Oregon State College, n.d.

Sand, Jan. Tero's apple, *Creative Computing*, 1981, 7(5), 62-63.

Schneider, I. A. Product news: Microprocessors. *School Product News*, May 1981, pp. 56-57.

Thomas, R. Our computer skills are lacking. *Counterpoint*, 1980, *1*(2), 1-4.

Wilson, K. Managing the administrative morass of special needs. *Classroom Computer News*, 1981, *1*(4), 8-9.

ADDITIONAL REFERENCES

Dwyer, T. A., & Kaufman, M. S. *A guided tour of computer programming in BASIC.* Geneva, IL: Houghton Mifflin, n.d., pp. 10-50.

Fitelson, N. Education on-line. *Apple*, 1981, *2*(1), 17-19.

Hawkins, H. Microcomputers. *Industrial Education.* New York: Harcourt Brace Jovanovich Publications, May/June 1981, pp. 15-16.

Hughes, E. M. A beginner's guide to memory. *On computing*, 1981, pp. 18-26.

Morgan, C. Editor's message. *On Computing*, 1981, Summer, 4.

Sloane, E. Workshop at Western Michigan University, Special Education Department, 1981, from Dade County Schools, Miami, FL.

Thornburg, D. D. How to select a personal computer. *Recreational Computing*, 1981, *10*(1), 9-13.

Watts, N. A dozen uses for the computer in education. *Educational Technology*, 1981, *21*(4), 18-22.

SOURCES OF INFORMATION
ON INSTRUCTIONAL USE OF MICROCOMPUTERS

Billings, K., & Moursund, D. *Are you computer literate?* Portland, OR: Dilithium Press, 1979.

Chirhan, P. M. *Understanding computers.* Portland, OR: Dilithium Press, 1978.

Classroom Computer News, Box 266, Cambridge, MA 02138.

Computing Teacher, Computing Center, Eastern Oregon State College, La Grande, OR 97850.

Creative Computing, PO Box 789-M, Morristown, NJ 07960.

Educational Computer Magazine, PO Box 535, Cupertino, CA 95015.

Educational Technology, 140 Sylvan Ave., Englewood Cliffs, NJ 07632.

InforWorld, 375 Cochitvate Rd. Route 30, Framingham, MA 01701.

Journal of Special Education Technology, Association for Special Education Technology, Exceptional Child Center, Utah State University, Logan, UT 84322.

MARCK, 280 Linden Ave., Branfort, CT 06405.

Microcomputers in Education, Queue, Inc., 5 Chapel Hill Dr., Fairfield, CT 06432.

Resource Guide, Marketing Services Dept., Apple Computer, Inc., 10260 Bandley Dr., Cupertino, CA 95014.

School Microware — A Directory of Educational Software, Dresden Associates, PO Box 246, Dresden, MA 04342.

Spencer, H. W. Fundamentals of Digital Computers (2nd ed.). Indianapolis, IN: Howard W. Sams & Co., n.d.

Author Index